The Essence of Being a Muse

1

Aya Fumino

CONTENTS

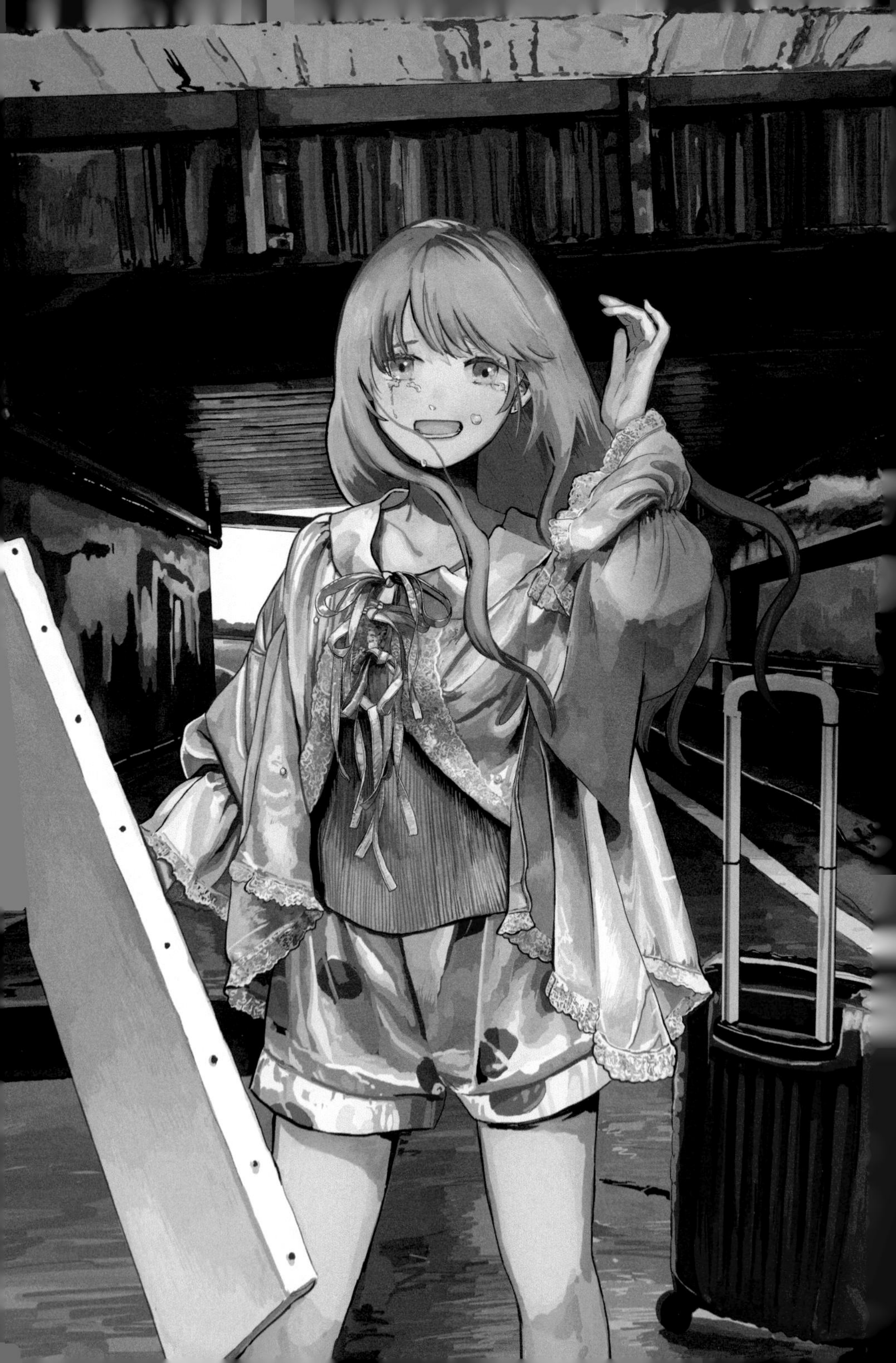

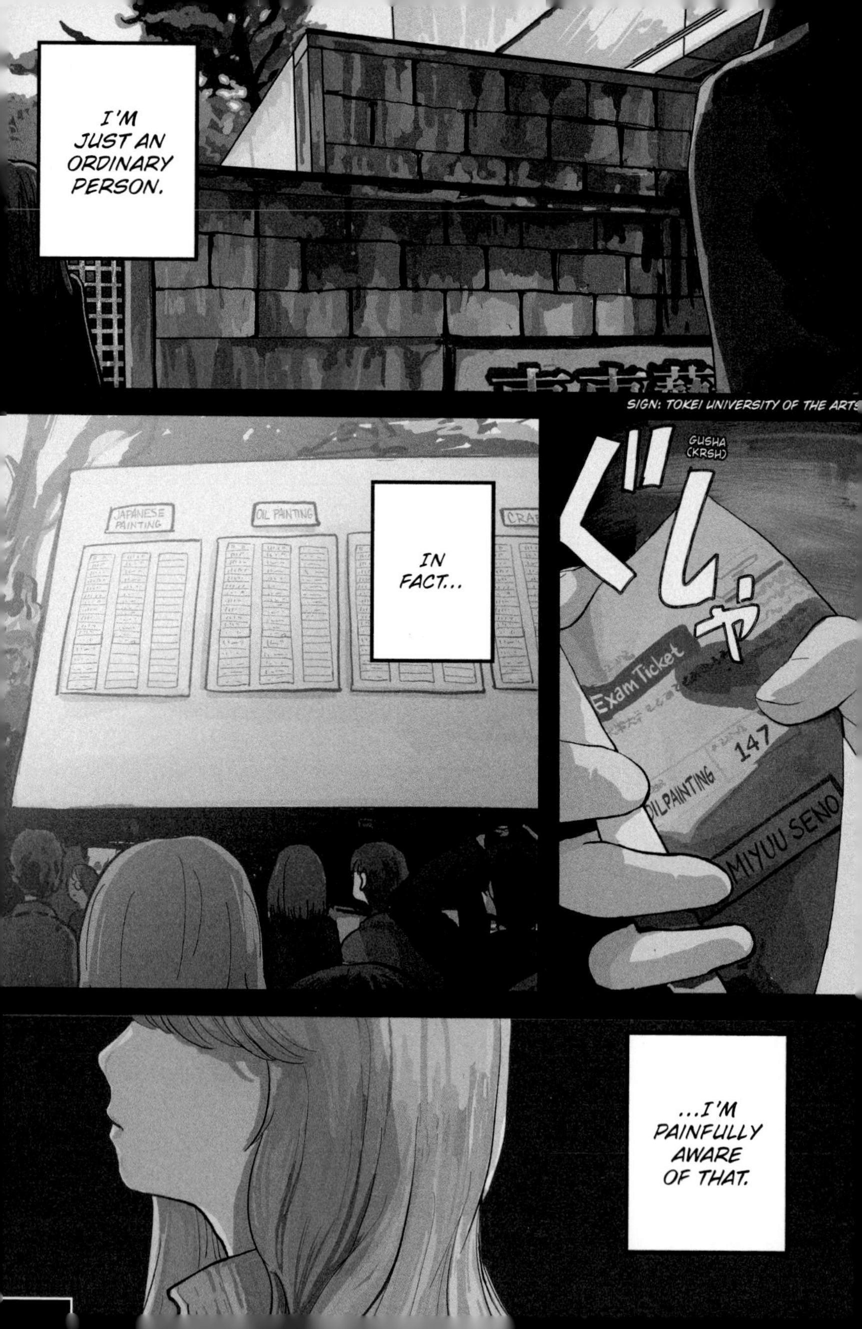
I'M JUST AN ORDINARY PERSON.
SIGN: TOKEI UNIVERSITY OF THE ARTS
ぐしゃ
GUSHA (KRSH)
Exam Ticket
147
OILPAINTING
MIYUU SENO
JAPANESE PAINTING
OIL PAINTING
IN FACT...
...I'M PAINFULLY AWARE OF THAT.

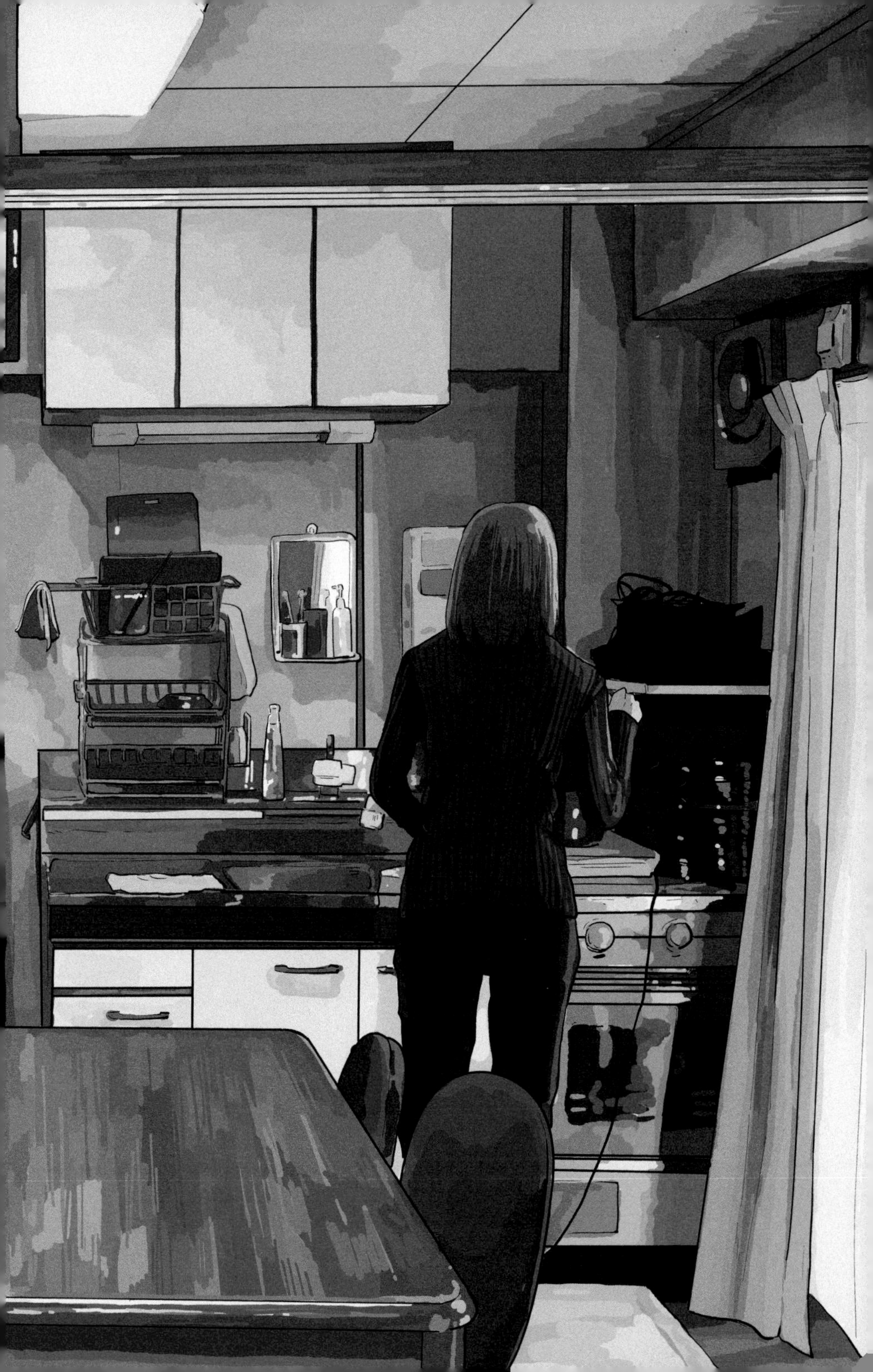

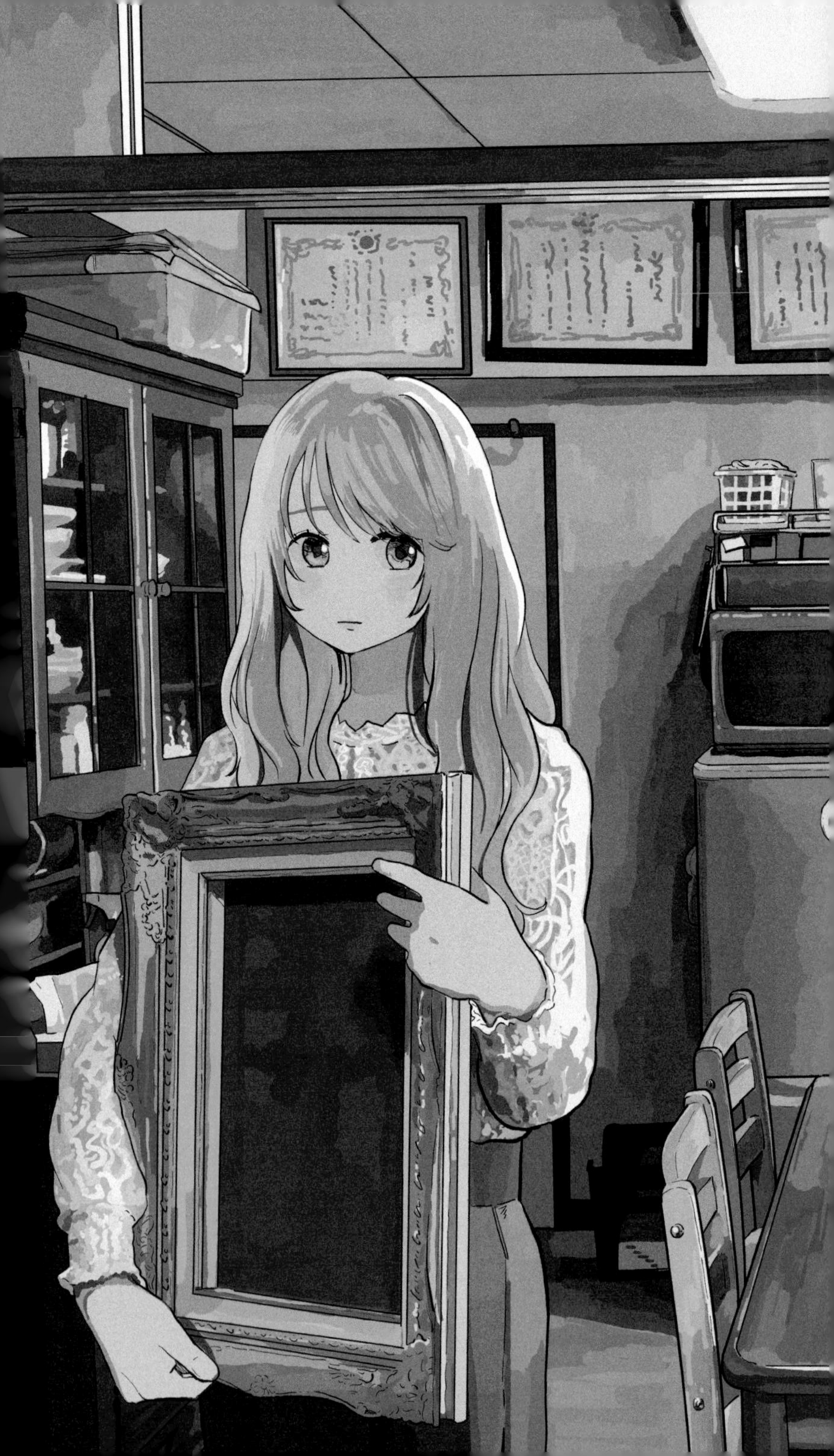

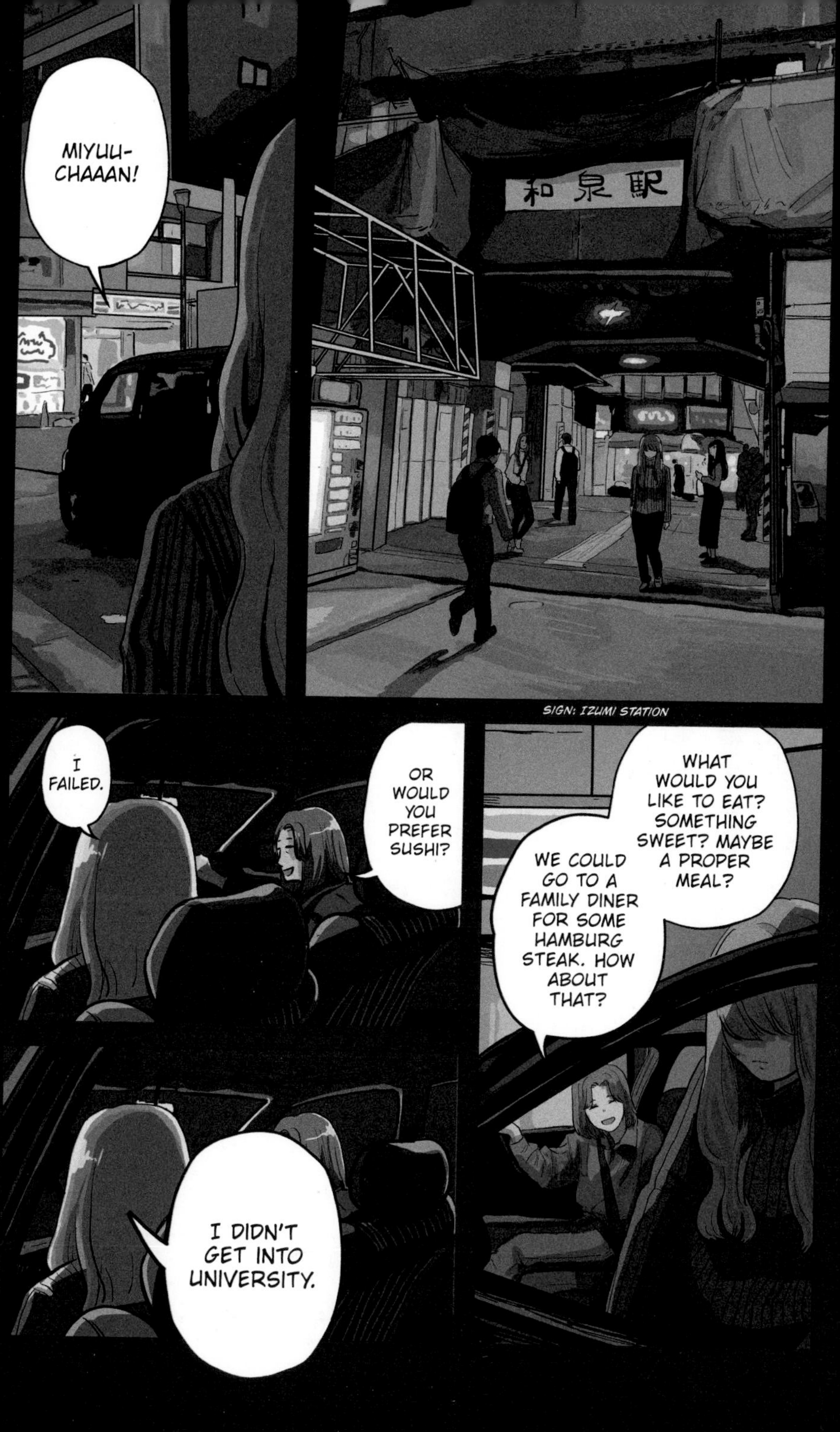

和泉駅
MIYUU-CHAAAN!
SIGN: IZUMI STATION
WHAT WOULD YOU LIKE TO EAT? SOMETHING SWEET? MAYBE A PROPER MEAL?
WE COULD GO TO A FAMILY DINER FOR SOME HAMBURG STEAK. HOW ABOUT THAT?
OR WOULD YOU PREFER SUSHI?
I FAILED.
I DIDN'T GET INTO UNIVERSITY.

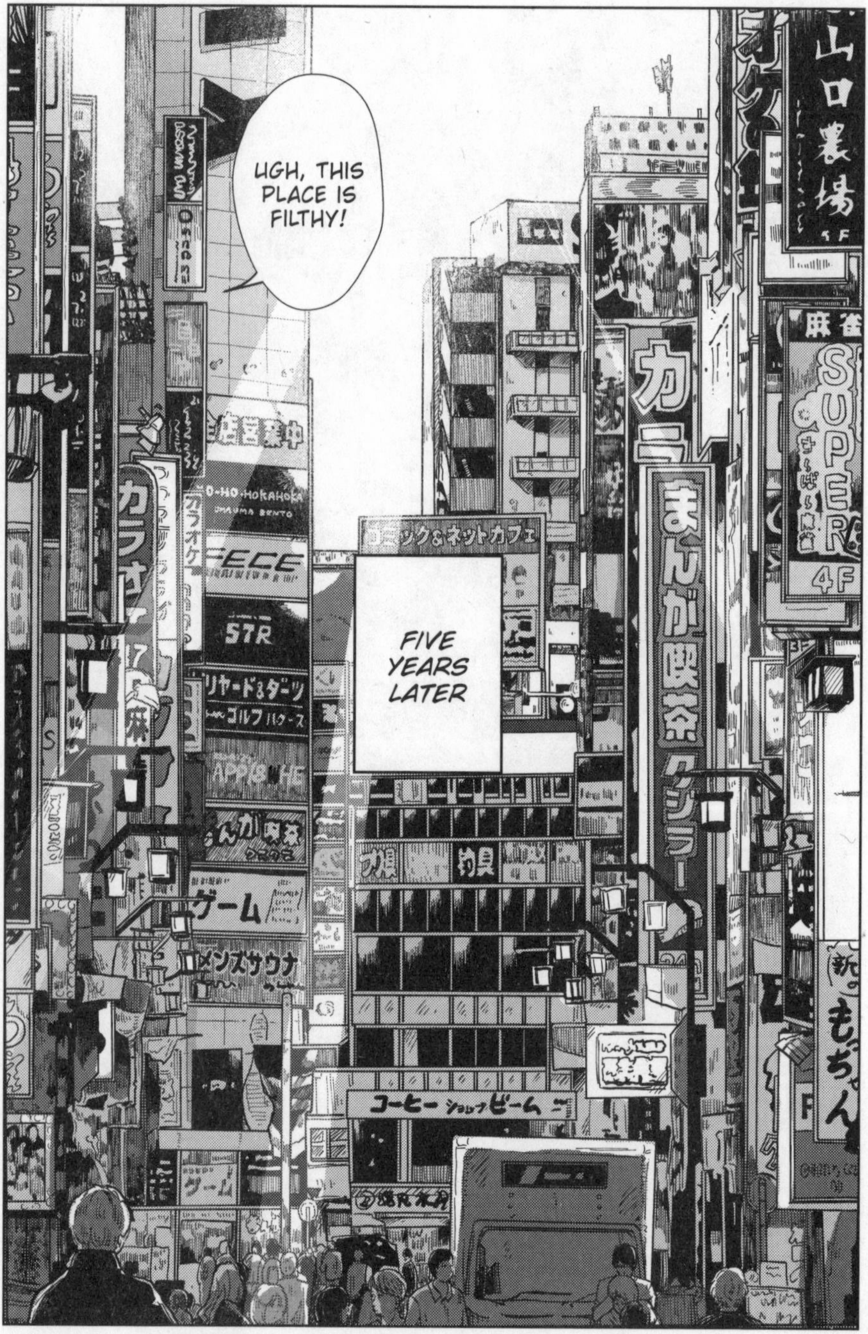
UGH, THIS PLACE IS FILTHY!
FIVE YEARS LATER
山口農場
麻雀
SUPER
4F
まんが喫茶
コミック&ネットカフェ
ゲーム
メンズサウナ
コーヒー ショップ ビーム

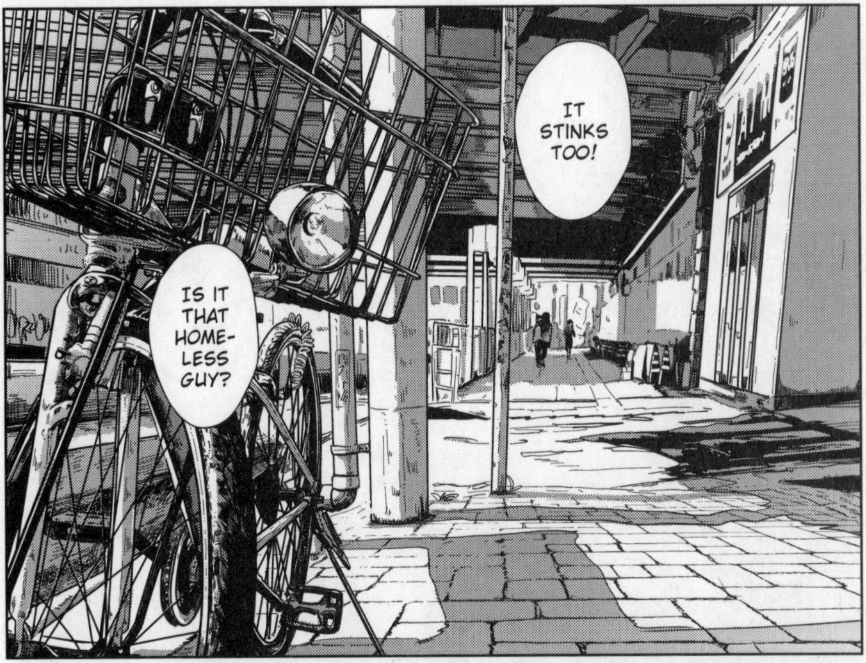
IT STINKS TOO!
IS IT THAT HOME-LESS GUY?

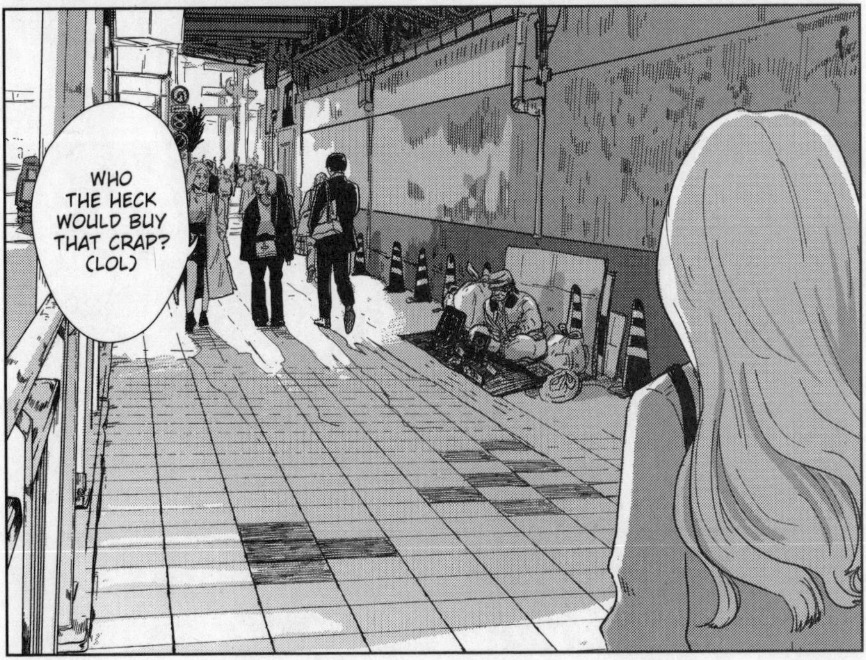
WHO THE HECK WOULD BUY THAT CRAP? (LOL)

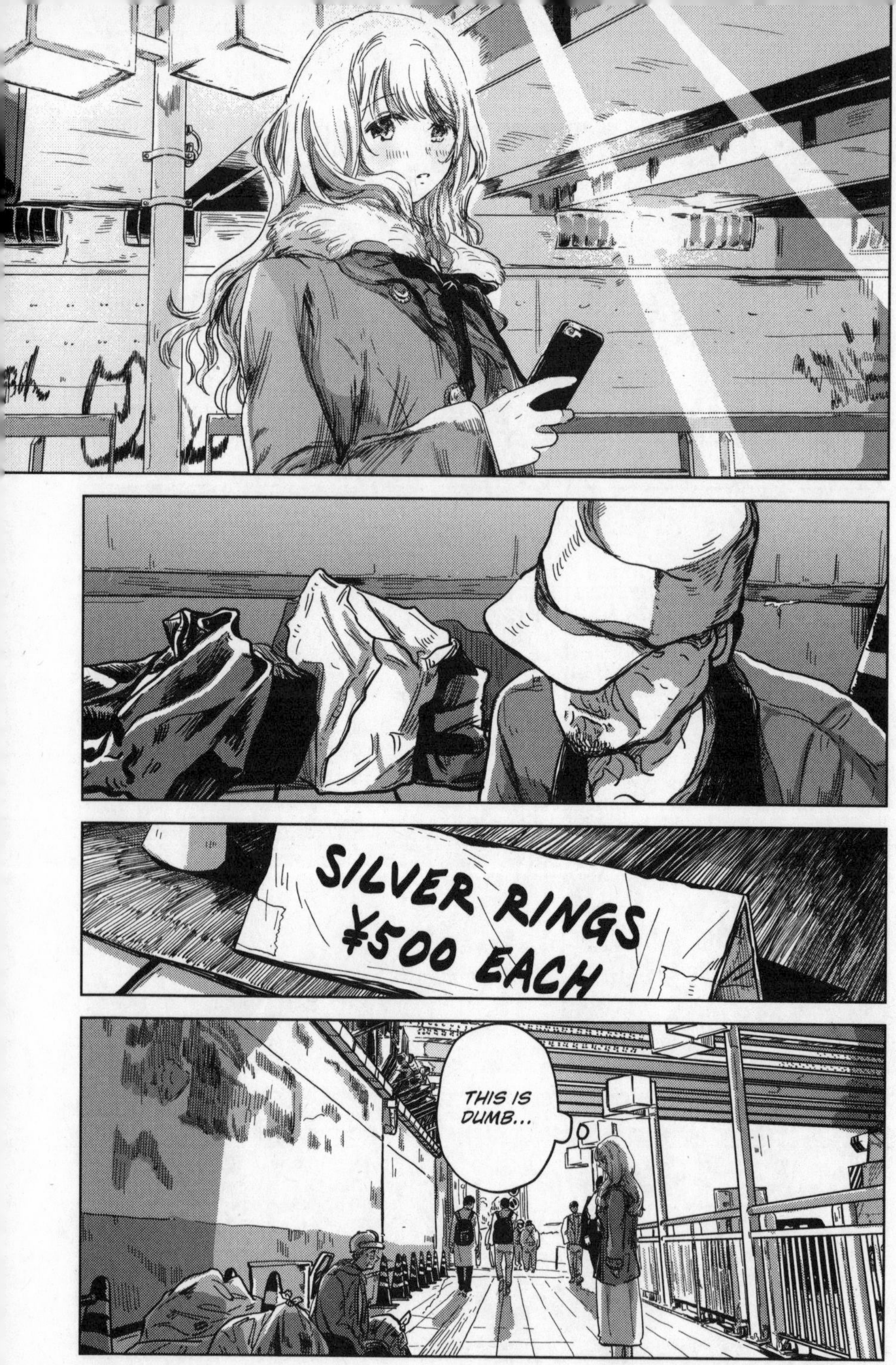
SILVER RINGS
¥500 EACH
THIS IS DUMB...

SIGNS: RAMEN, SOBA KING / GRILLED OFFAL / YASUBE

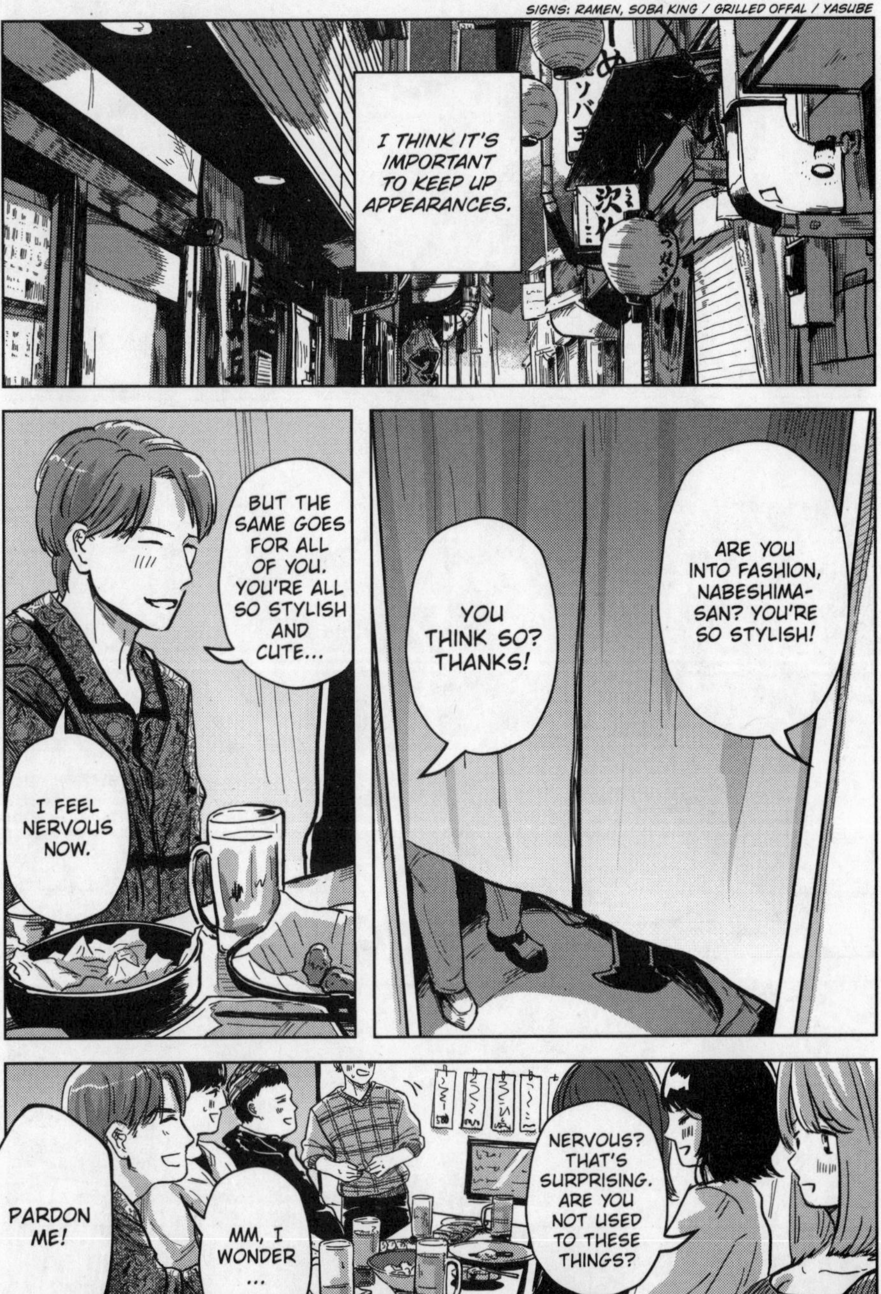
I THINK IT'S IMPORTANT TO KEEP UP APPEARANCES.
ARE YOU INTO FASHION, NABESHIMA-SAN? YOU'RE SO STYLISH!
YOU THINK SO? THANKS!
BUT THE SAME GOES FOR ALL OF YOU. YOU'RE ALL SO STYLISH AND CUTE...
I FEEL NERVOUS NOW.
NERVOUS? THAT'S SURPRISING. ARE YOU NOT USED TO THESE THINGS?
MM, I WONDER ...
PARDON ME!

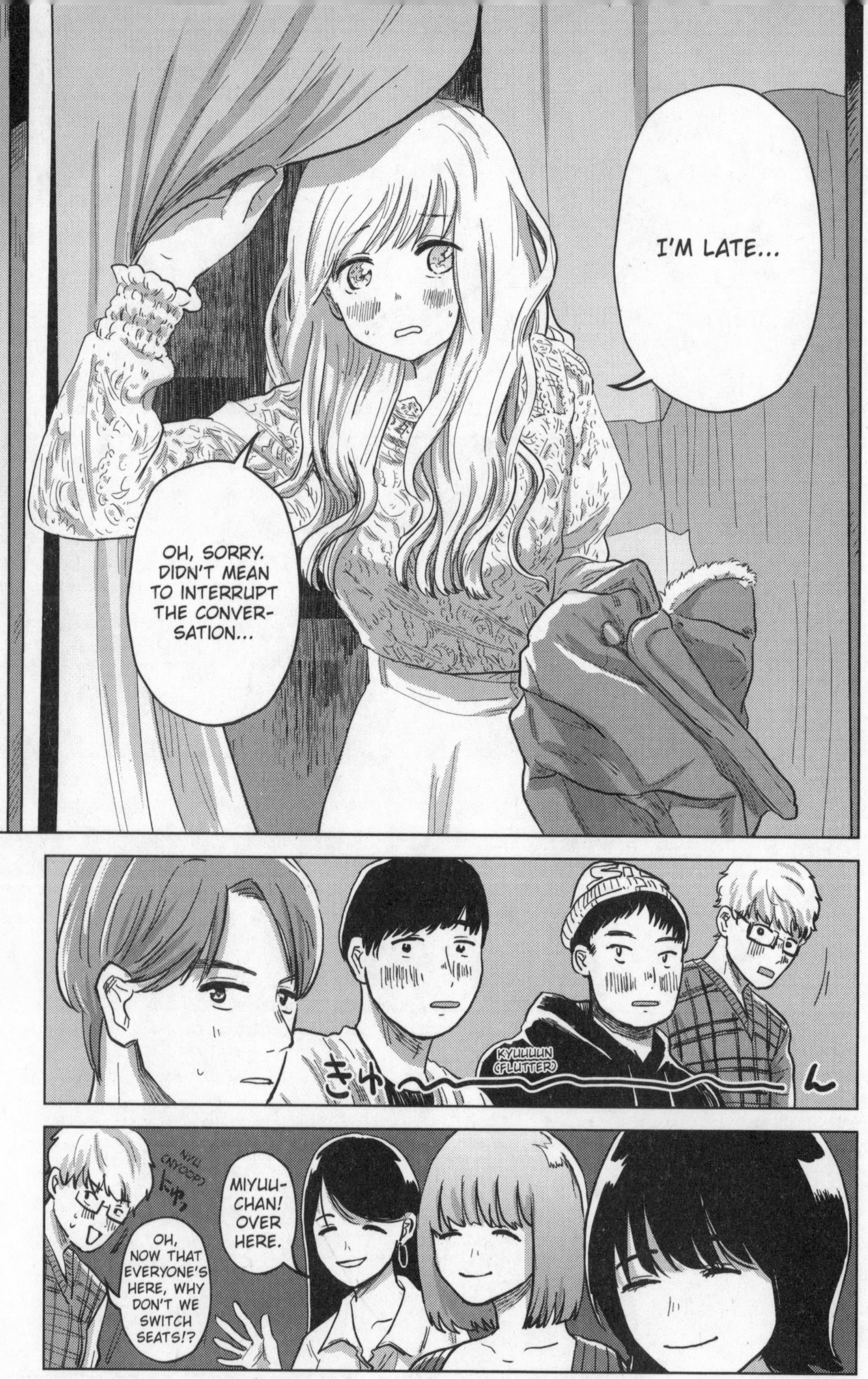
I'M LATE...
OH, SORRY. DIDN'T MEAN TO INTERRUPT THE CONVER-SATION...
KYULLLLN (FLUTTER)
MIYUU-CHAN! OVER HERE.
OH, NOW THAT EVERYONE'S HERE, WHY DON'T WE SWITCH SEATS!?

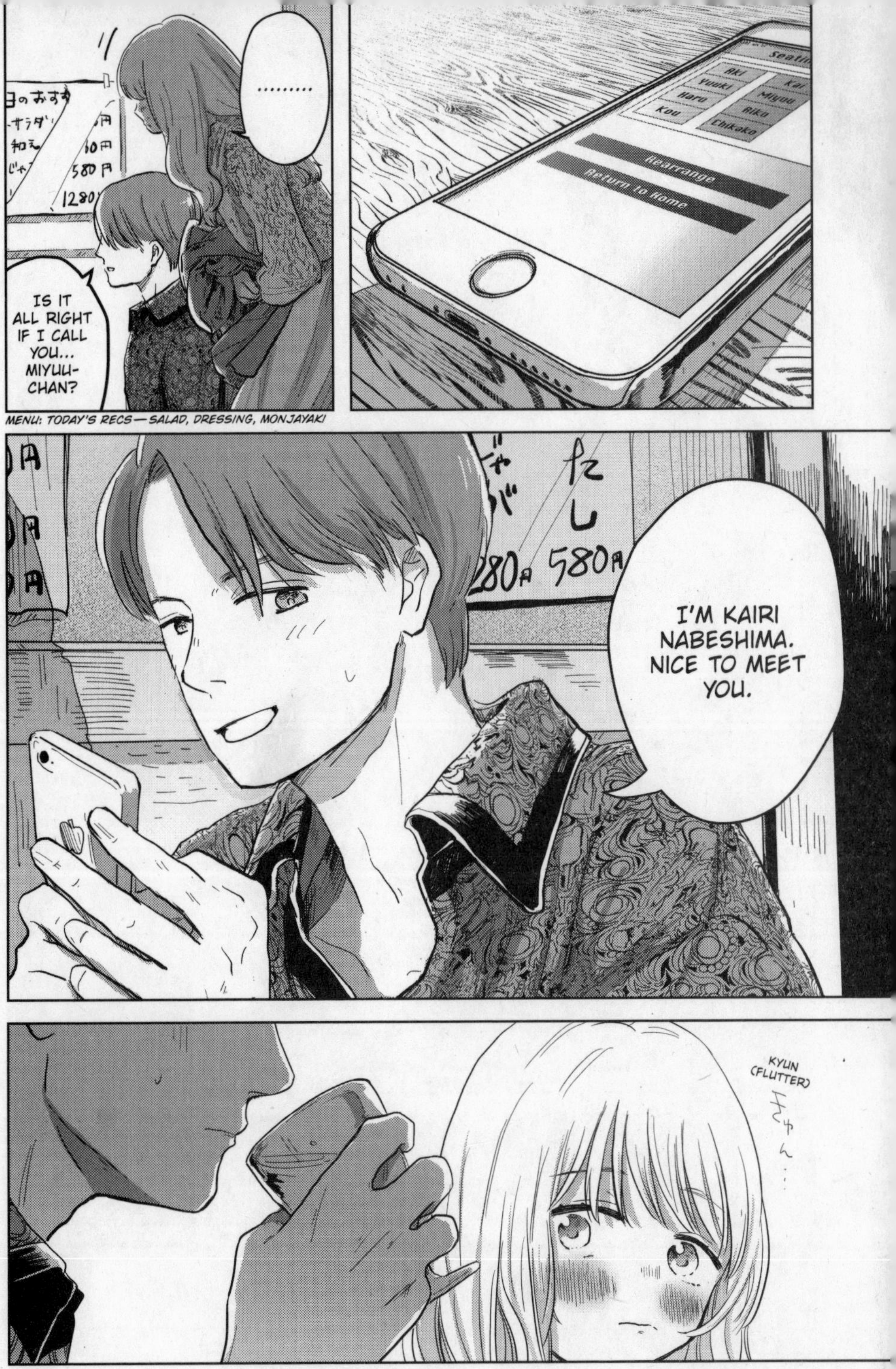
Aki
Kai
Yuuki
Miyuu
Haru
Riko
Kou
Chikako
Rearrange
Return to Home
....
IS IT ALL RIGHT IF I CALL YOU... MIYUU-CHAN?
MENU: TODAY'S RECS—SALAD, DRESSING, MONJAYAKI
I'M KAIRI NABESHIMA. NICE TO MEET YOU.
KYUN (FLUTTER)
きゅん…

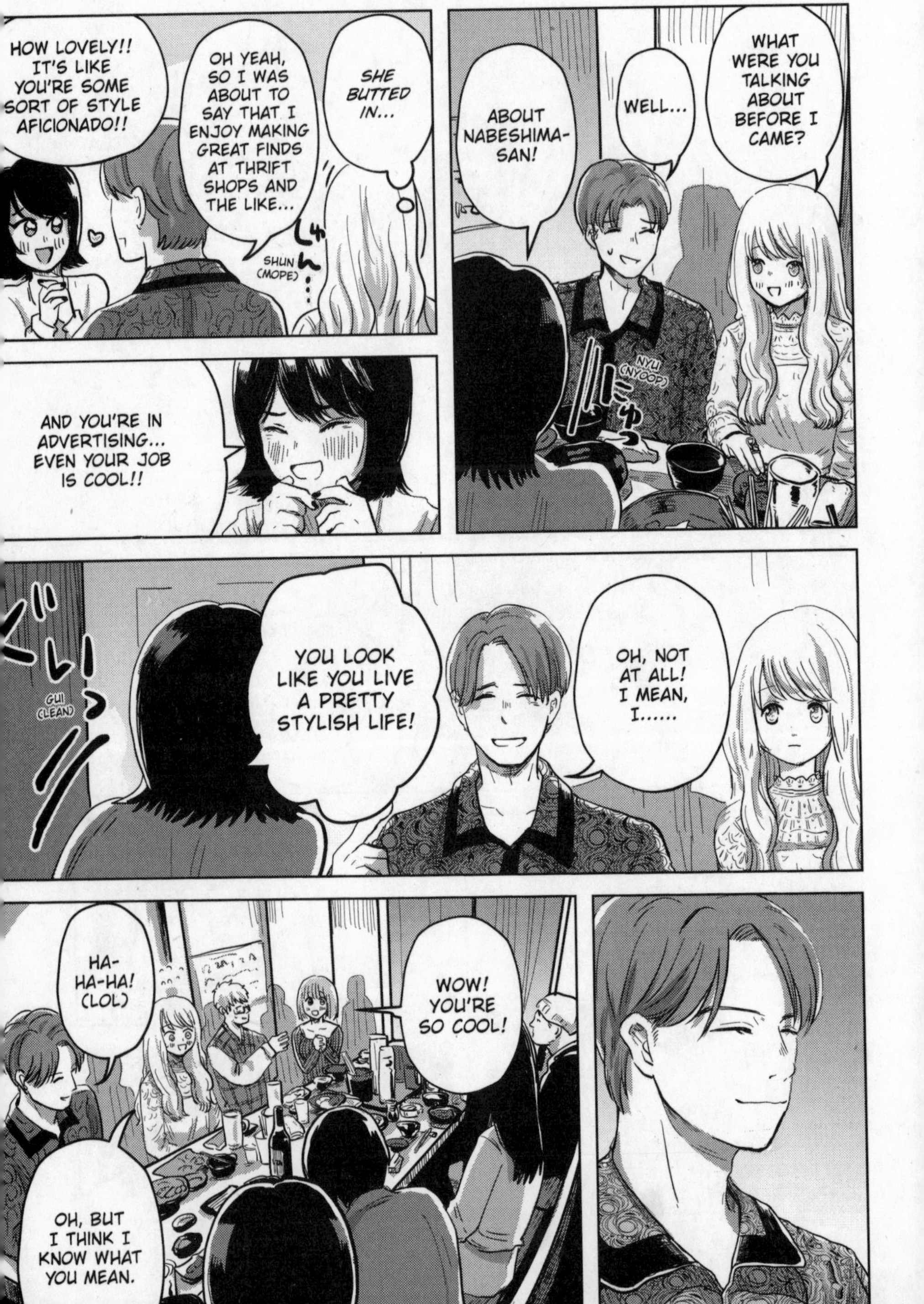
WHAT WERE YOU TALKING ABOUT BEFORE I CAME?
WELL...
ABOUT NABESHIMA-SAN!
NYU (NYOOP)
SHE BUTTED IN...
OH YEAH, SO I WAS ABOUT TO SAY THAT I ENJOY MAKING GREAT FINDS AT THRIFT SHOPS AND THE LIKE...
HOW LOVELY!! IT'S LIKE YOU'RE SOME SORT OF STYLE AFICIONADO!!
SHUN (MOPE)
AND YOU'RE IN ADVERTISING... EVEN YOUR JOB IS COOL!!
OH, NOT AT ALL! I MEAN, I......
YOU LOOK LIKE YOU LIVE A PRETTY STYLISH LIFE!
GUI (CLEAN)
WOW! YOU'RE SO COOL!
HA-HA-HA! (LOL)
OH, BUT I THINK I KNOW WHAT YOU MEAN.

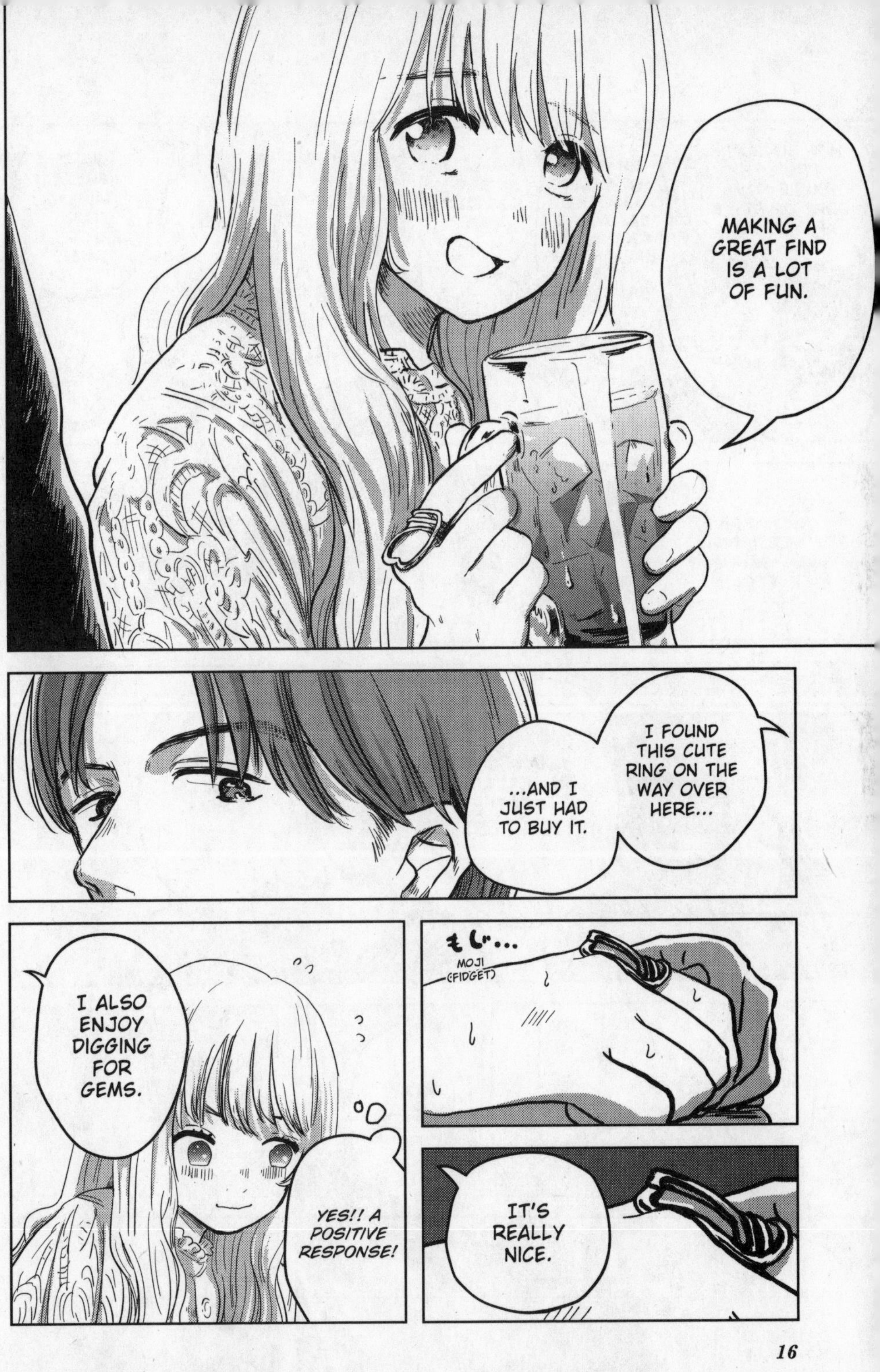
MAKING A GREAT FIND IS A LOT OF FUN.
I FOUND THIS CUTE RING ON THE WAY OVER HERE...
...AND I JUST HAD TO BUY IT.
もじ…
MOJI (FIDGET)
IT'S REALLY NICE.
I ALSO ENJOY DIGGING FOR GEMS.
YES!! A POSITIVE RESPONSE!

SIGN: JR SHINJUKU STATION

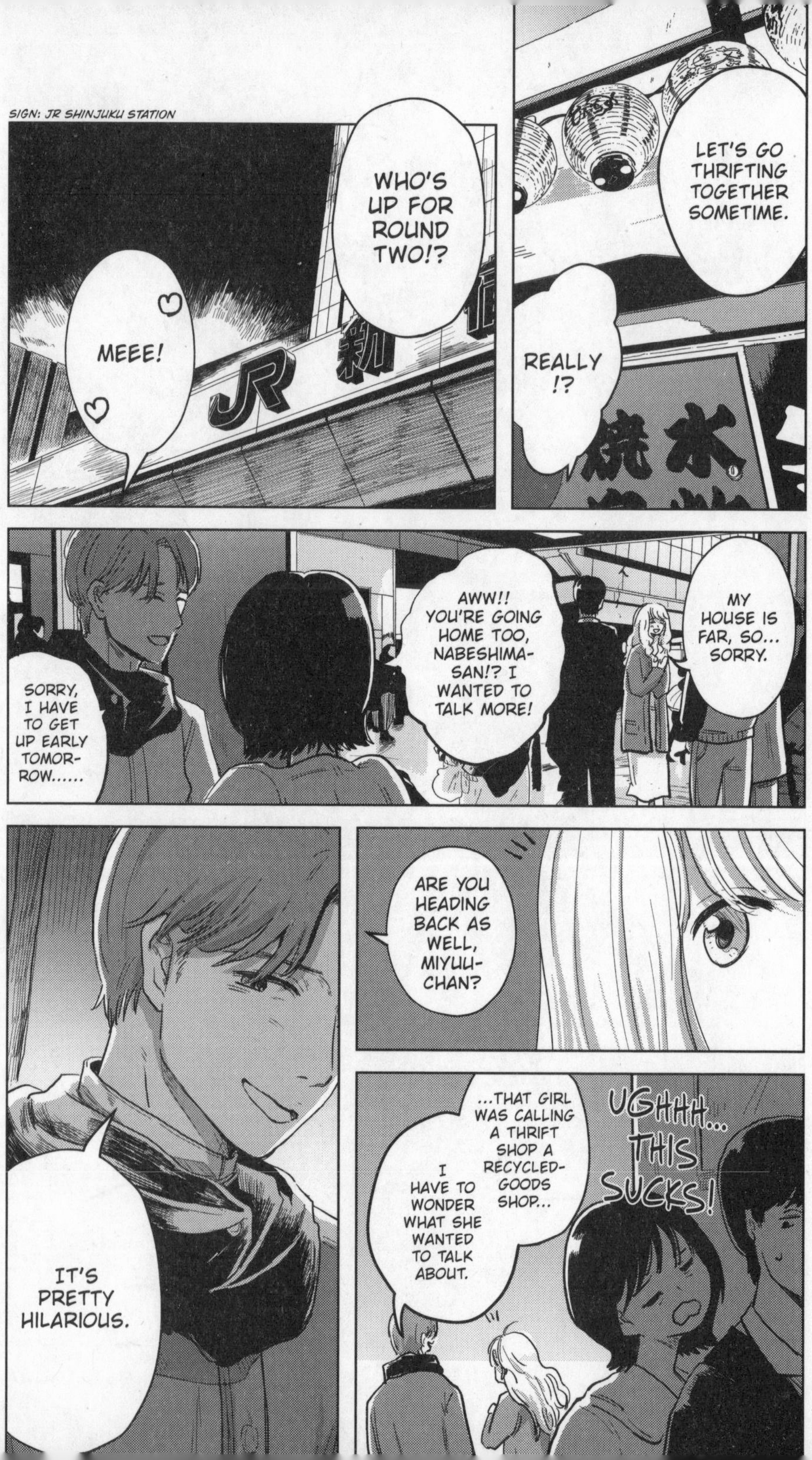

LET'S GO THRIFTING TOGETHER SOMETIME.
REALLY !?
WHO'S UP FOR ROUND TWO!?
MEEE!
MY HOUSE IS FAR, SO... SORRY.
AWW!! YOU'RE GOING HOME TOO, NABESHIMA-SAN!? I WANTED TO TALK MORE!
SORRY, I HAVE TO GET UP EARLY TOMOR-ROW......
ARE YOU HEADING BACK AS WELL, MIYUU-CHAN?
UGHHH... THIS SUCKS!
...THAT GIRL WAS CALLING A THRIFT SHOP A RECYCLED-GOODS SHOP...
I HAVE TO WONDER WHAT SHE WANTED TO TALK ABOUT.
IT'S PRETTY HILARIOUS.

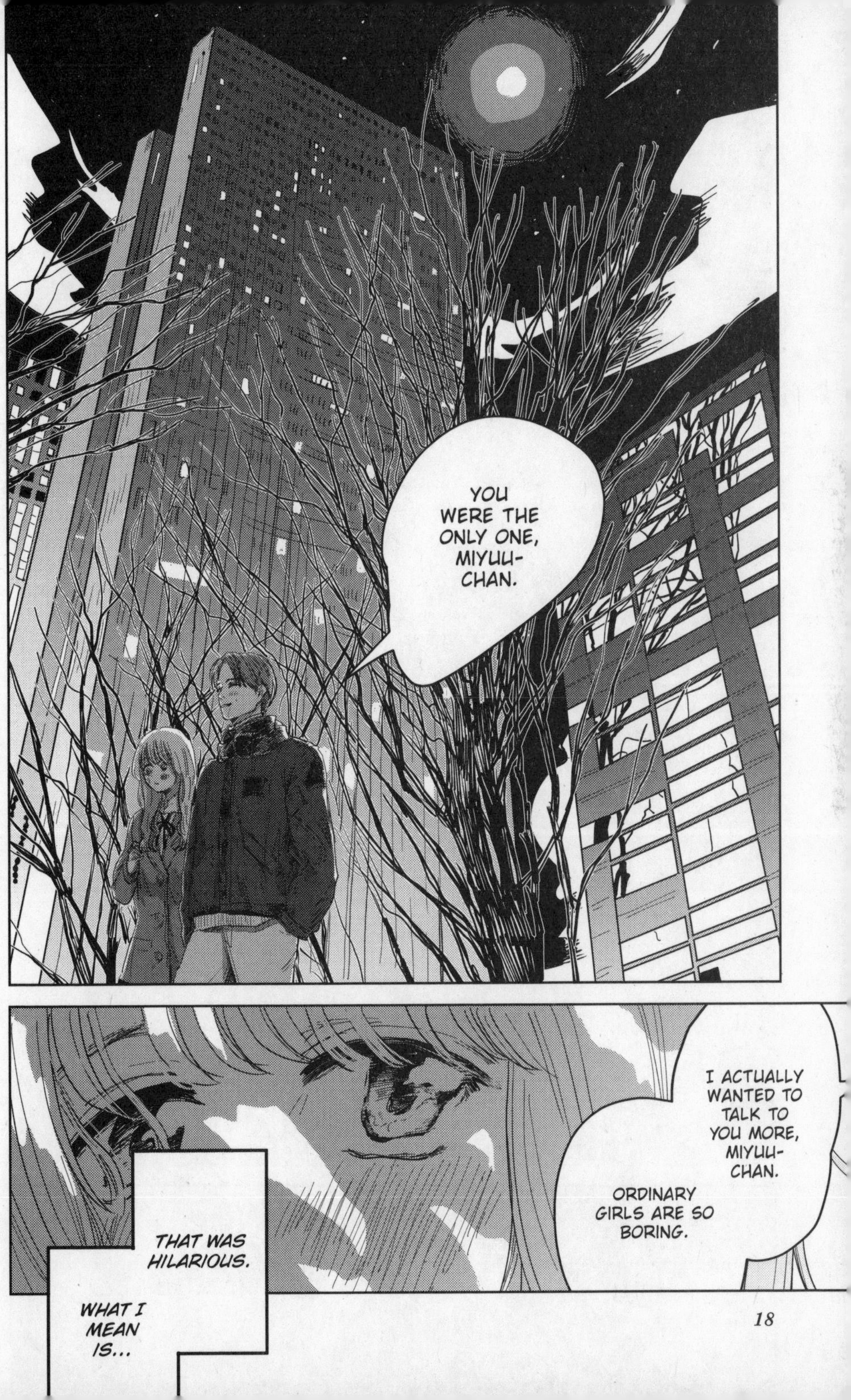
YOU WERE THE ONLY ONE, MIYUU-CHAN.
I ACTUALLY WANTED TO TALK TO YOU MORE, MIYUU-CHAN.
ORDINARY GIRLS ARE SO BORING.
THAT WAS HILARIOUS.
WHAT I MEAN IS...

...I'VE FALLEN FOR HIM.

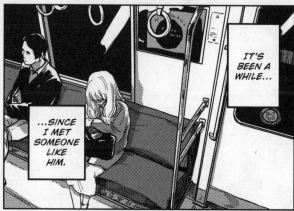

IT'S BEEN A WHILE...

...SINCE I MET SOMEONE LIKE HIM.

I'M HOME!

SOMEONE WHO GETS IT.

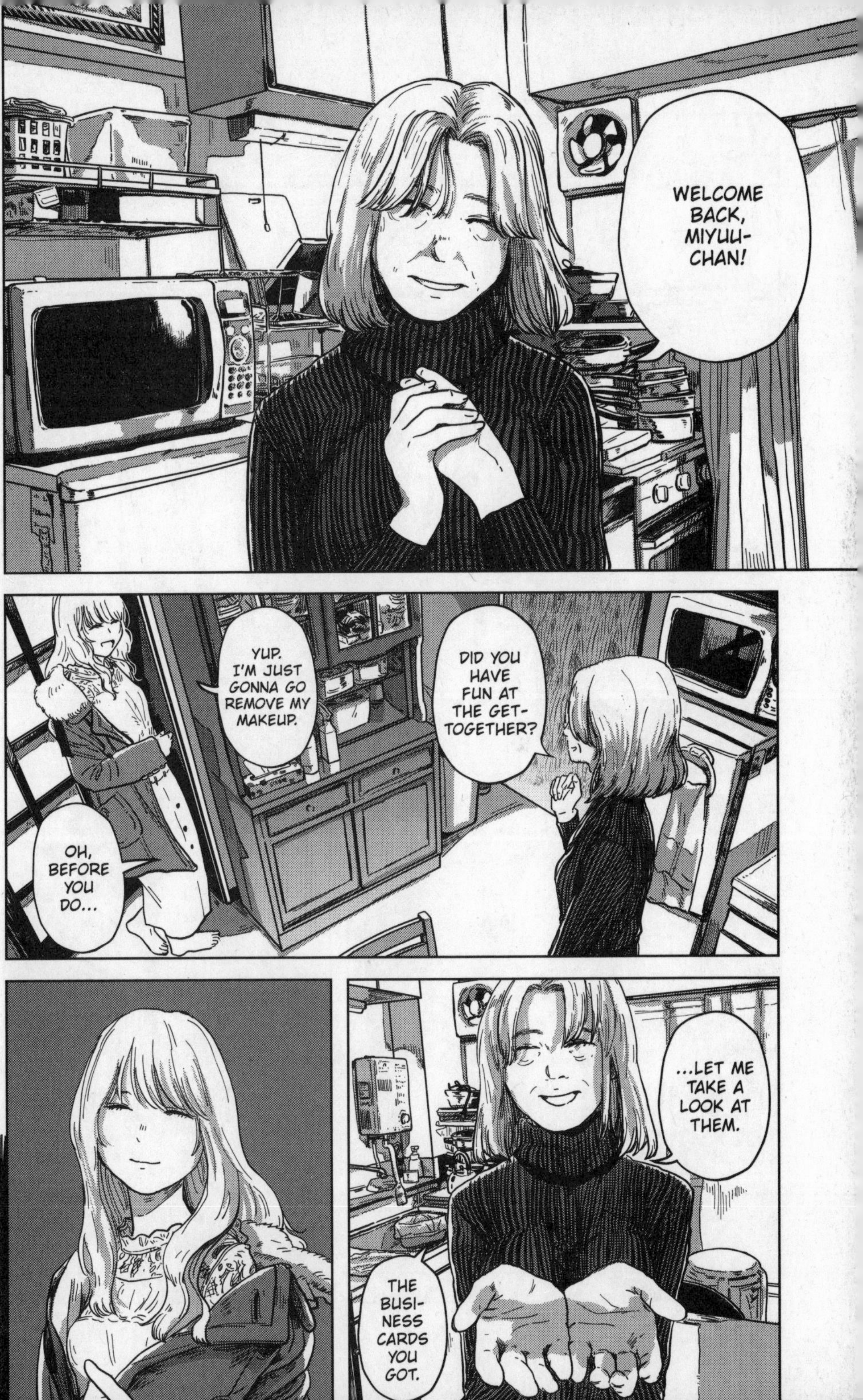
WELCOME BACK, MIYUU-CHAN!
DID YOU HAVE FUN AT THE GET-TOGETHER?
YUP. I'M JUST GONNA GO REMOVE MY MAKEUP.
OH, BEFORE YOU DO...
...LET ME TAKE A LOOK AT THEM.
THE BUSINESS CARDS YOU GOT.

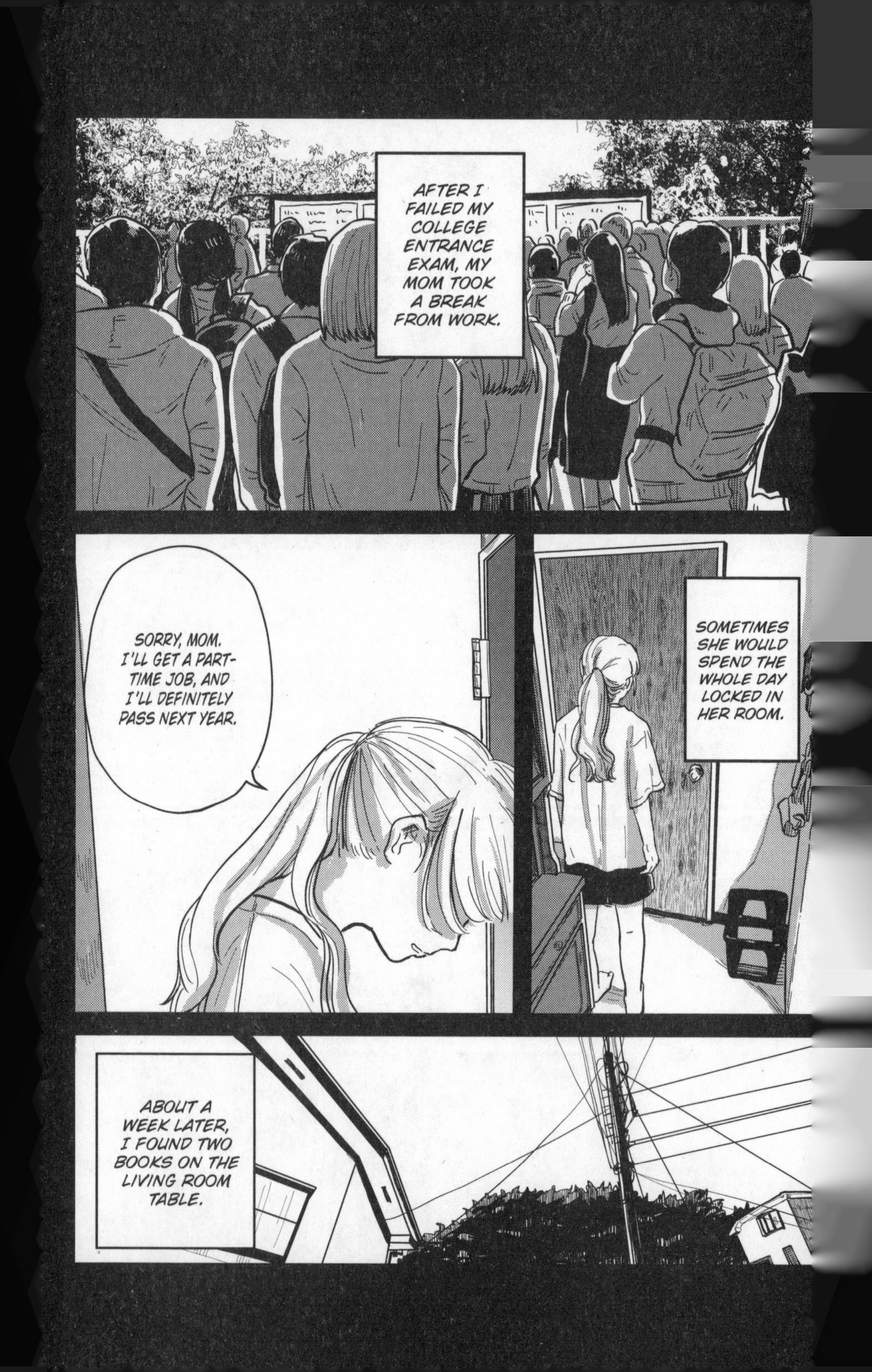
AFTER I FAILED MY COLLEGE ENTRANCE EXAM, MY MOM TOOK A BREAK FROM WORK.
SOMETIMES SHE WOULD SPEND THE WHOLE DAY LOCKED IN HER ROOM.
SORRY, MOM. I'LL GET A PART-TIME JOB, AND I'LL DEFINITELY PASS NEXT YEAR.
ABOUT A WEEK LATER, I FOUND TWO BOOKS ON THE LIVING ROOM TABLE.

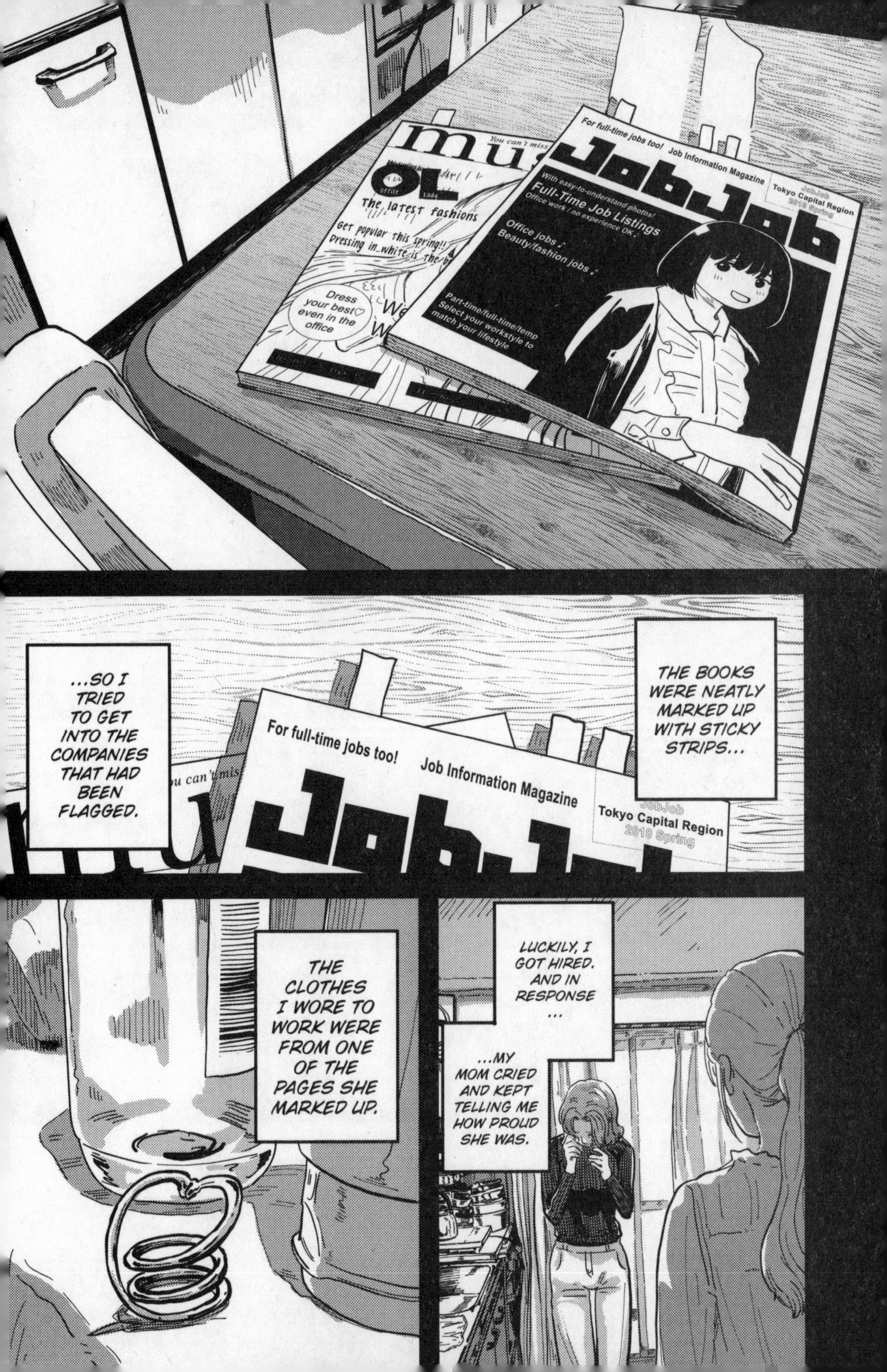
For full-time jobs too!
Job Information Magazine
JobJob
JobJob
Tokyo Capital Region
2018 Spring
With easy-to-understand photos!
Full-Time Job Listings
Office work / no experience OK.
Office jobs♪
Beauty/fashion jobs♪
Part-time/full-time/temp
Select your workstyle to match your lifestyle
You can't miss
OL
Office Lady
The latest fashions
Dress your best♡ even in the office
THE BOOKS WERE NEATLY MARKED UP WITH STICKY STRIPS...
...SO I TRIED TO GET INTO THE COMPANIES THAT HAD BEEN FLAGGED.
For full-time jobs too!
Job Information Magazine
JobJob
Tokyo Capital Region
2018 Spring
LUCKILY, I GOT HIRED. AND IN RESPONSE...
...MY MOM CRIED AND KEPT TELLING ME HOW PROUD SHE WAS.
THE CLOTHES I WORE TO WORK WERE FROM ONE OF THE PAGES SHE MARKED UP.

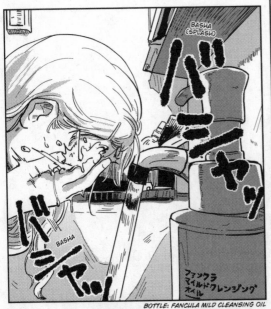

JAAAAA (SHHHHH)
BASHA (SPLASH)
バシャッ
BASHA
バシャッ
ファンクラ マイルドクレンジング オイル
BOTTLE: FANCULA MILD CLEANSING OIL
MIYUU-CHAN!
THEY'RE ALL MARRIAGE MATERIAL! WHO'RE YOU GOING FOR? NABESHIMA-SAN?
I JUST CAN'T WAIT TO SEE MY CUTE LITTLE GIRL GET MARRIED!

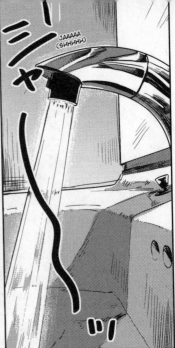

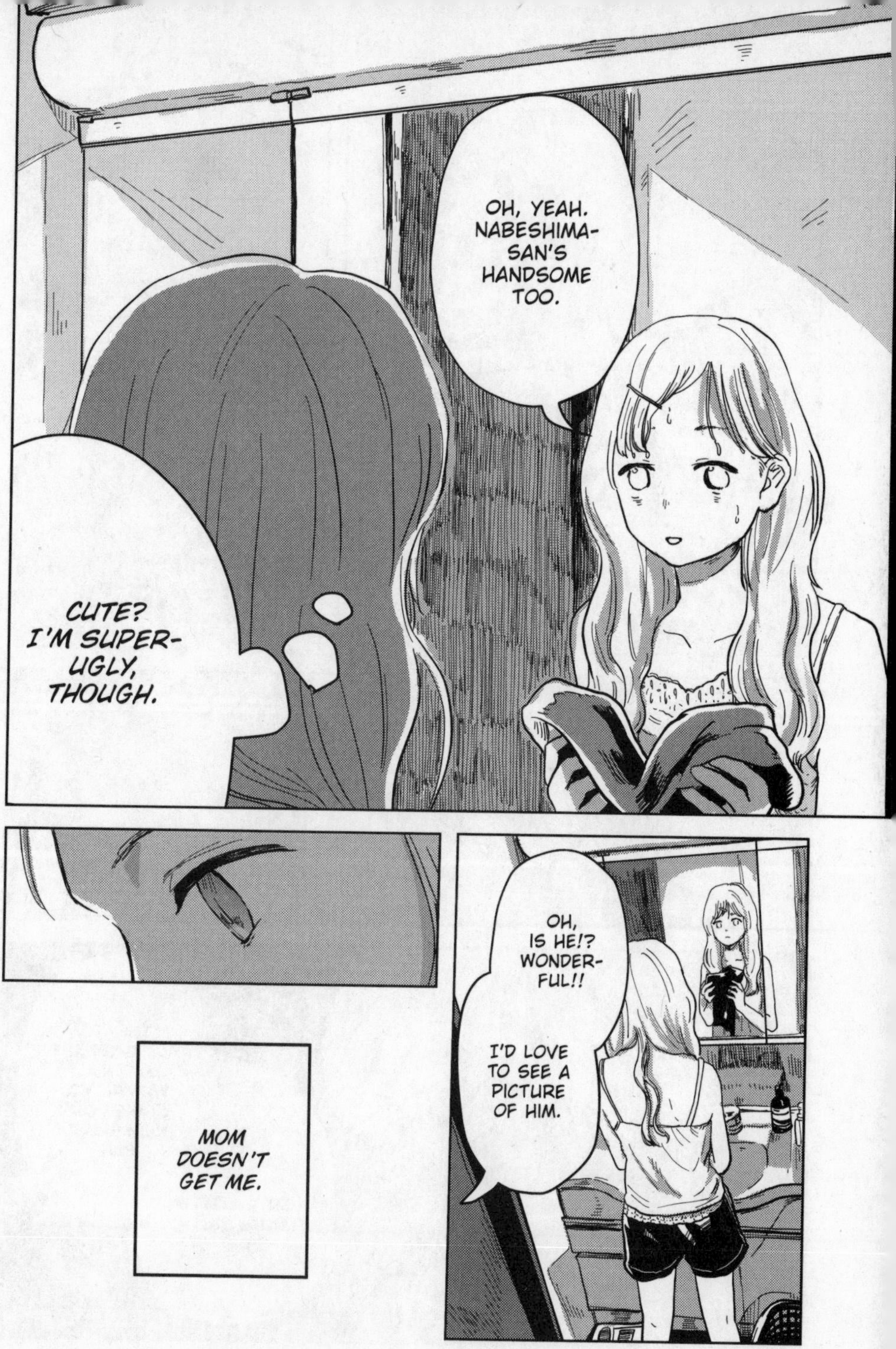
OH, YEAH. NABESHIMA-SAN'S HANDSOME TOO.
CUTE? I'M SUPER-UGLY, THOUGH.
OH, IS HE!? WONDERFUL!!
I'D LOVE TO SEE A PICTURE OF HIM.
MOM DOESN'T GET ME.

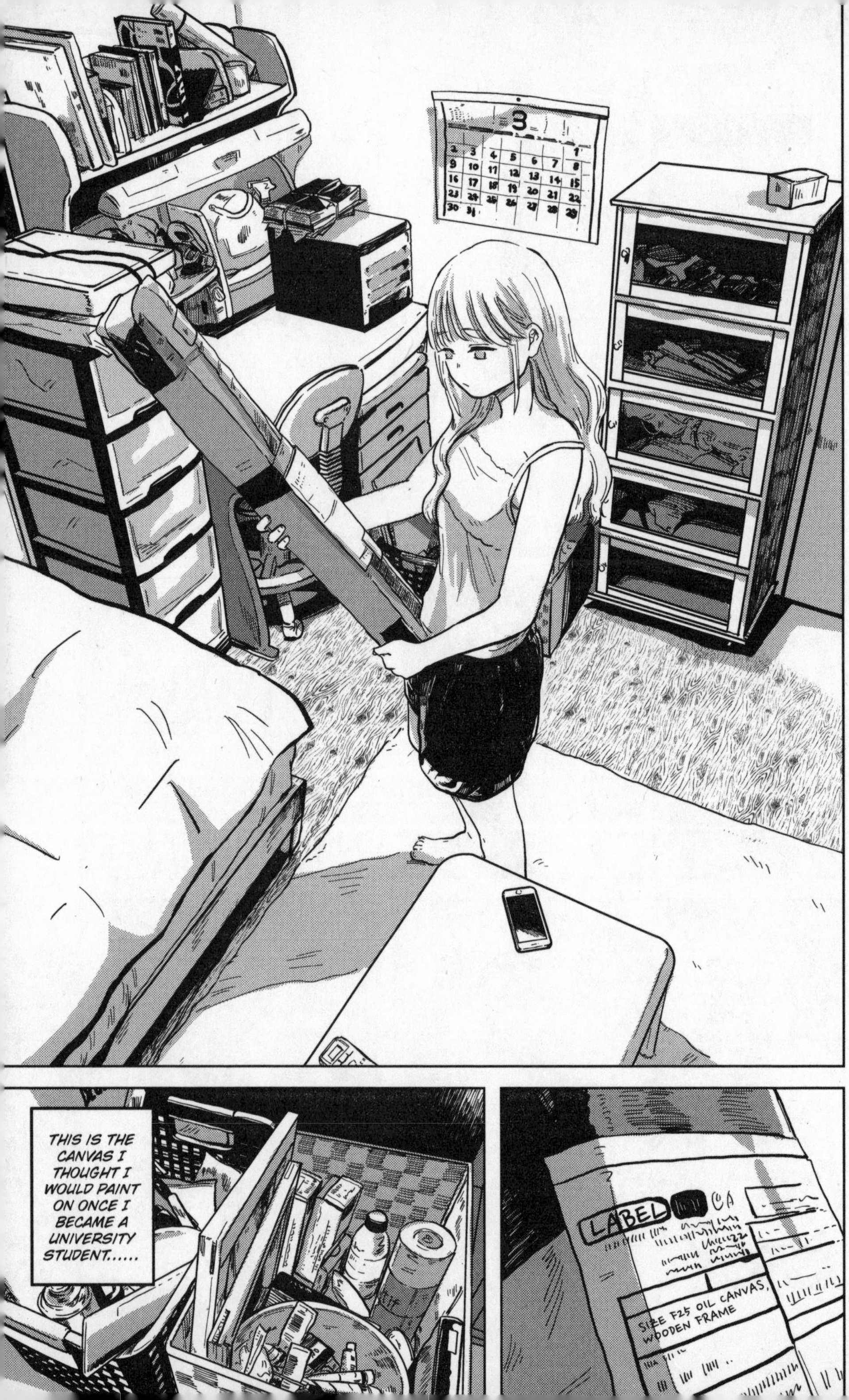
LABEL
SIZE F25 OIL CANVAS, WOODEN FRAME
THIS IS THE CANVAS I THOUGHT I WOULD PAINT ON ONCE I BECAME A UNIVERSITY STUDENT......

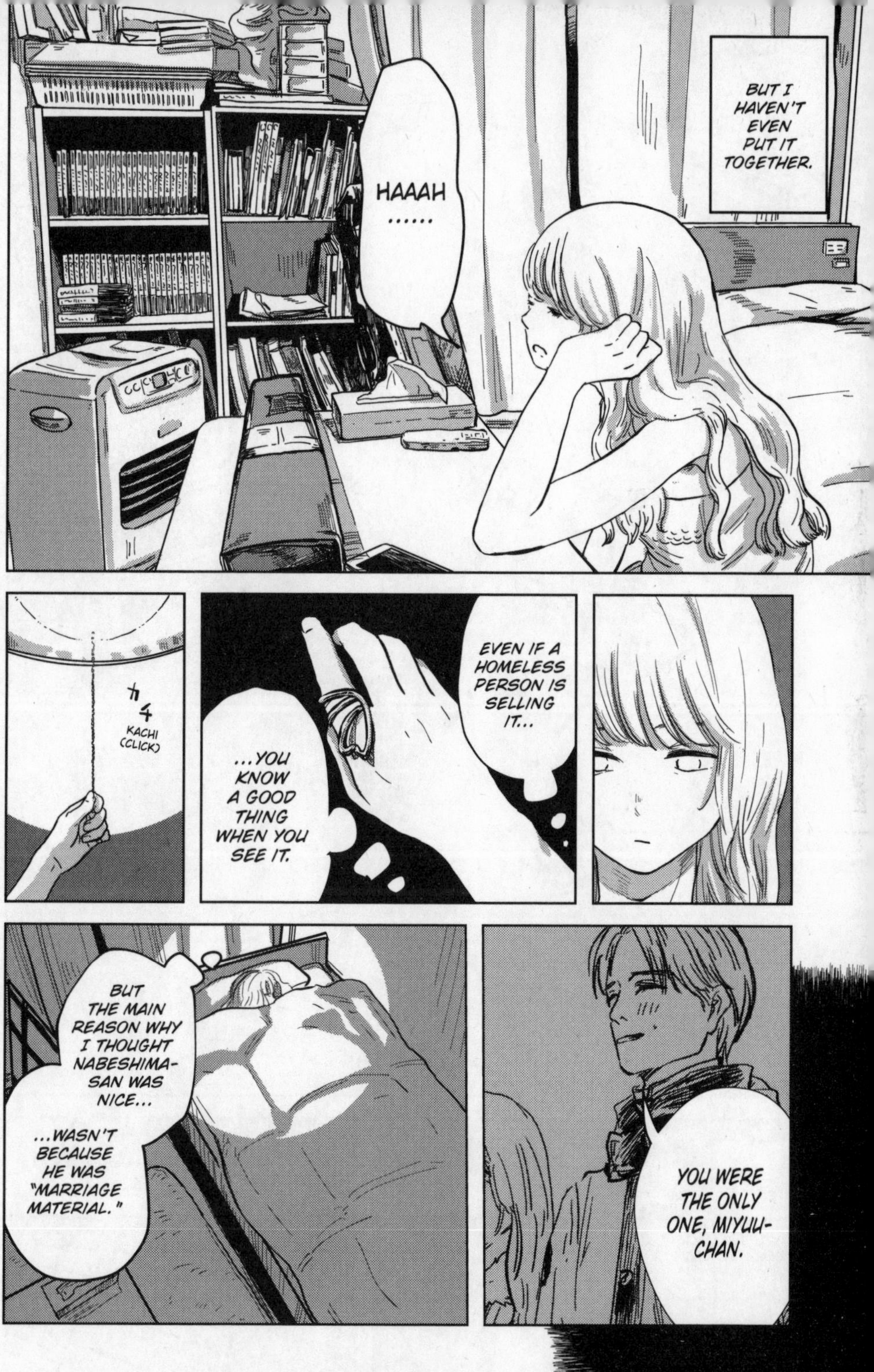
BUT I HAVEN'T EVEN PUT IT TOGETHER.
HAAAH ......
EVEN IF A HOMELESS PERSON IS SELLING IT...
...YOU KNOW A GOOD THING WHEN YOU SEE IT.
カチ
KACHI (CLICK)
YOU WERE THE ONLY ONE, MIYUU-CHAN.
BUT THE MAIN REASON WHY I THOUGHT NABESHIMA-SAN WAS NICE...
...WASN'T BECAUSE HE WAS "MARRIAGE MATERIAL."

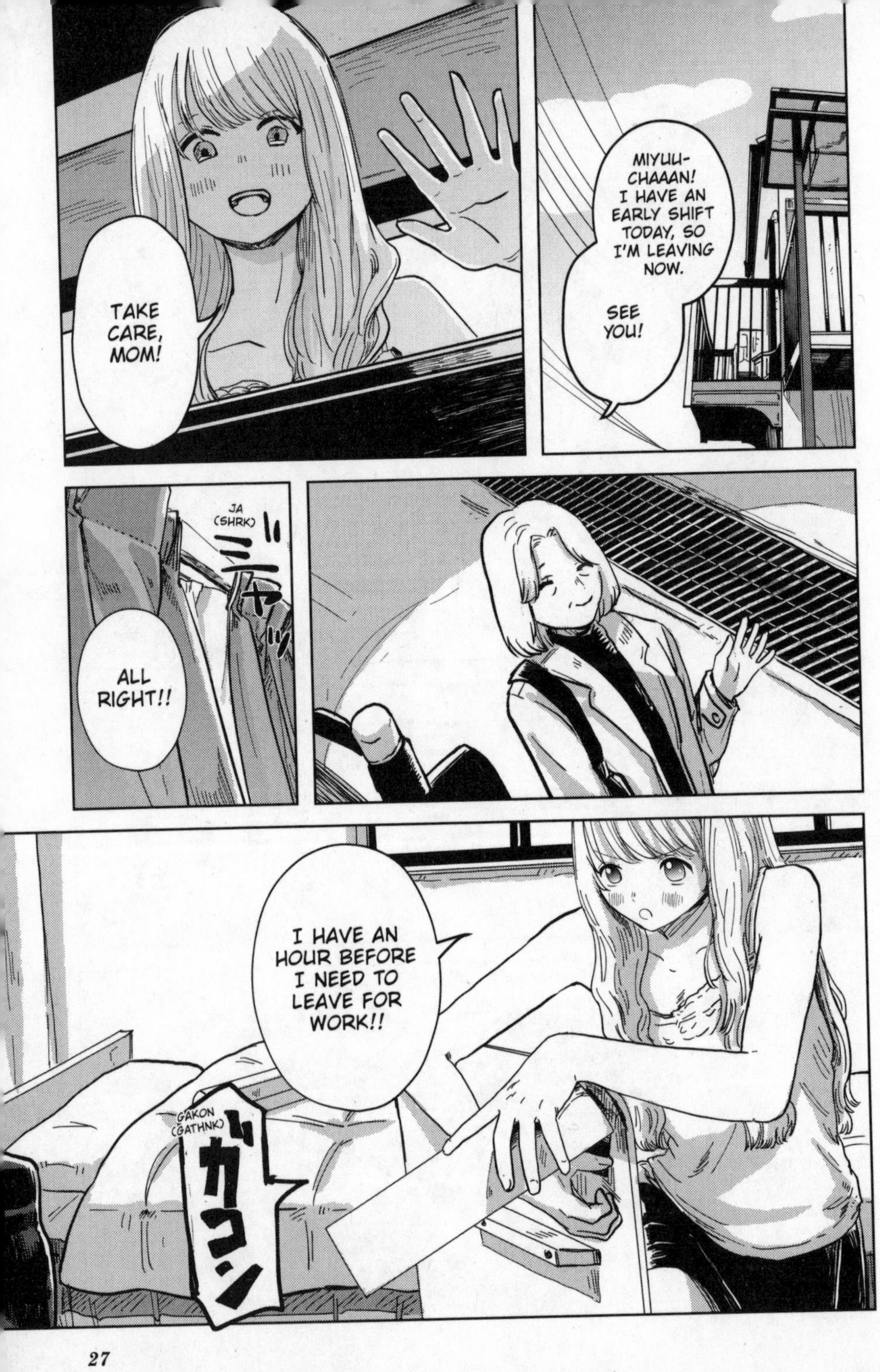
MIYUU-CHAAAN! I HAVE AN EARLY SHIFT TODAY, SO I'M LEAVING NOW.
SEE YOU!
TAKE CARE, MOM!
JA (SHRK)
ジャッ
ALL RIGHT!!
I HAVE AN HOUR BEFORE I NEED TO LEAVE FOR WORK!!
GAKON (GATHNK)
ガコン

BASA
(FWAP)

JOKI
(SNIP)

ジョキ
JOKI

ジョキ
JOKI

ジョキ
JOKI

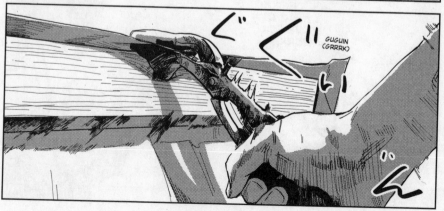

ぐくい
GUGUIN
(GRRRK)

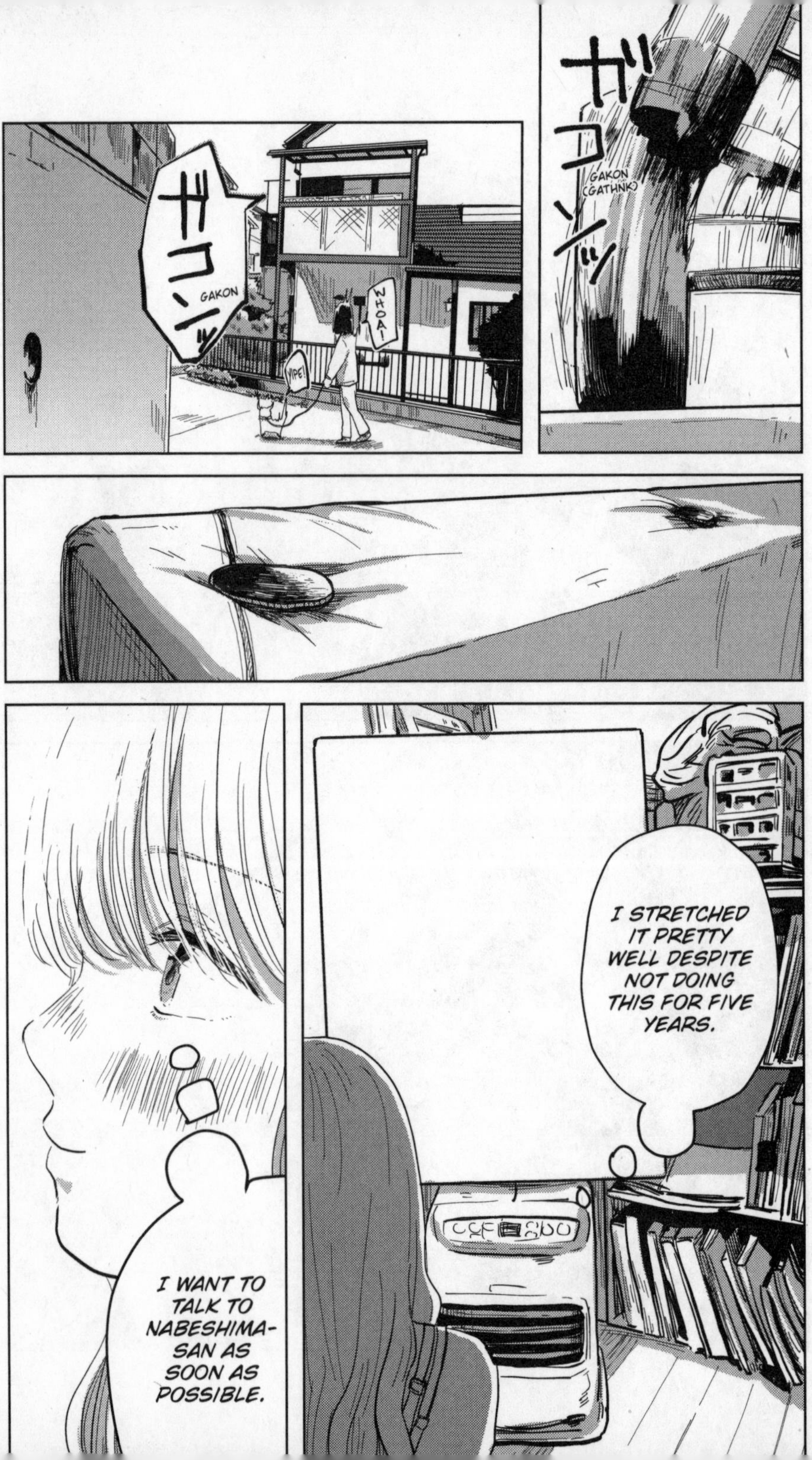
ガコンッ
GAKON (GATHNK)
ガコンッ
GAKON
WHOA!
YIPE!
I STRETCHED IT PRETTY WELL DESPITE NOT DOING THIS FOR FIVE YEARS.
I WANT TO TALK TO NABESHIMA-SAN AS SOON AS POSSIBLE.

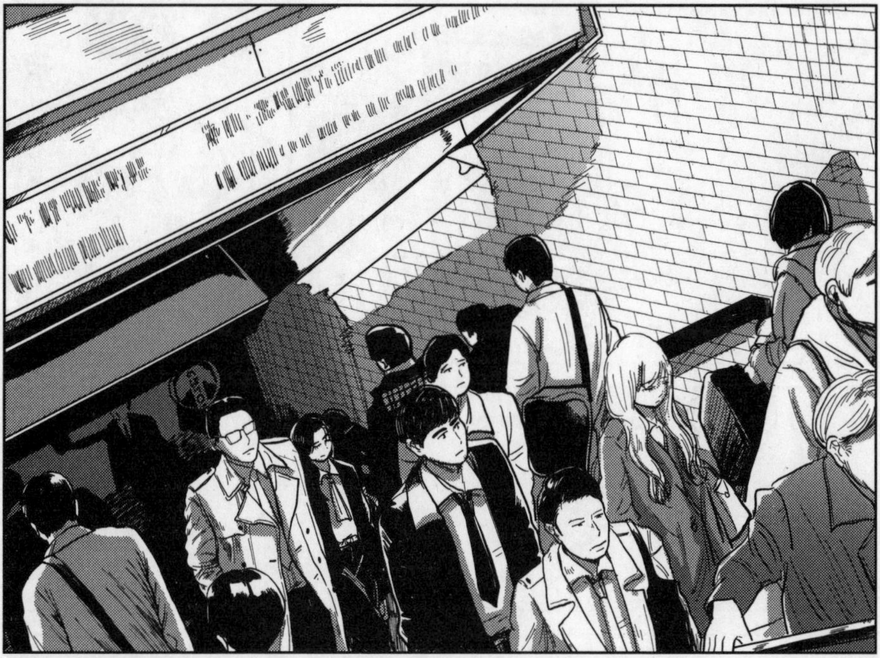

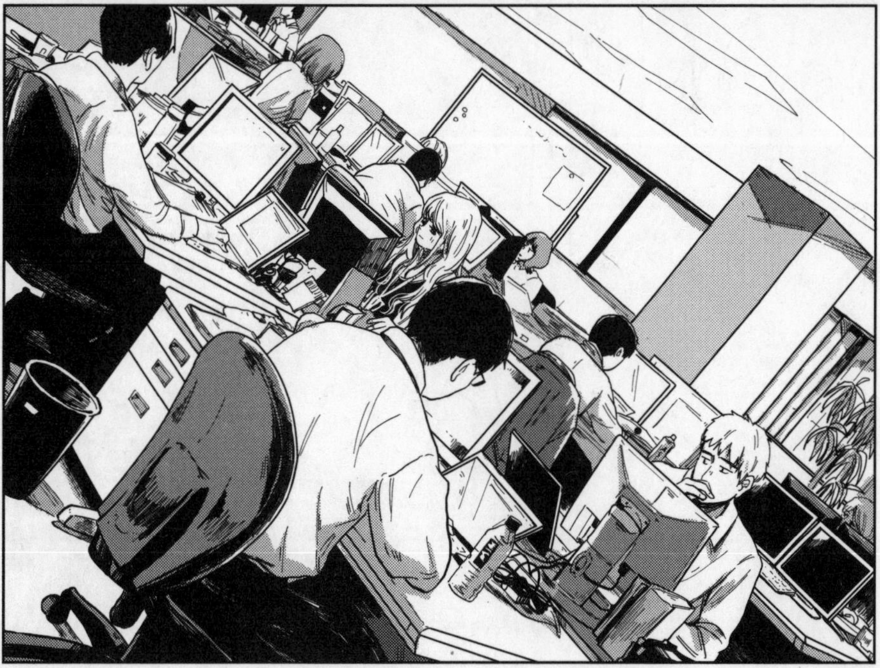

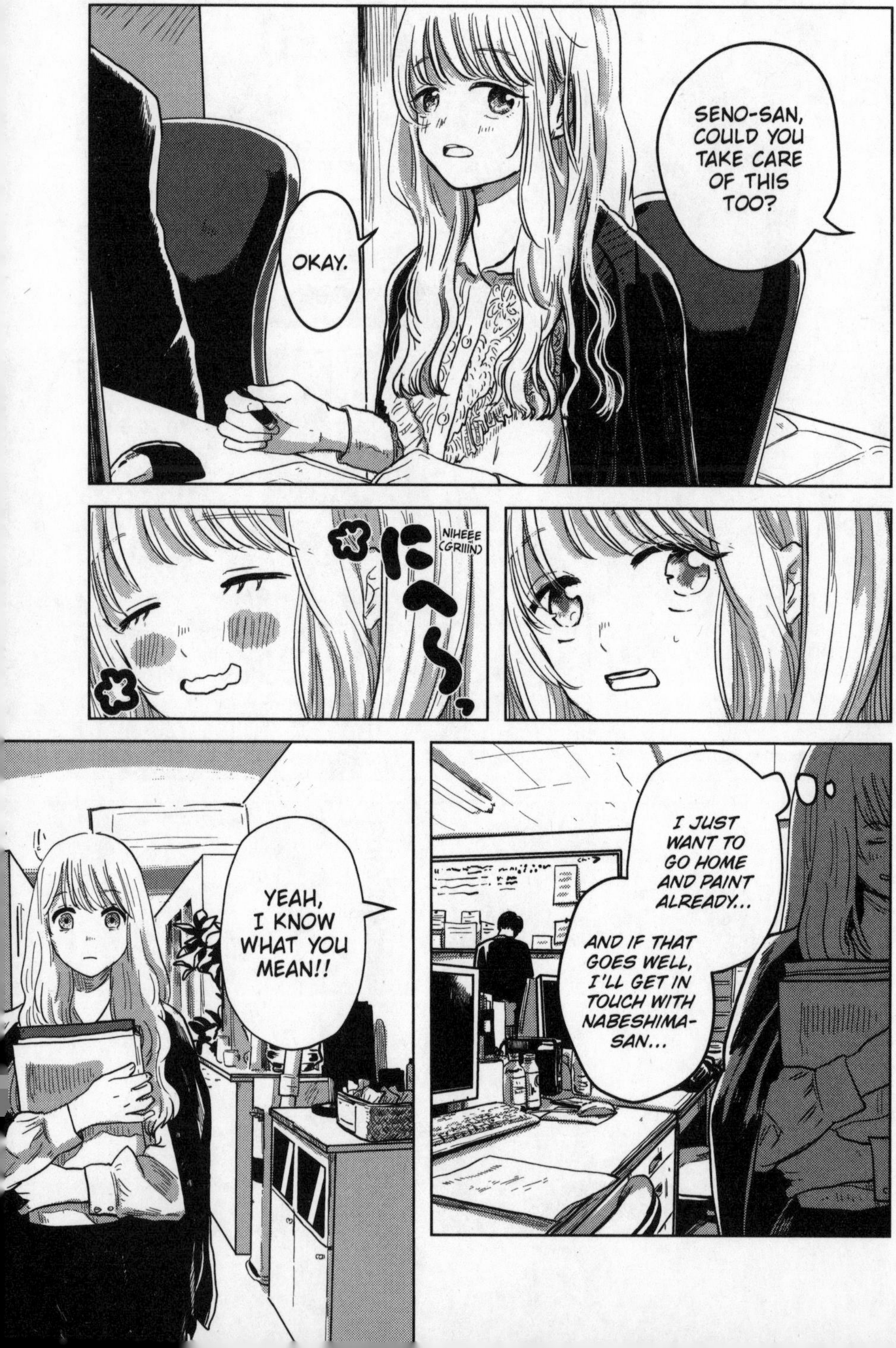
SENO-SAN, COULD YOU TAKE CARE OF THIS TOO?
OKAY.
にへら
NIHEEE (GRIIIN)
I JUST WANT TO GO HOME AND PAINT ALREADY...
AND IF THAT GOES WELL, I'LL GET IN TOUCH WITH NABESHIMA-SAN...
YEAH, I KNOW WHAT YOU MEAN!!

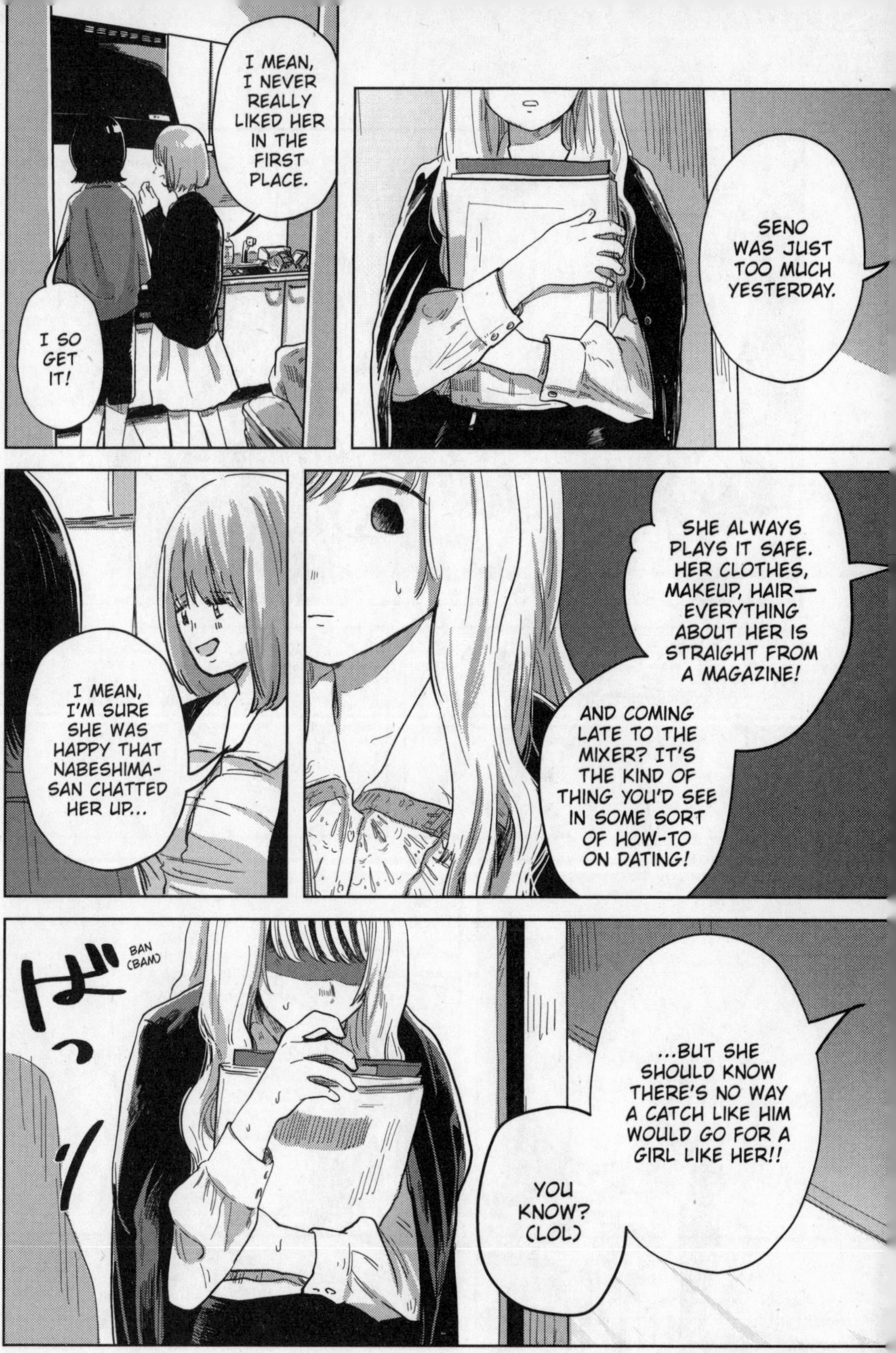
SENO WAS JUST TOO MUCH YESTERDAY.
I MEAN, I NEVER REALLY LIKED HER IN THE FIRST PLACE.
I SO GET IT!
SHE ALWAYS PLAYS IT SAFE. HER CLOTHES, MAKEUP, HAIR—EVERYTHING ABOUT HER IS STRAIGHT FROM A MAGAZINE!
AND COMING LATE TO THE MIXER? IT'S THE KIND OF THING YOU'D SEE IN SOME SORT OF HOW-TO ON DATING!
I MEAN, I'M SURE SHE WAS HAPPY THAT NABESHIMA-SAN CHATTED HER UP...
...BUT SHE SHOULD KNOW THERE'S NO WAY A CATCH LIKE HIM WOULD GO FOR A GIRL LIKE HER!!
YOU KNOW? (LOL)
ばっ
BAN (BAM)

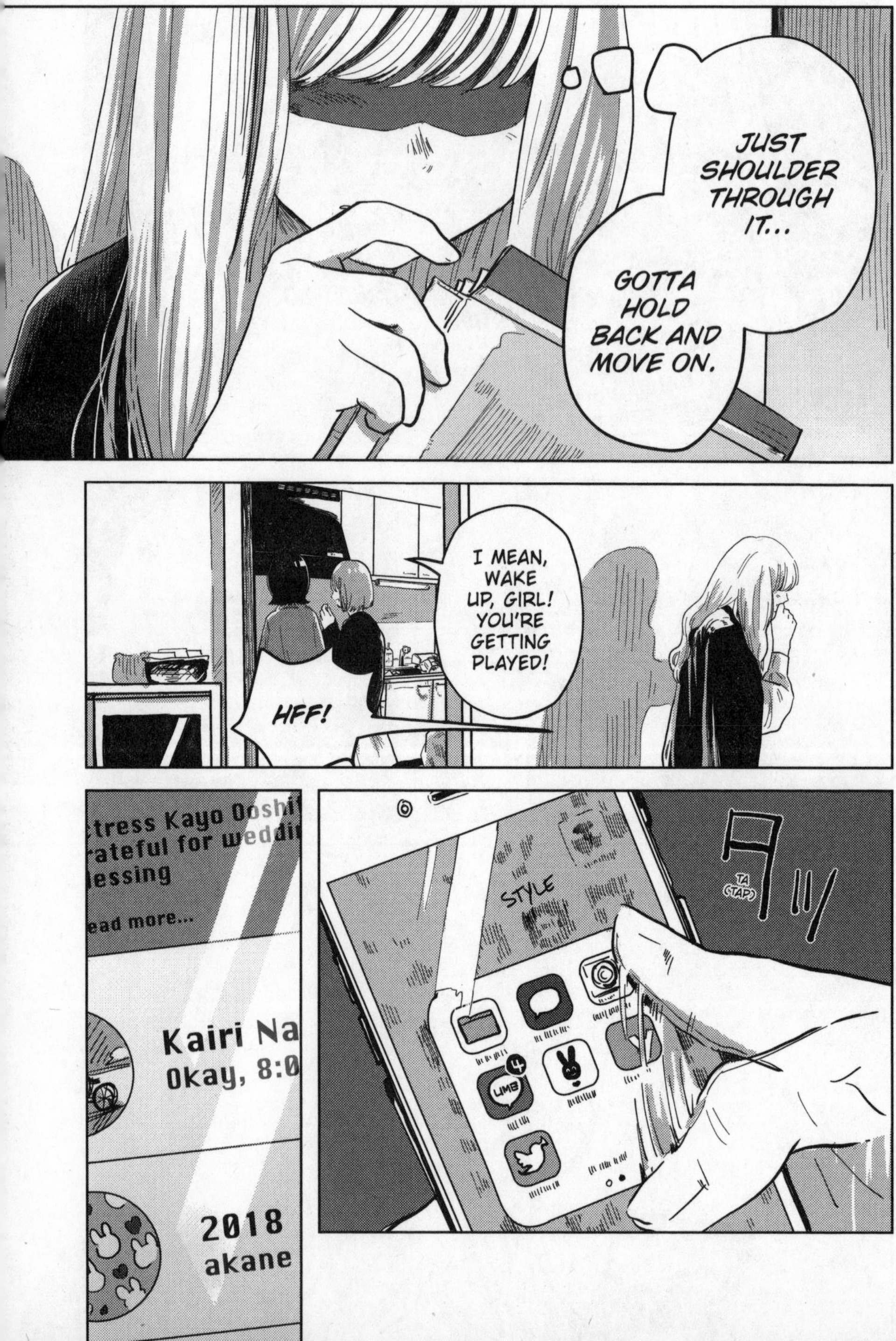
JUST SHOULDER THROUGH IT...
GOTTA HOLD BACK AND MOVE ON.
I MEAN, WAKE UP, GIRL! YOU'RE GETTING PLAYED!
HFF!
STYLE
TA (TAP)
ctress Kayo Ooshi
rateful for weddi
lessing
ead more...
Kairi Na
Okay, 8:0
2018
akane

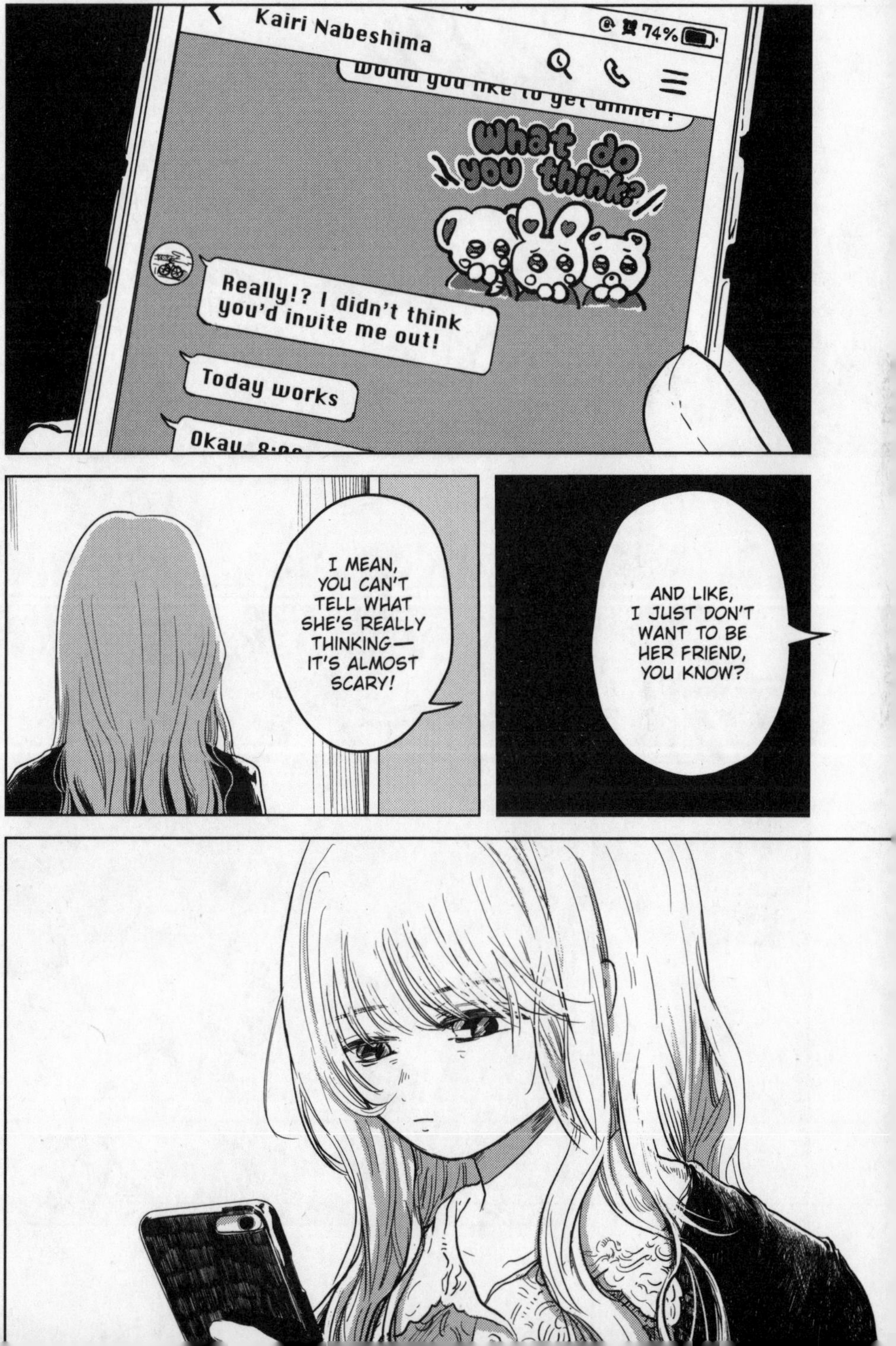
Kairi Nabeshima
74%
What do you think?
Really!? I didn't think you'd invite me out!
Today works
AND LIKE, I JUST DON'T WANT TO BE HER FRIEND, YOU KNOW?
I MEAN, YOU CAN'T TELL WHAT SHE'S REALLY THINKING—IT'S ALMOST SCARY!

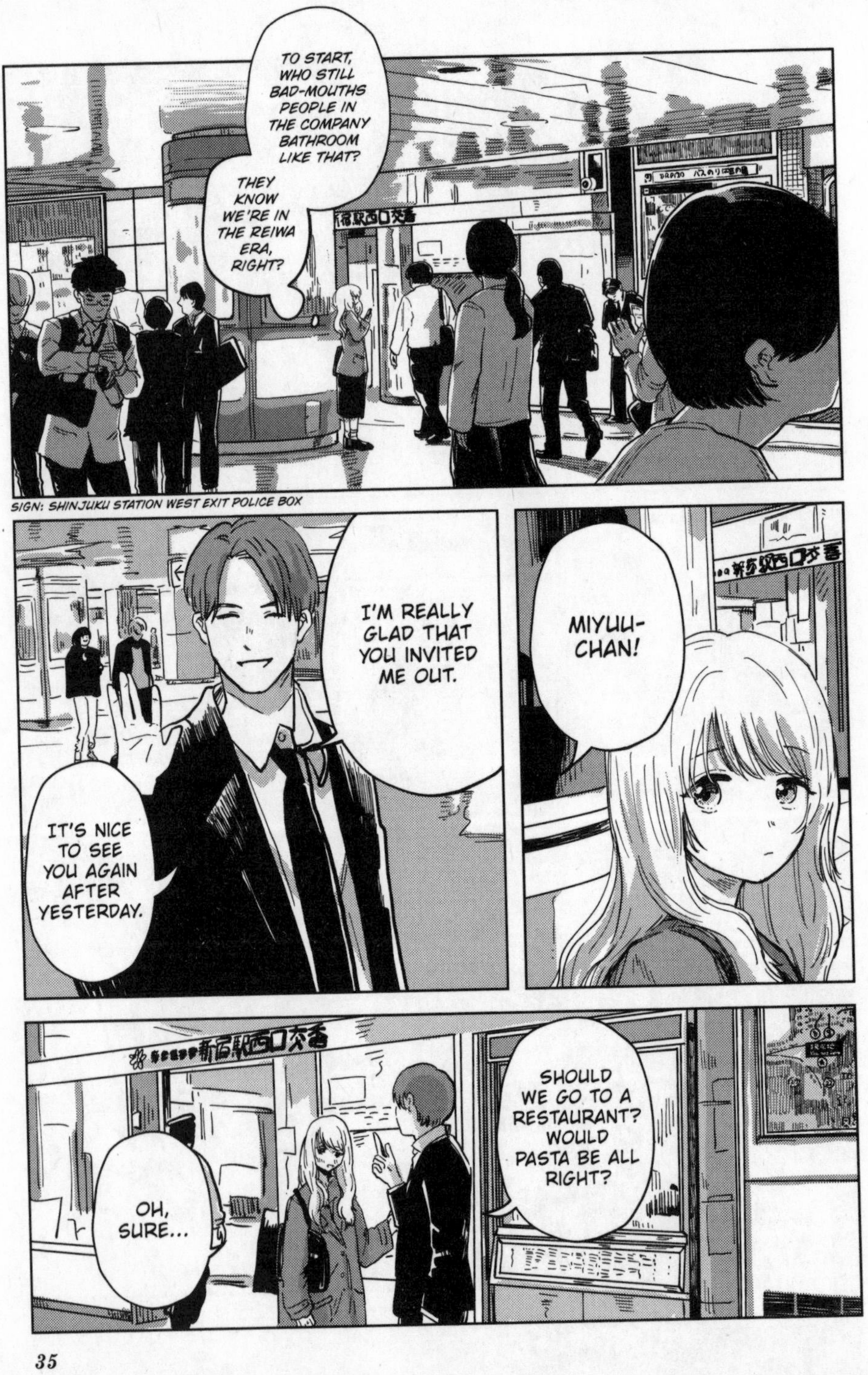
TO START, WHO STILL BAD-MOUTHS PEOPLE IN THE COMPANY BATHROOM LIKE THAT?
THEY KNOW WE'RE IN THE REIWA ERA, RIGHT?
SIGN: SHINJUKU STATION WEST EXIT POLICE BOX
MIYUU-CHAN!
I'M REALLY GLAD THAT YOU INVITED ME OUT.
IT'S NICE TO SEE YOU AGAIN AFTER YESTERDAY.
SHOULD WE GO TO A RESTAURANT? WOULD PASTA BE ALL RIGHT?
OH, SURE...

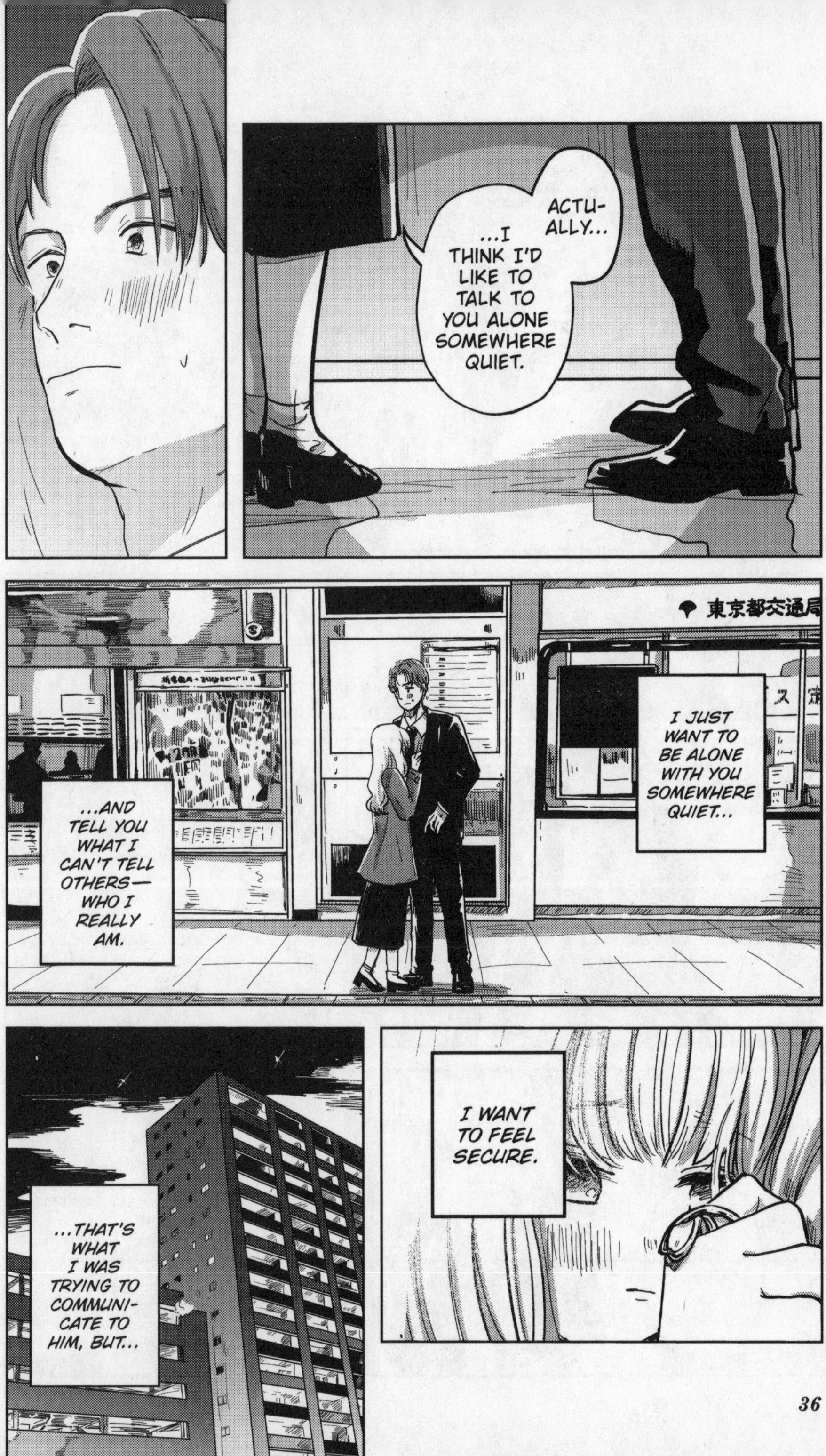
ACTUALLY... ...I THINK I'D LIKE TO TALK TO YOU ALONE SOMEWHERE QUIET.
東京都交通局
I JUST WANT TO BE ALONE WITH YOU SOMEWHERE QUIET...
...AND TELL YOU WHAT I CAN'T TELL OTHERS—WHO I REALLY AM.
I WANT TO FEEL SECURE.
...THAT'S WHAT I WAS TRYING TO COMMUNICATE TO HIM, BUT...

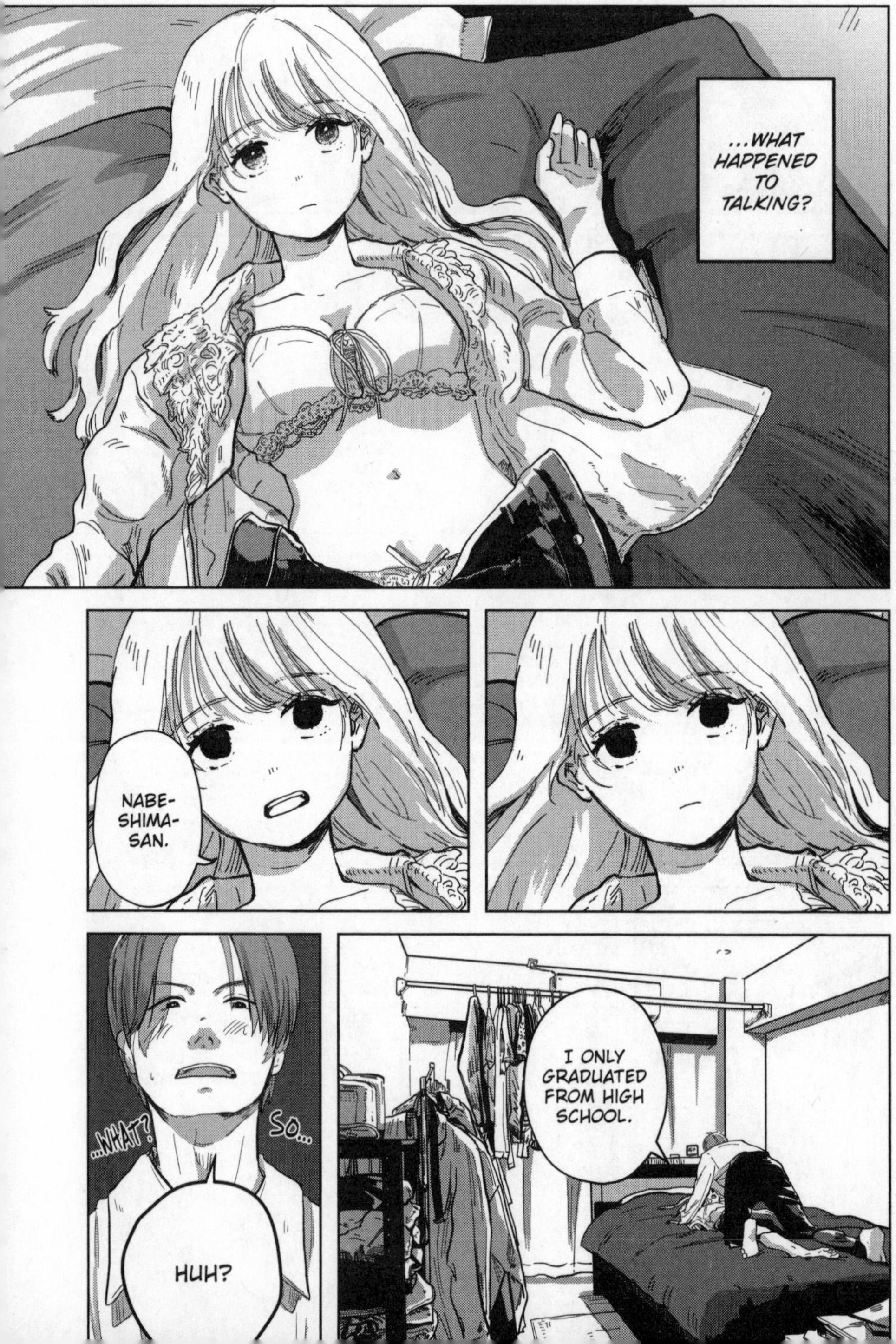
...WHAT HAPPENED TO TALKING?
NABE-SHIMA-SAN.
I ONLY GRADUATED FROM HIGH SCHOOL.
SO...
...WHAT?
HUH?

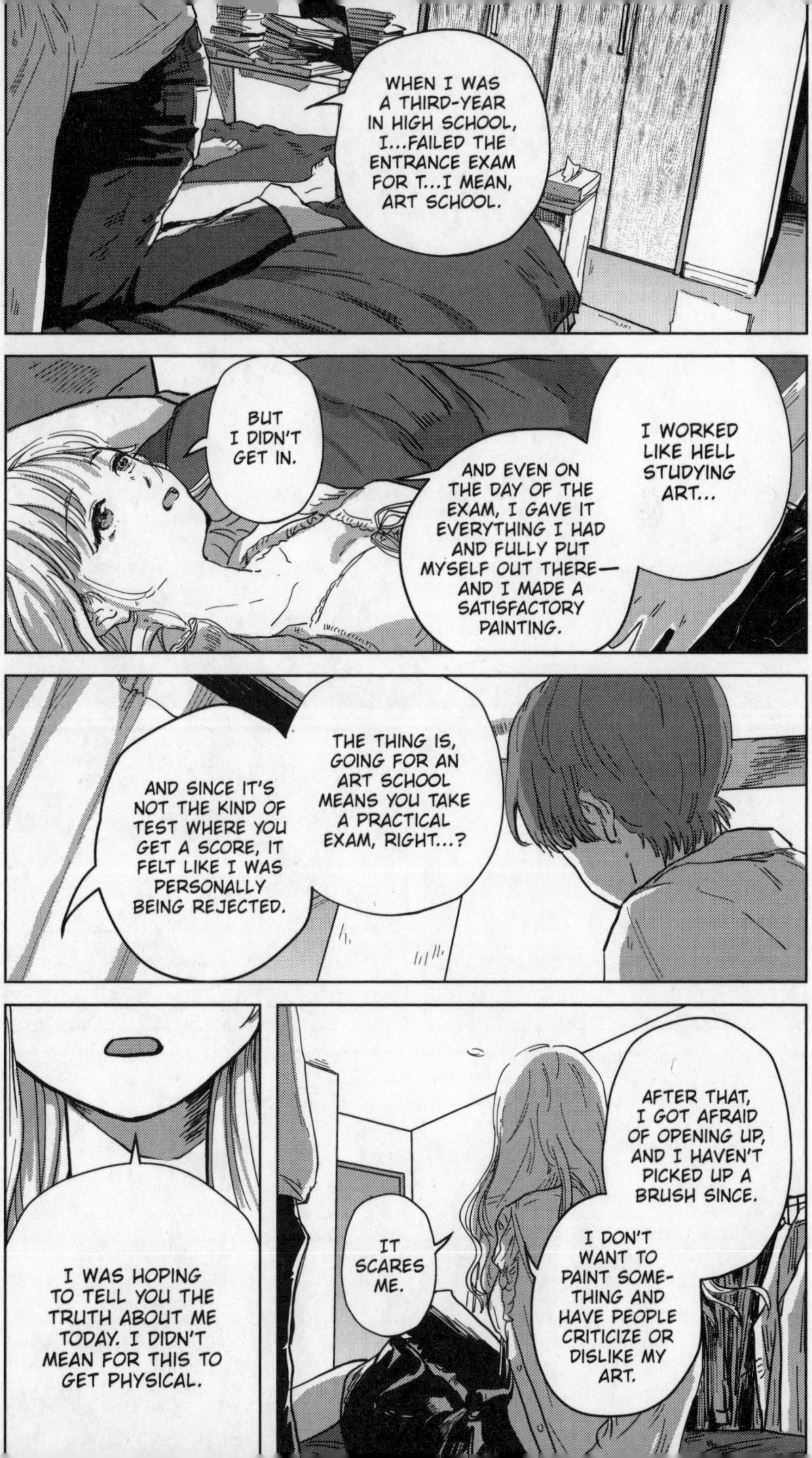
WHEN I WAS A THIRD-YEAR IN HIGH SCHOOL, I...FAILED THE ENTRANCE EXAM FOR T...I MEAN, ART SCHOOL.
I WORKED LIKE HELL STUDYING ART...
AND EVEN ON THE DAY OF THE EXAM, I GAVE IT EVERYTHING I HAD AND FULLY PUT MYSELF OUT THERE—AND I MADE A SATISFACTORY PAINTING.
BUT I DIDN'T GET IN.
THE THING IS, GOING FOR AN ART SCHOOL MEANS YOU TAKE A PRACTICAL EXAM, RIGHT...?
AND SINCE IT'S NOT THE KIND OF TEST WHERE YOU GET A SCORE, IT FELT LIKE I WAS PERSONALLY BEING REJECTED.
AFTER THAT, I GOT AFRAID OF OPENING UP, AND I HAVEN'T PICKED UP A BRUSH SINCE.
I DON'T WANT TO PAINT SOME-THING AND HAVE PEOPLE CRITICIZE OR DISLIKE MY ART.
IT SCARES ME.
I WAS HOPING TO TELL YOU THE TRUTH ABOUT ME TODAY. I DIDN'T MEAN FOR THIS TO GET PHYSICAL.

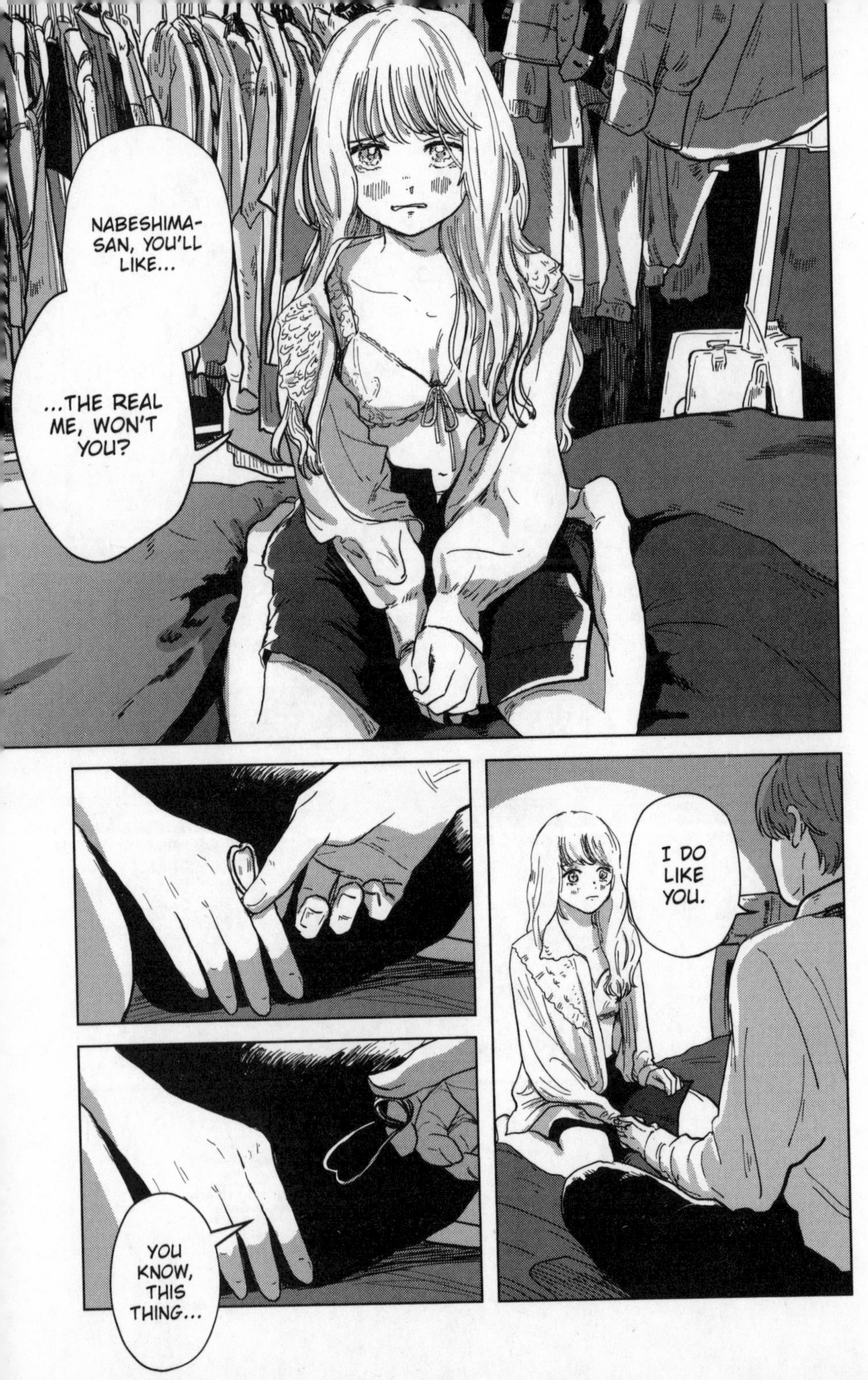
NABESHIMA-SAN, YOU'LL LIKE...
...THE REAL ME, WON'T YOU?
I DO LIKE YOU.
YOU KNOW, THIS THING...

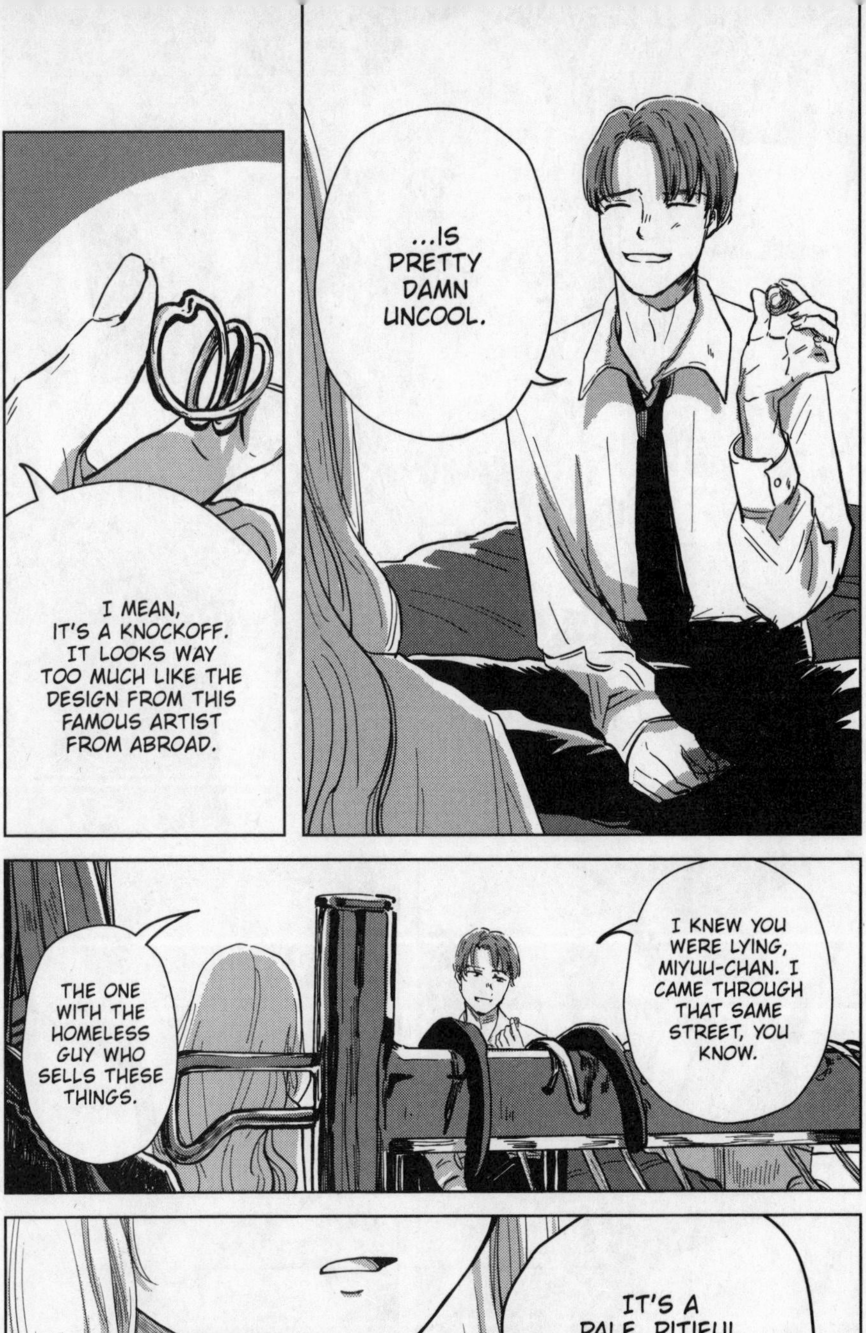
...IS PRETTY DAMN UNCOOL.
I MEAN, IT'S A KNOCKOFF. IT LOOKS WAY TOO MUCH LIKE THE DESIGN FROM THIS FAMOUS ARTIST FROM ABROAD.
I KNEW YOU WERE LYING, MIYUU-CHAN. I CAME THROUGH THAT SAME STREET, YOU KNOW.
THE ONE WITH THE HOMELESS GUY WHO SELLS THESE THINGS.
IT'S A PALE, PITIFUL IMITATION.

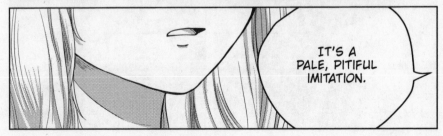

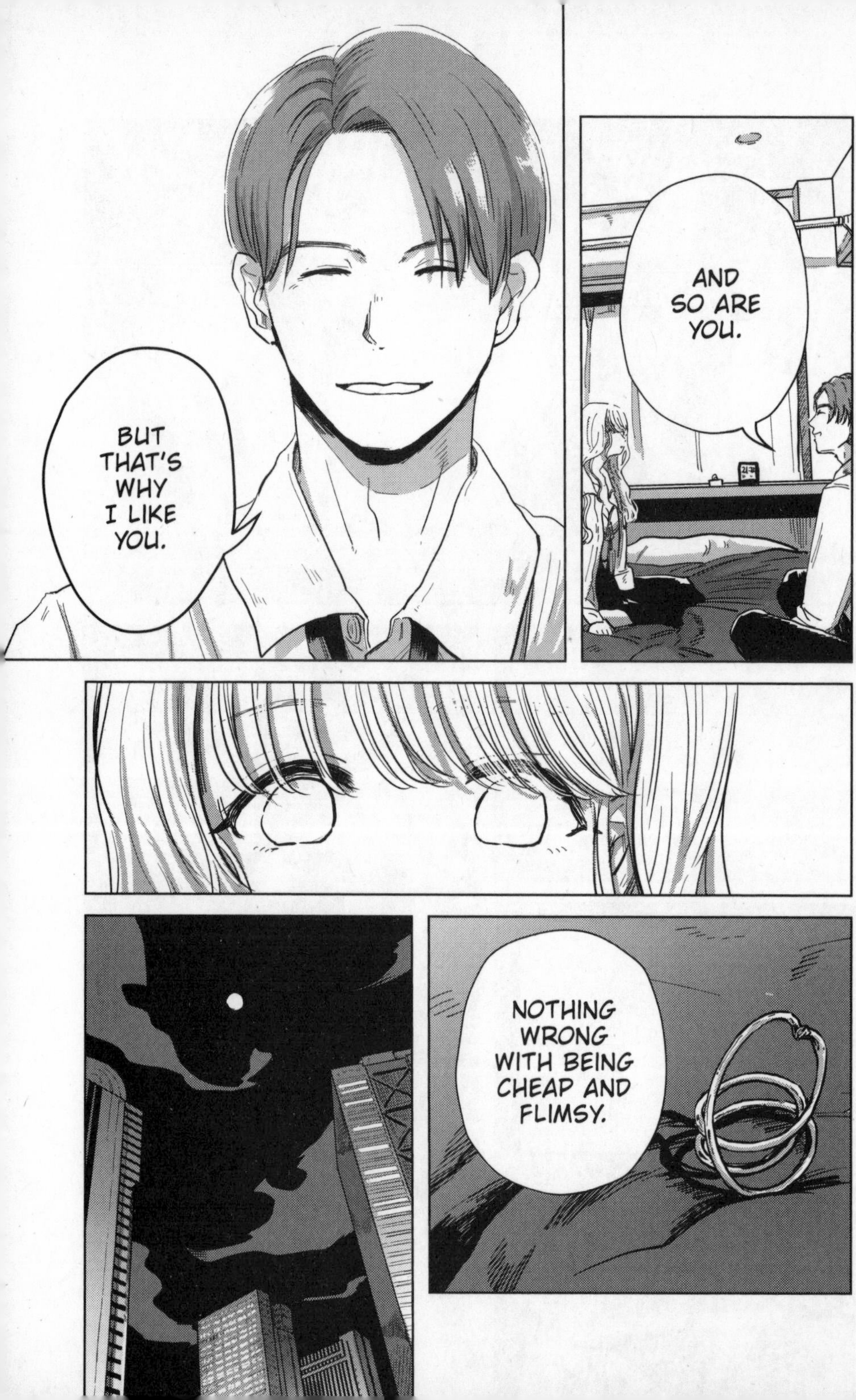
AND SO ARE YOU.
BUT THAT'S WHY I LIKE YOU.
NOTHING WRONG WITH BEING CHEAP AND FLIMSY.

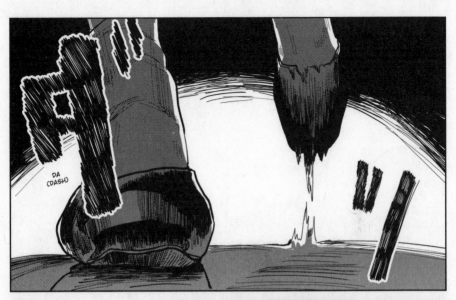

DA
(DASH)

I'M SO ASHAMED. I WAS ARROGANT, AND I EXPECTED TOO MUCH FROM MYSELF.

WHEN DID I BECOME SUCH A FAKE?

42

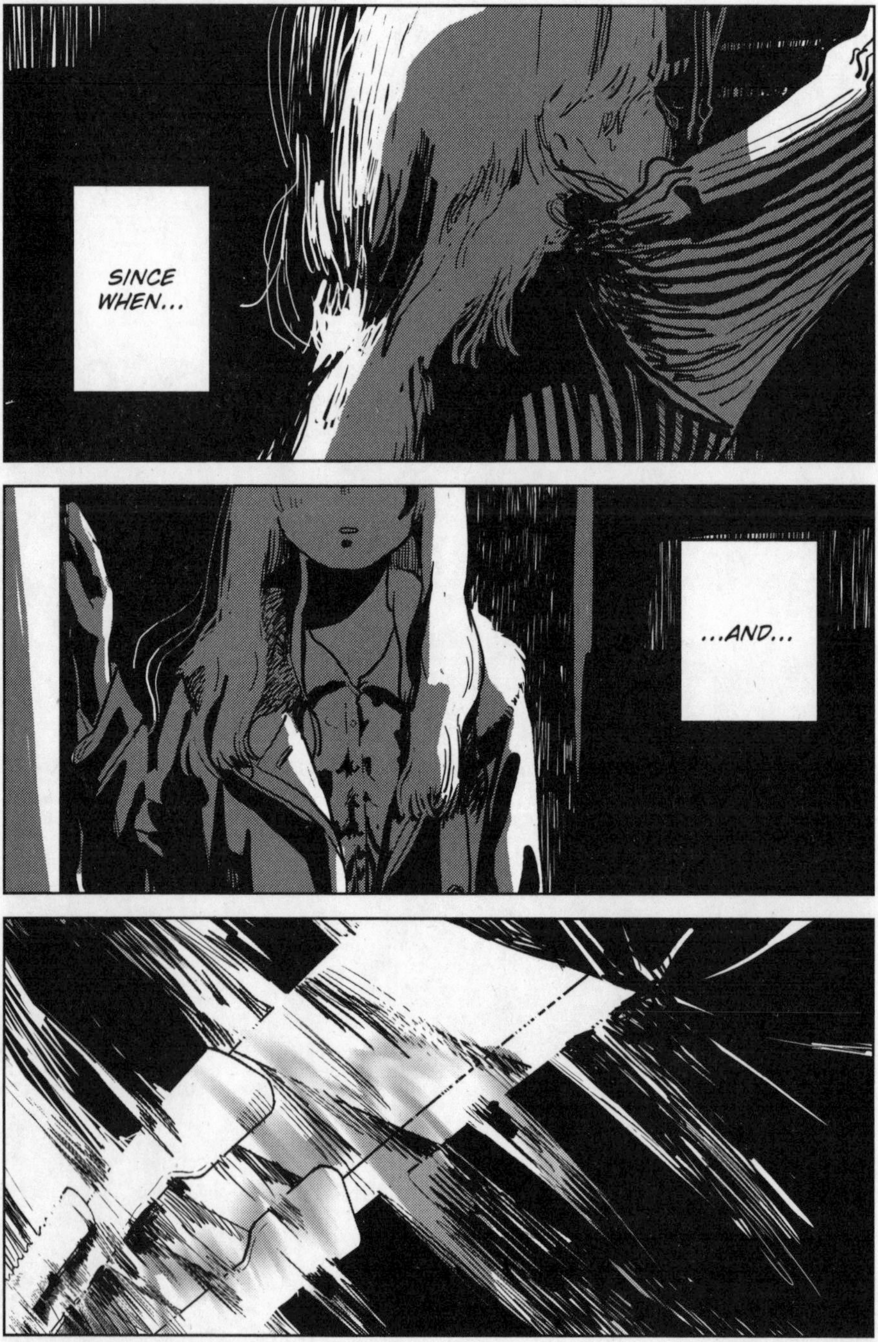
SINCE WHEN...
...AND...

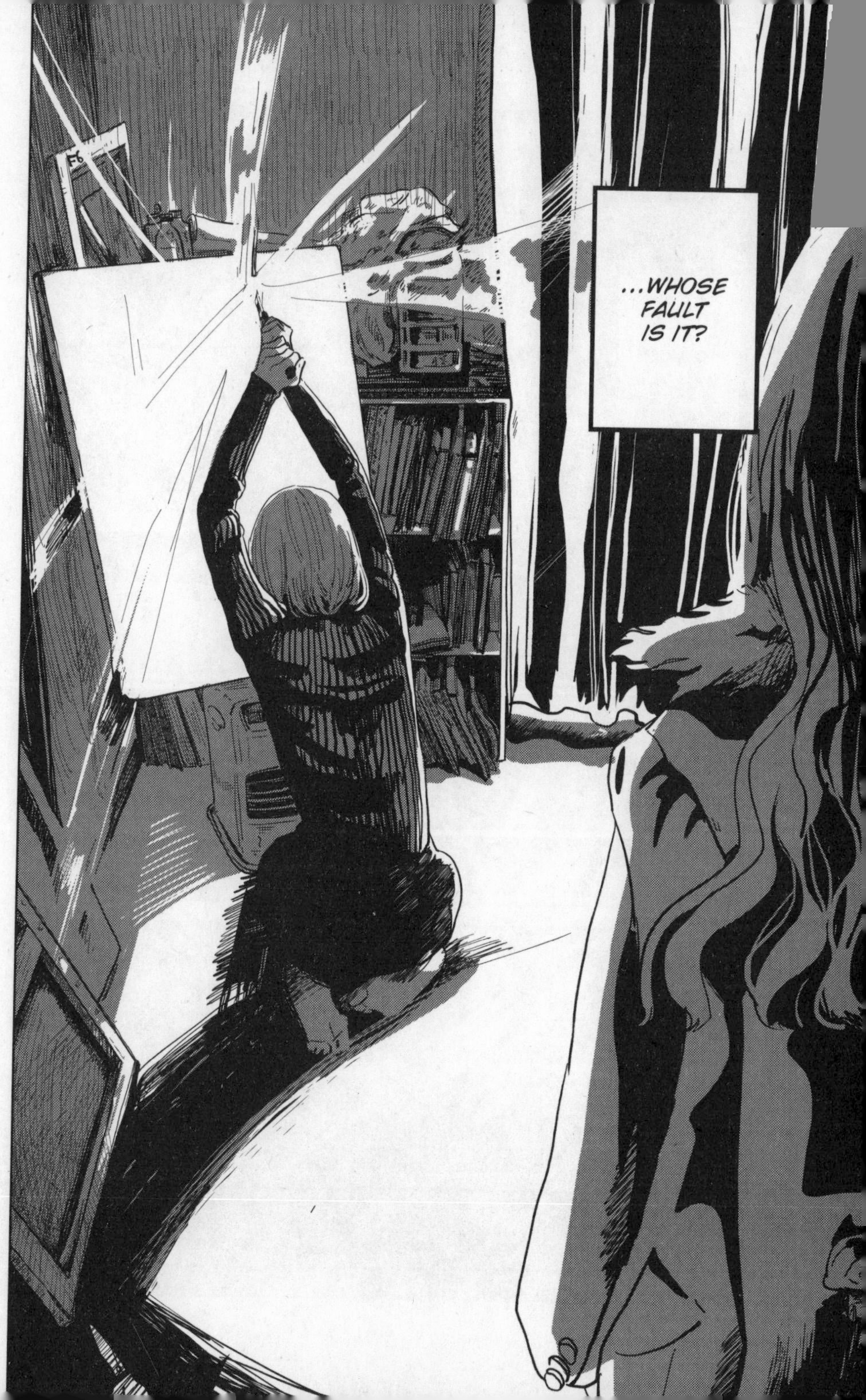
...WHOSE FAULT IS IT?

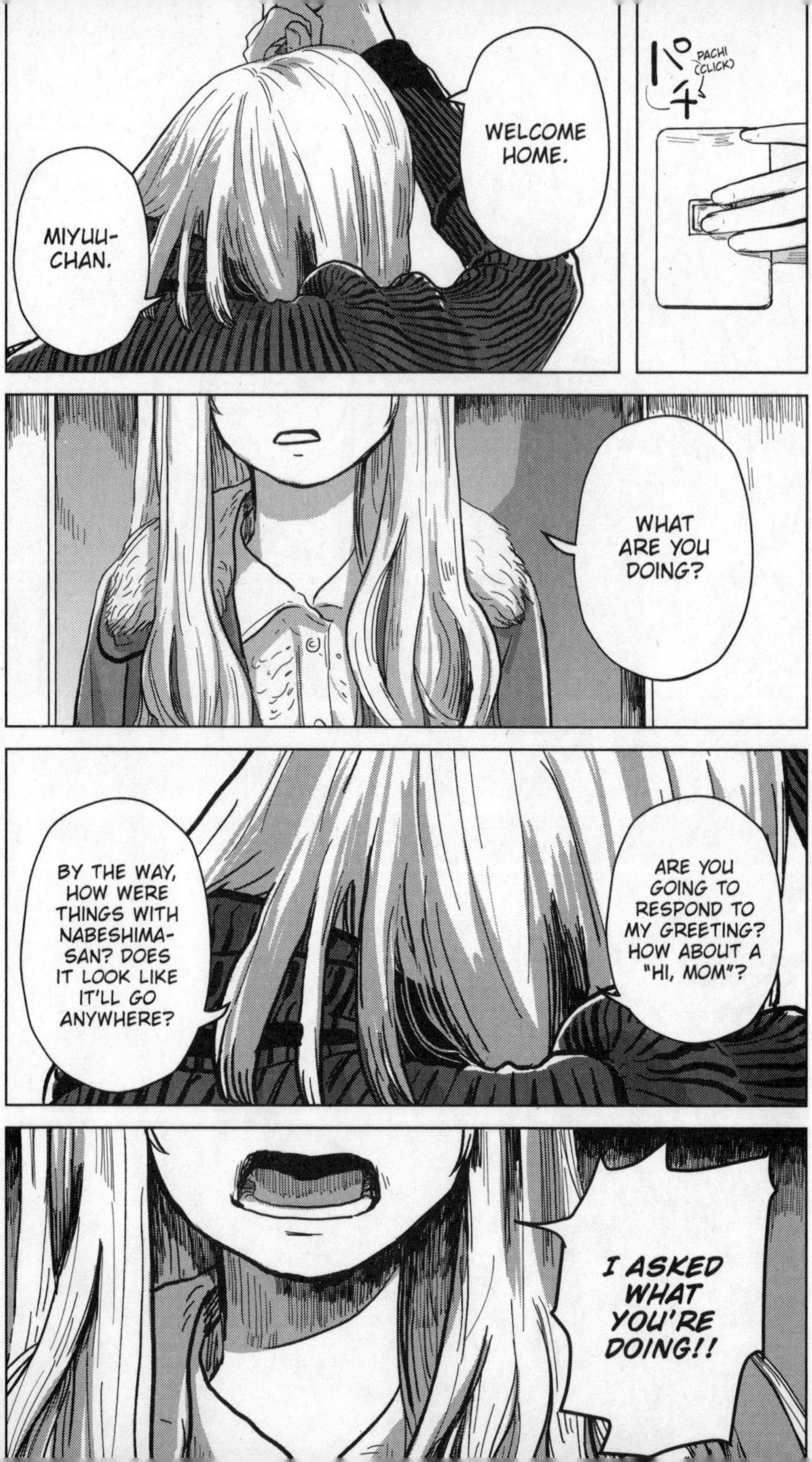
パチ
PACHI (CLICK)
WELCOME HOME.
MIYUU-CHAN.
WHAT ARE YOU DOING?
ARE YOU GOING TO RESPOND TO MY GREETING? HOW ABOUT A "HI, MOM"?
BY THE WAY, HOW WERE THINGS WITH NABESHIMA-SAN? DOES IT LOOK LIKE IT'LL GO ANYWHERE?
I ASKED WHAT YOU'RE DOING!!

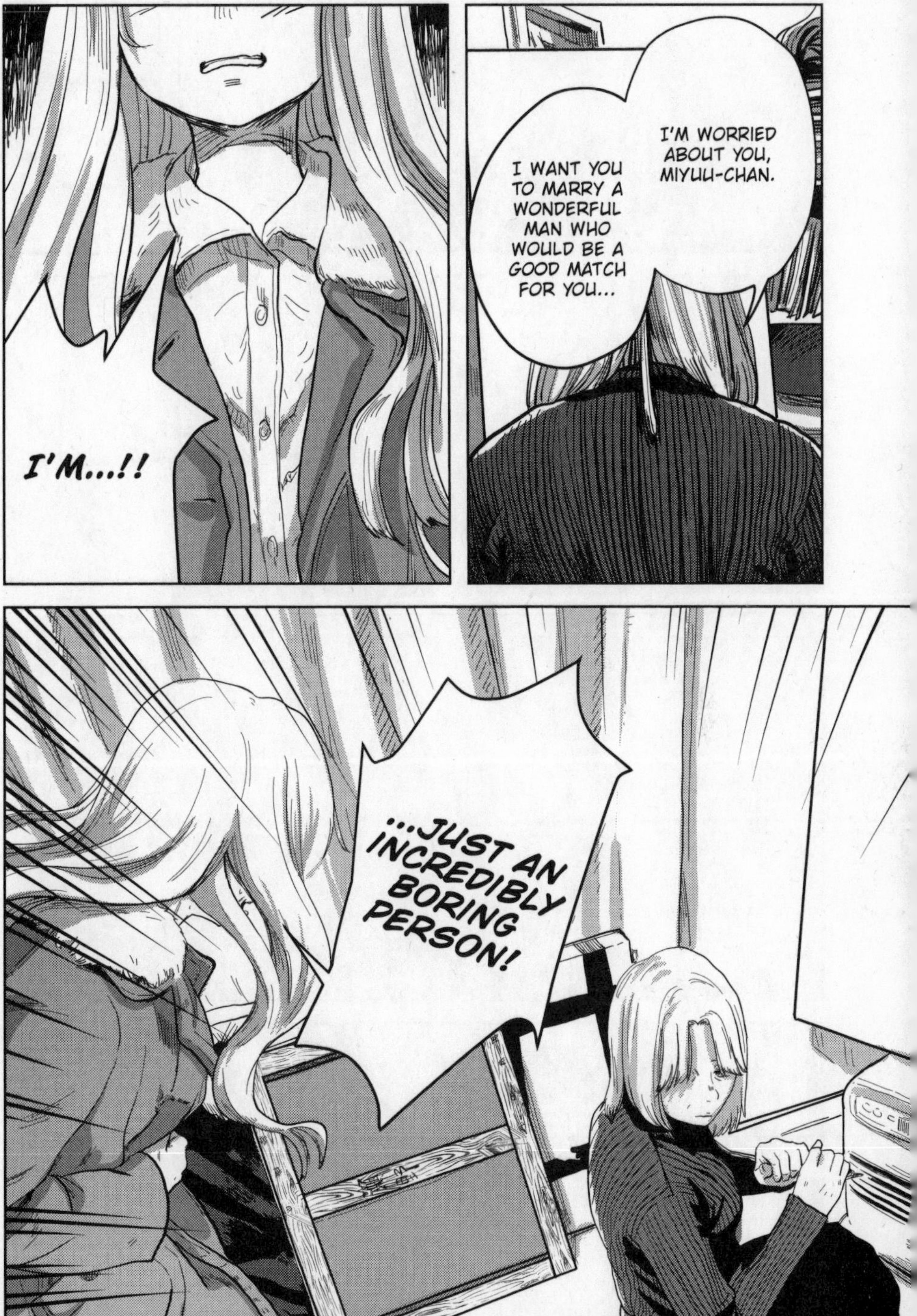
I'M WORRIED ABOUT YOU, MIYUU-CHAN.
I WANT YOU TO MARRY A WONDERFUL MAN WHO WOULD BE A GOOD MATCH FOR YOU...
I'M...!!
...JUST AN INCREDIBLY BORING PERSON!

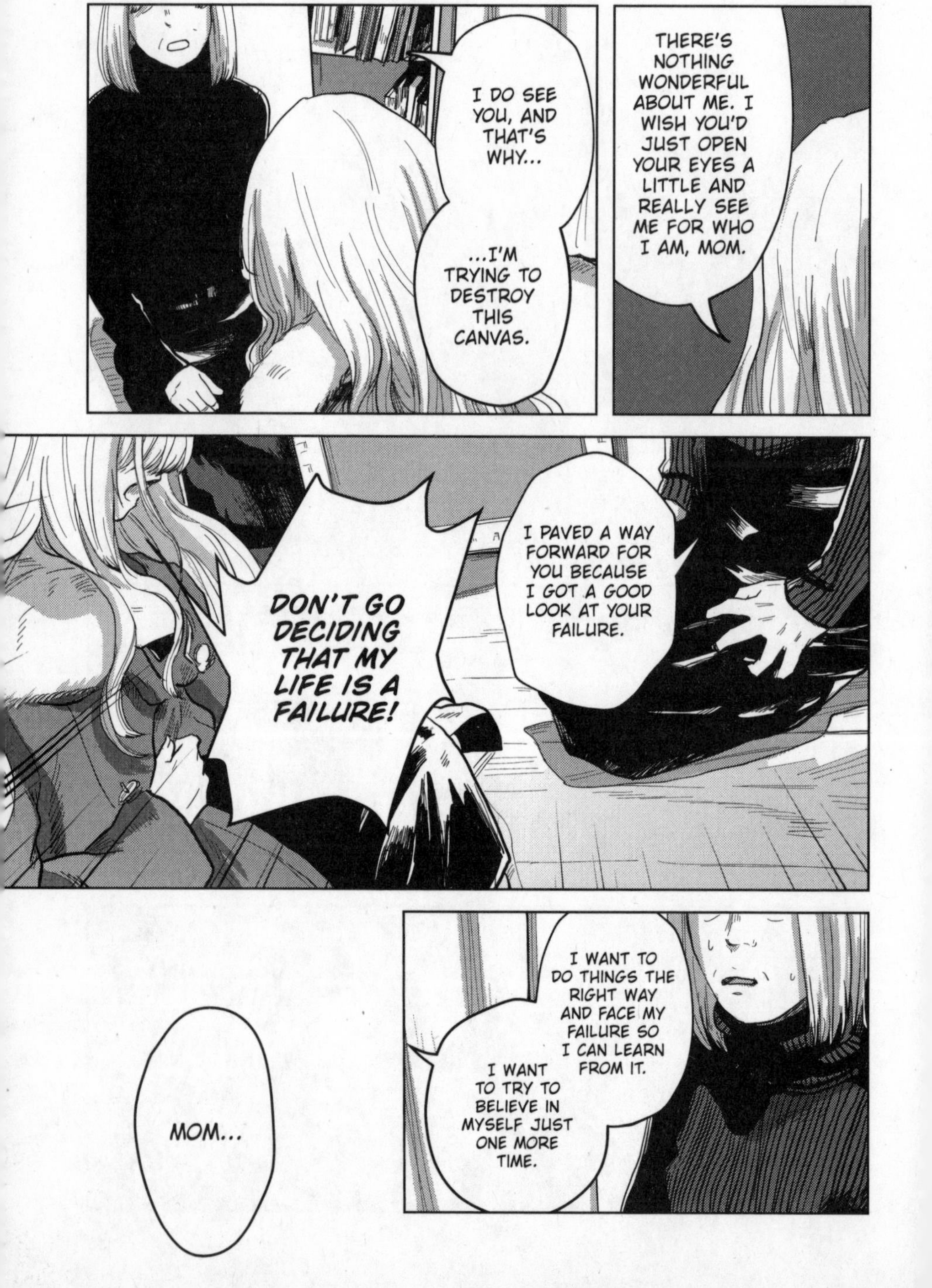
THERE'S NOTHING WONDERFUL ABOUT ME. I WISH YOU'D JUST OPEN YOUR EYES A LITTLE AND REALLY SEE ME FOR WHO I AM, MOM.
I DO SEE YOU, AND THAT'S WHY...
...I'M TRYING TO DESTROY THIS CANVAS.
I PAVED A WAY FORWARD FOR YOU BECAUSE I GOT A GOOD LOOK AT YOUR FAILURE.
DON'T GO DECIDING THAT MY LIFE IS A FAILURE!
I WANT TO DO THINGS THE RIGHT WAY AND FACE MY FAILURE SO I CAN LEARN FROM IT.
I WANT TO TRY TO BELIEVE IN MYSELF JUST ONE MORE TIME.
MOM...

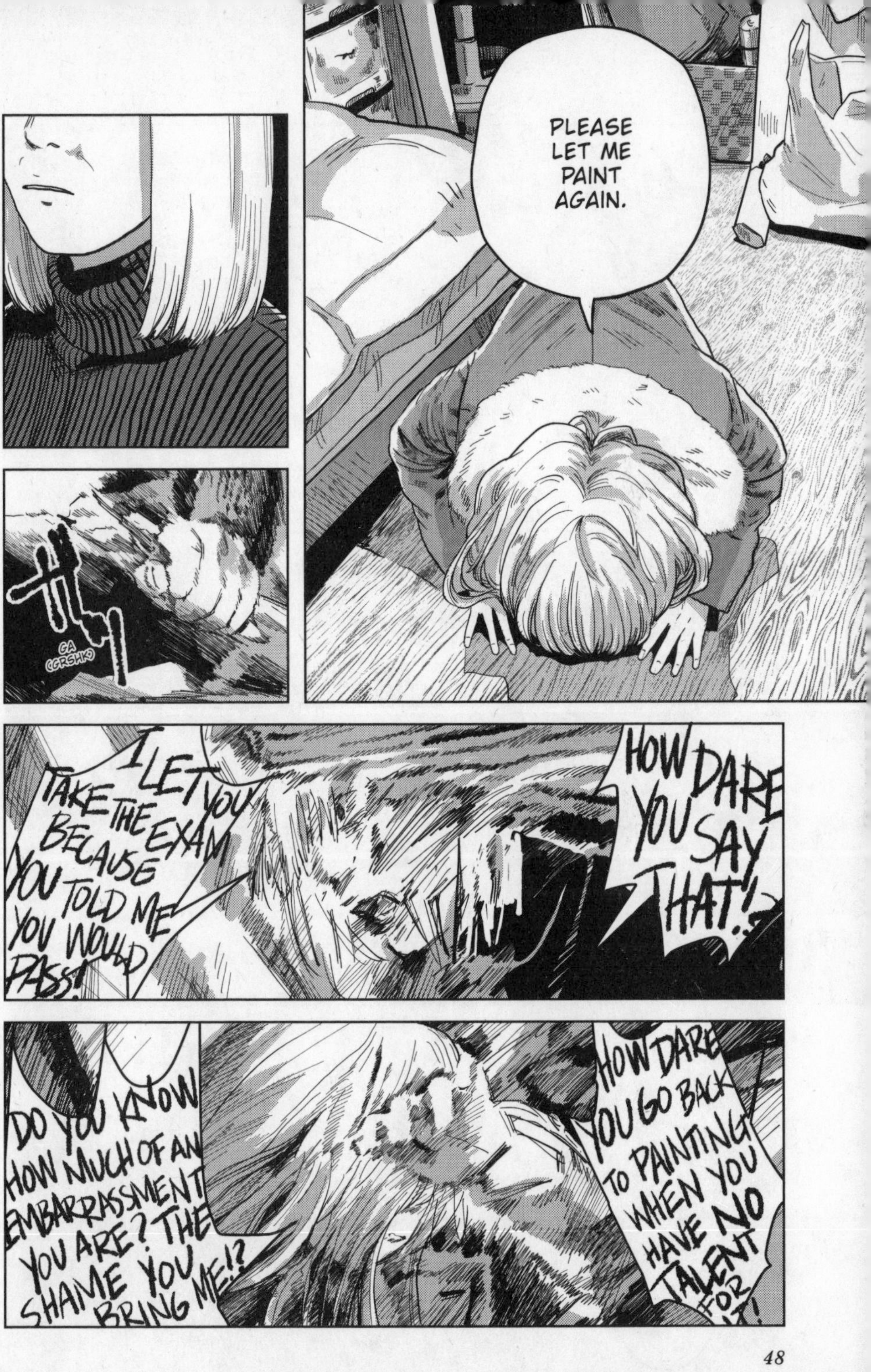
PLEASE LET ME PAINT AGAIN.
GA (GRSHK)
HOW DARE YOU SAY THAT!
I LET YOU TAKE THE EXAM BECAUSE YOU TOLD ME YOU WOULD PASS!
HOW DARE YOU GO BACK TO PAINTING WHEN YOU HAVE NO TALENT FOR
DO YOU KNOW HOW MUCH OF AN EMBARRASSMENT YOU ARE? THE SHAME YOU BRING ME!?

BUT I WANT TO TRY PAINTING AGAIN.

SORRY.

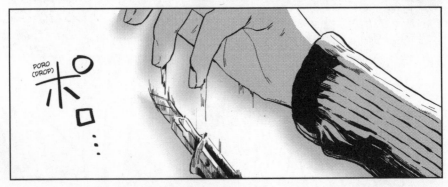

PORO
(DROP)

ポロ...

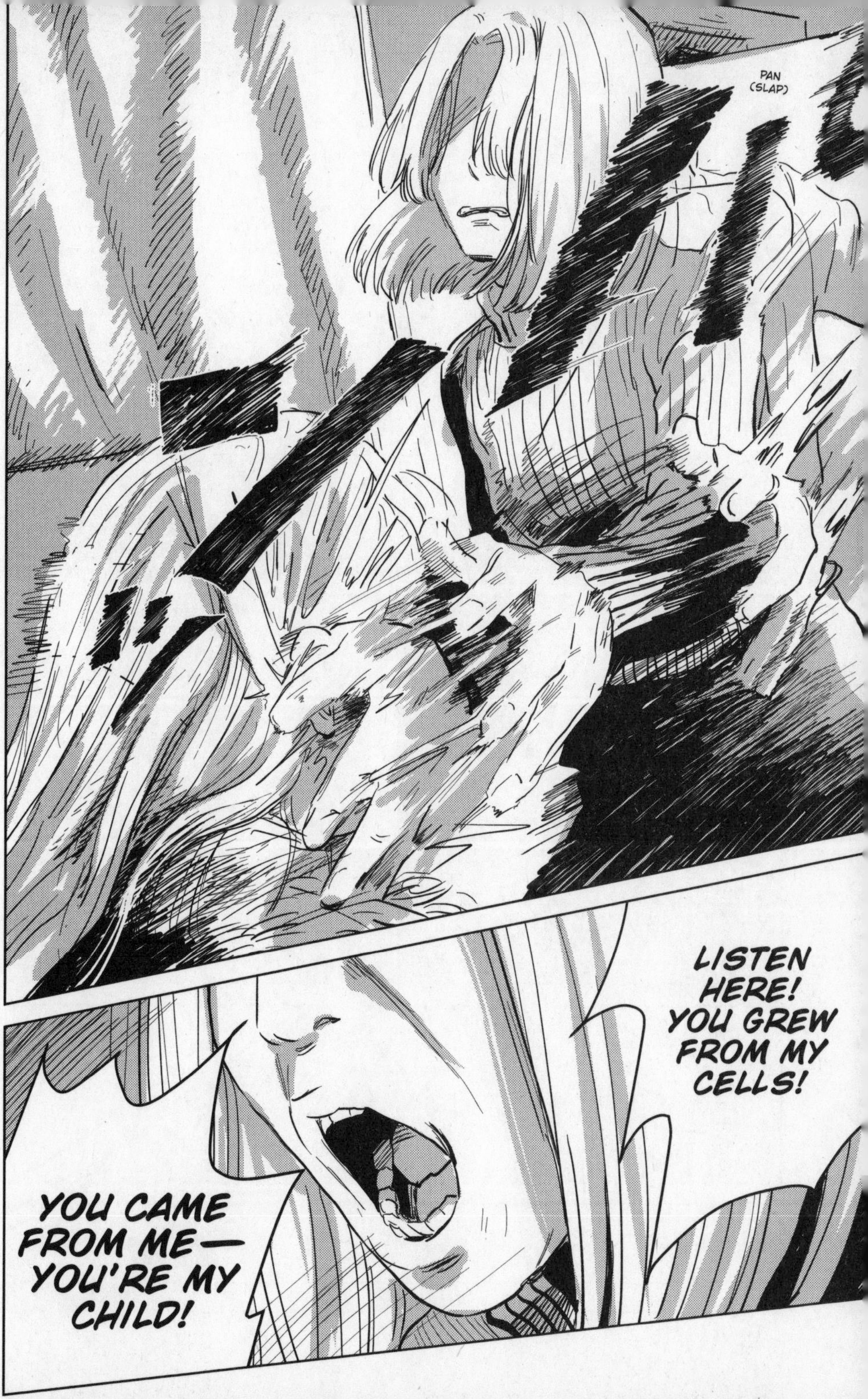
PAN
(SLAP)
LISTEN HERE! YOU GREW FROM MY CELLS!
YOU CAME FROM ME— YOU'RE MY CHILD!

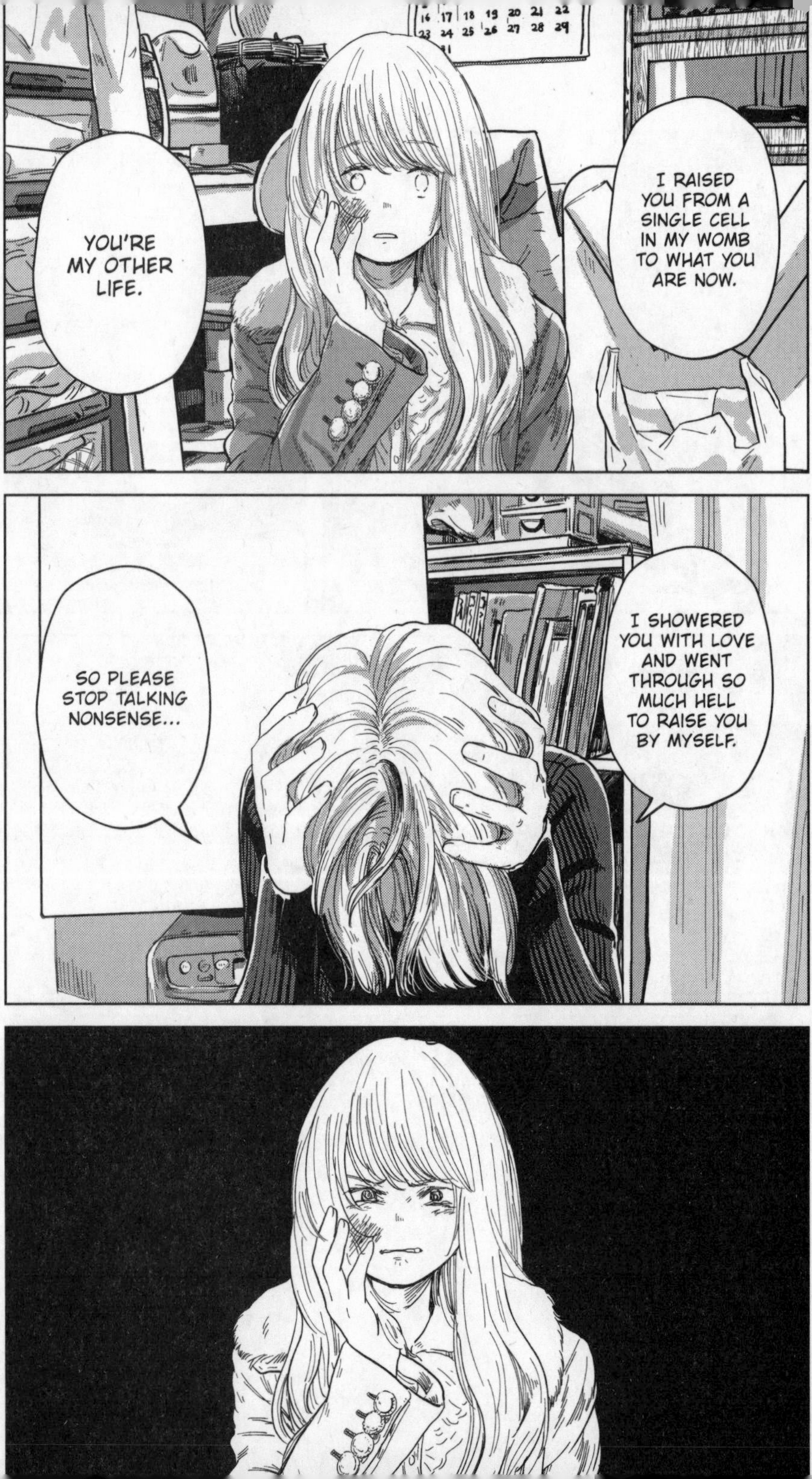
I RAISED YOU FROM A SINGLE CELL IN MY WOMB TO WHAT YOU ARE NOW.
YOU'RE MY OTHER LIFE.
I SHOWERED YOU WITH LOVE AND WENT THROUGH SO MUCH HELL TO RAISE YOU BY MYSELF.
SO PLEASE STOP TALKING NONSENSE...

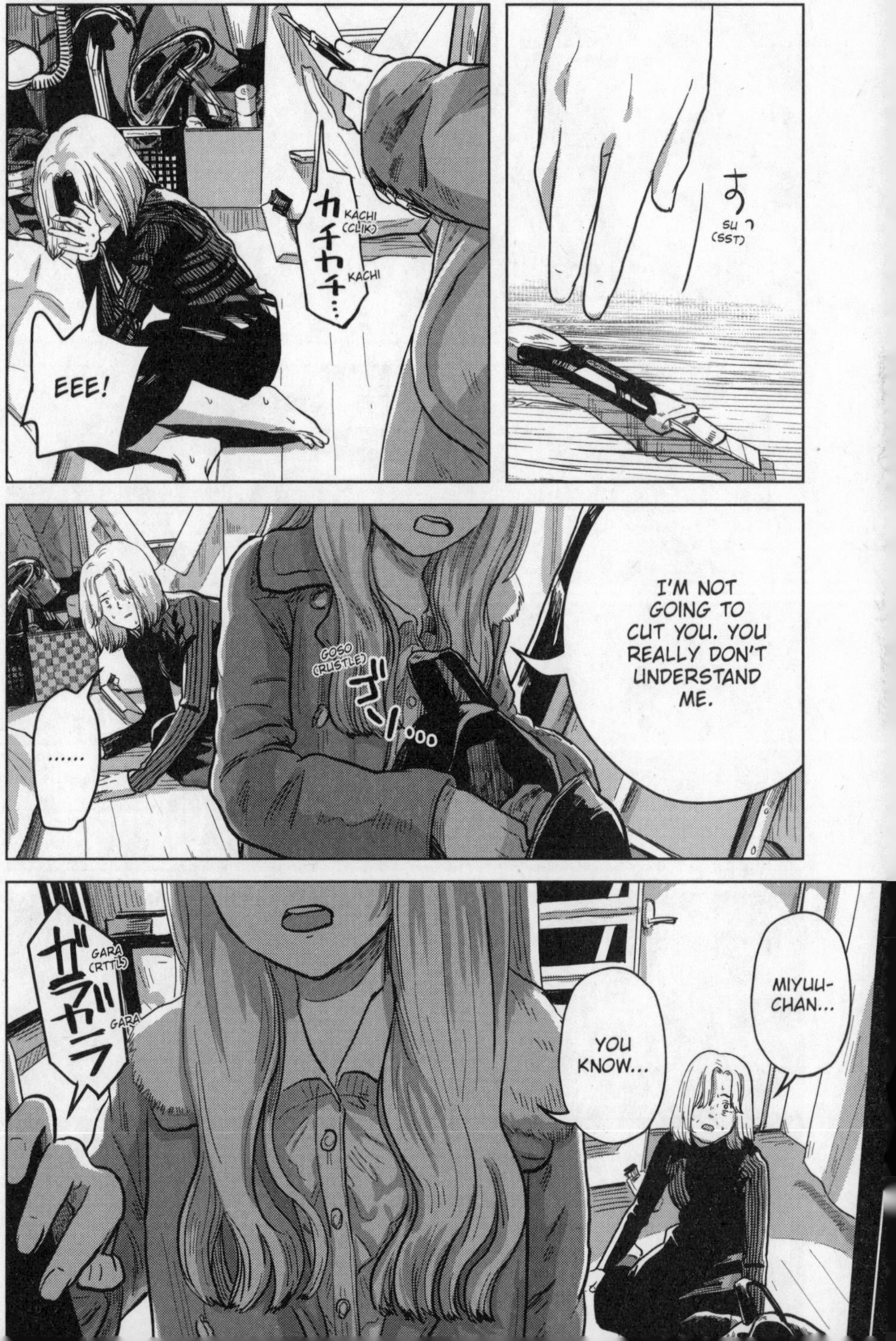
す
SU (SST)
カチカチ…
KACHI (CLIK) KACHI
EEE!
I'M NOT GOING TO CUT YOU. YOU REALLY DON'T UNDERSTAND ME.
GOSO (RUSTLE)
......
MIYUU-CHAN...
YOU KNOW...
ガラガラ
GARA (RTTL) GARA

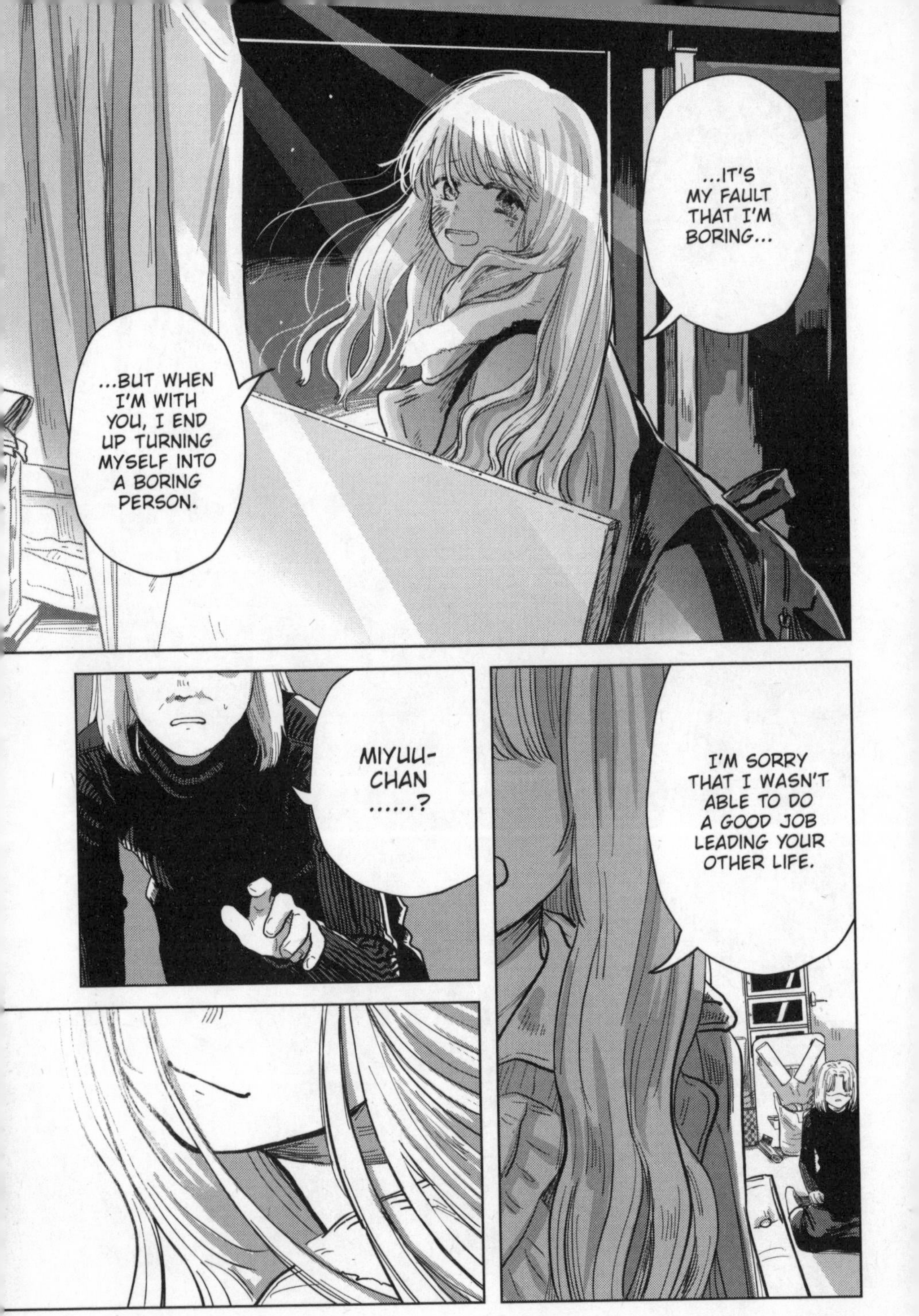
...IT'S MY FAULT THAT I'M BORING...
...BUT WHEN I'M WITH YOU, I END UP TURNING MYSELF INTO A BORING PERSON.
I'M SORRY THAT I WASN'T ABLE TO DO A GOOD JOB LEADING YOUR OTHER LIFE.
MIYUU-CHAN ......?

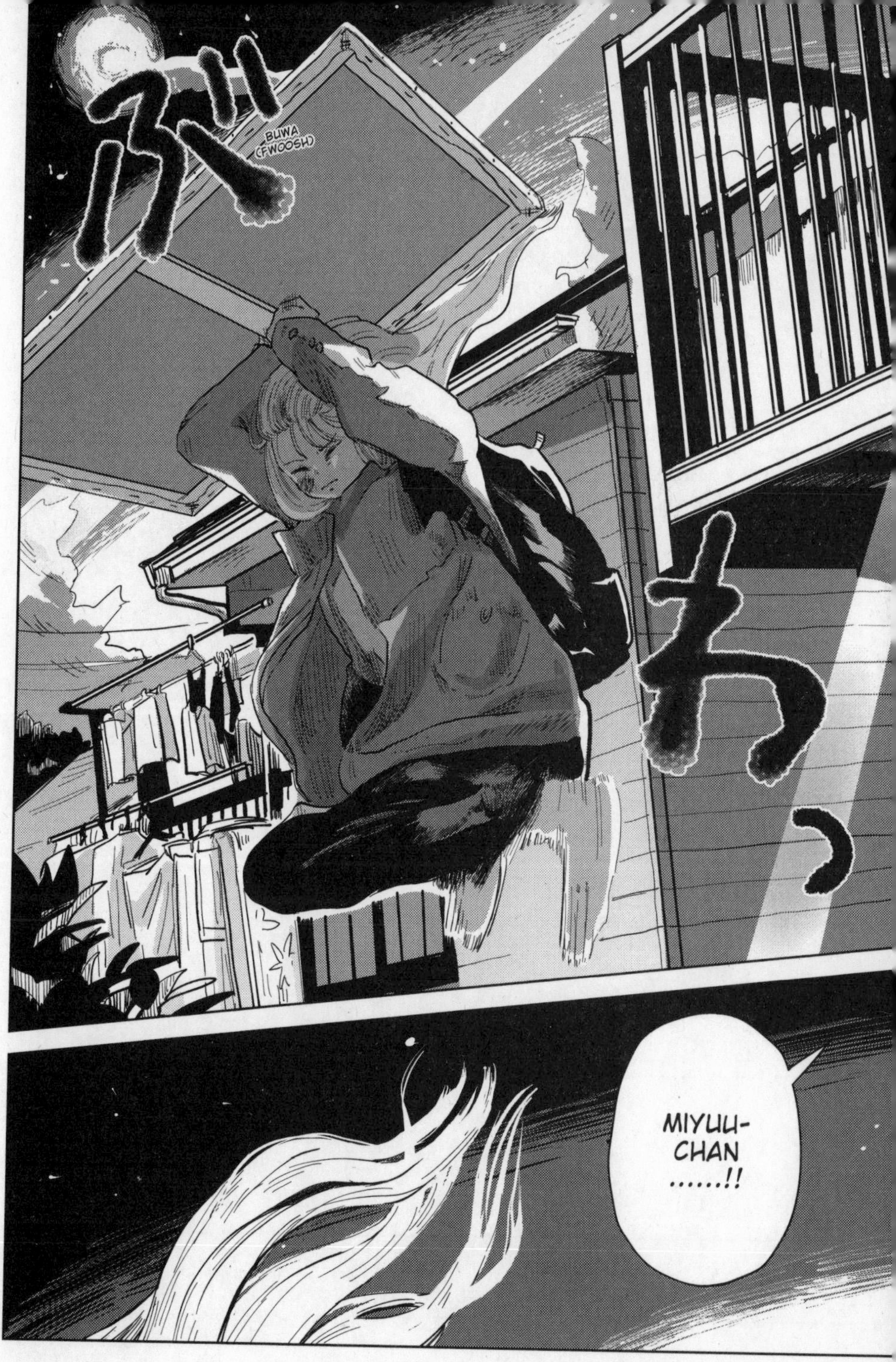
BUWA (FWOOSH)
MIYUU-CHAN ......!!

......HEH.

......

BASA
(FWAP)

AH HA HA!

AIR RESISTANCE! I GLIDED DOWN BECAUSE OF AIR RESISTANCE!!

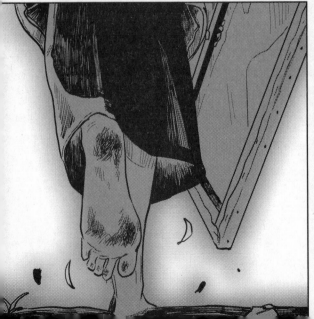

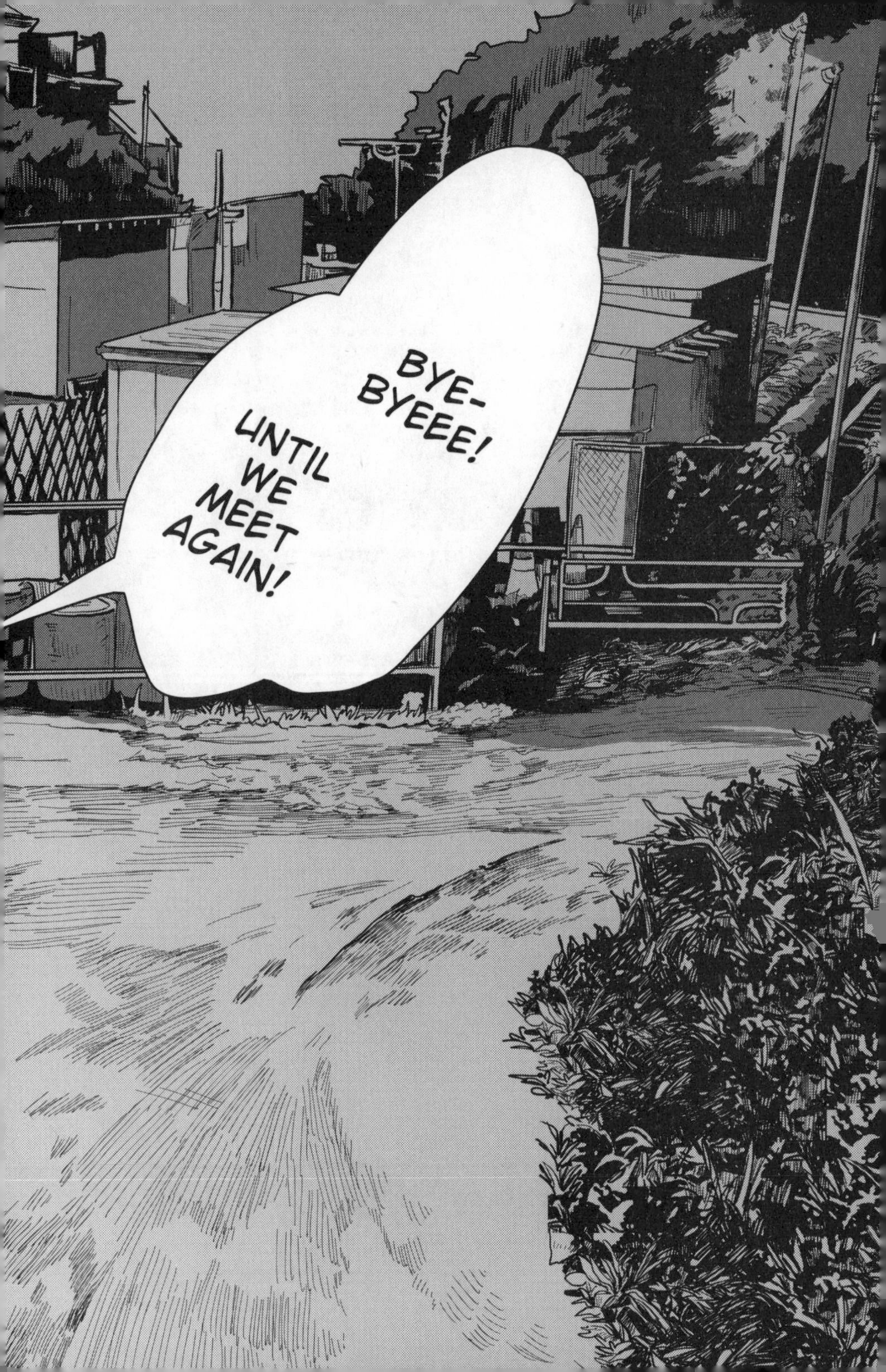
BYE-BYEEEE! UNTIL WE MEET AGAIN!

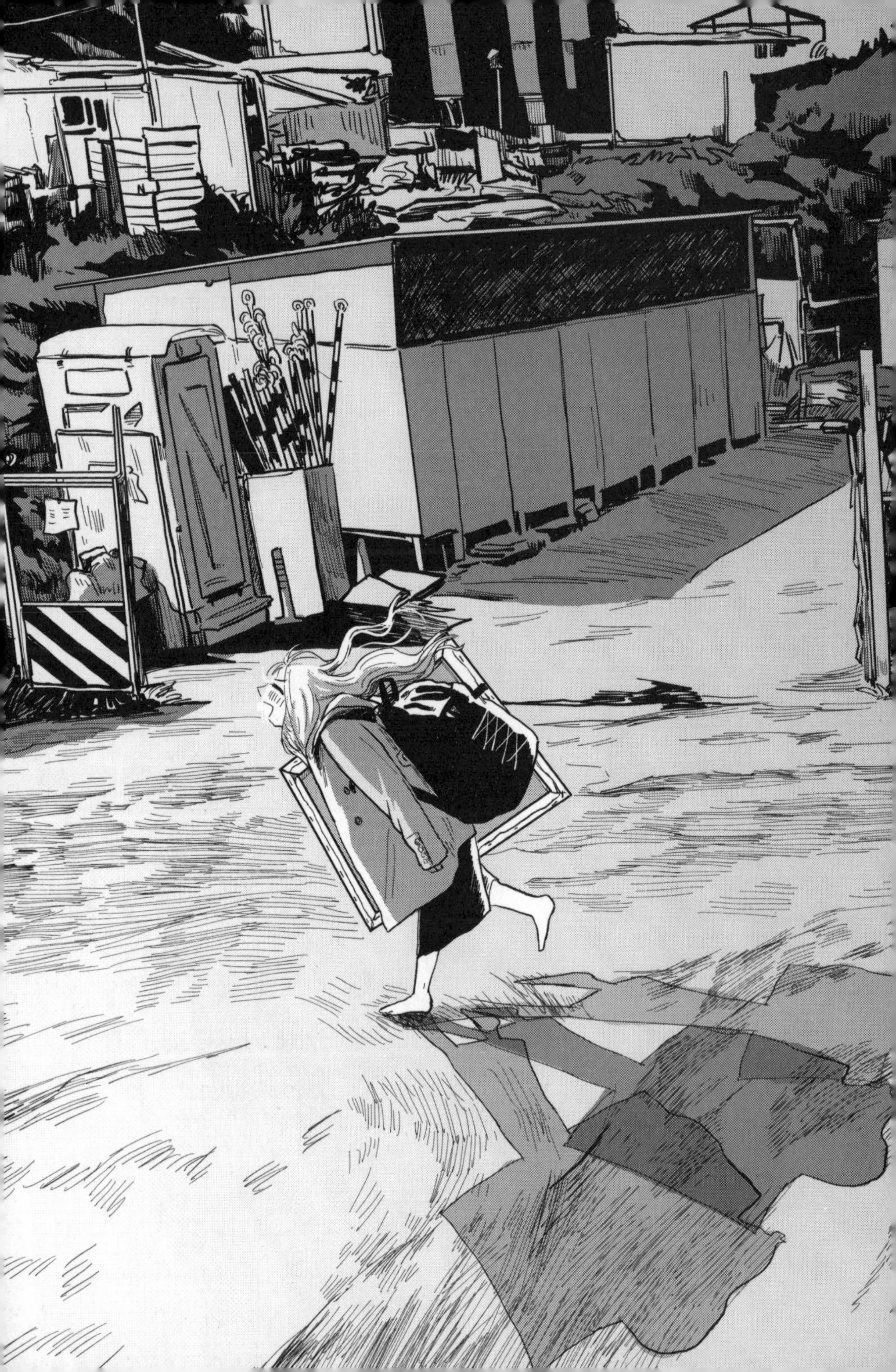

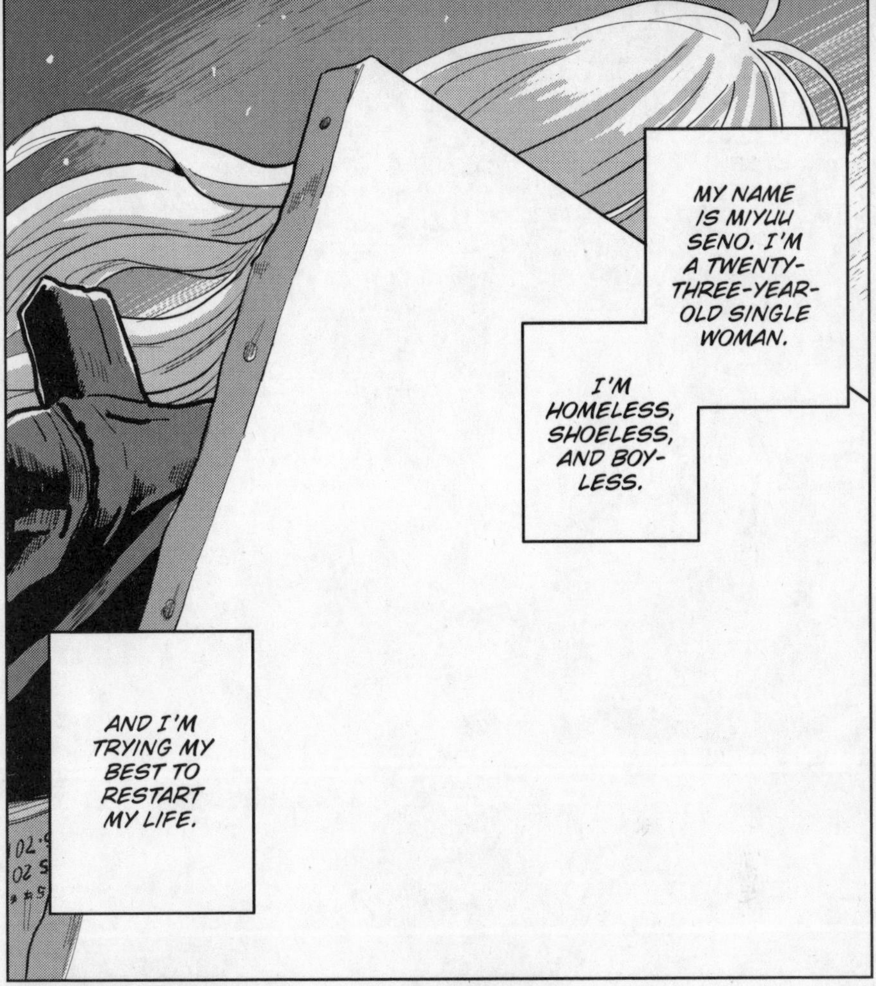
MY NAME IS MIYUU SENO. I'M A TWENTY-THREE-YEAR-OLD SINGLE WOMAN.
I'M HOMELESS, SHOELESS, AND BOY-LESS.
AND I'M TRYING MY BEST TO RESTART MY LIFE.

LABEL: ART SCHOOLS ENTRANCE EXAM MATERIAL COLLECTION, 2016 EDITION

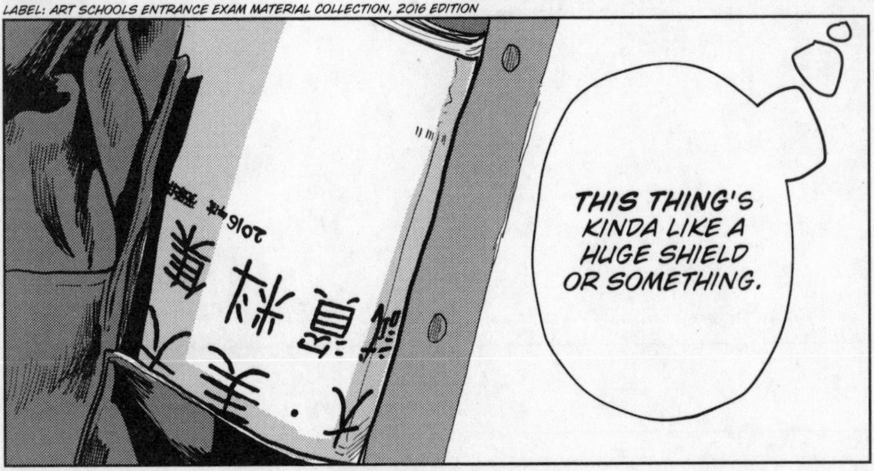
THIS THING'S KINDA LIKE A HUGE SHIELD OR SOMETHING.

Chapter 1 / END

FUN FACT...

HEY, ARE YOU LOOKING FOR SOMETHING?

ARE YOU IN HIGH SCHOOL? HOW ABOUT I TREAT YOU TO SOME STARBUCKS?

SORRY, I'M IN A RUSH...

FORGETTING TO ZIP UP YOUR BACKPACK...

...INCREASES THE RATE AT WHICH RANDOM OLDER GUYS WILL TALK TO YOU.

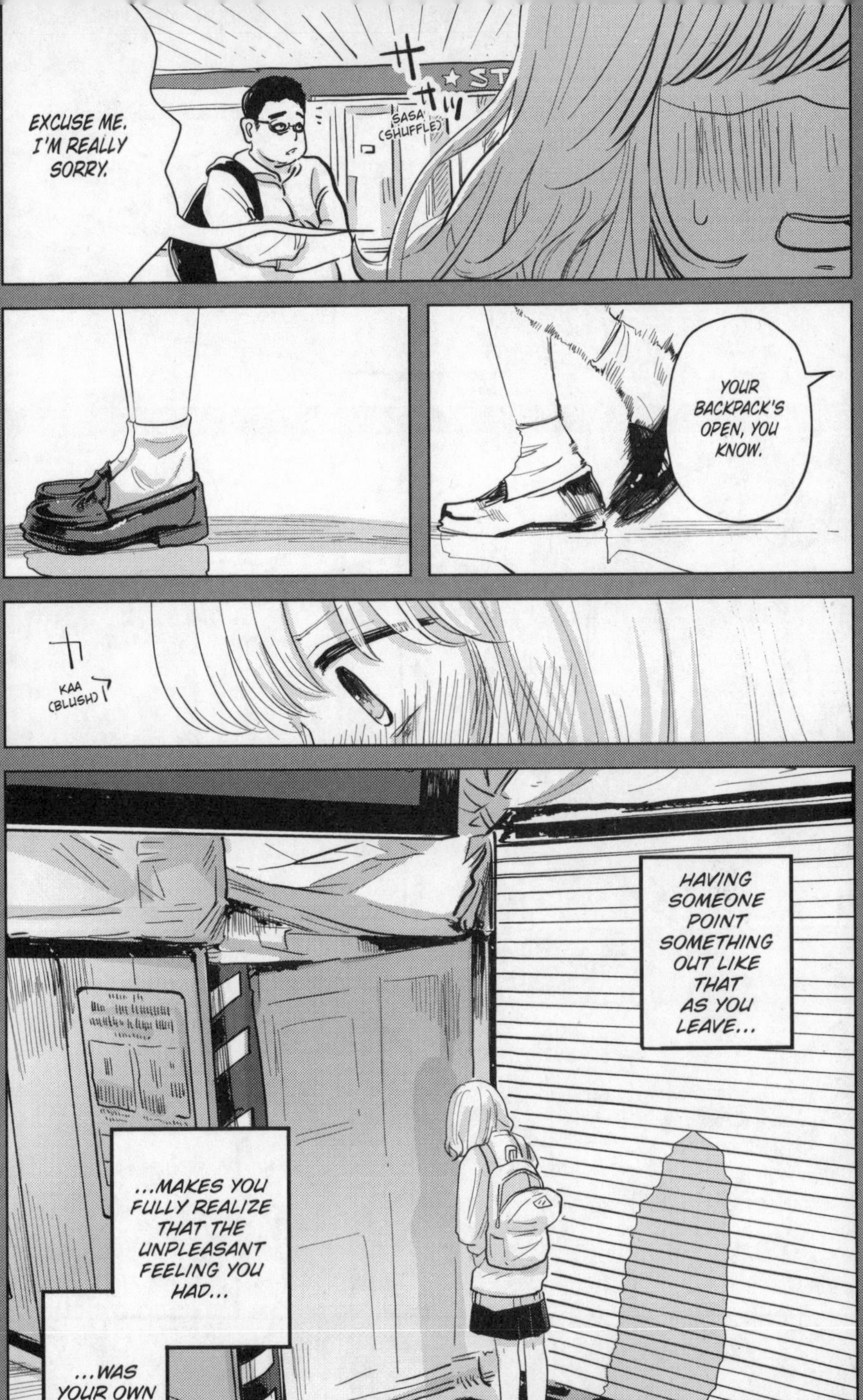
SASA (SHUFFLE)
EXCUSE ME. I'M REALLY SORRY.
YOUR BACKPACK'S OPEN, YOU KNOW.
KAA (BLUSH)
HAVING SOMEONE POINT SOMETHING OUT LIKE THAT AS YOU LEAVE...
...MAKES YOU FULLY REALIZE THAT THE UNPLEASANT FEELING YOU HAD...
...WAS YOUR OWN FAULT.

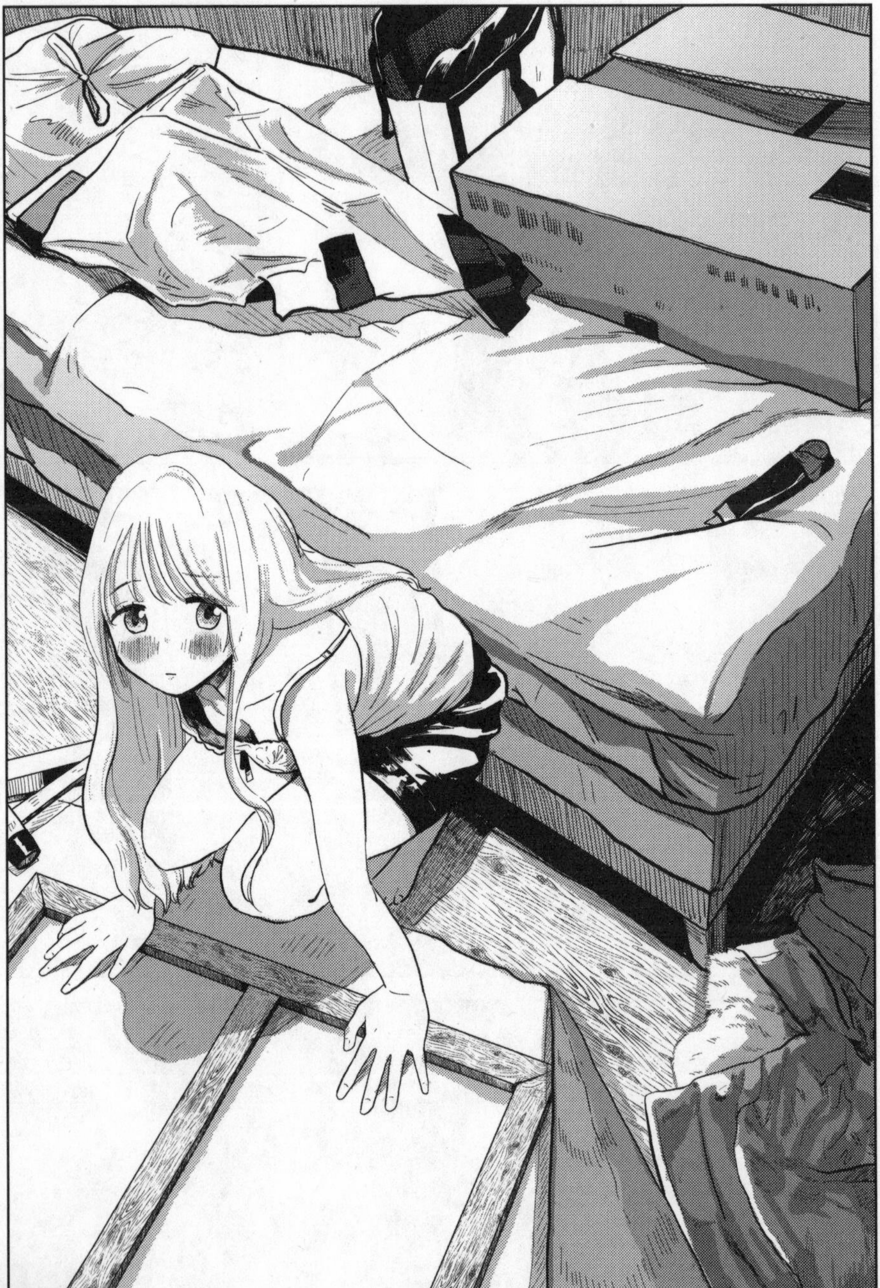

Chapter 2

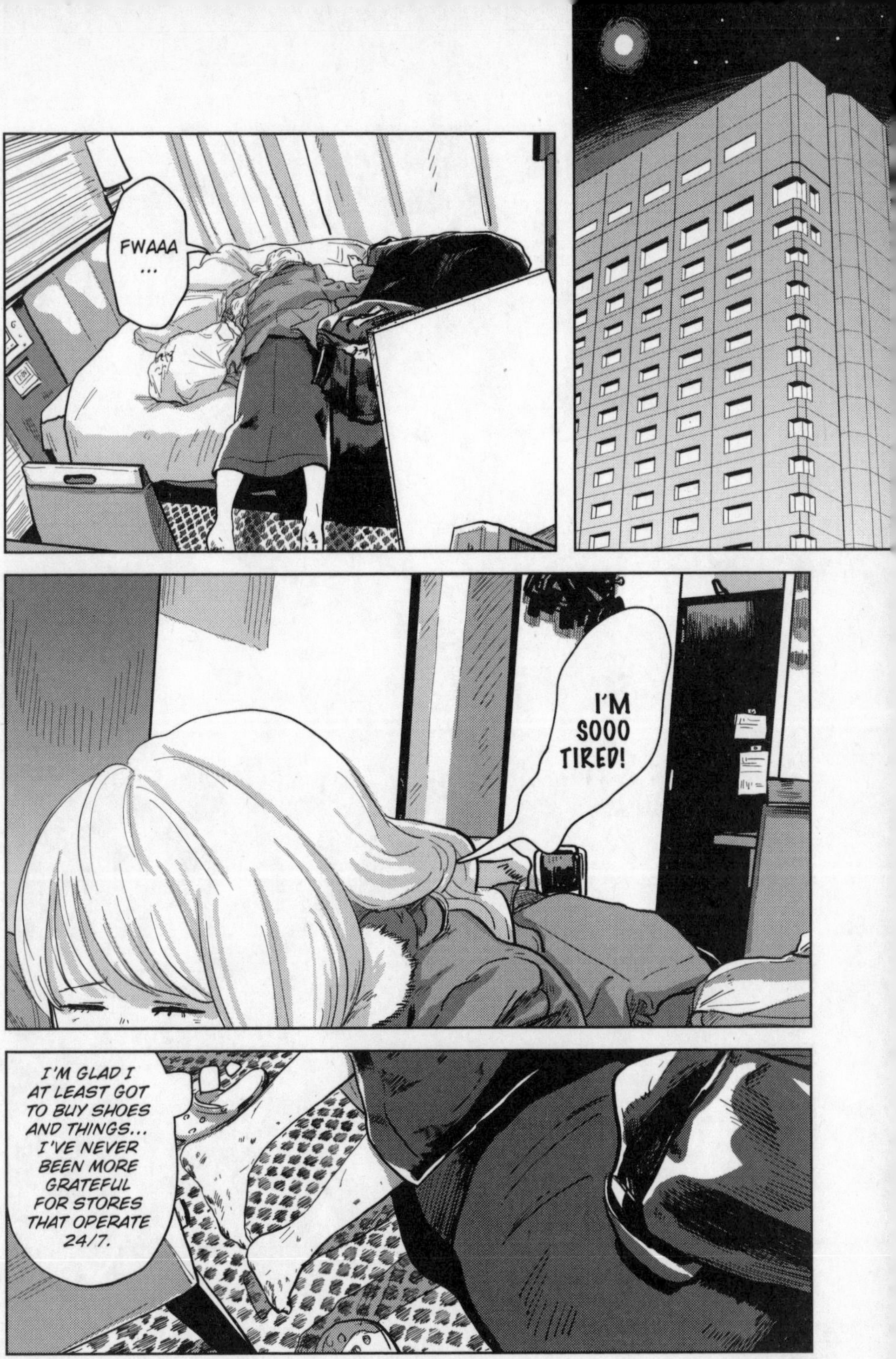
FWAAA ...
I'M SOOO TIRED!
I'M GLAD I AT LEAST GOT TO BUY SHOES AND THINGS... I'VE NEVER BEEN MORE GRATEFUL FOR STORES THAT OPERATE 24/7.

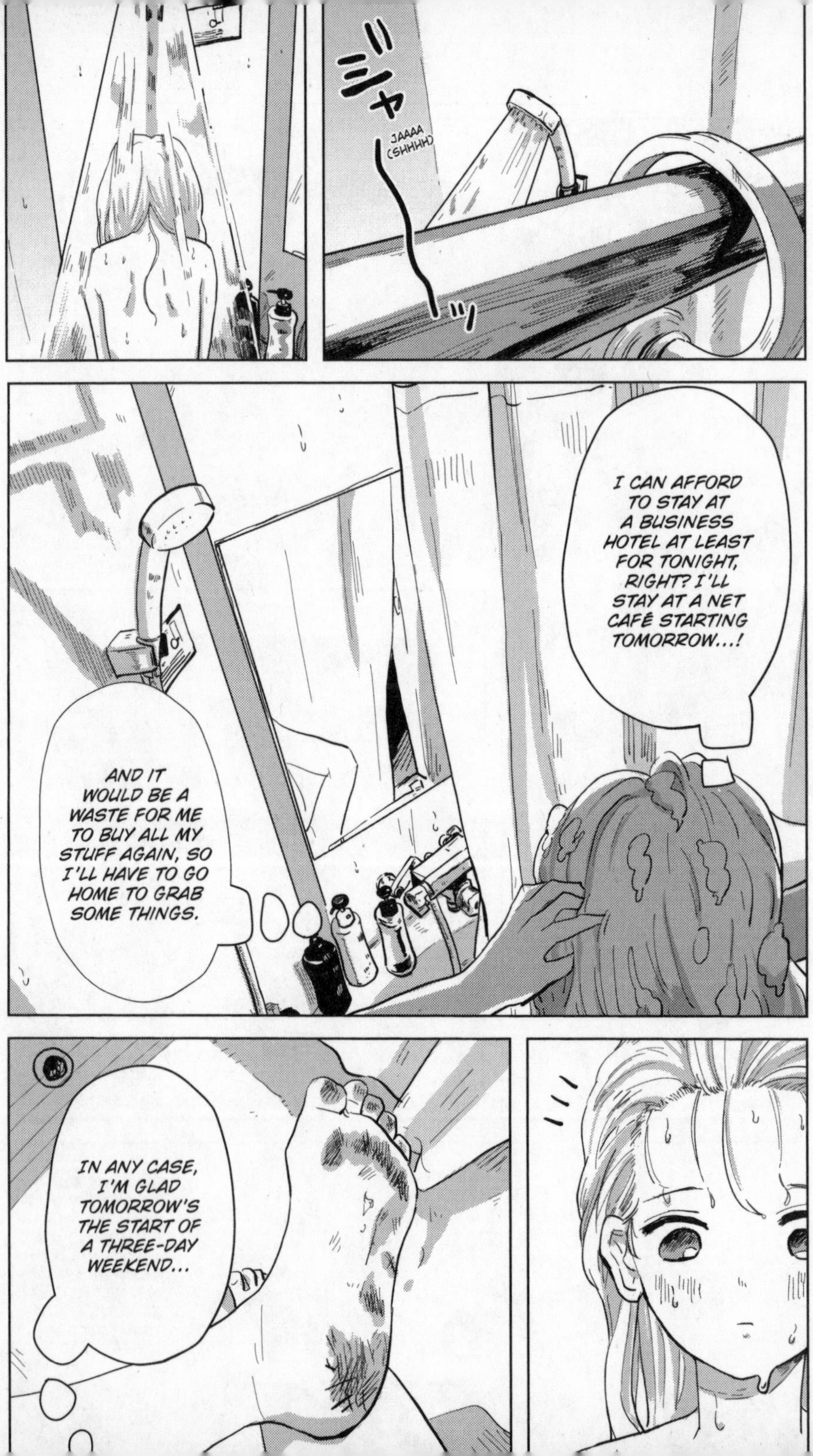
ジャー
JAAAA (SHHHH)
I CAN AFFORD TO STAY AT A BUSINESS HOTEL AT LEAST FOR TONIGHT, RIGHT? I'LL STAY AT A NET CAFÉ STARTING TOMORROW...!
AND IT WOULD BE A WASTE FOR ME TO BUY ALL MY STUFF AGAIN, SO I'LL HAVE TO GO HOME TO GRAB SOME THINGS.
IN ANY CASE, I'M GLAD TOMORROW'S THE START OF A THREE-DAY WEEKEND...

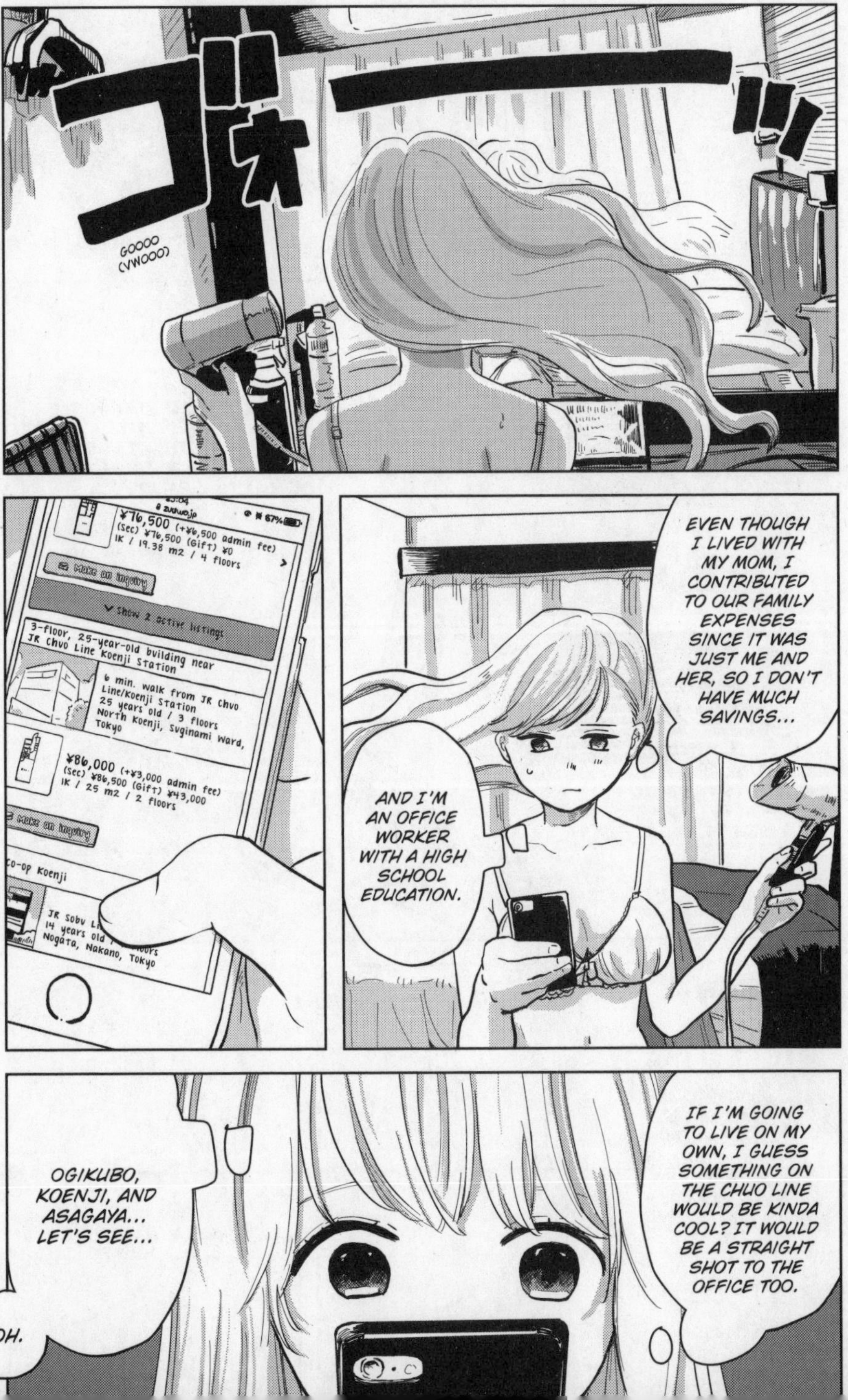
GOOOO (VWOOO)
EVEN THOUGH I LIVED WITH MY MOM, I CONTRIBUTED TO OUR FAMILY EXPENSES SINCE IT WAS JUST ME AND HER, SO I DON'T HAVE MUCH SAVINGS...
AND I'M AN OFFICE WORKER WITH A HIGH SCHOOL EDUCATION.
¥76,500 (+¥6,500 admin fee)
(Sec) ¥76,500 (Gift) ¥0
1K / 19.38 m2 / 4 floors
Make an inquiry
Show 2 active listings
3-floor, 25-year-old building near JR Chuo Line Koenji Station
6 min. walk from JR Chuo Line/Koenji Station
25 years old / 3 floors
North Koenji, Suginami Ward, Tokyo
¥86,000 (+¥3,000 admin fee)
(Sec) ¥86,500 (Gift) ¥43,000
1K / 25 m2 / 2 floors
Make an inquiry
Co-op Koenji
14 years old
Nogata, Nakano, Tokyo
IF I'M GOING TO LIVE ON MY OWN, I GUESS SOMETHING ON THE CHUO LINE WOULD BE KINDA COOL? IT WOULD BE A STRAIGHT SHOT TO THE OFFICE TOO.
OGIKUBO, KOENJI, AND ASAGAYA... LET'S SEE...
OH.

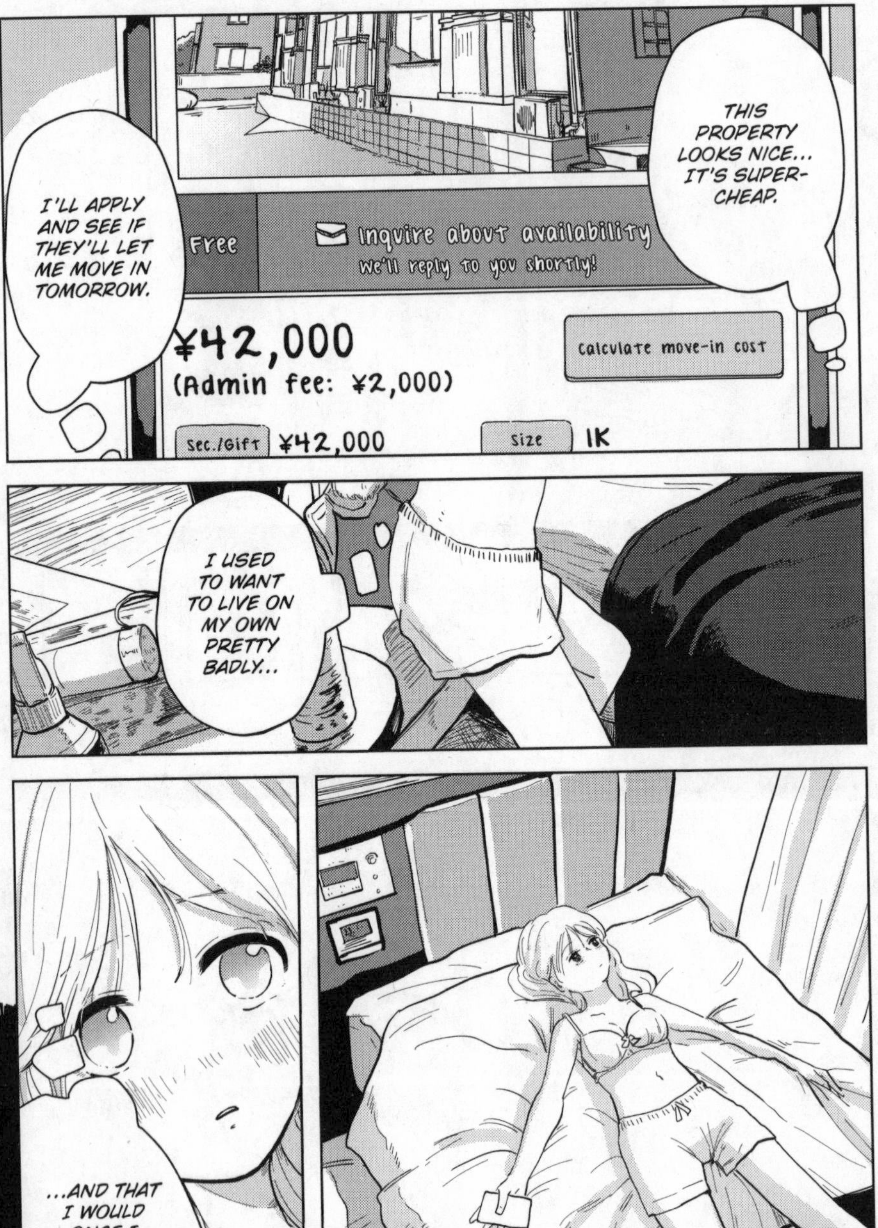
THIS PROPERTY LOOKS NICE... IT'S SUPER-CHEAP.
I'LL APPLY AND SEE IF THEY'LL LET ME MOVE IN TOMORROW.
Free
Inquire about availability
We'll reply to you shortly!
¥42,000
(Admin fee: ¥2,000)
Calculate move-in cost
Sec./Gift ¥42,000
Size 1K
I USED TO WANT TO LIVE ON MY OWN PRETTY BADLY...
...AND THAT I WOULD ONCE I GOT INTO UNIVERSITY...

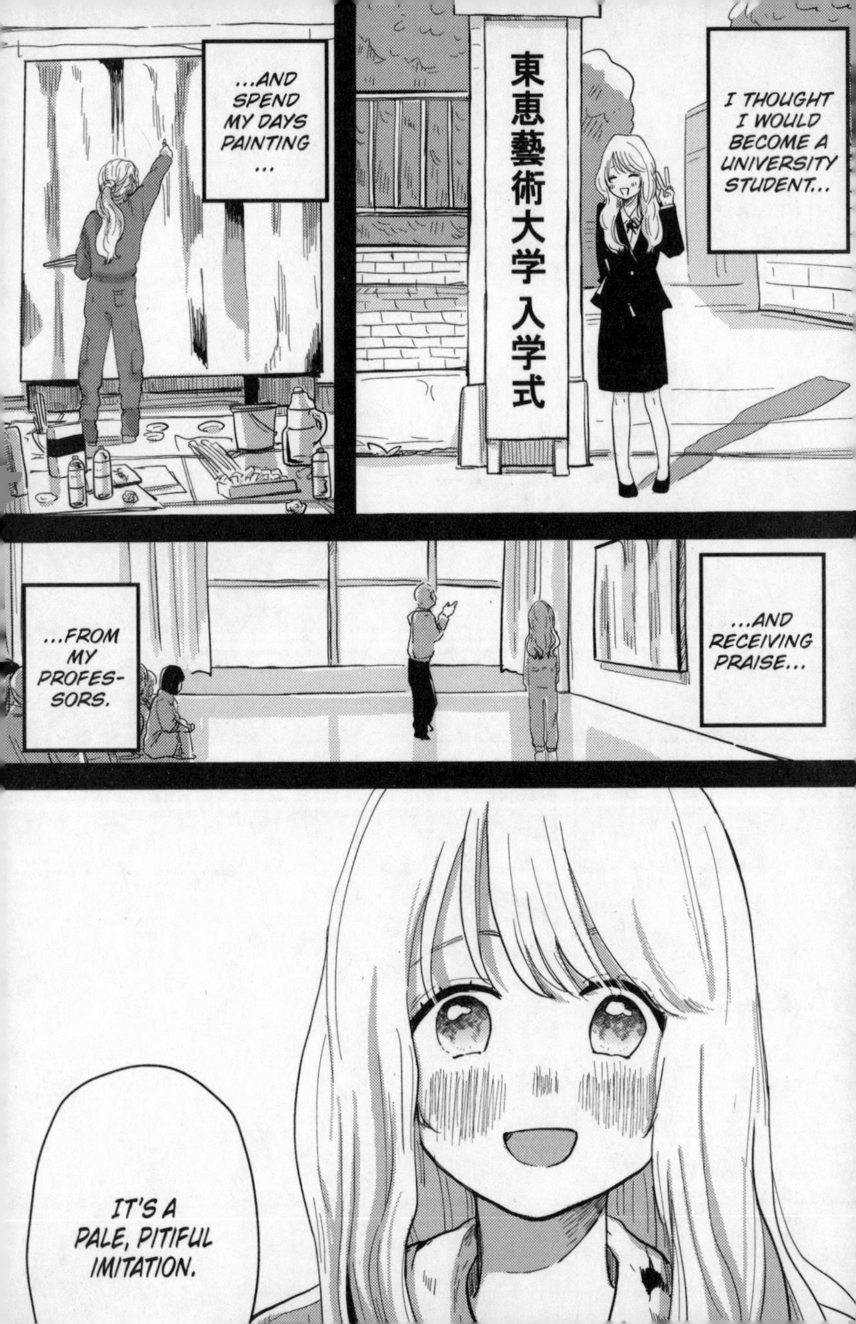

東恵藝術大学 入学式
I THOUGHT I WOULD BECOME A UNIVERSITY STUDENT...
...AND SPEND MY DAYS PAINTING...
...AND RECEIVING PRAISE...
...FROM MY PROFES-SORS.
IT'S A PALE, PITIFUL IMITATION.

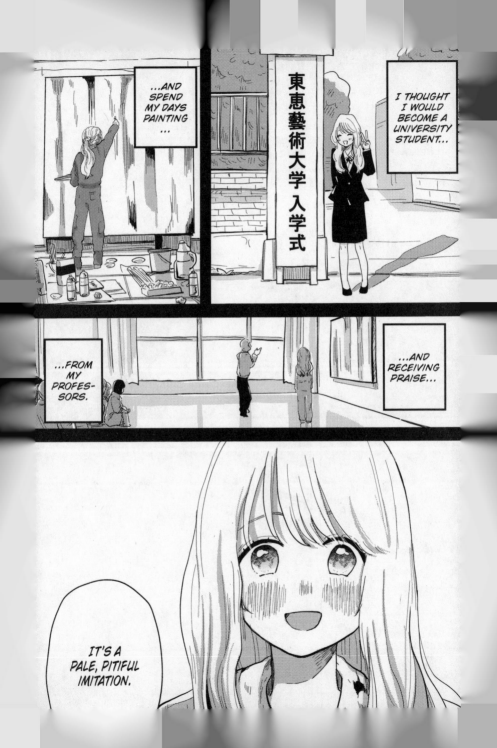

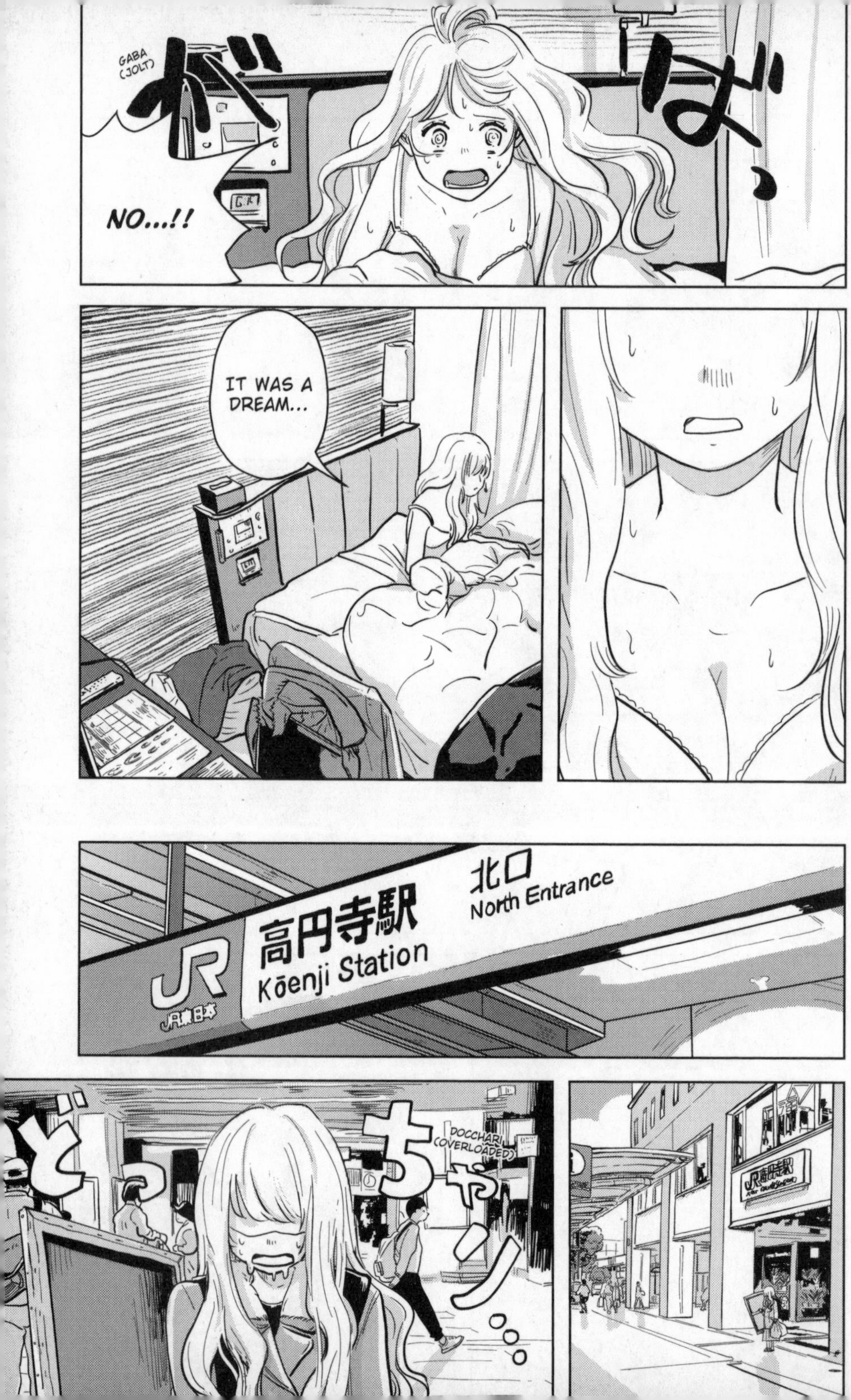
GABA (JOLT)
NO...!!
IT WAS A DREAM...
高円寺駅
Kōenji Station
北口
North Entrance
DOCCHARI (OVERLOADED)

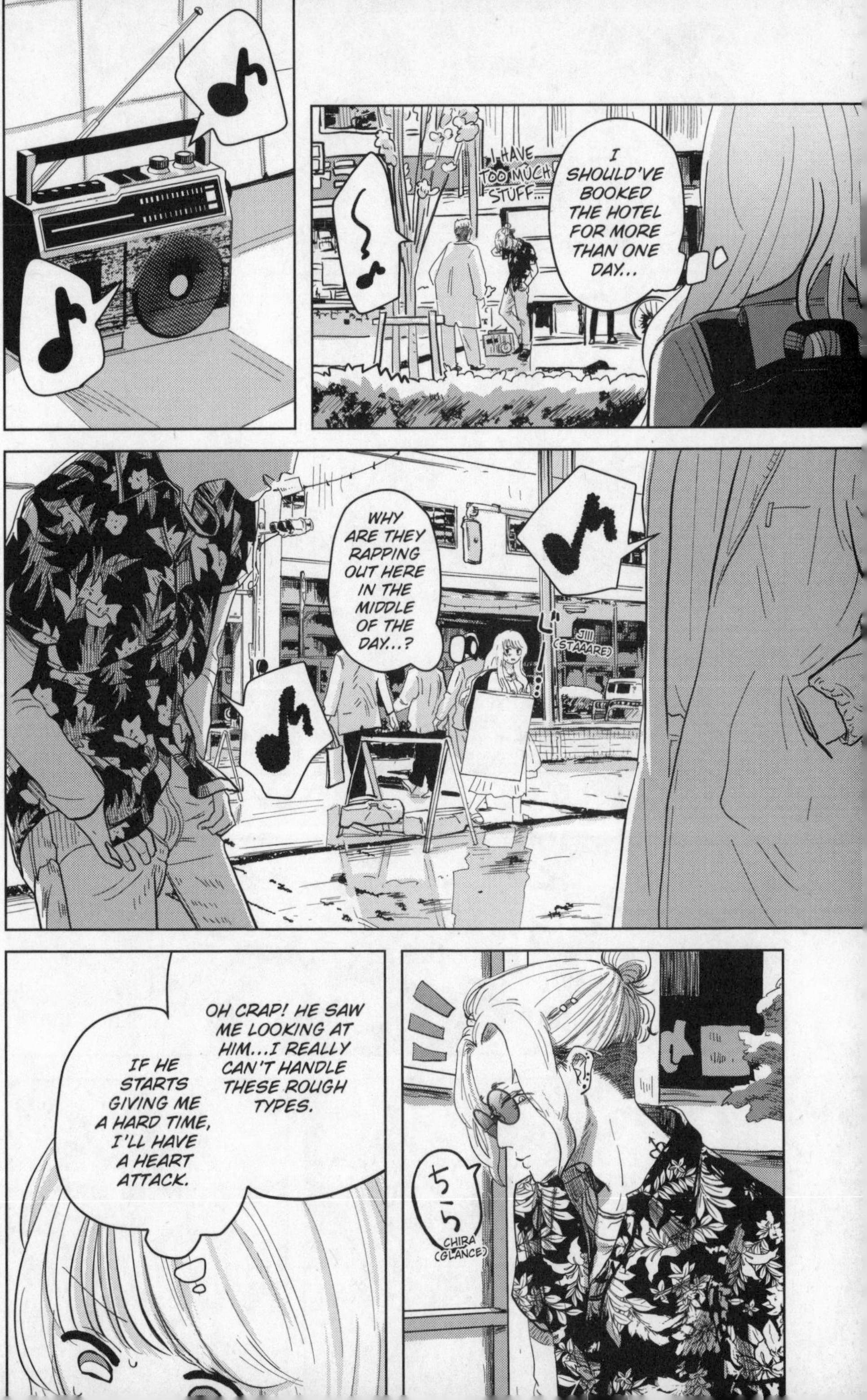
I SHOULD'VE BOOKED THE HOTEL FOR MORE THAN ONE DAY...
I HAVE TOO MUCH STUFF...
じー
JIII (STAAARE)
WHY ARE THEY RAPPING OUT HERE IN THE MIDDLE OF THE DAY...?
ちら
CHIRA (GLANCE)
OH CRAP! HE SAW ME LOOKING AT HIM...I REALLY CAN'T HANDLE THESE ROUGH TYPES.
IF HE STARTS GIVING ME A HARD TIME, I'LL HAVE A HEART ATTACK.

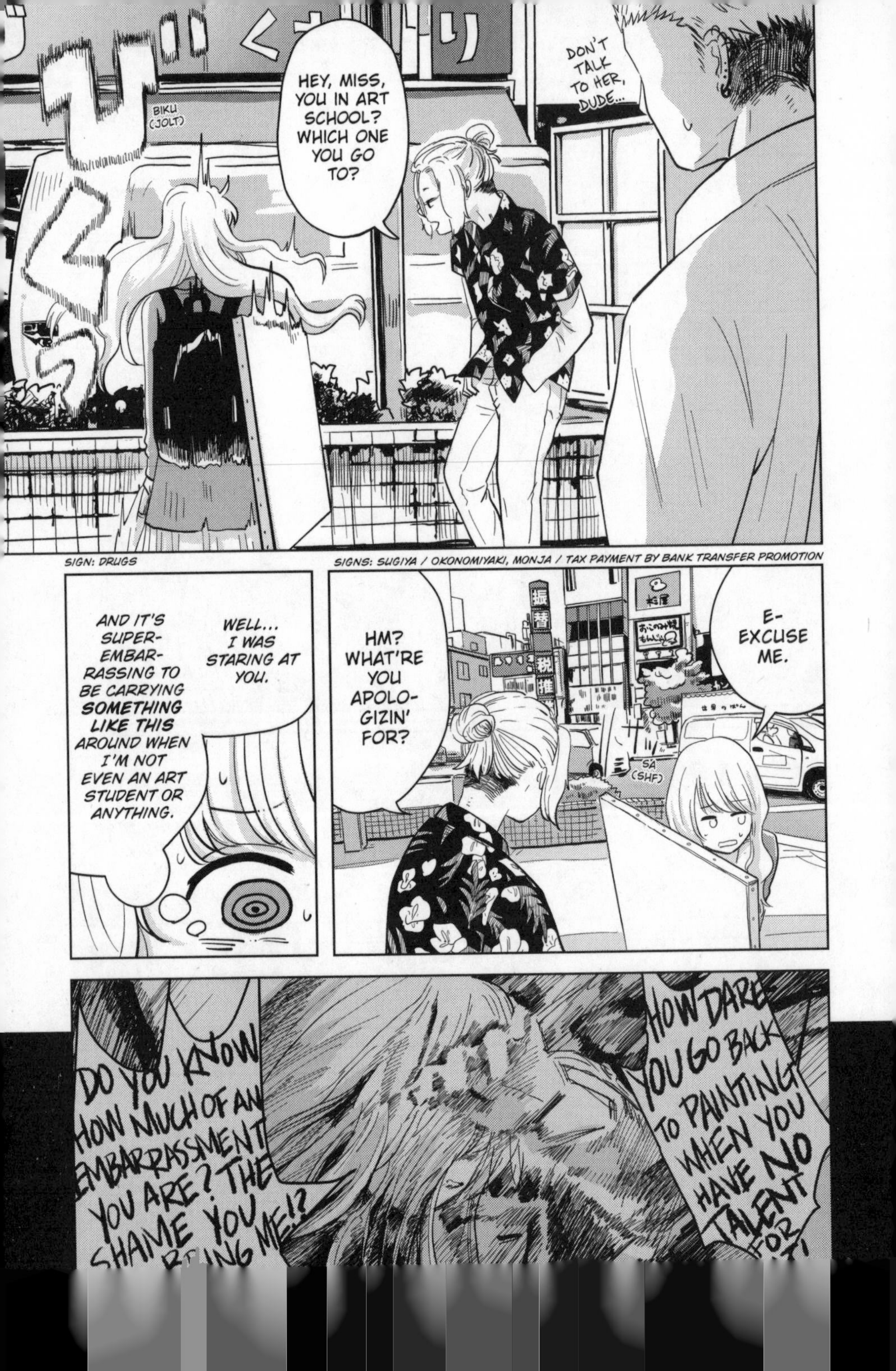
DON'T TALK TO HER, DUDE...
HEY, MISS, YOU IN ART SCHOOL? WHICH ONE YOU GO TO?
BIKU (JOLT)
SIGN: DRUGS
SIGNS: SUGIYA / OKONOMIYAKI, MONJA / TAX PAYMENT BY BANK TRANSFER PROMOTION
E-EXCUSE ME.
SA (SHF)
HM? WHAT'RE YOU APOLOGIZIN' FOR?
WELL... I WAS STARING AT YOU.
AND IT'S SUPER-EMBARRASSING TO BE CARRYING SOMETHING LIKE THIS AROUND WHEN I'M NOT EVEN AN ART STUDENT OR ANYTHING.
HOW DARE YOU GO BACK TO PAINTING WHEN YOU HAVE NO TALENT FOR
DO YOU KNOW HOW MUCH OF AN EMBARRASSMENT YOU ARE? THE SHAME YOU BRING ME!?

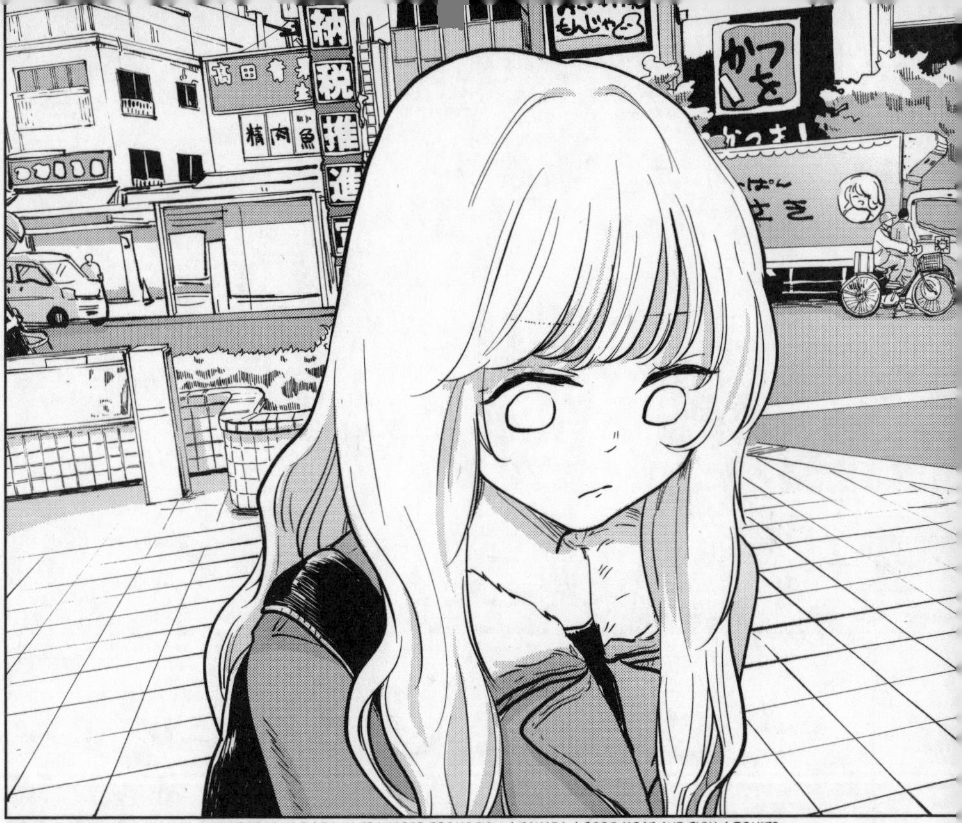

SIGNS: OKONOMIYAKI, MONJA / TAX PAYMENT BY BANK TRANSFER PROMOTION / TAKADA / GOOD MEAT AND FISH / BONITO

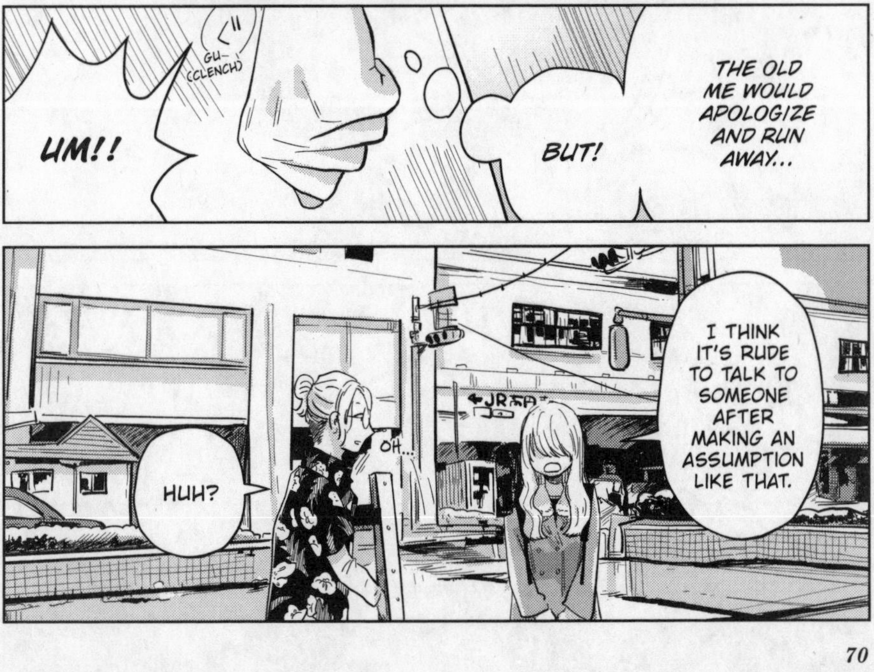
THE OLD ME WOULD APOLOGIZE AND RUN AWAY...
BUT!
GU- (CLENCH)
UM!!
I THINK IT'S RUDE TO TALK TO SOMEONE AFTER MAKING AN ASSUMPTION LIKE THAT.
OH...
HUH?

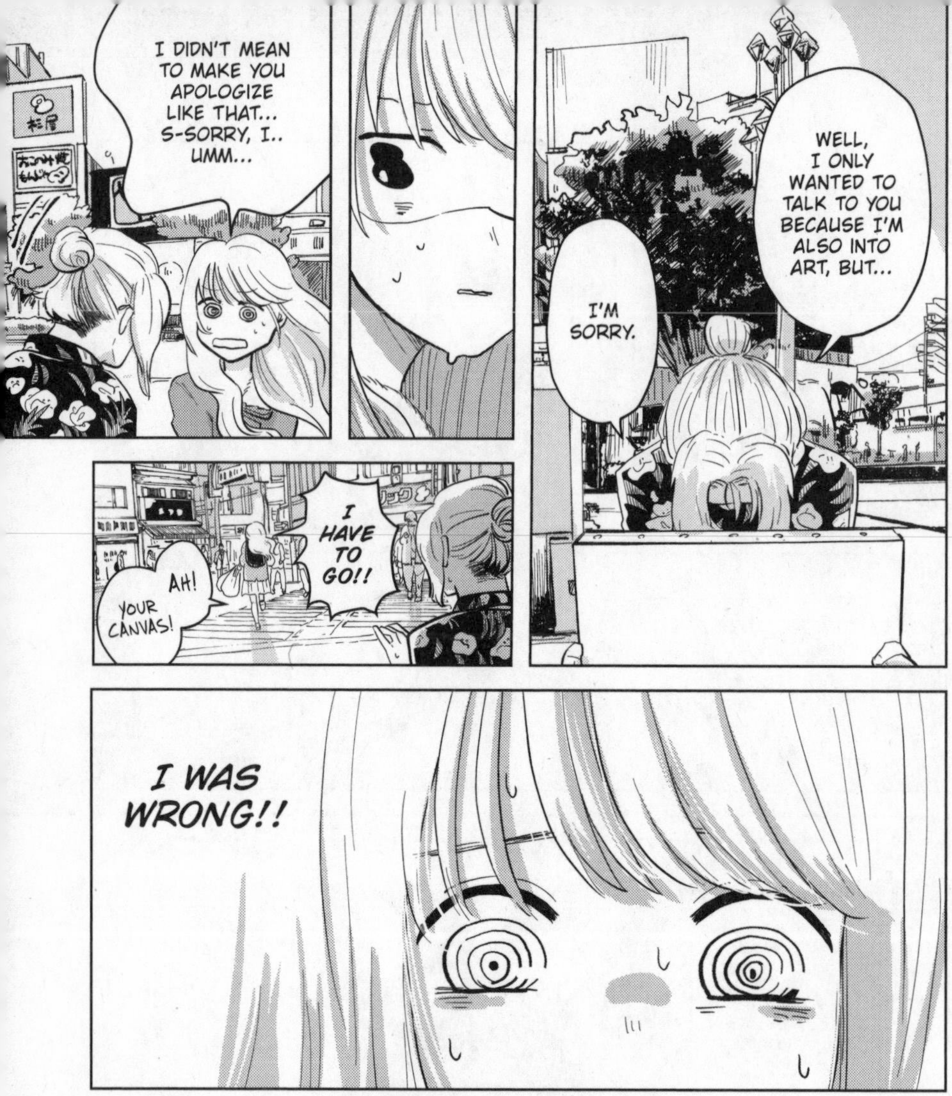
WELL, I ONLY WANTED TO TALK TO YOU BECAUSE I'M ALSO INTO ART, BUT...
I'M SORRY.
I DIDN'T MEAN TO MAKE YOU APOLOGIZE LIKE THAT... S-SORRY, I.. UMM...
I HAVE TO GO!!
AH!
YOUR CANVAS!
I WAS WRONG!!

SIGNS: CITY REAL ESTATE BROKER "HOME FINDERS" / RENTALS & SALES

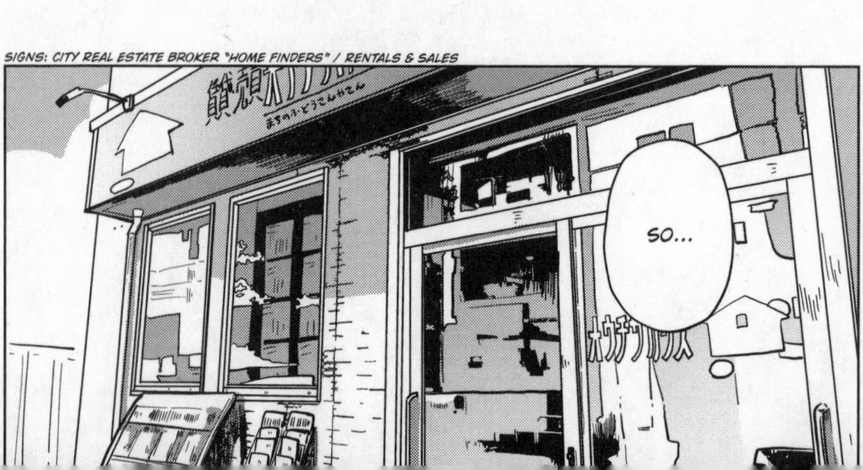
SO...

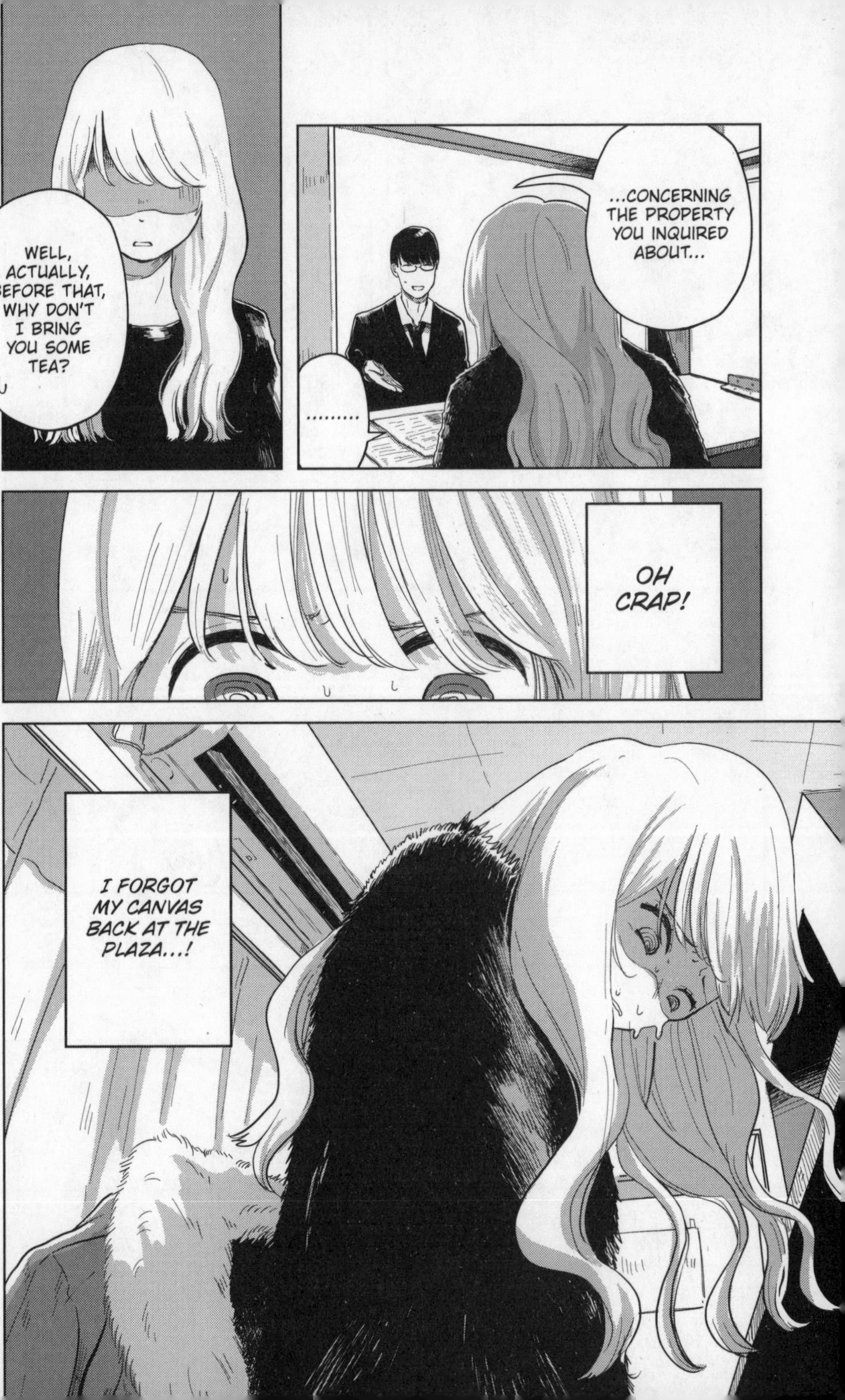
...CONCERNING THE PROPERTY YOU INQUIRED ABOUT...
....
WELL, ACTUALLY, BEFORE THAT, WHY DON'T I BRING YOU SOME TEA?
OH CRAP!
I FORGOT MY CANVAS BACK AT THE PLAZA...!

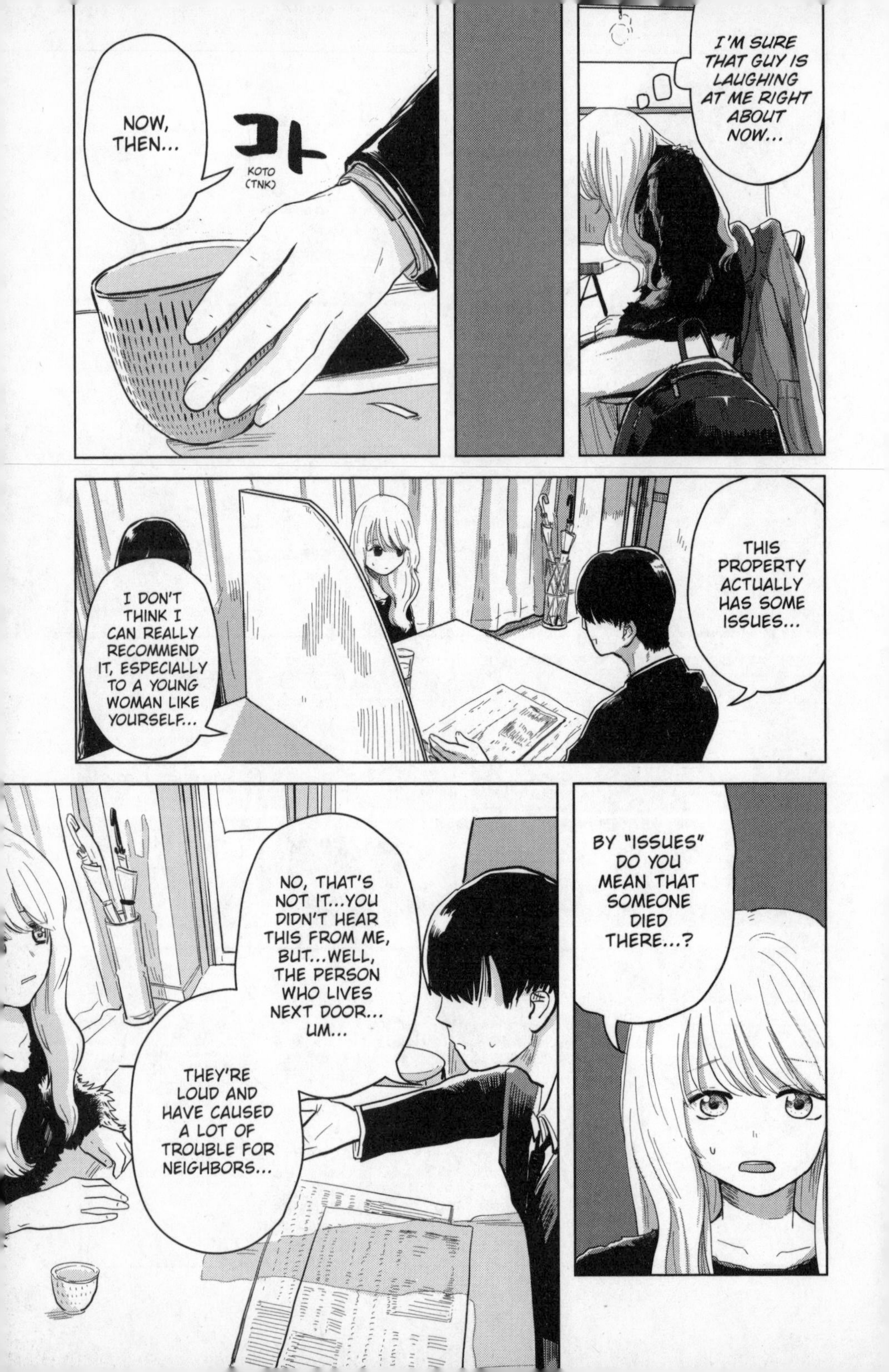
I'M SURE THAT GUY IS LAUGHING AT ME RIGHT ABOUT NOW...
NOW, THEN...
KOTO (TNK)
THIS PROPERTY ACTUALLY HAS SOME ISSUES...
I DON'T THINK I CAN REALLY RECOMMEND IT, ESPECIALLY TO A YOUNG WOMAN LIKE YOURSELF...
BY "ISSUES" DO YOU MEAN THAT SOMEONE DIED THERE...?
NO, THAT'S NOT IT...YOU DIDN'T HEAR THIS FROM ME, BUT...WELL, THE PERSON WHO LIVES NEXT DOOR... UM...
THEY'RE LOUD AND HAVE CAUSED A LOT OF TROUBLE FOR NEIGHBORS...

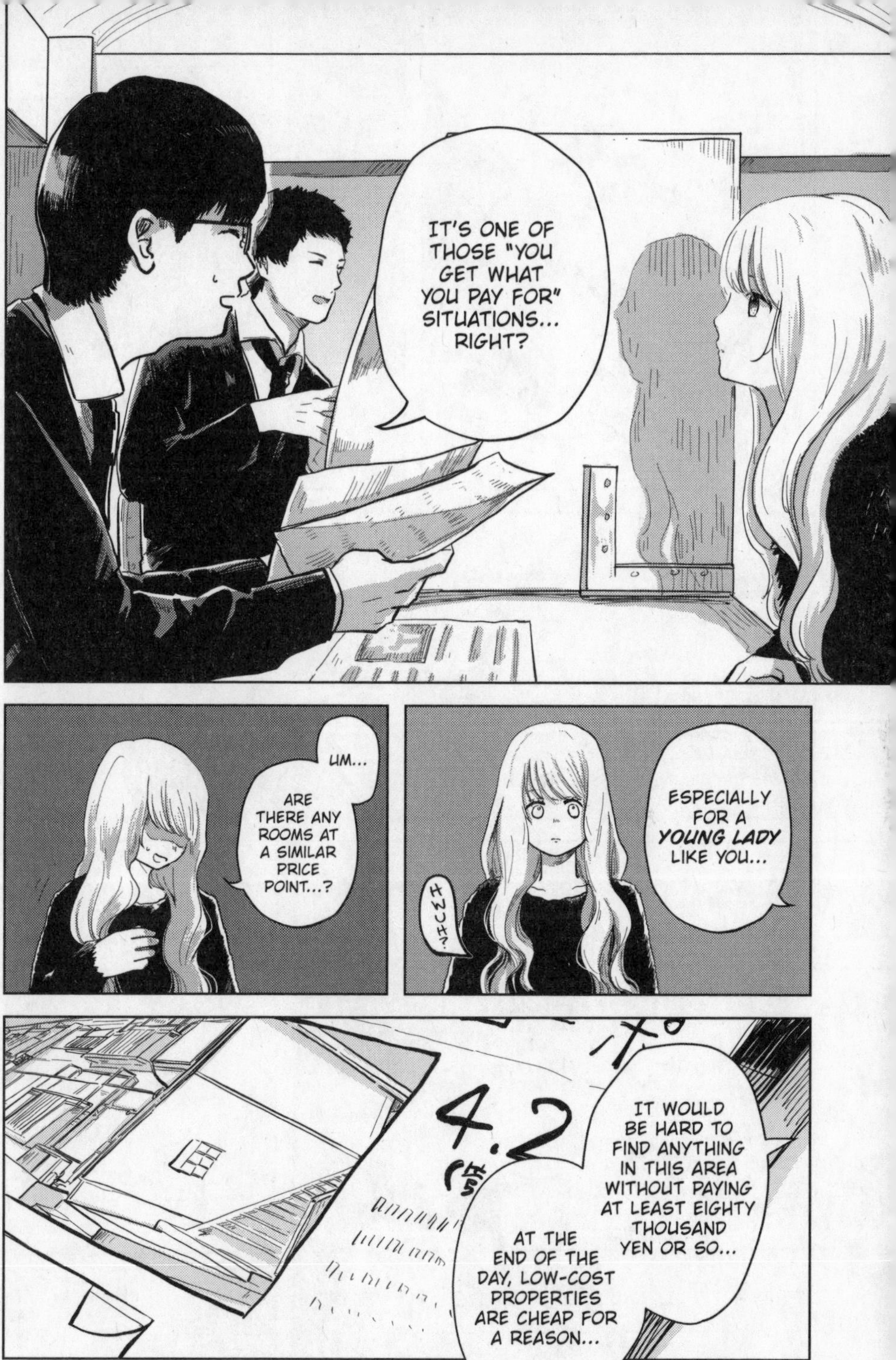
IT'S ONE OF THOSE "YOU GET WHAT YOU PAY FOR" SITUATIONS... RIGHT?
ESPECIALLY FOR A *YOUNG LADY* LIKE YOU...
HWUH?
UM...
ARE THERE ANY ROOMS AT A SIMILAR PRICE POINT...?
4.2
IT WOULD BE HARD TO FIND ANYTHING IN THIS AREA WITHOUT PAYING AT LEAST EIGHTY THOUSAND YEN OR SO...
AT THE END OF THE DAY, LOW-COST PROPERTIES ARE CHEAP FOR A REASON...

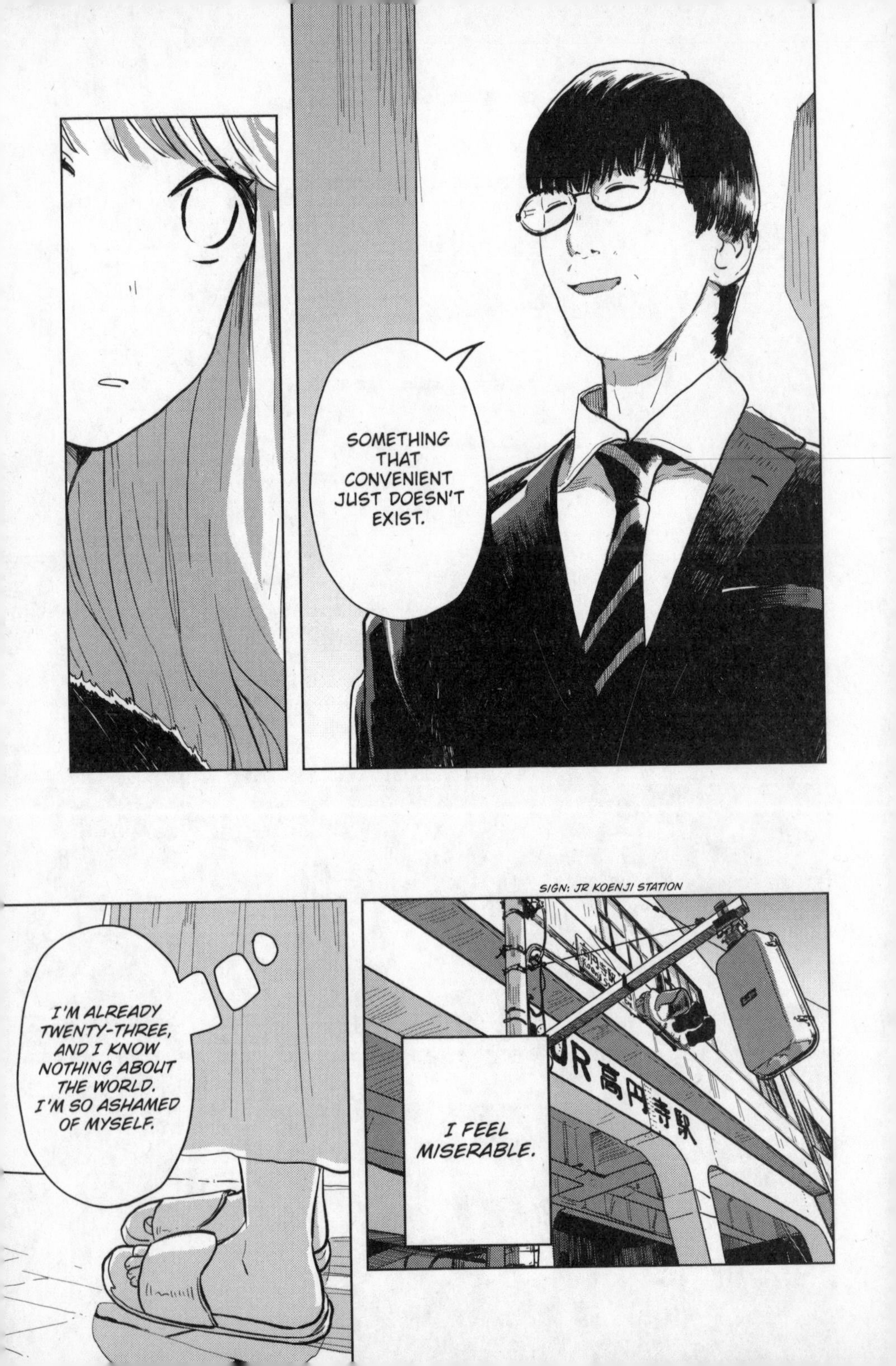
SOMETHING THAT CONVENIENT JUST DOESN'T EXIST.
SIGN: JR KOENJI STATION
JR 高円寺駅
I FEEL MISERABLE.
I'M ALREADY TWENTY-THREE, AND I KNOW NOTHING ABOUT THE WORLD. I'M SO ASHAMED OF MYSELF.

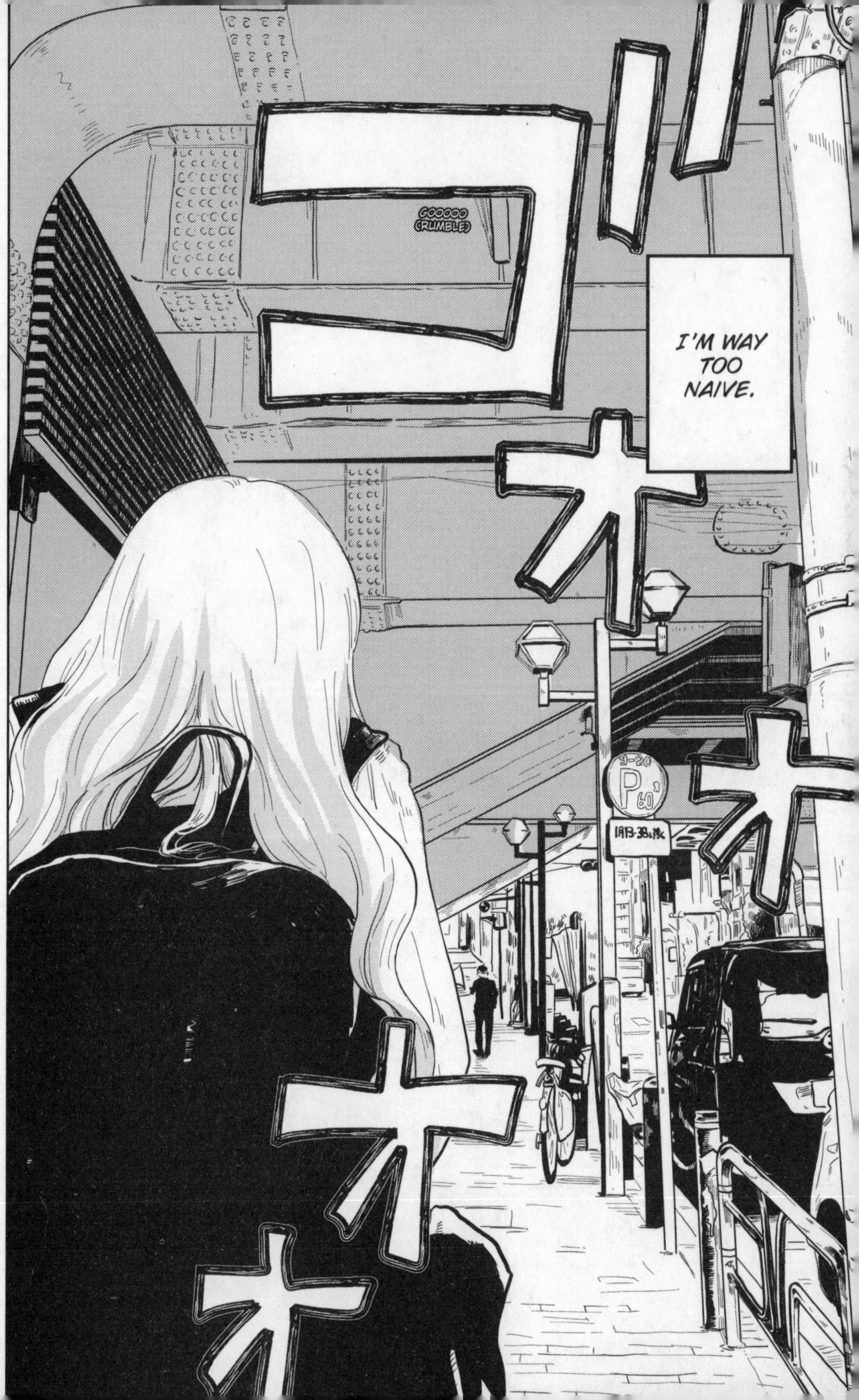
GOOOOO (RUMBLE)
I'M WAY TOO NAIVE.

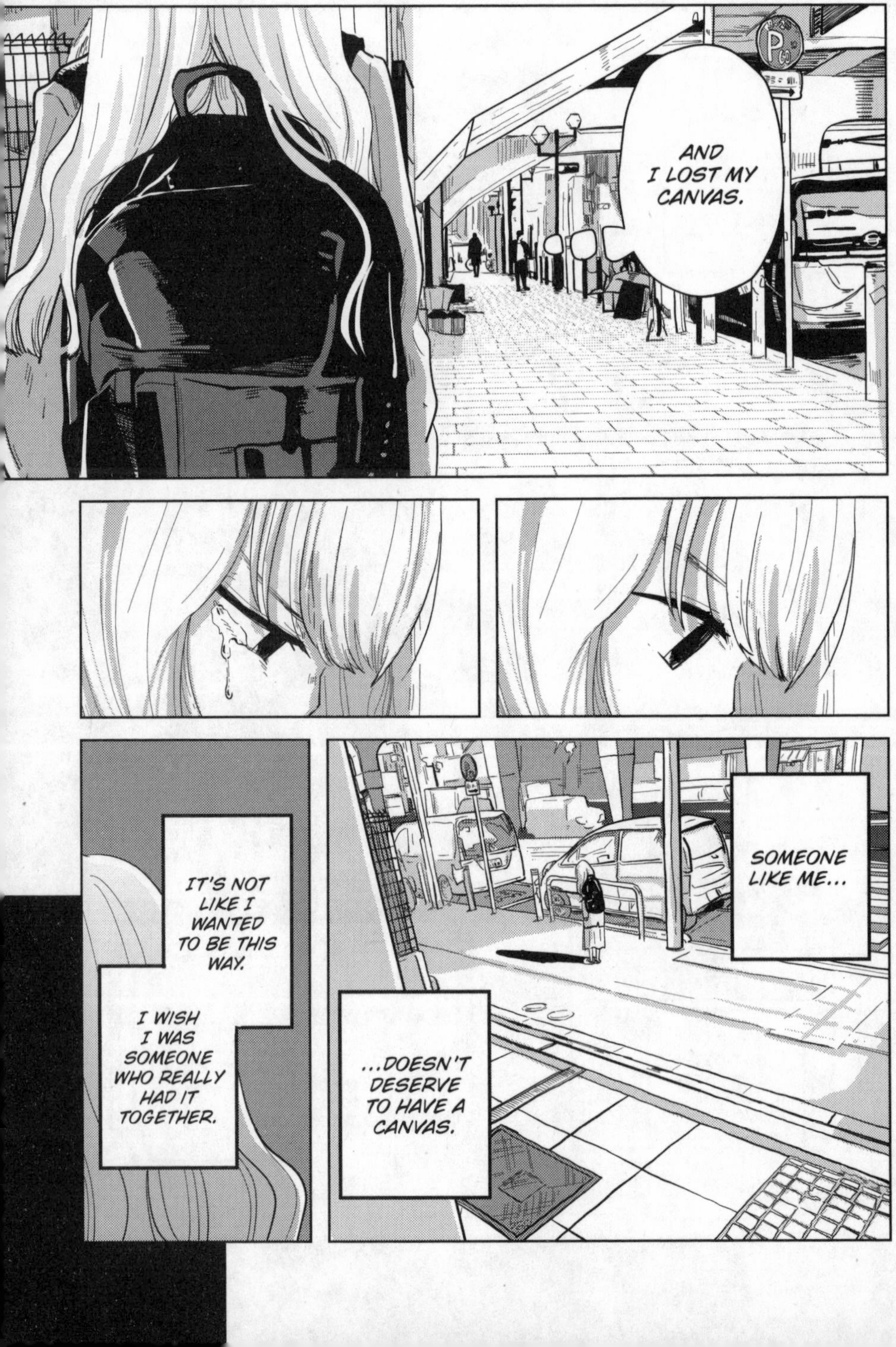
AND I LOST MY CANVAS.
SOMEONE LIKE ME...
...DOESN'T DESERVE TO HAVE A CANVAS.
IT'S NOT LIKE I WANTED TO BE THIS WAY.
I WISH I WAS SOMEONE WHO REALLY HAD IT TOGETHER.

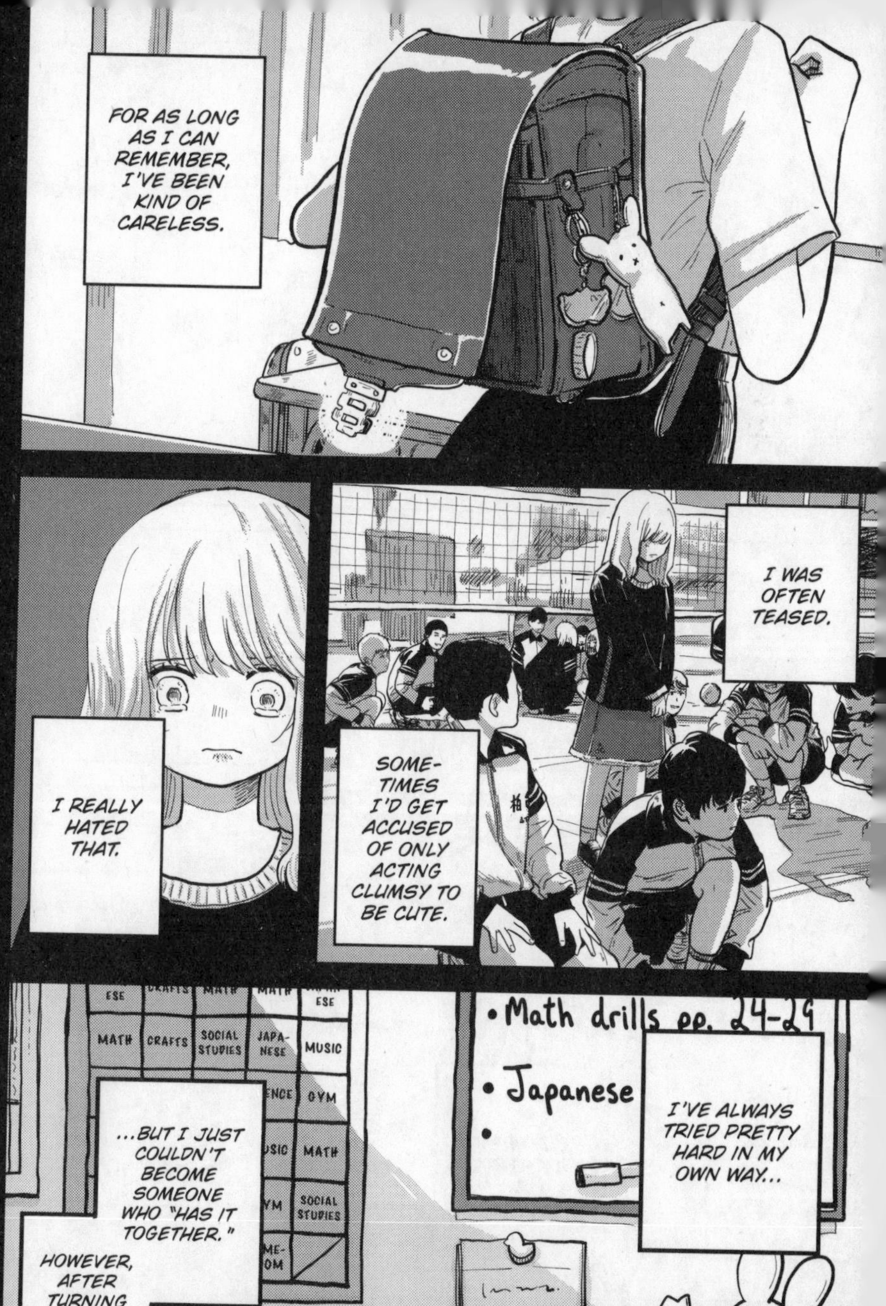
FOR AS LONG AS I CAN REMEMBER, I'VE BEEN KIND OF CARELESS.
I WAS OFTEN TEASED.
SOME-TIMES I'D GET ACCUSED OF ONLY ACTING CLUMSY TO BE CUTE.
I REALLY HATED THAT.
• Math drills pp. 24-29
• Japanese
I'VE ALWAYS TRIED PRETTY HARD IN MY OWN WAY...
...BUT I JUST COULDN'T BECOME SOMEONE WHO "HAS IT TOGETHER."
HOWEVER, AFTER TURNING

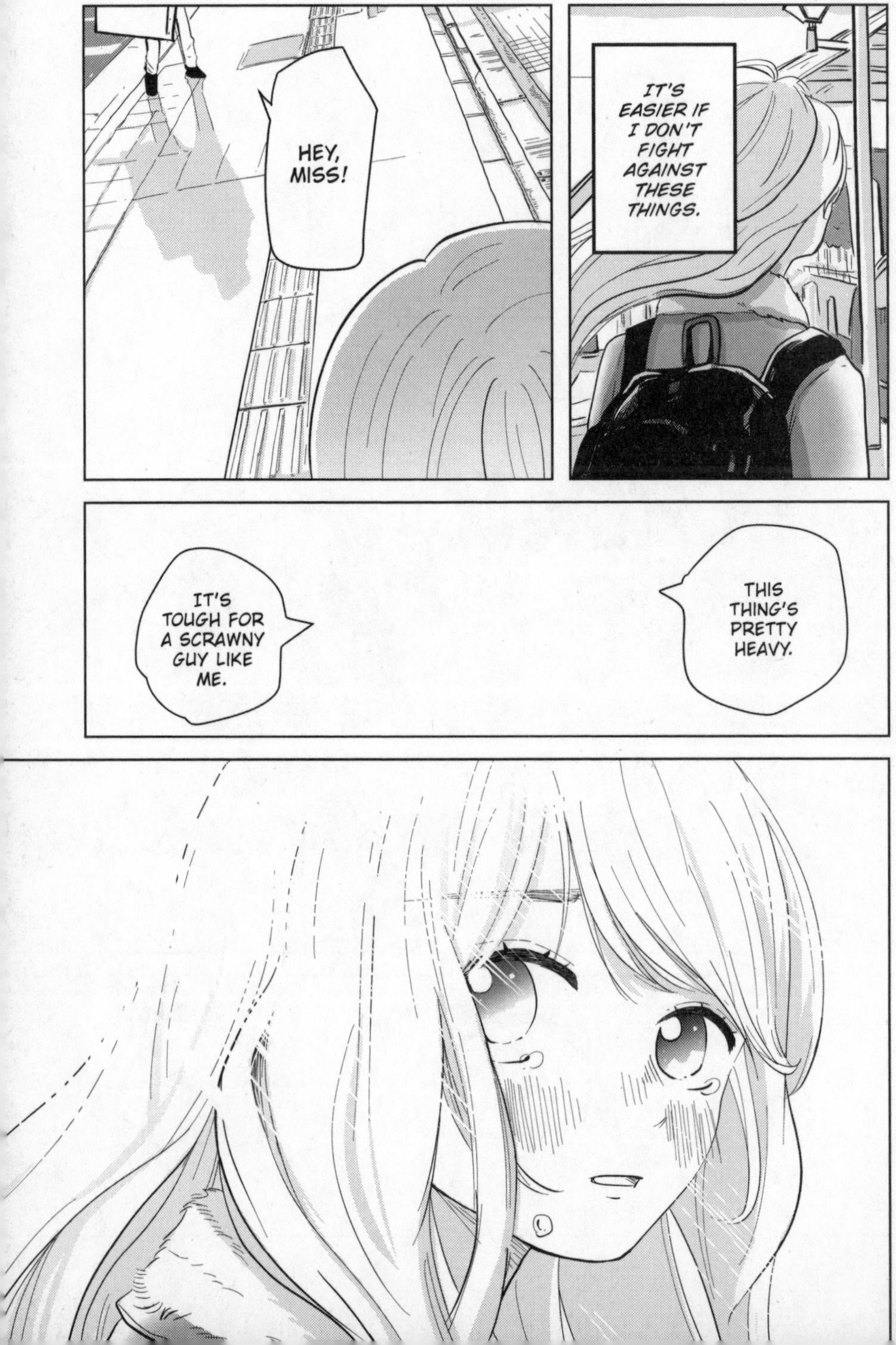
IT'S EASIER IF I DON'T FIGHT AGAINST THESE THINGS.
HEY, MISS!
THIS THING'S PRETTY HEAVY.
IT'S TOUGH FOR A SCRAWNY GUY LIKE ME.

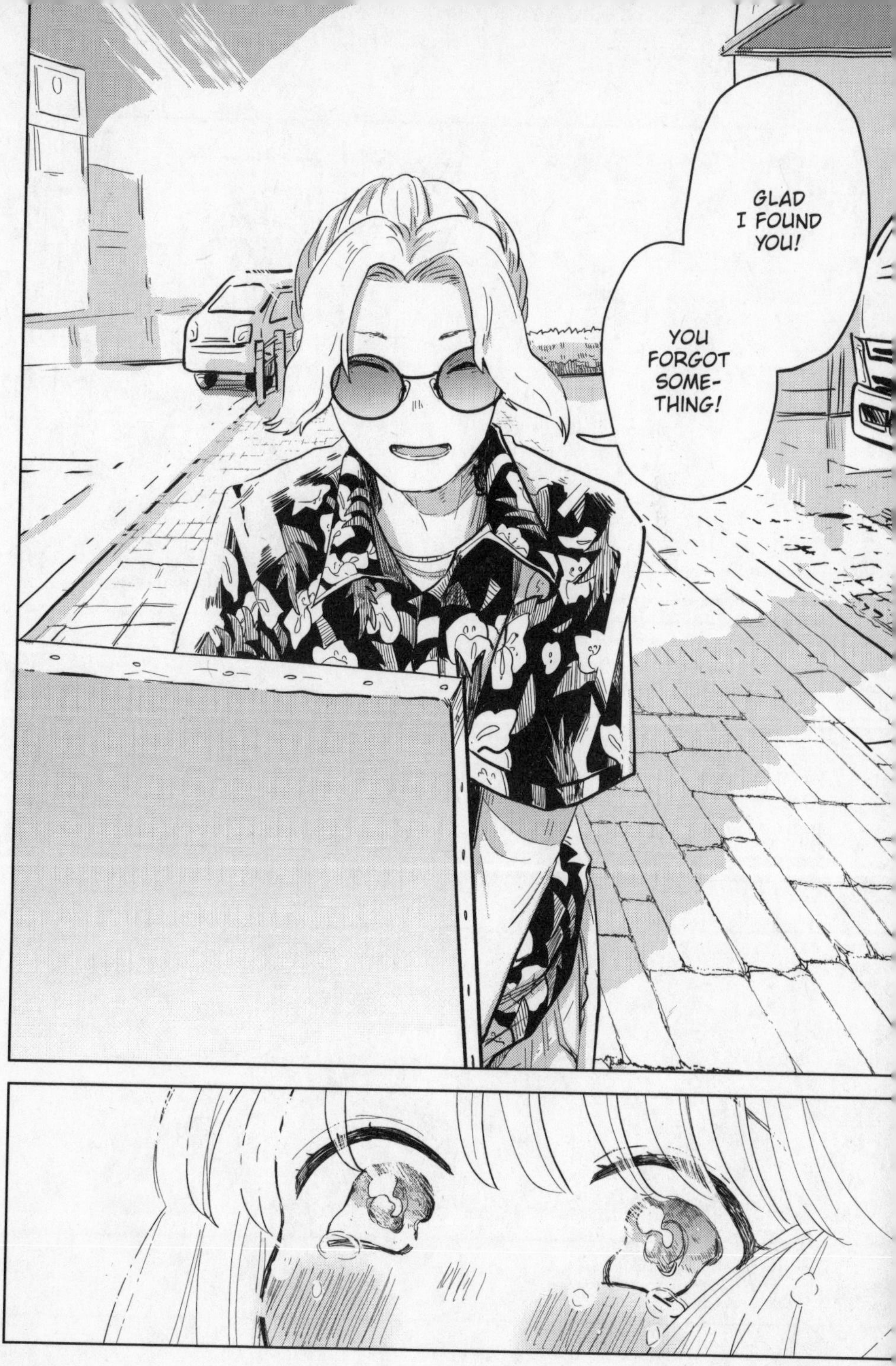
GLAD I FOUND YOU!
YOU FORGOT SOME-THING!

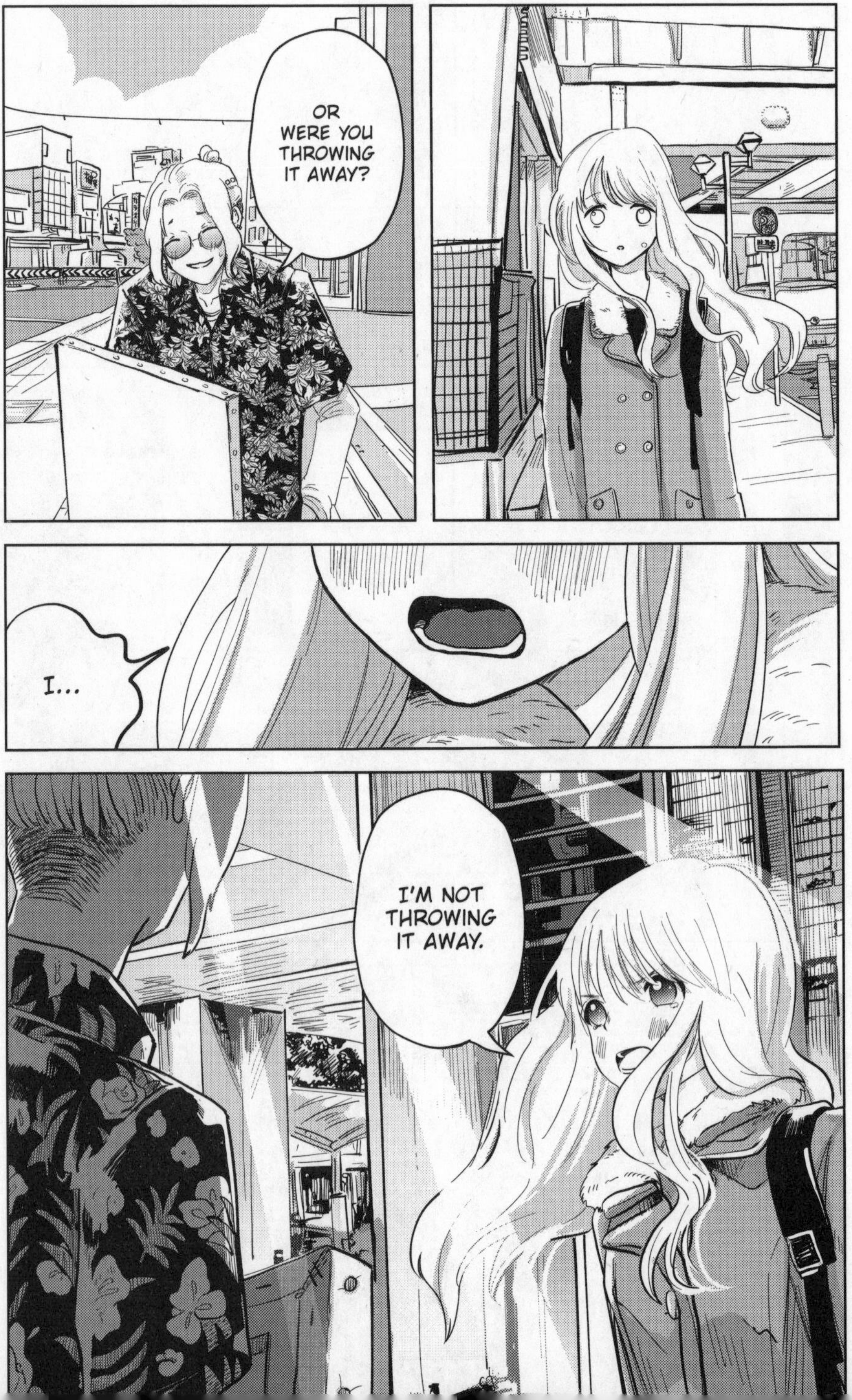
OR WERE YOU THROWING IT AWAY?
I...
I'M NOT THROWING IT AWAY.

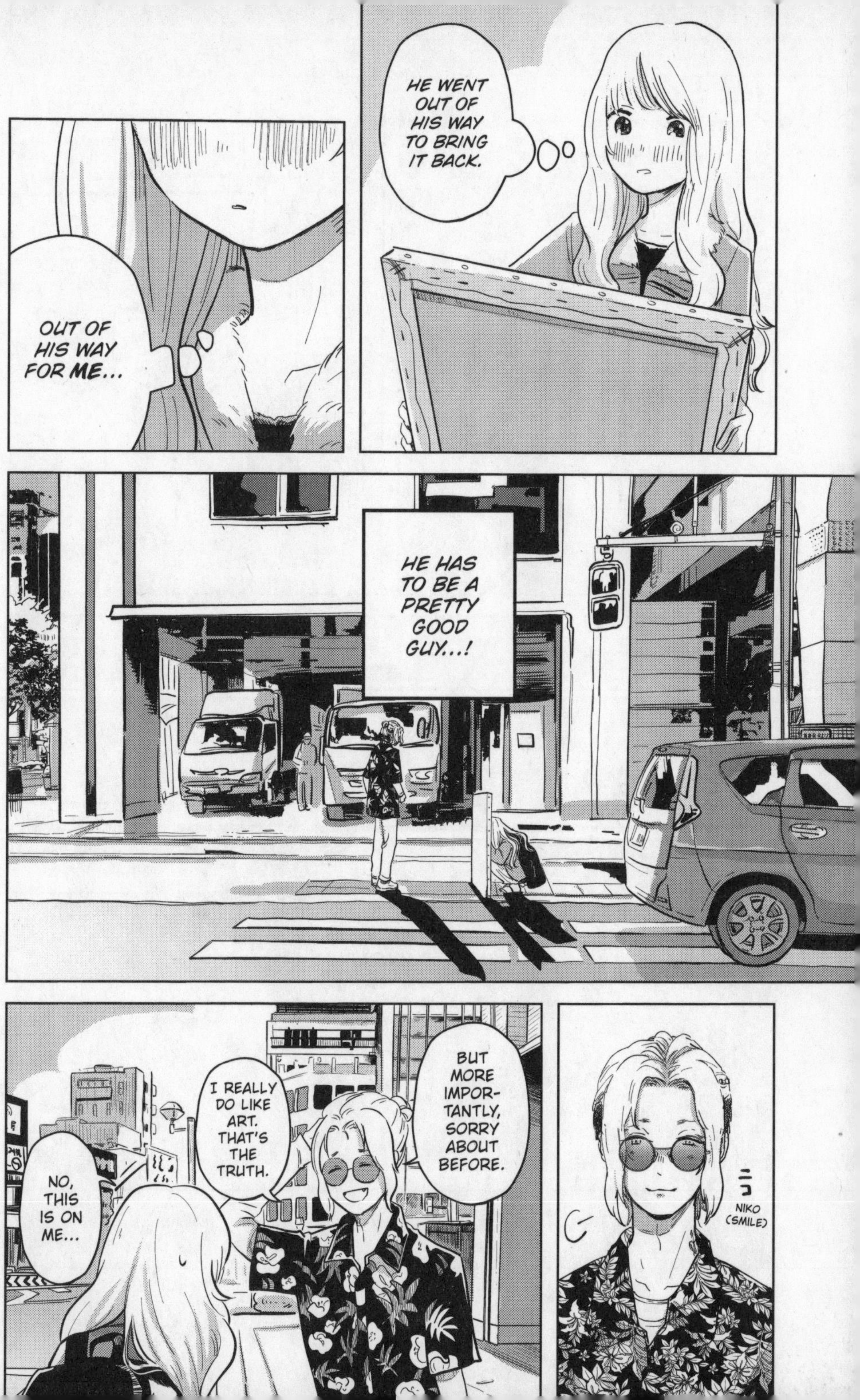
HE WENT OUT OF HIS WAY TO BRING IT BACK.
OUT OF HIS WAY FOR **ME**...
HE HAS TO BE A PRETTY GOOD GUY...!
ニコ
NIKO (SMILE)
BUT MORE IMPORTANTLY, SORRY ABOUT BEFORE.
I REALLY DO LIKE ART. THAT'S THE TRUTH.
NO, THIS IS ON ME...

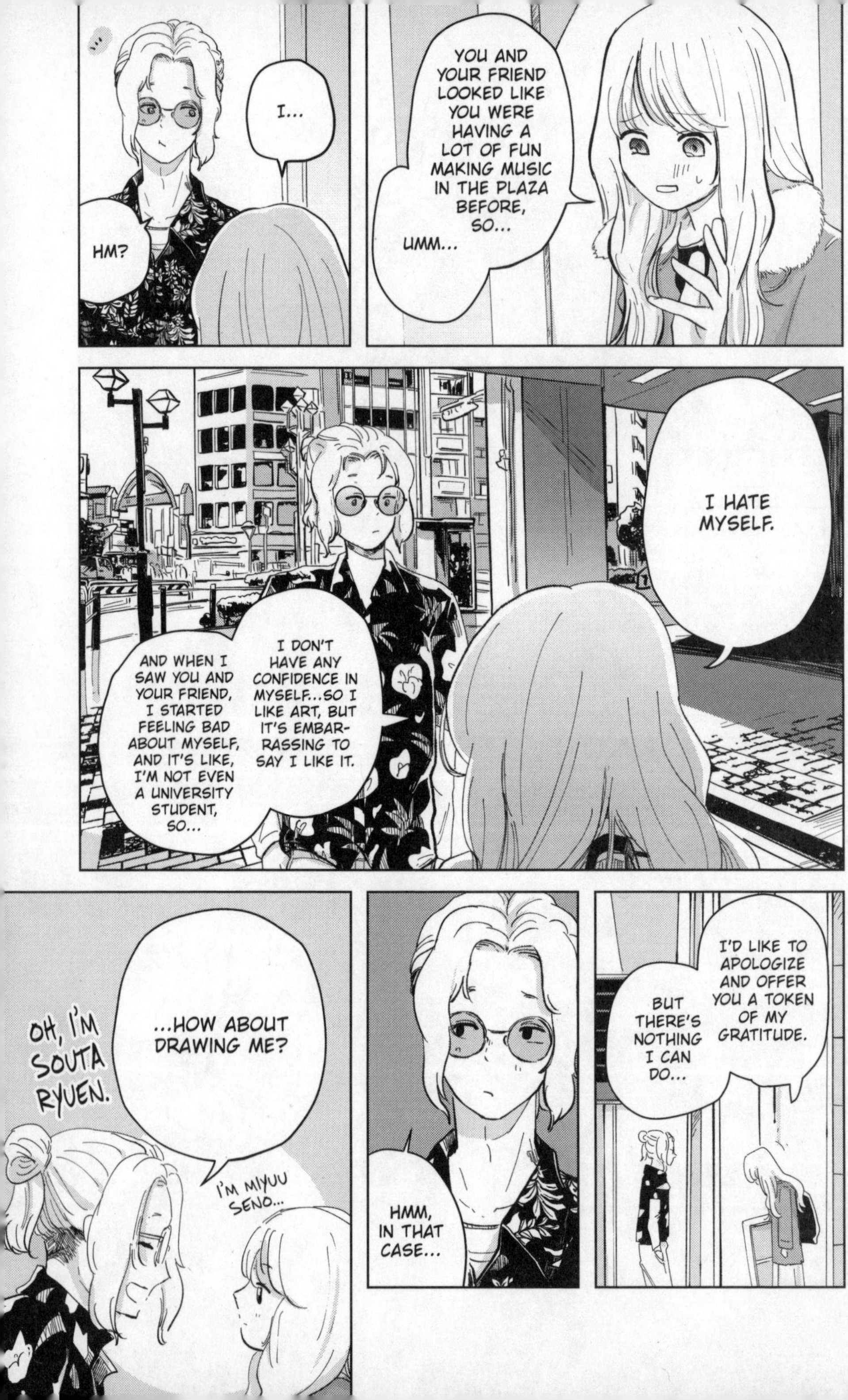
YOU AND YOUR FRIEND LOOKED LIKE YOU WERE HAVING A LOT OF FUN MAKING MUSIC IN THE PLAZA BEFORE, SO...
UMM...
I...
...
HM?
I HATE MYSELF.
I DON'T HAVE ANY CONFIDENCE IN MYSELF...SO I LIKE ART, BUT IT'S EMBARRASSING TO SAY I LIKE IT.
AND WHEN I SAW YOU AND YOUR FRIEND, I STARTED FEELING BAD ABOUT MYSELF, AND IT'S LIKE, I'M NOT EVEN A UNIVERSITY STUDENT, SO...
I'D LIKE TO APOLOGIZE AND OFFER YOU A TOKEN OF MY GRATITUDE.
BUT THERE'S NOTHING I CAN DO...
HMM, IN THAT CASE...
...HOW ABOUT DRAWING ME?
OH, I'M SOUTA RYUEN.
I'M MIYUU SENO...

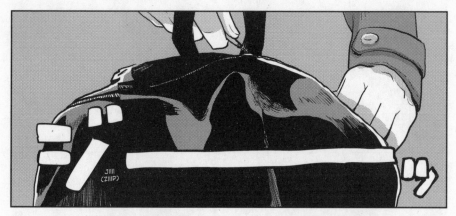

JIIII
(ZIIIP)

I SAID I WANTED TO THANK HIM, BUT...

SKETCH

パカ
PAKA
(PLCK)

SIGN: DRUG STORE "OKUSURIX"

RYUEN-SAN, DON'T YOU FEEL EMBARRASSED TO HAVE SOMEONE DRAWING YOU OUT HERE?

WHY?

?

IT MUST BE NICE TO HAVE CONFIDENCE IN YOURSELF.

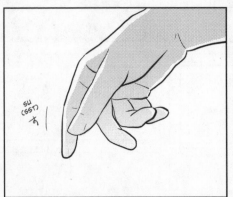

SU (SST)
す

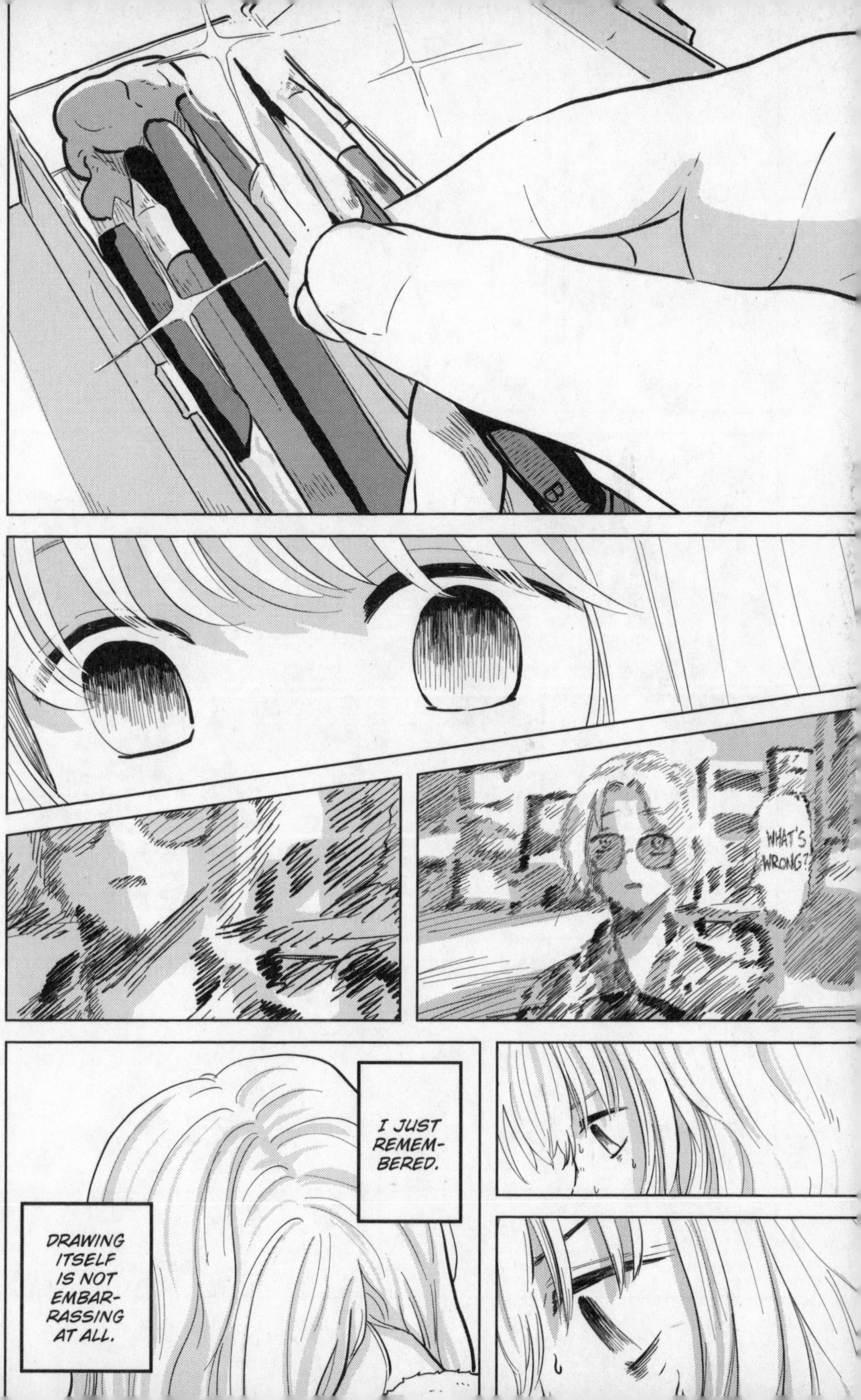
WHAT'S WRONG?
I JUST REMEMBERED.
DRAWING ITSELF IS NOT EMBARRASSING AT ALL.

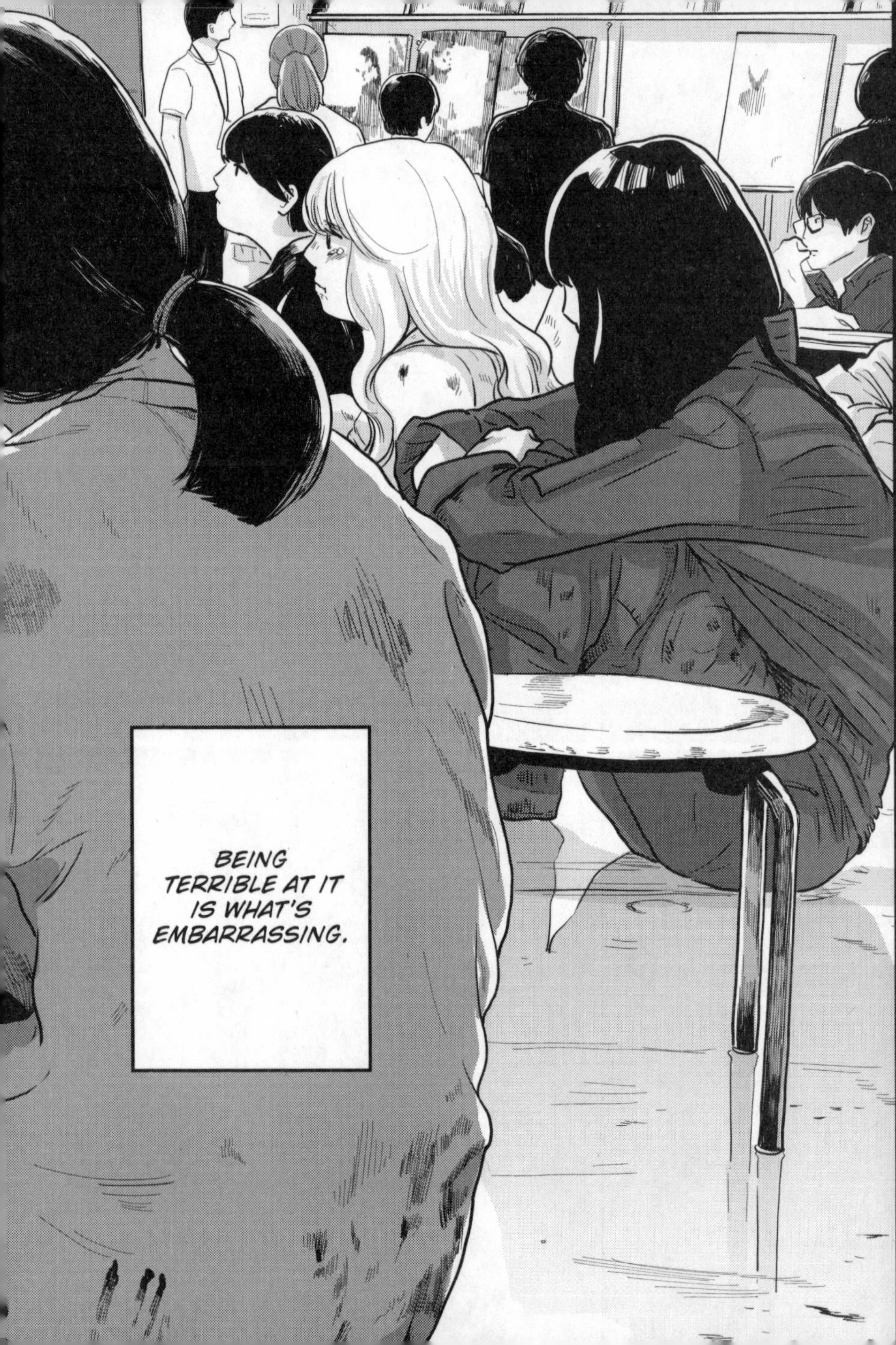
BEING TERRIBLE AT IT IS WHAT'S EMBARRASSING.

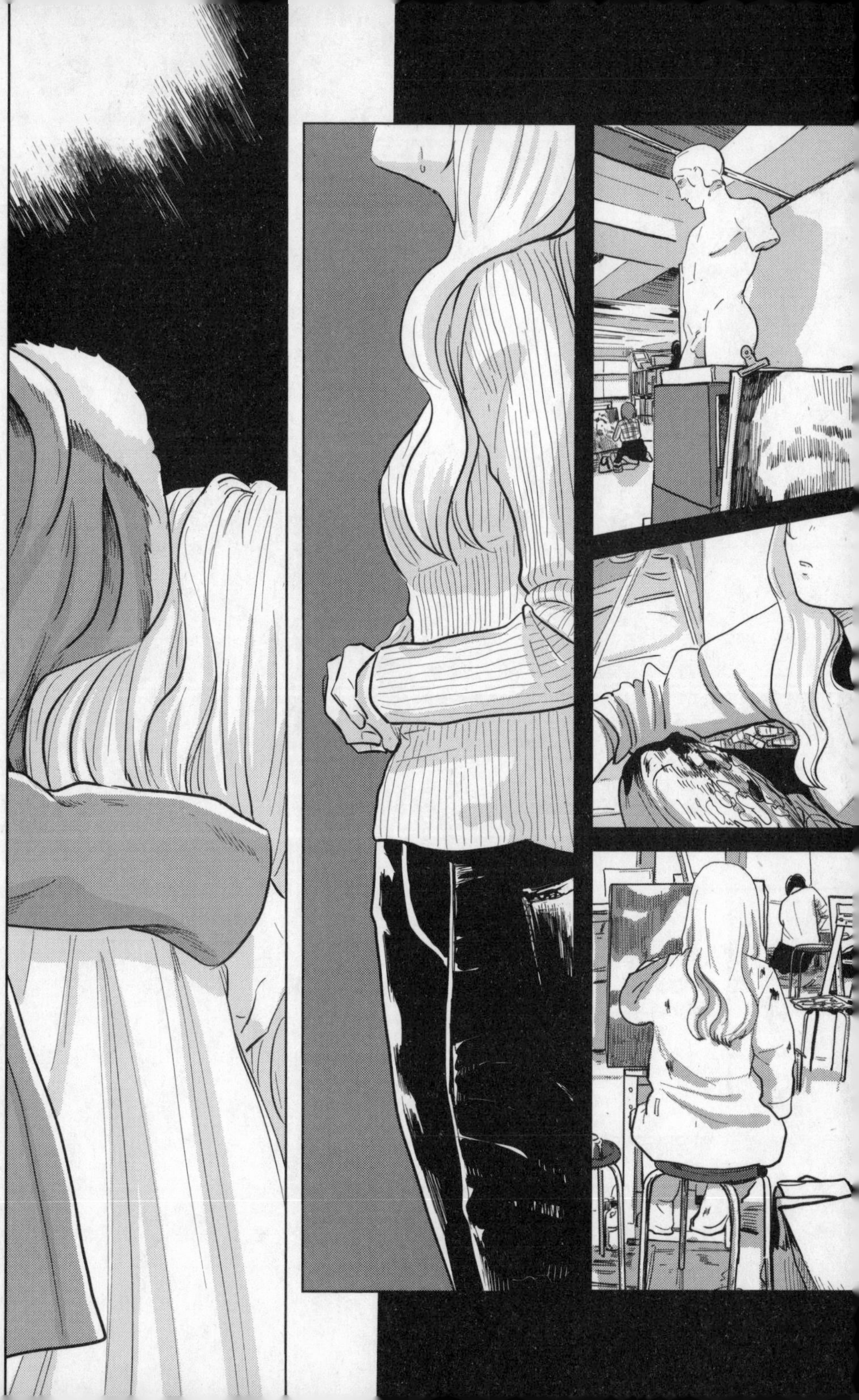

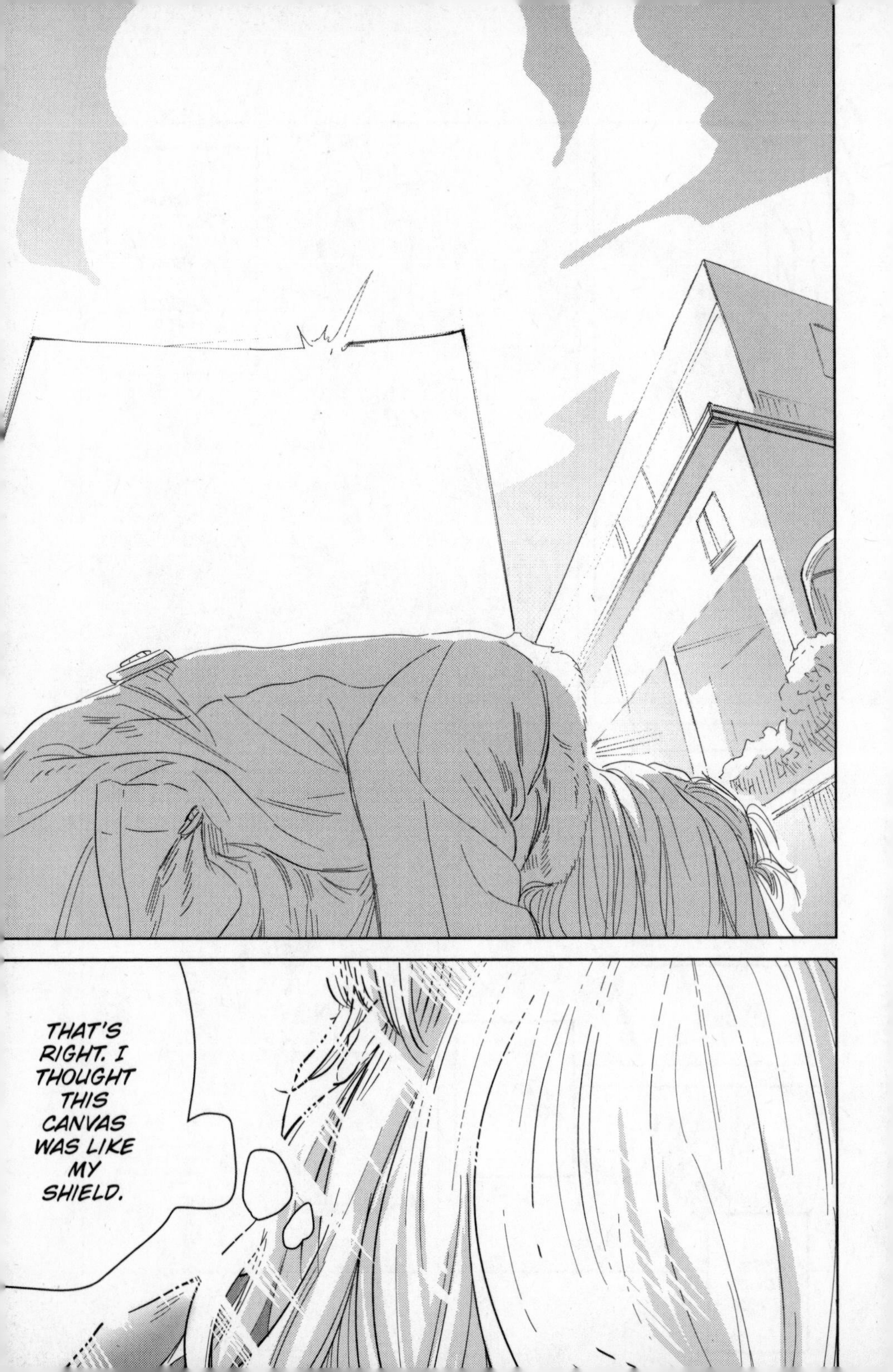
THAT'S RIGHT. I THOUGHT THIS CANVAS WAS LIKE MY SHIELD.

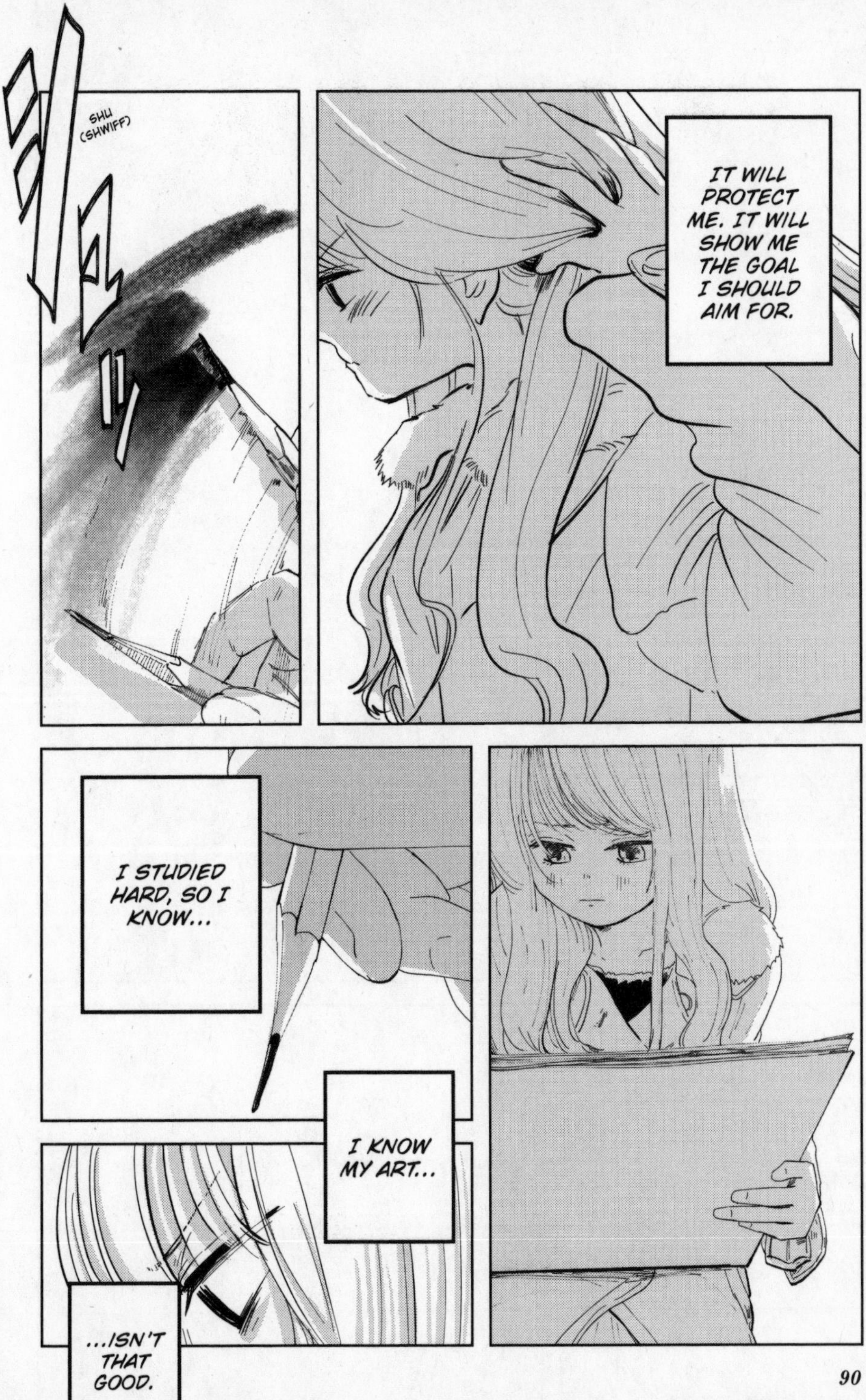
IT WILL PROTECT ME. IT WILL SHOW ME THE GOAL I SHOULD AIM FOR.
SHU (SHWIFF)
I STUDIED HARD, SO I KNOW...
I KNOW MY ART...
...ISN'T THAT GOOD.

BUT IT'S STRANGE...

MY HEART IS RACING...

MY BODY FEELS WARM AND KIND OF FUNNY.

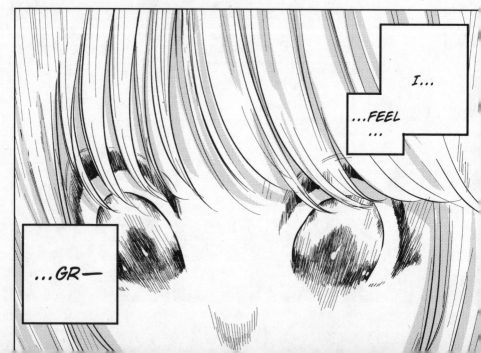

I...

...FEEL...

...GR—

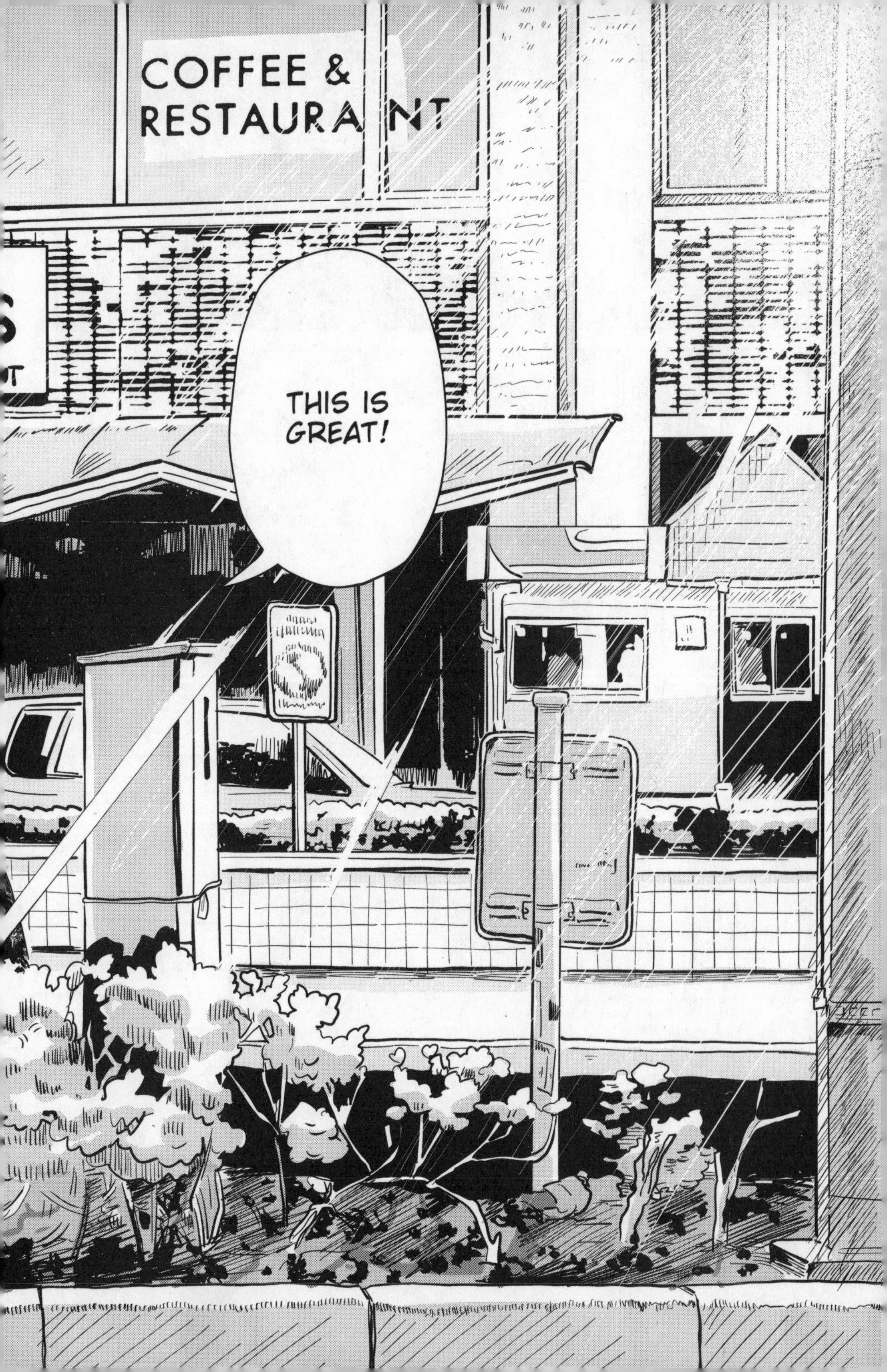
COFFEE &
RESTAURANT
THIS IS GREAT!

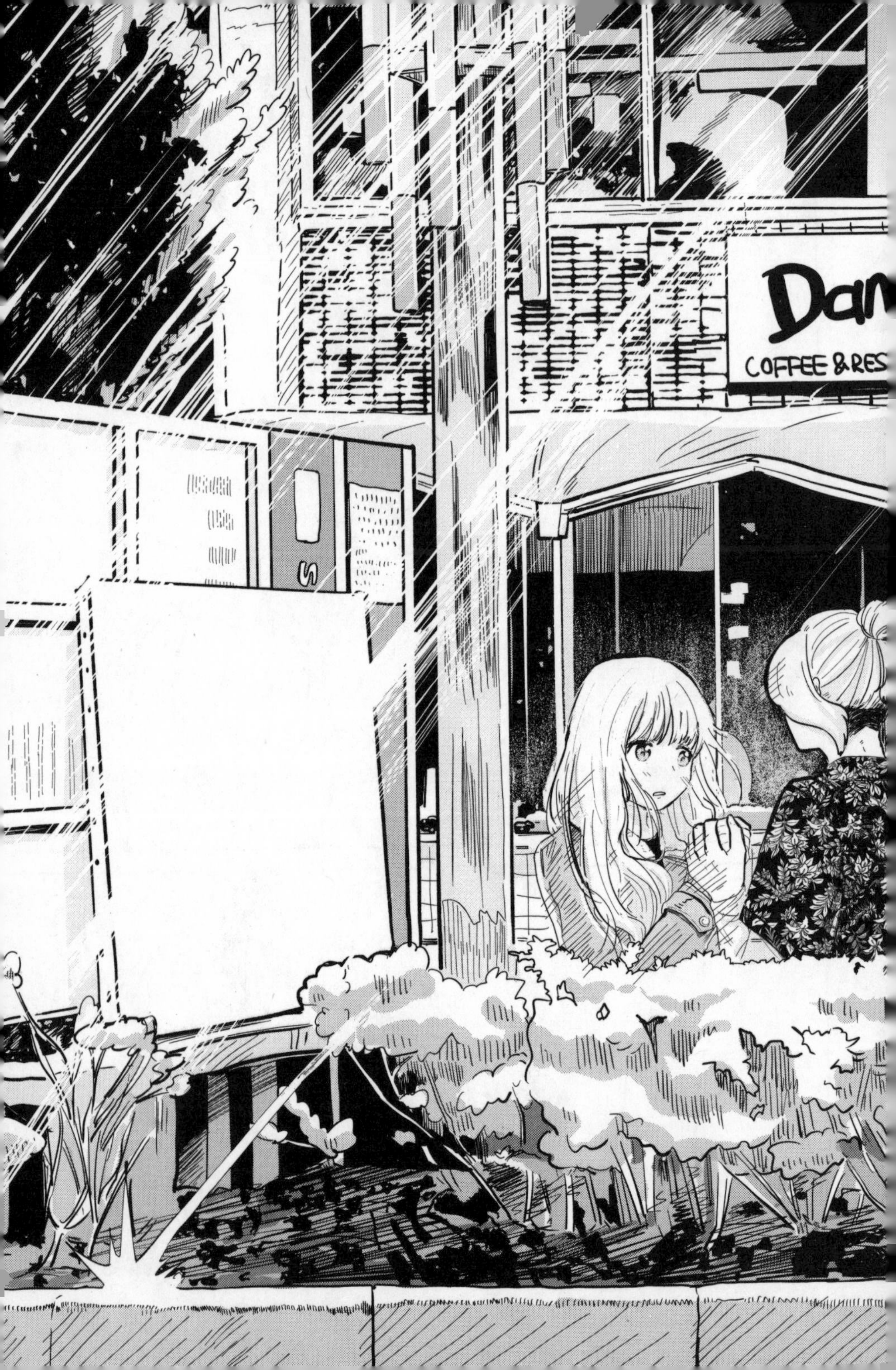
Dan
COFFEE &RES

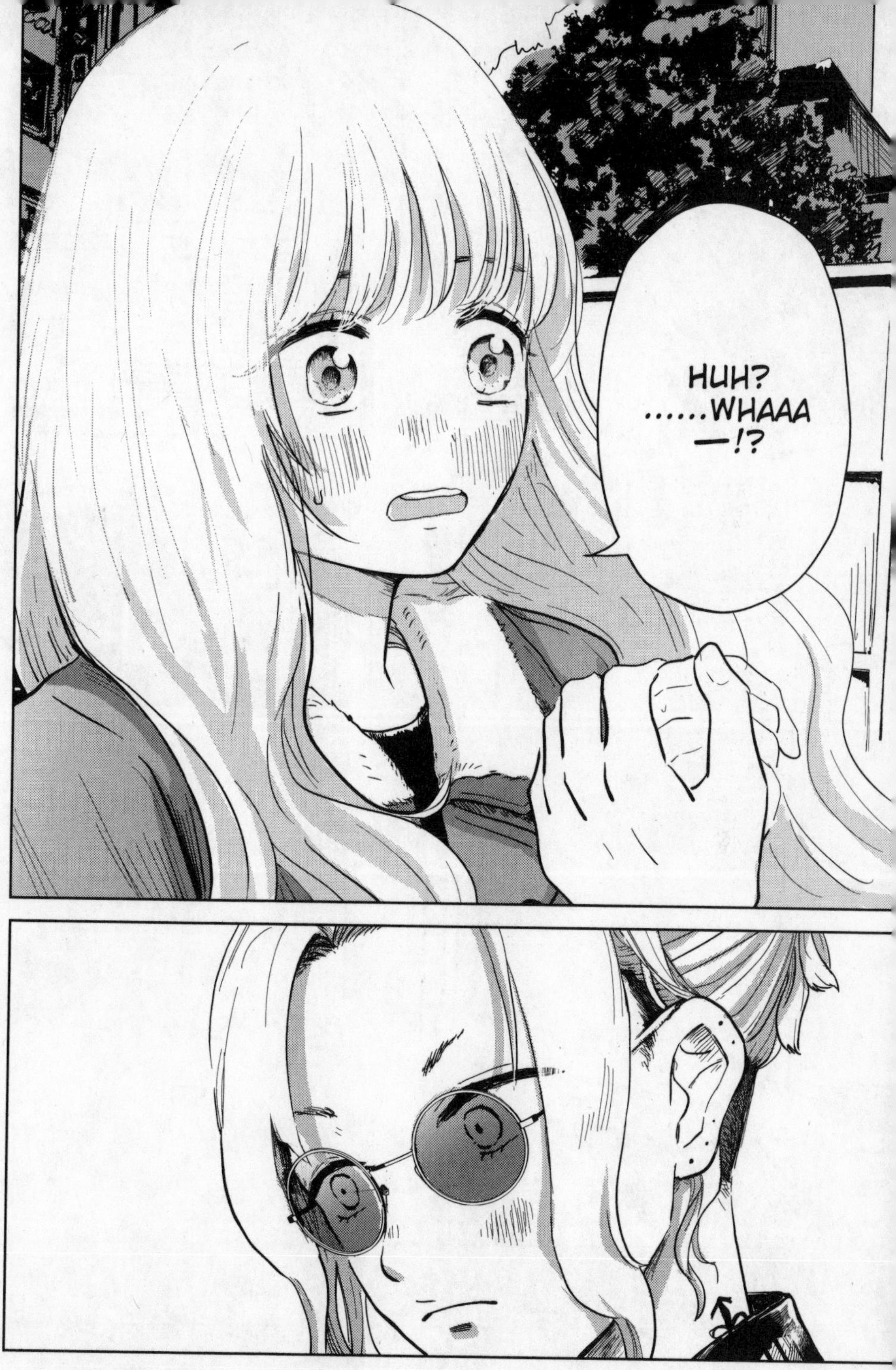
HUH? ......WHAAA—!?

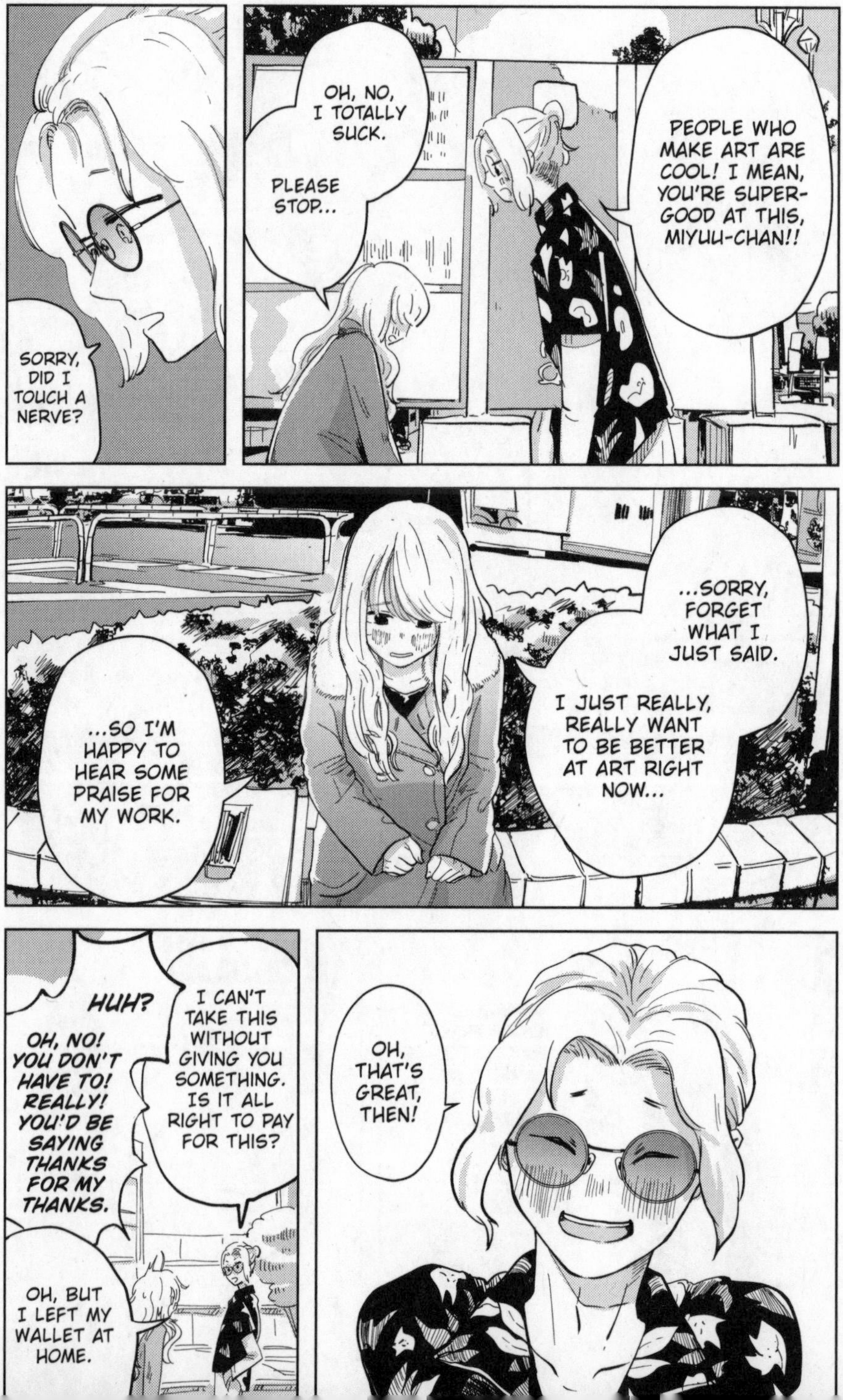
PEOPLE WHO MAKE ART ARE COOL! I MEAN, YOU'RE SUPER-GOOD AT THIS, MIYUU-CHAN!!
OH, NO, I TOTALLY SUCK.
PLEASE STOP...
SORRY, DID I TOUCH A NERVE?
...SORRY, FORGET WHAT I JUST SAID.
I JUST REALLY, REALLY WANT TO BE BETTER AT ART RIGHT NOW...
...SO I'M HAPPY TO HEAR SOME PRAISE FOR MY WORK.
OH, THAT'S GREAT, THEN!
I CAN'T TAKE THIS WITHOUT GIVING YOU SOMETHING. IS IT ALL RIGHT TO PAY FOR THIS?
HUH?
OH, NO! YOU DON'T HAVE TO! REALLY! YOU'D BE SAYING THANKS FOR MY THANKS.
OH, BUT I LEFT MY WALLET AT HOME.

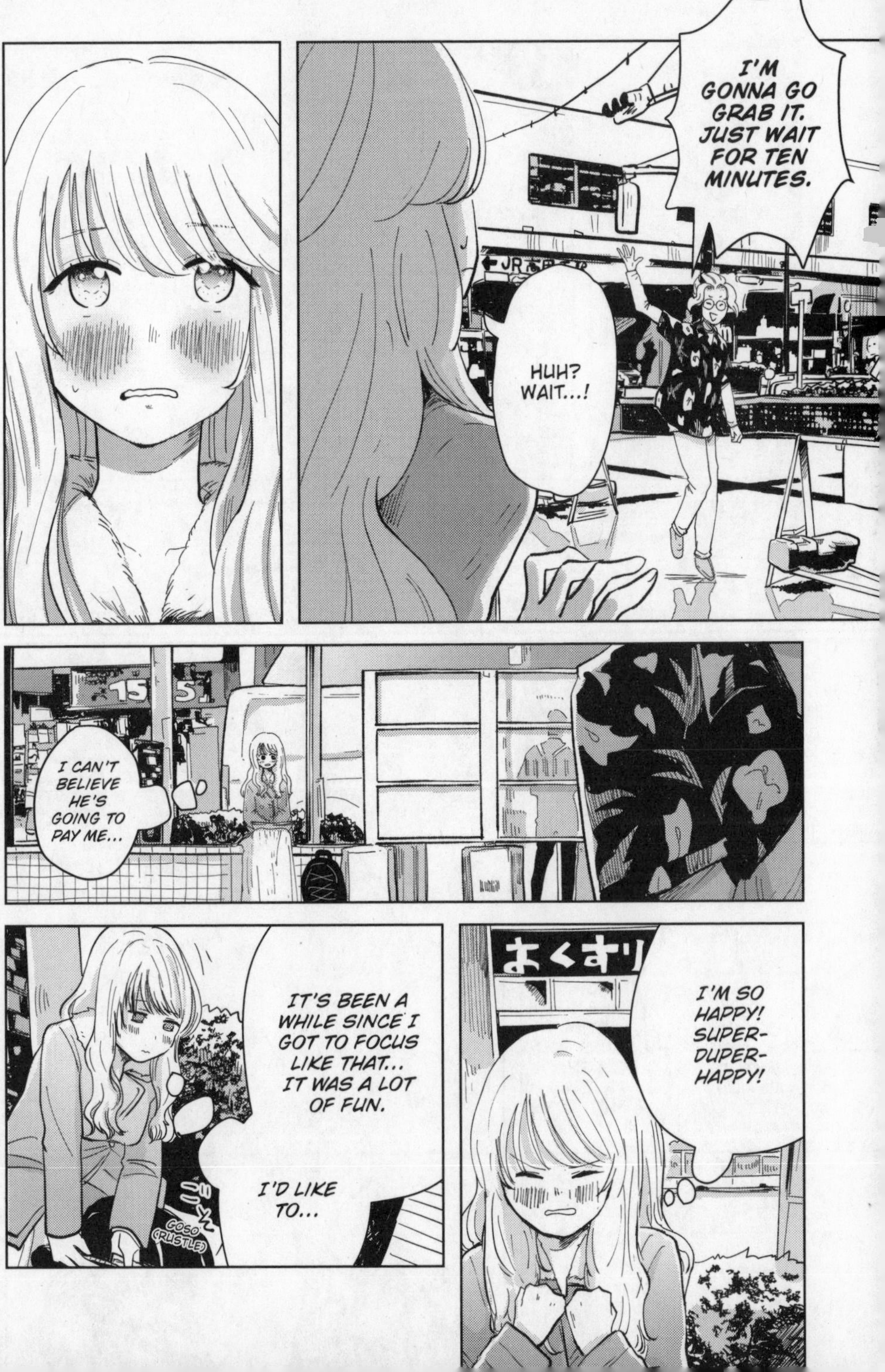
I'M GONNA GO GRAB IT. JUST WAIT FOR TEN MINUTES.
HUH? WAIT...!
I CAN'T BELIEVE HE'S GOING TO PAY ME...
おくすり
I'M SO HAPPY! SUPER-DUPER-HAPPY!
IT'S BEEN A WHILE SINCE I GOT TO FOCUS LIKE THAT... IT WAS A LOT OF FUN.
I'D LIKE TO...
GOSO (RUSTLE)

SU
(SHF)
すっ

I'D LIKE TO GET MUCH BETTER.

Art School & Art University Exams
East Nakano Art Preparatory Academy
HIGABI

HIGABI2021

Take your first step toward passing the exams! Now accepting students for our 2021 courses

TAPU
(TAP)
たぷ

Q Search / Enter site name

Bookmark

Comics Humor

Comics Humor

Show fewer it

MIYUU-CHAN?

Request documen

TAPU
たぷ
：

Higabi informatio

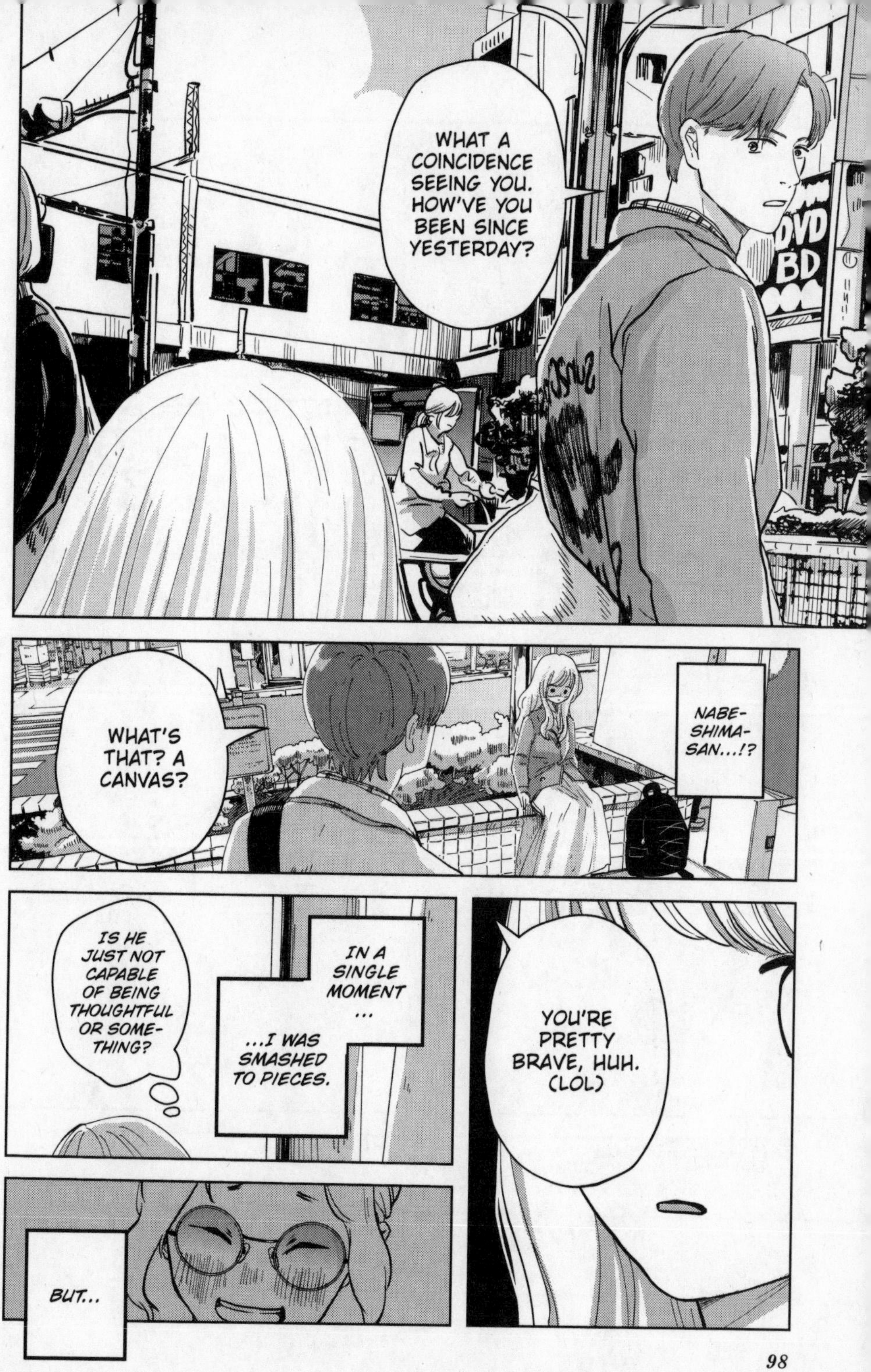

WHAT A COINCIDENCE SEEING YOU. HOW'VE YOU BEEN SINCE YESTERDAY?
DVD BD
NABE-SHIMA-SAN...!?
WHAT'S THAT? A CANVAS?
YOU'RE PRETTY BRAVE, HUH. (LOL)
IN A SINGLE MOMENT...
...I WAS SMASHED TO PIECES.
IS HE JUST NOT CAPABLE OF BEING THOUGHTFUL OR SOME-THING?
BUT...

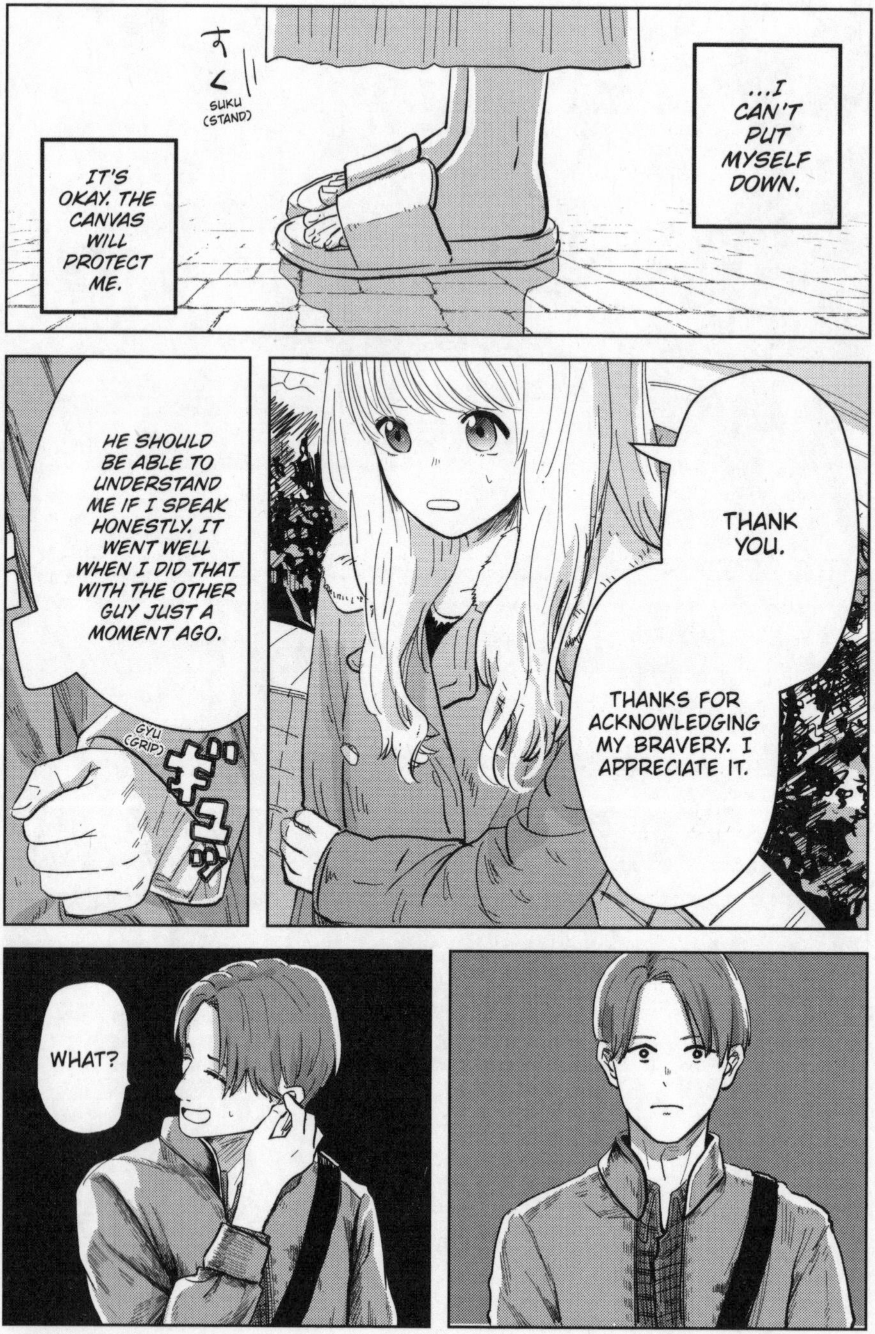
...I CAN'T PUT MYSELF DOWN.
すく
SUKU (STAND)
IT'S OKAY. THE CANVAS WILL PROTECT ME.
THANK YOU.
THANKS FOR ACKNOWLEDGING MY BRAVERY. I APPRECIATE IT.
HE SHOULD BE ABLE TO UNDERSTAND ME IF I SPEAK HONESTLY. IT WENT WELL WHEN I DID THAT WITH THE OTHER GUY JUST A MOMENT AGO.
ギュッ
GYU (GRIP)
WHAT?

YOU'RE THE TYPE OF PERSON WHO ALWAYS TAKES THINGS LITERALLY, AREN'T YOU, MIYUU-CHAN?

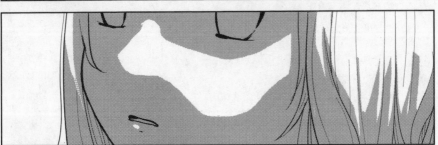

...I KNOW WHO I AM.

...CAN EASILY BE PIERCED.

SHIELDS...

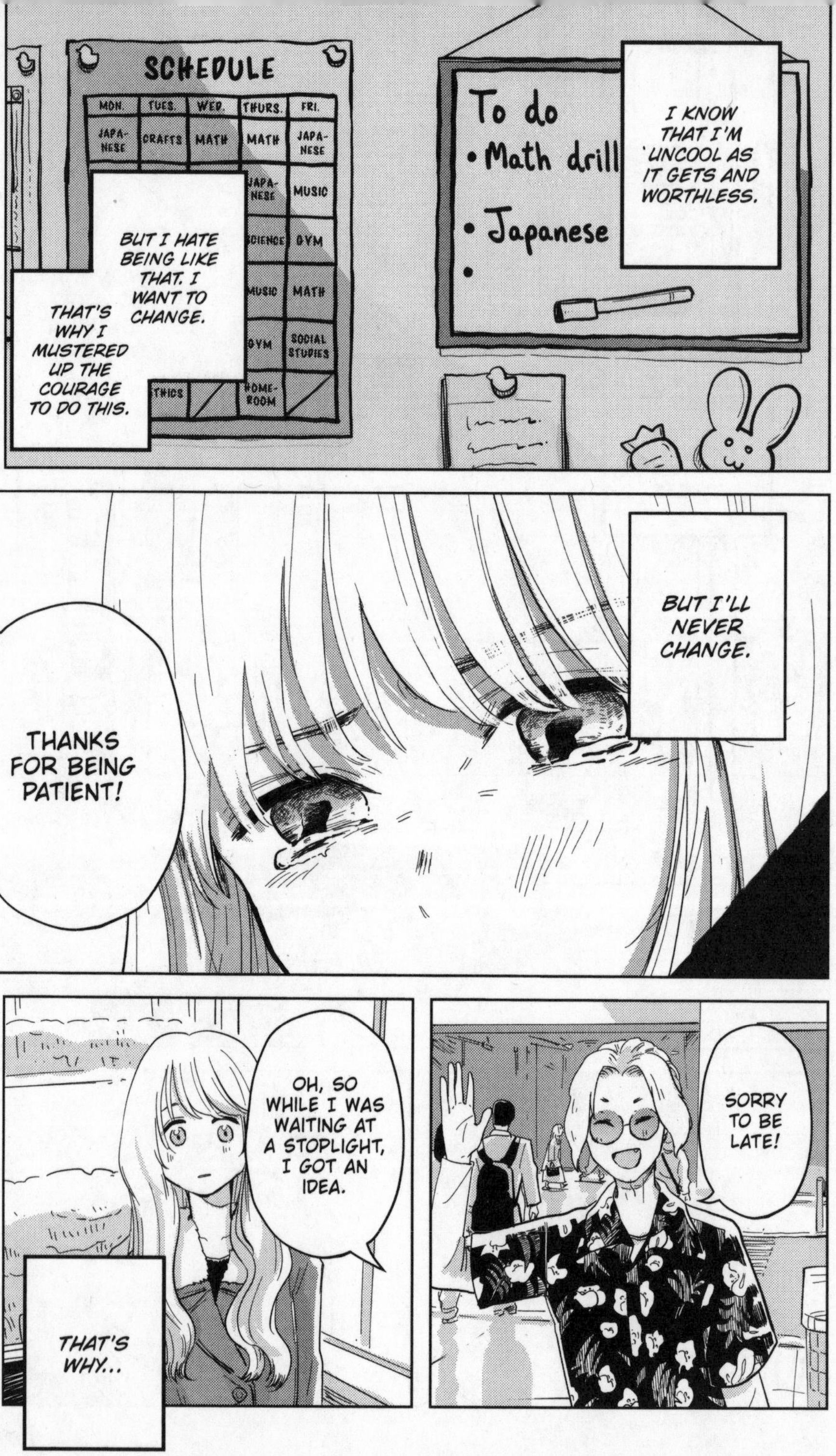
I KNOW THAT I'M UNCOOL AS IT GETS AND WORTHLESS.
To do
• Math drill
• Japanese
SCHEDULE
BUT I HATE BEING LIKE THAT. I WANT TO CHANGE.
THAT'S WHY I MUSTERED UP THE COURAGE TO DO THIS.
BUT I'LL NEVER CHANGE.
THANKS FOR BEING PATIENT!
SORRY TO BE LATE!
OH, SO WHILE I WAS WAITING AT A STOPLIGHT, I GOT AN IDEA.
THAT'S WHY...

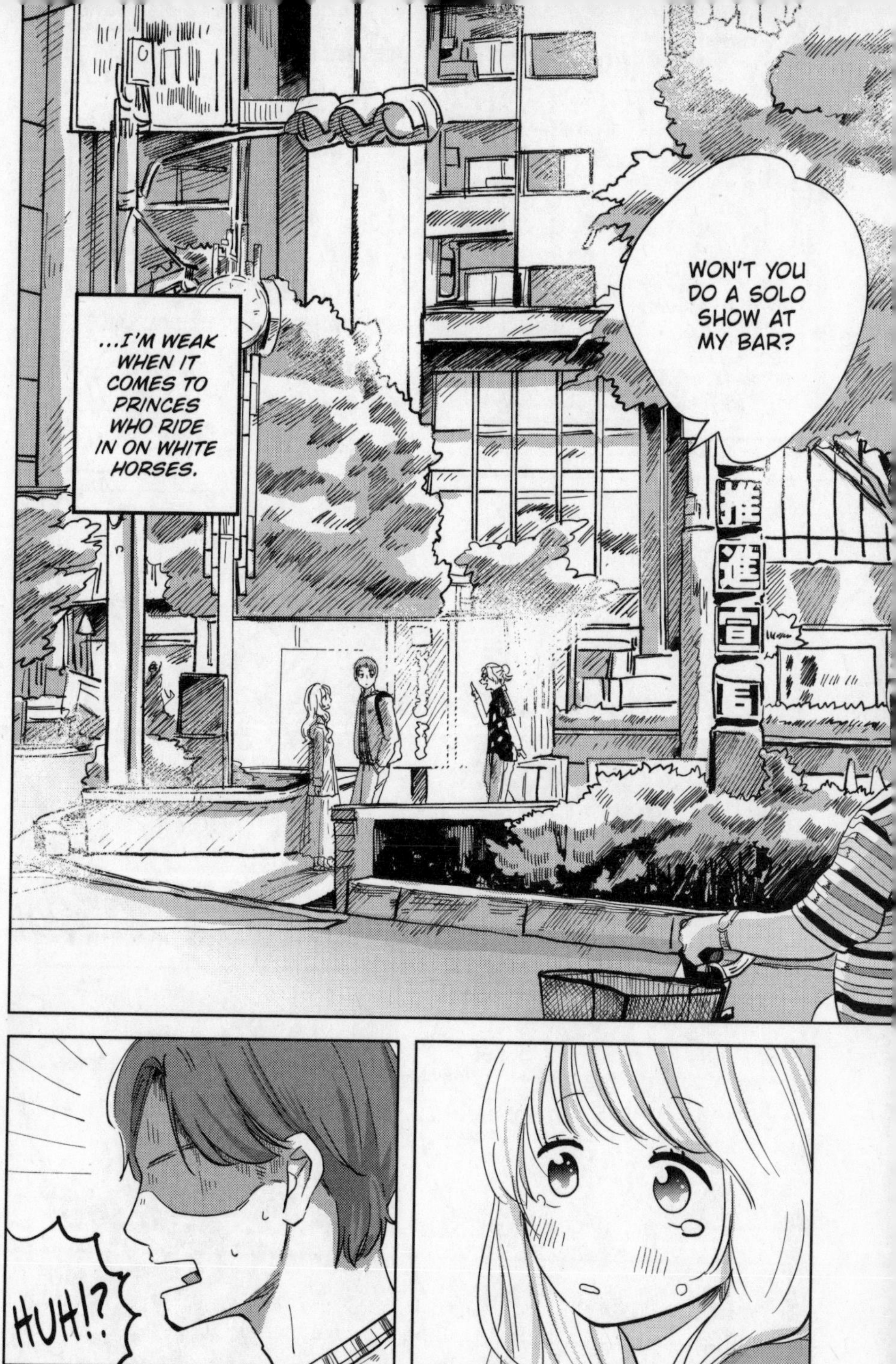
WON'T YOU DO A SOLO SHOW AT MY BAR?
...I'M WEAK WHEN IT COMES TO PRINCES WHO RIDE IN ON WHITE HORSES.
推進宣言
HUH!?

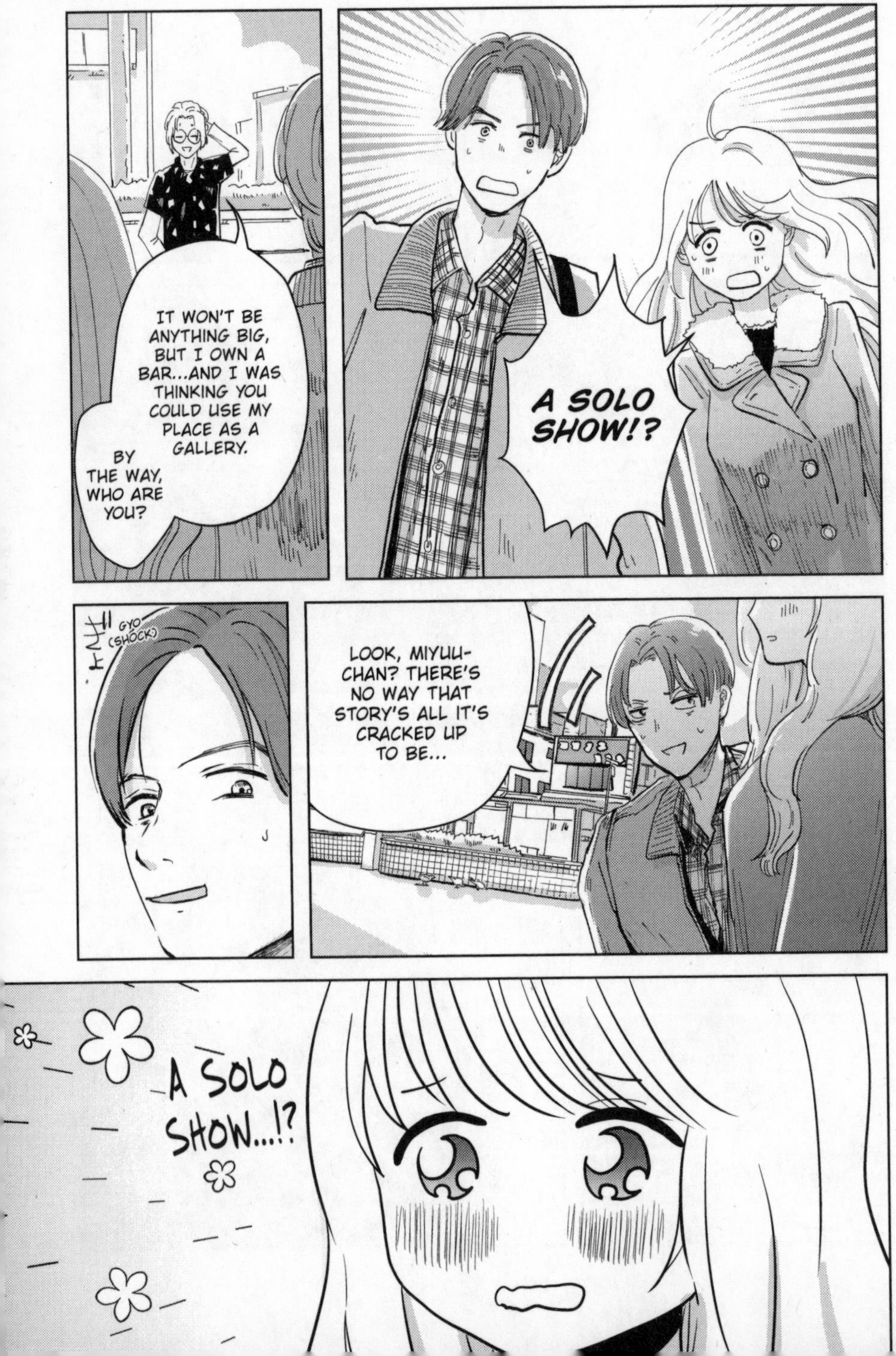

A SOLO SHOW!?
IT WON'T BE ANYTHING BIG, BUT I OWN A BAR...AND I WAS THINKING YOU COULD USE MY PLACE AS A GALLERY.
BY THE WAY, WHO ARE YOU?
LOOK, MIYUU-CHAN? THERE'S NO WAY THAT STORY'S ALL IT'S CRACKED UP TO BE...
GYO (SHOCK)
A SOLO SHOW...!?

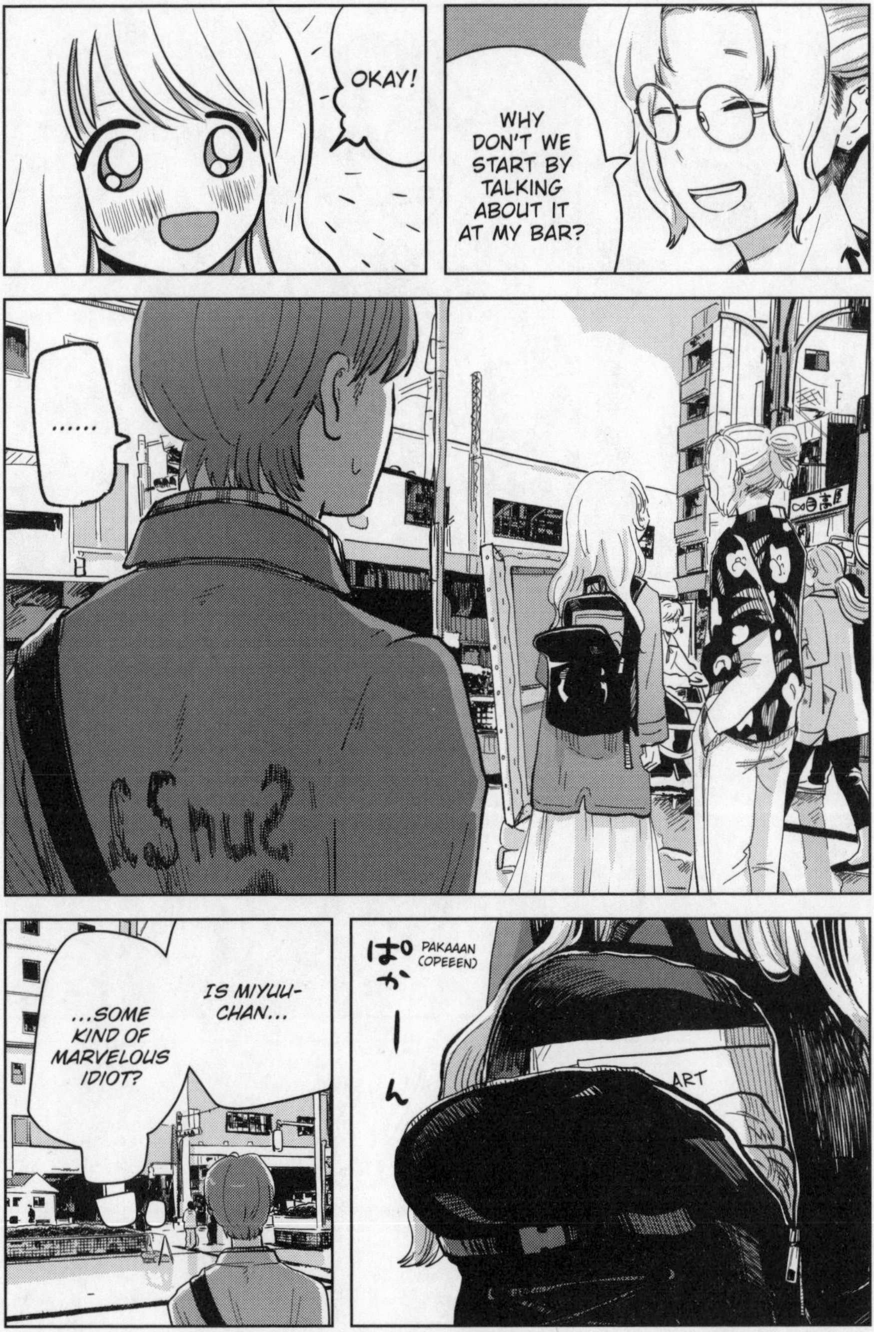
WHY DON'T WE START BY TALKING ABOUT IT AT MY BAR?
OKAY!
....
ぱかーん
PAKAAAN (OPEEEN)
ART
IS MIYUU-CHAN...
...SOME KIND OF MARVELOUS IDIOT?

Chapter 2 / END

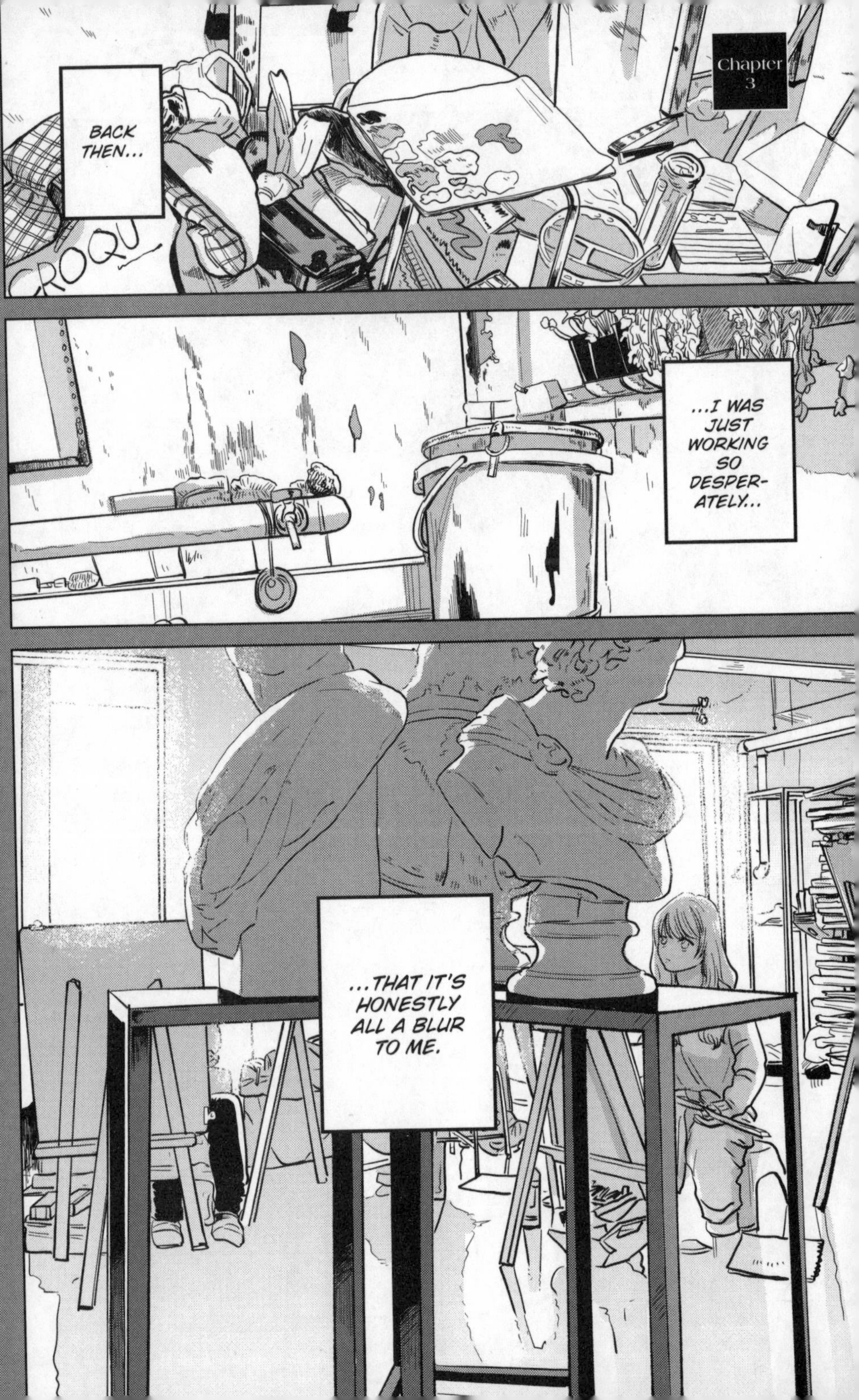
Chapter
3
BACK THEN...
CROQU
...I WAS JUST WORKING SO DESPERATELY...
...THAT IT'S HONESTLY ALL A BLUR TO ME.

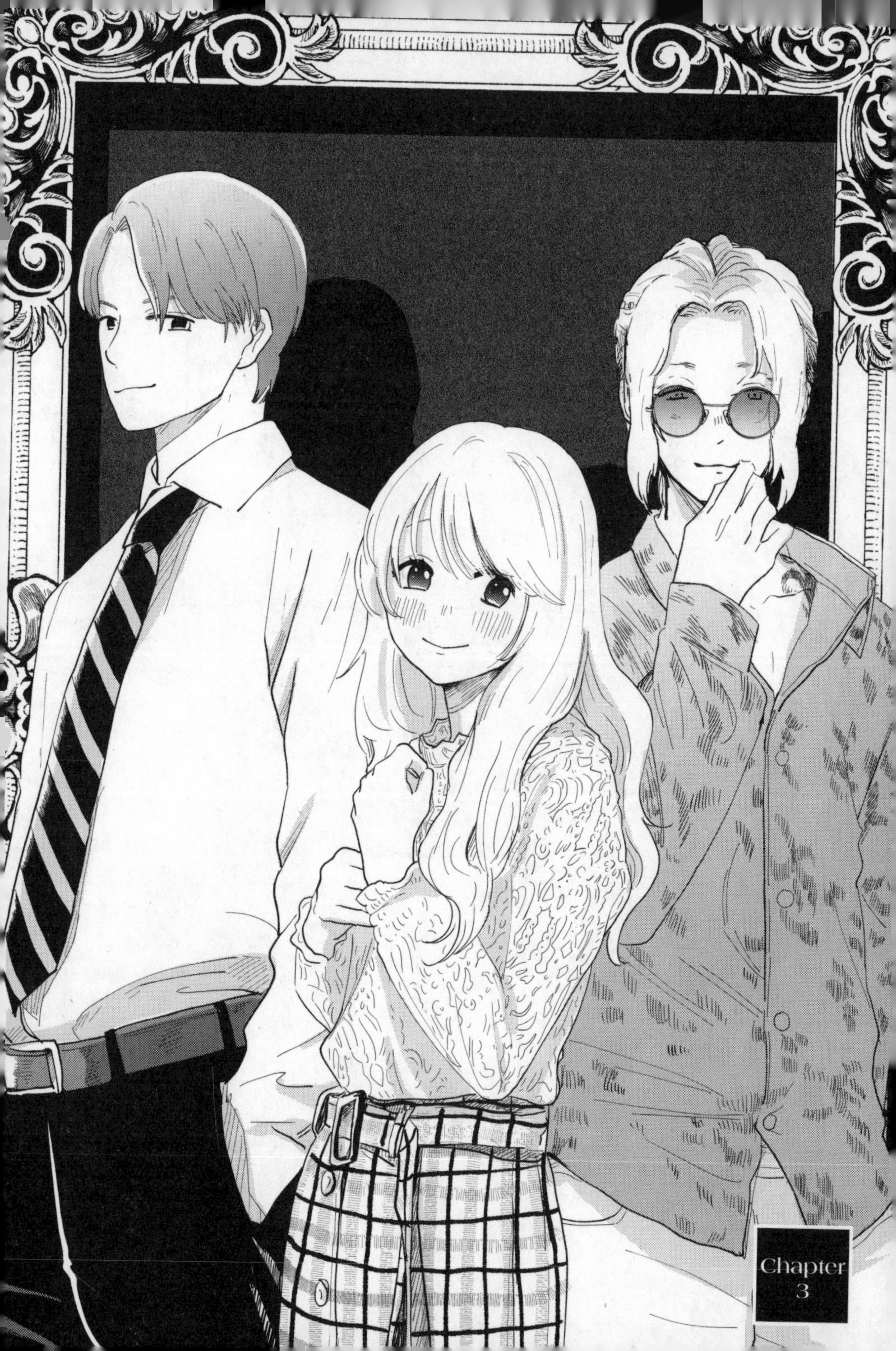
Chapter
3

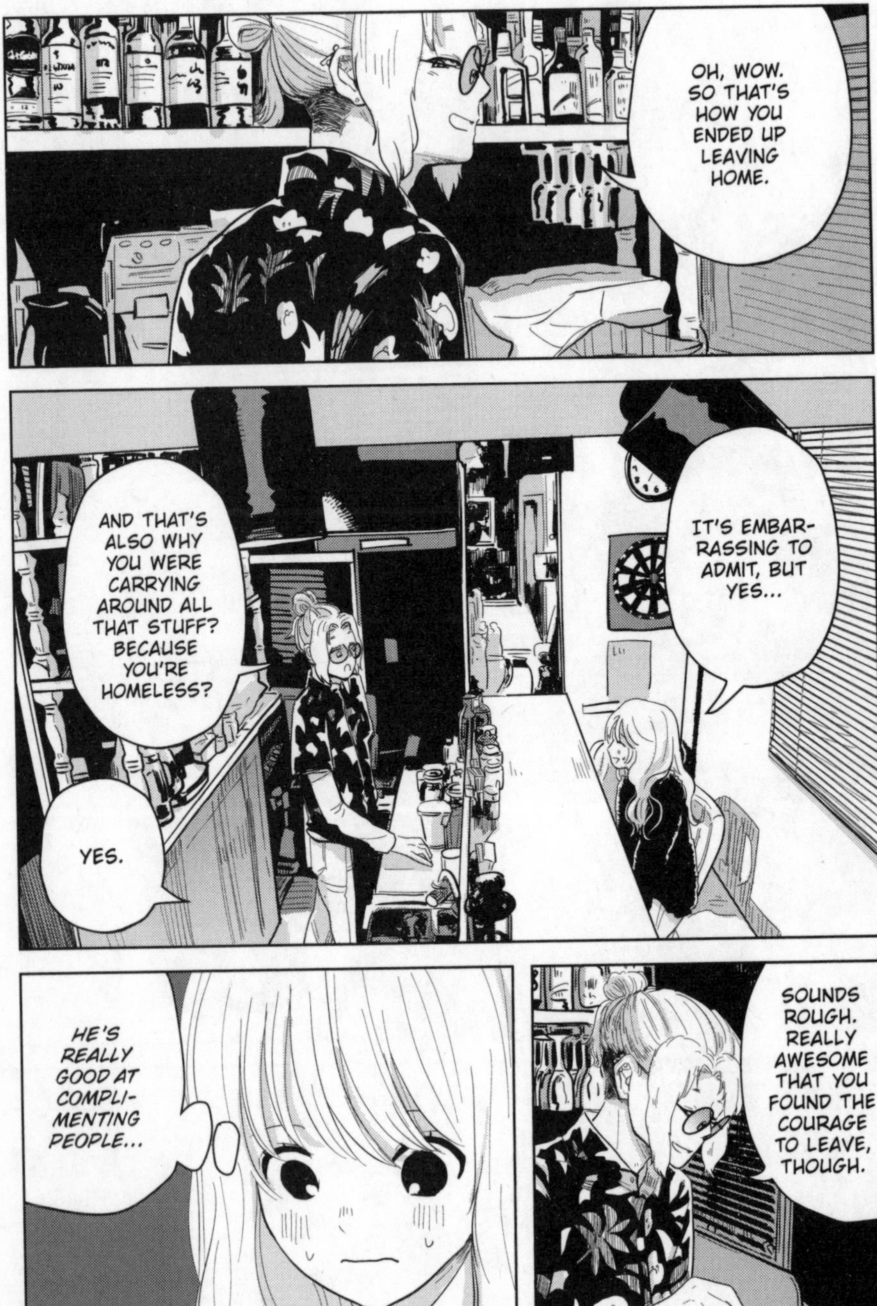
OH, WOW. SO THAT'S HOW YOU ENDED UP LEAVING HOME.
IT'S EMBAR-RASSING TO ADMIT, BUT YES...
AND THAT'S ALSO WHY YOU WERE CARRYING AROUND ALL THAT STUFF? BECAUSE YOU'RE HOMELESS?
YES.
SOUNDS ROUGH. REALLY AWESOME THAT YOU FOUND THE COURAGE TO LEAVE, THOUGH.
HE'S REALLY GOOD AT COMPLI-MENTING PEOPLE...

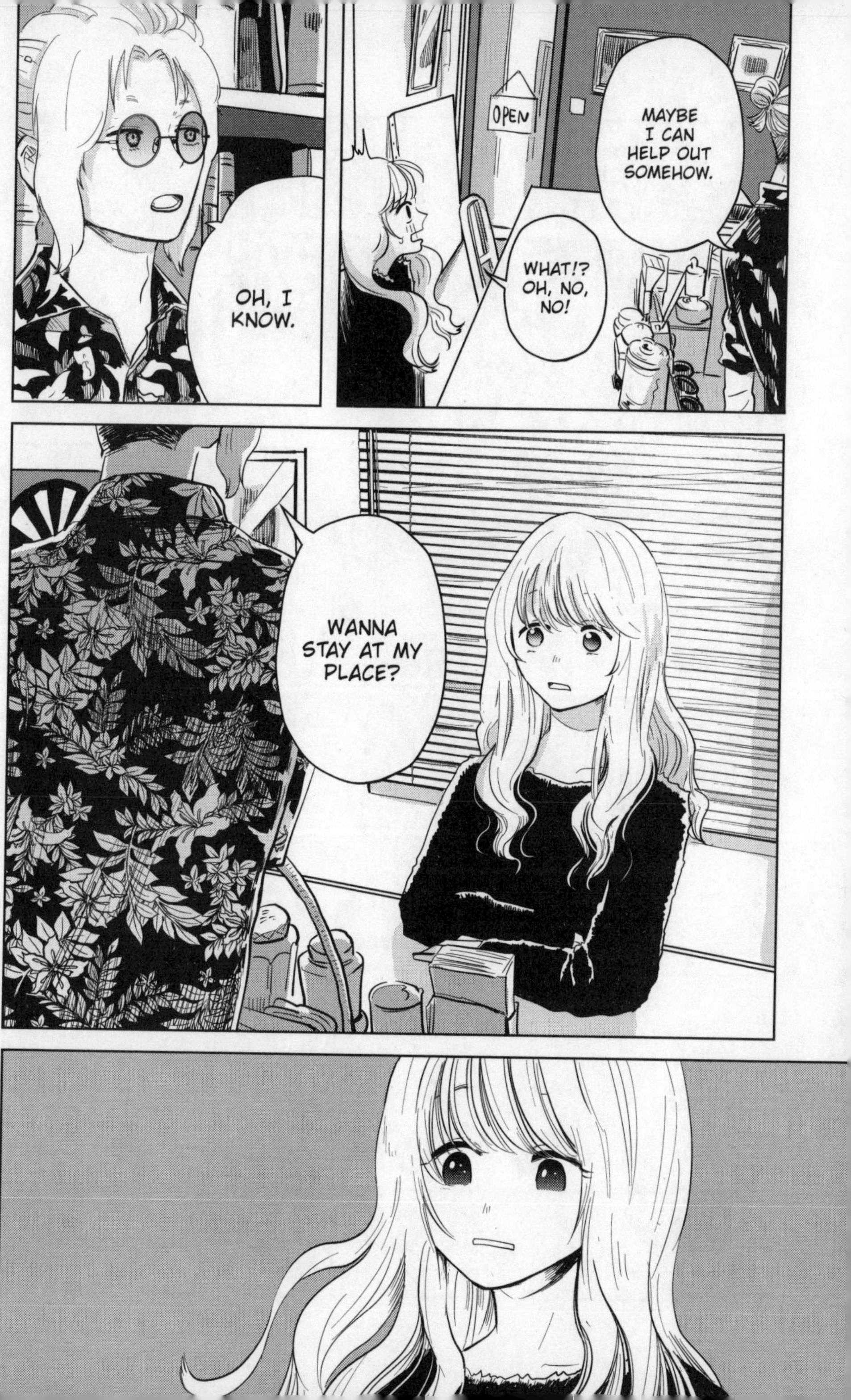
MAYBE I CAN HELP OUT SOMEHOW.
OPEN
WHAT!? OH, NO, NO!
OH, I KNOW.
WANNA STAY AT MY PLACE?

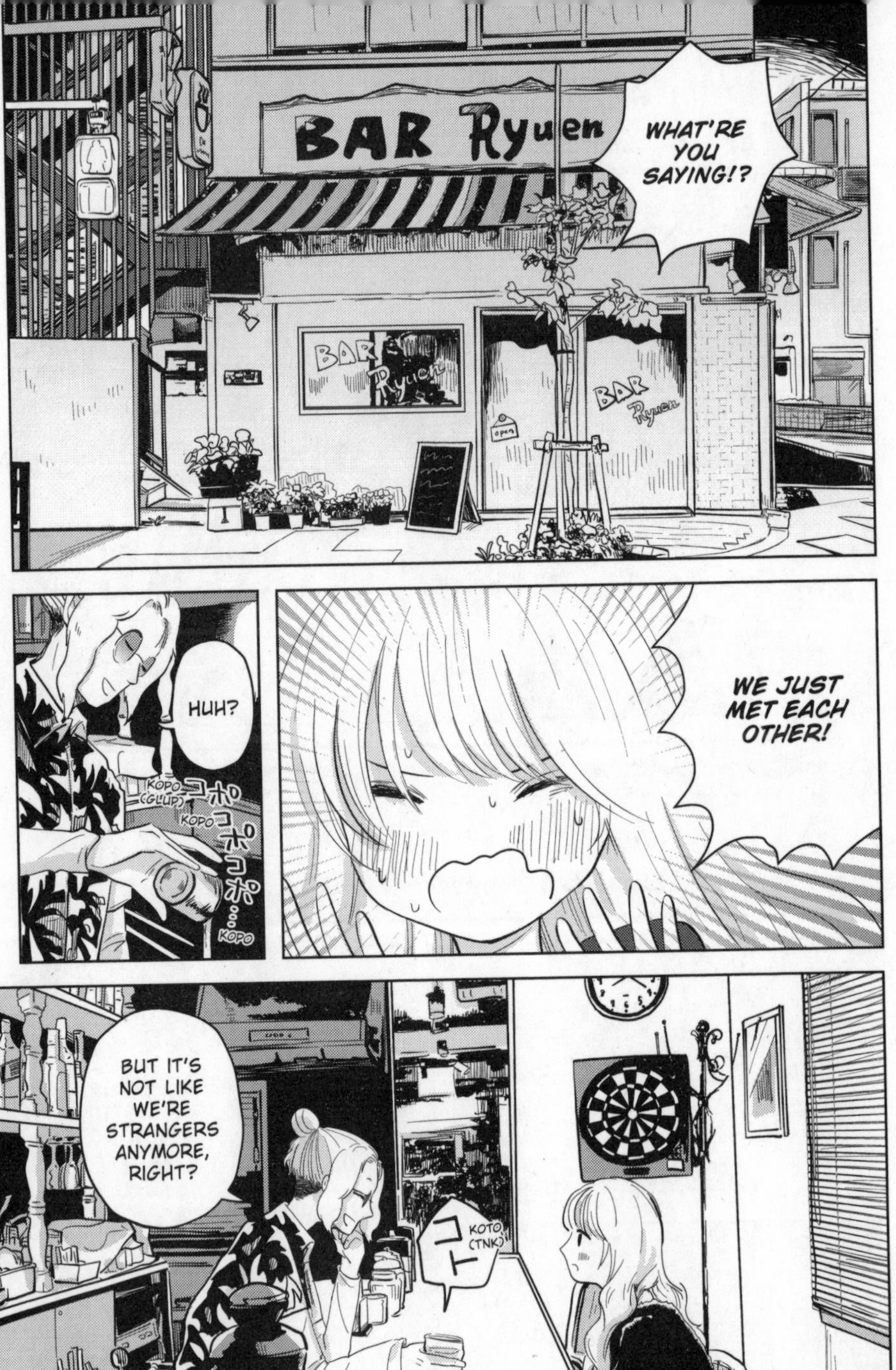
BAR Ryuen
WHAT'RE YOU SAYING!?
WE JUST MET EACH OTHER!
HUH?
KOPO (GLUP) KOPO KOPO
BUT IT'S NOT LIKE WE'RE STRANGERS ANYMORE, RIGHT?
KOTO (TNK)

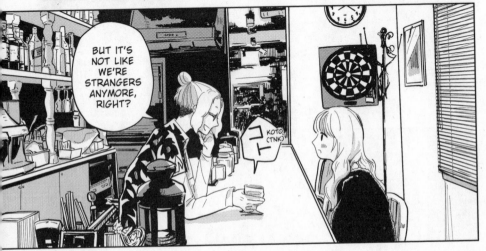

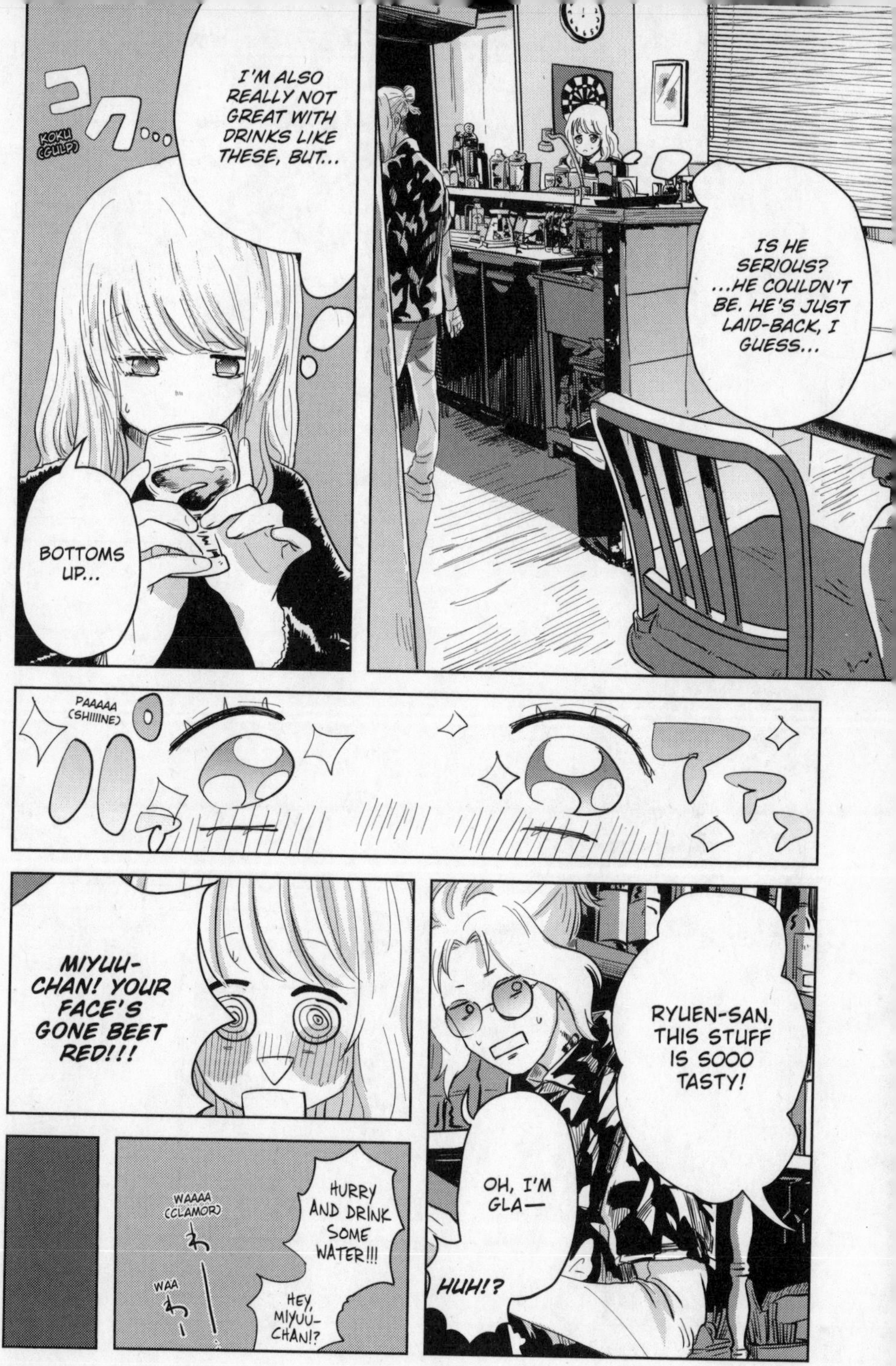
IS HE SERIOUS? ...HE COULDN'T BE. HE'S JUST LAID-BACK, I GUESS...
I'M ALSO REALLY NOT GREAT WITH DRINKS LIKE THESE, BUT...
コク...
KOKU (GULP)
BOTTOMS UP...
PAAAAA (SHIIINE)
RYUEN-SAN, THIS STUFF IS SOOO TASTY!
MIYUU-CHAN! YOUR FACE'S GONE BEET RED!!!
OH, I'M GLA—
HUH!?
HURRY AND DRINK SOME WATER!!!
HEY, MIYUU-CHAN!?
WAAAA (CLAMOR)
WAA

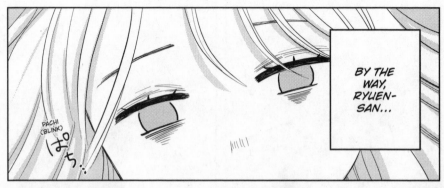

BY THE WAY, RYUEN-SAN...

PACHI
(BLINK)

...WHAT HAPPENED TO OUR TALK ABOUT ME DOING A SOLO SHOW?

CHUN
(TWEET)

CHUN

OH, SORRY. DIDN'T KNOW YOU WERE AWAKE.

GOT YOU SOME SNACKS AND WATER.

GASA
(GRSH)

...WHERE AM I?

KON
(KNOCK)

KON

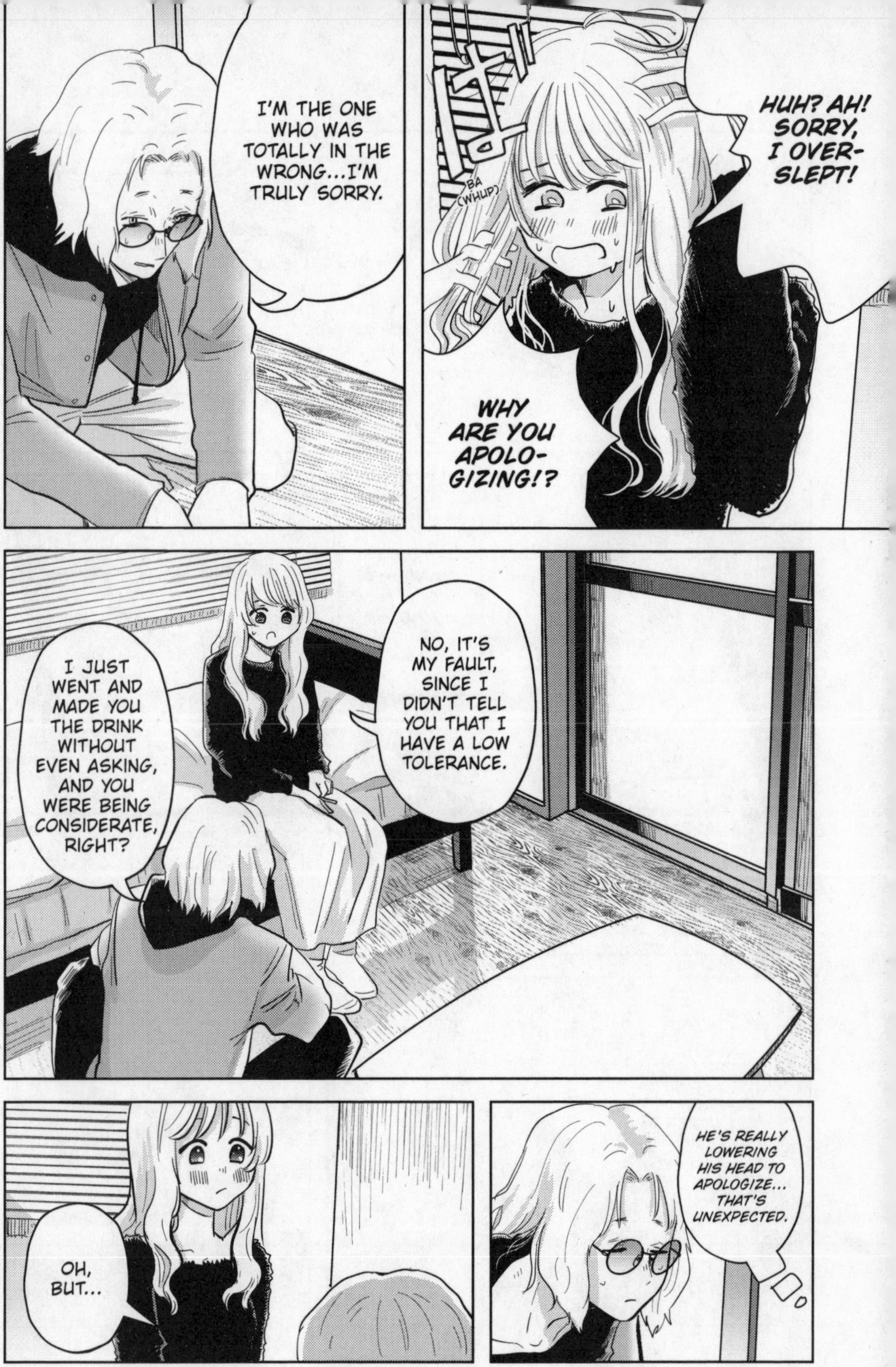

HUH? AH! SORRY, I OVER-SLEPT!
BA (WHUP)
WHY ARE YOU APOLO-GIZING!?
I'M THE ONE WHO WAS TOTALLY IN THE WRONG...I'M TRULY SORRY.
NO, IT'S MY FAULT, SINCE I DIDN'T TELL YOU THAT I HAVE A LOW TOLERANCE.
I JUST WENT AND MADE YOU THE DRINK WITHOUT EVEN ASKING, AND YOU WERE BEING CONSIDERATE, RIGHT?
HE'S REALLY LOWERING HIS HEAD TO APOLOGIZE... THAT'S UNEXPECTED.
OH, BUT...

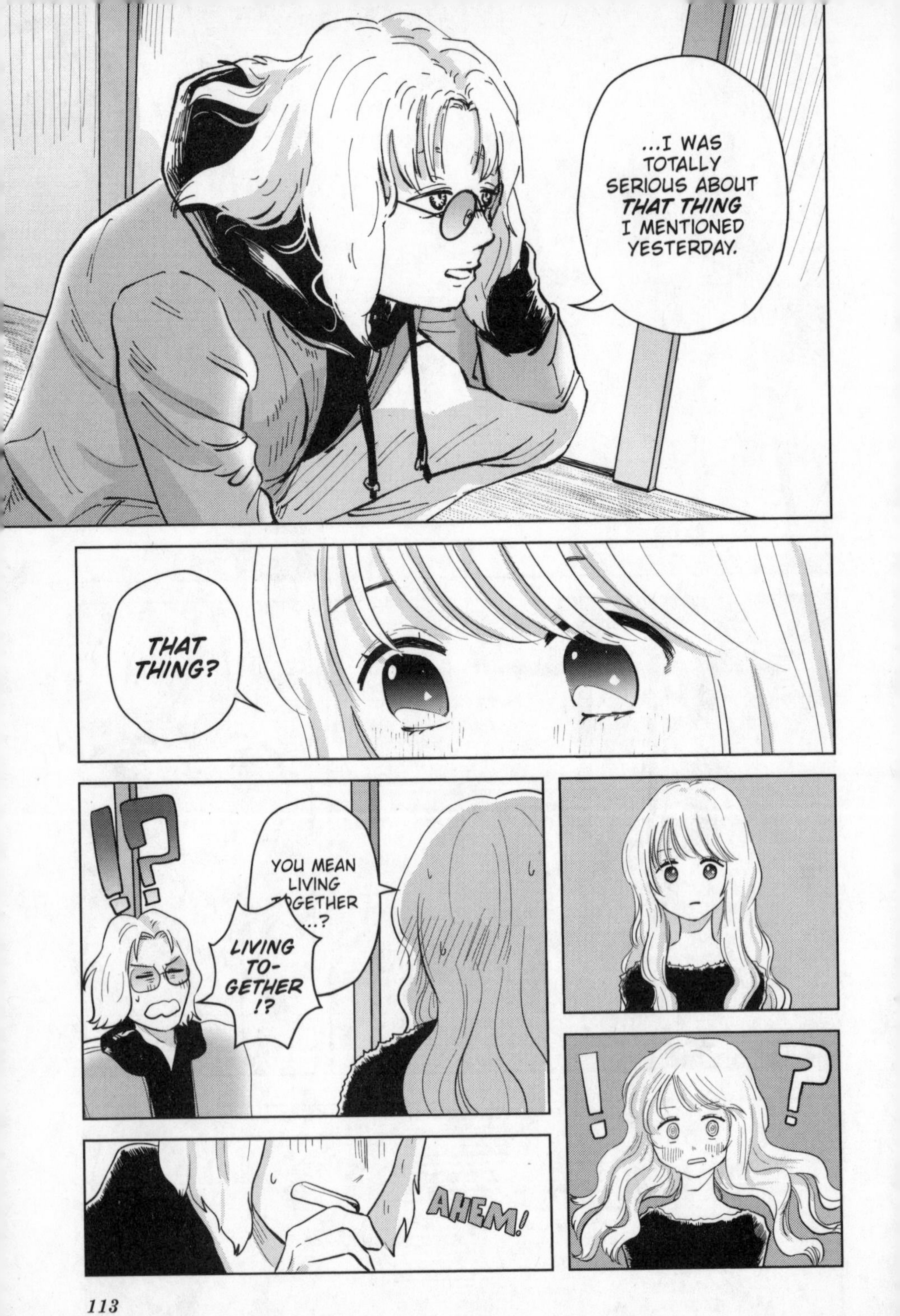
...I WAS TOTALLY SERIOUS ABOUT *THAT THING* I MENTIONED YESTERDAY.
THAT THING?
YOU MEAN LIVING TOGETHER ...?
LIVING TO-GETHER !?
!?
!?
AHEM!

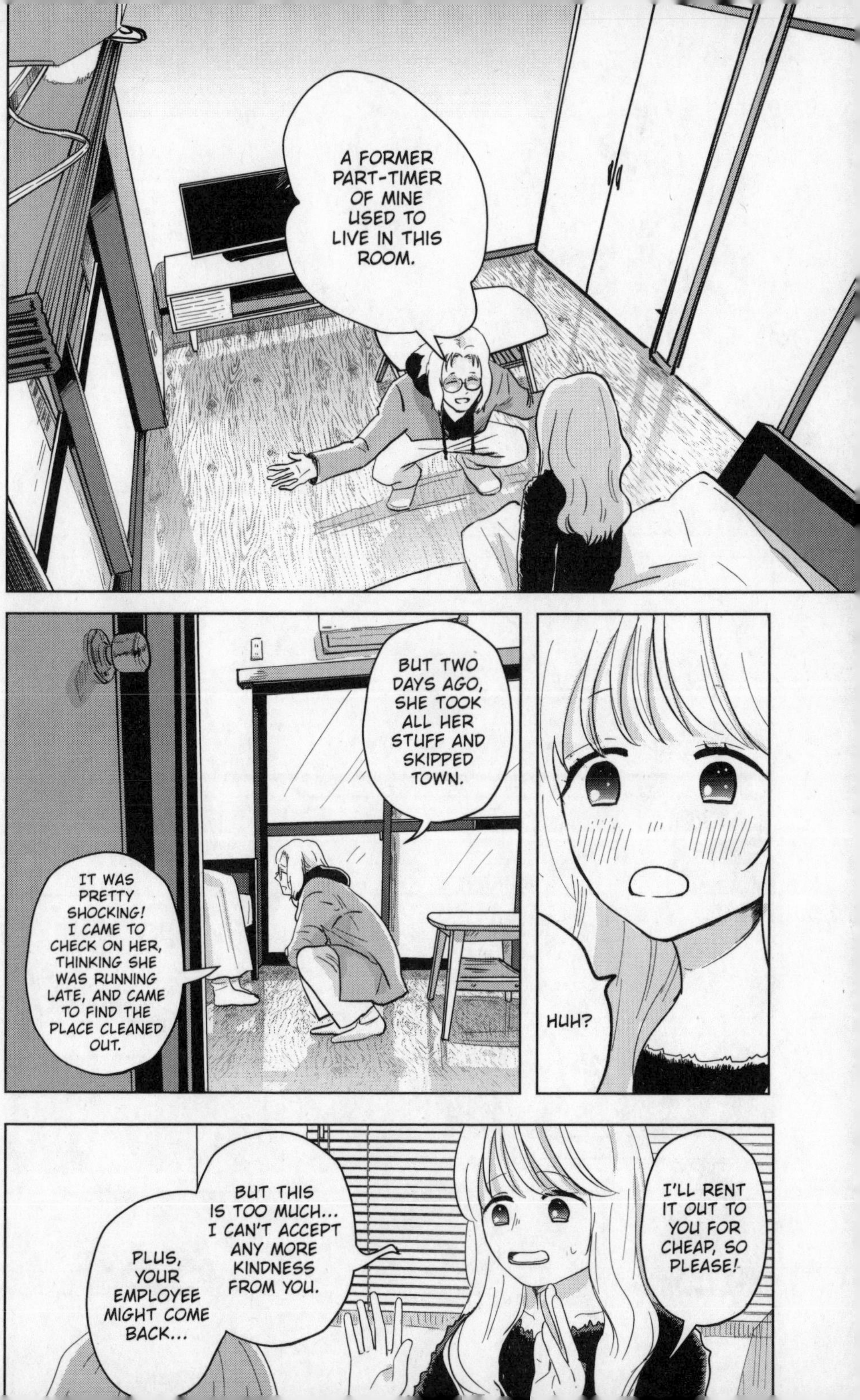
A FORMER PART-TIMER OF MINE USED TO LIVE IN THIS ROOM.
HUH?
BUT TWO DAYS AGO, SHE TOOK ALL HER STUFF AND SKIPPED TOWN.
IT WAS PRETTY SHOCKING! I CAME TO CHECK ON HER, THINKING SHE WAS RUNNING LATE, AND CAME TO FIND THE PLACE CLEANED OUT.
I'LL RENT IT OUT TO YOU FOR CHEAP, SO PLEASE!
BUT THIS IS TOO MUCH... I CAN'T ACCEPT ANY MORE KINDNESS FROM YOU.
PLUS, YOUR EMPLOYEE MIGHT COME BACK...

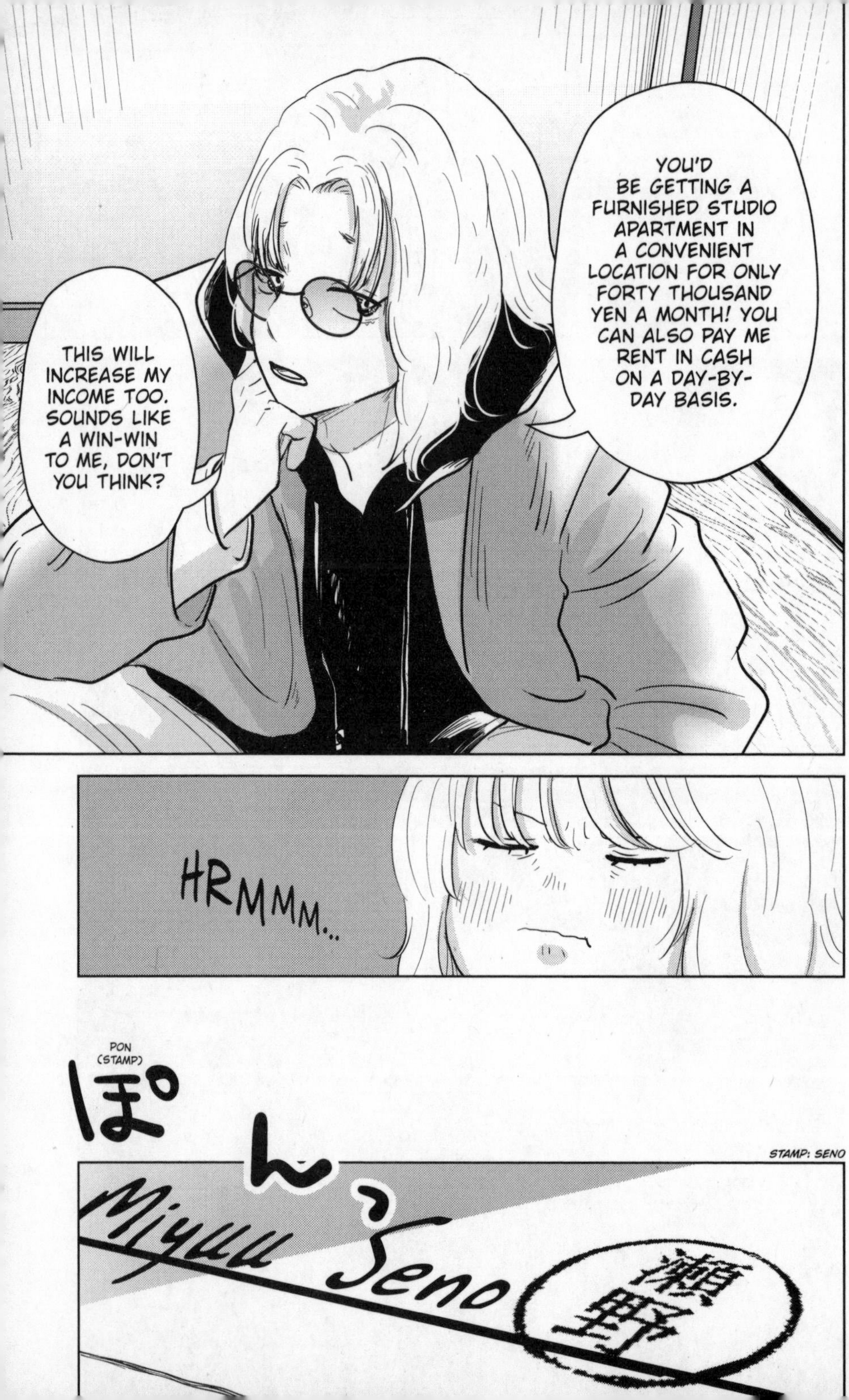
YOU'D BE GETTING A FURNISHED STUDIO APARTMENT IN A CONVENIENT LOCATION FOR ONLY FORTY THOUSAND YEN A MONTH! YOU CAN ALSO PAY ME RENT IN CASH ON A DAY-BY-DAY BASIS.
THIS WILL INCREASE MY INCOME TOO. SOUNDS LIKE A WIN-WIN TO ME, DON'T YOU THINK?
HRMMM...
PON (STAMP)
ぽんっ
STAMP: SENO
Miyuu Seno
瀬野

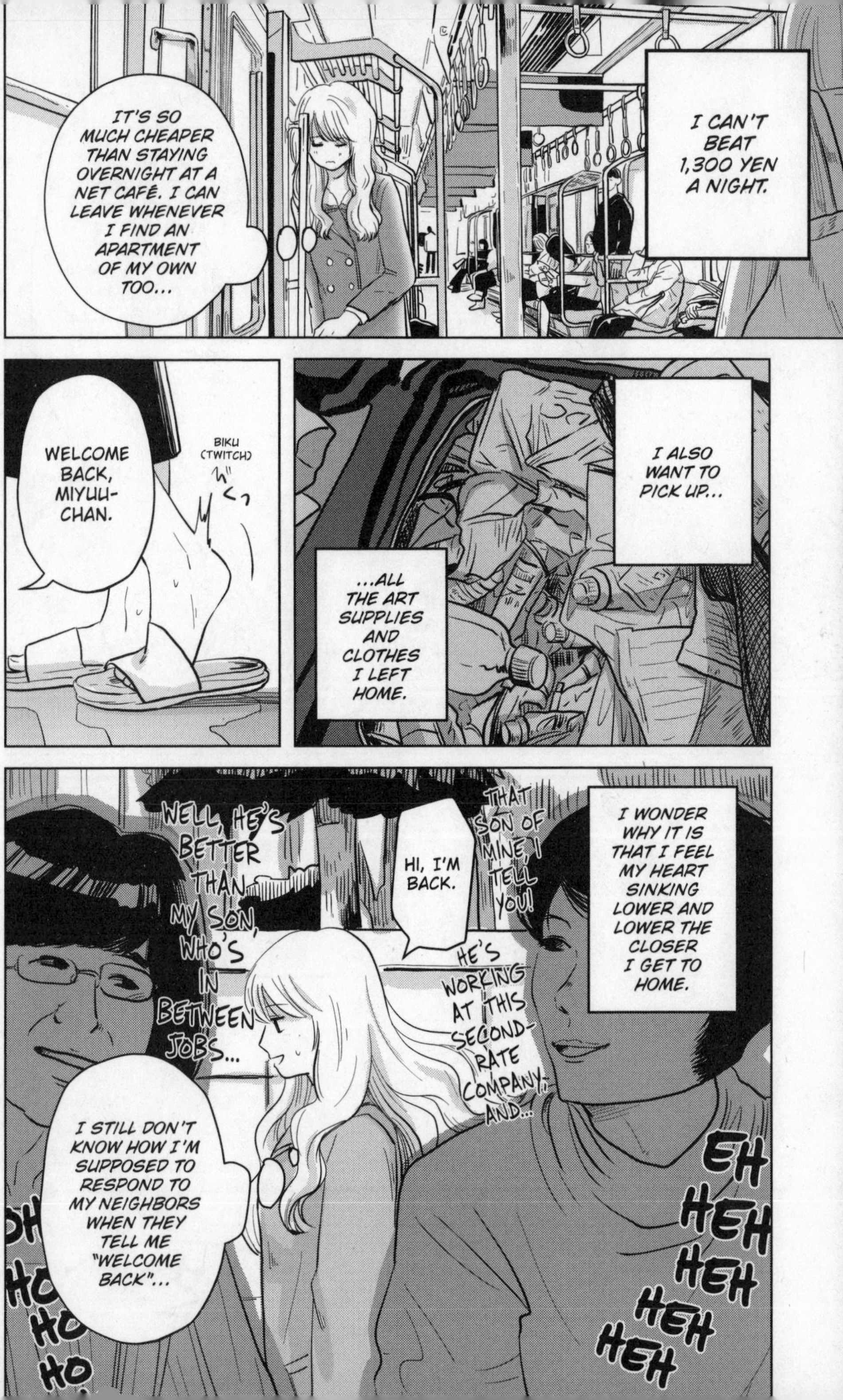
I CAN'T BEAT 1,300 YEN A NIGHT.
IT'S SO MUCH CHEAPER THAN STAYING OVERNIGHT AT A NET CAFÉ. I CAN LEAVE WHENEVER I FIND AN APARTMENT OF MY OWN TOO...
I ALSO WANT TO PICK UP...
...ALL THE ART SUPPLIES AND CLOTHES I LEFT HOME.
BIKU (TWITCH)
WELCOME BACK, MIYUU-CHAN.
I WONDER WHY IT IS THAT I FEEL MY HEART SINKING LOWER AND LOWER THE CLOSER I GET TO HOME.
THAT SON OF MINE, I TELL YOU!
HE'S WORKING AT THIS SECOND-RATE COMPANY, AND...
HI, I'M BACK.
WELL, HE'S BETTER THAN MY SON, WHO'S IN BETWEEN JOBS...
EH HEH HEH HEH HEH HEH
I STILL DON'T KNOW HOW I'M SUPPOSED TO RESPOND TO MY NEIGHBORS WHEN THEY TELL ME "WELCOME BACK"...
OHO HO HO HO

ALL RIGHT! THE LIGHTS AREN'T ON.
MIYUU-CHAN?

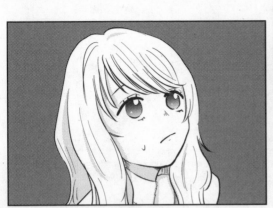

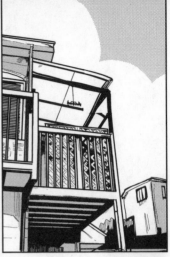

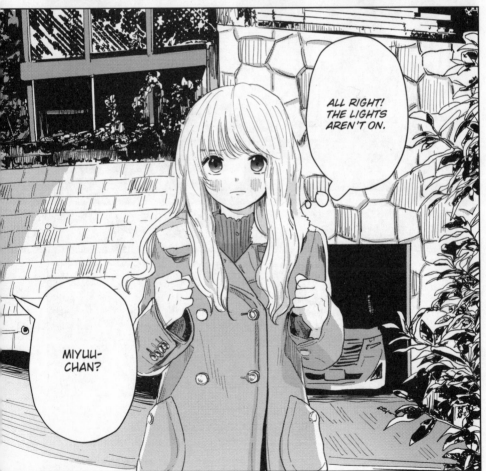

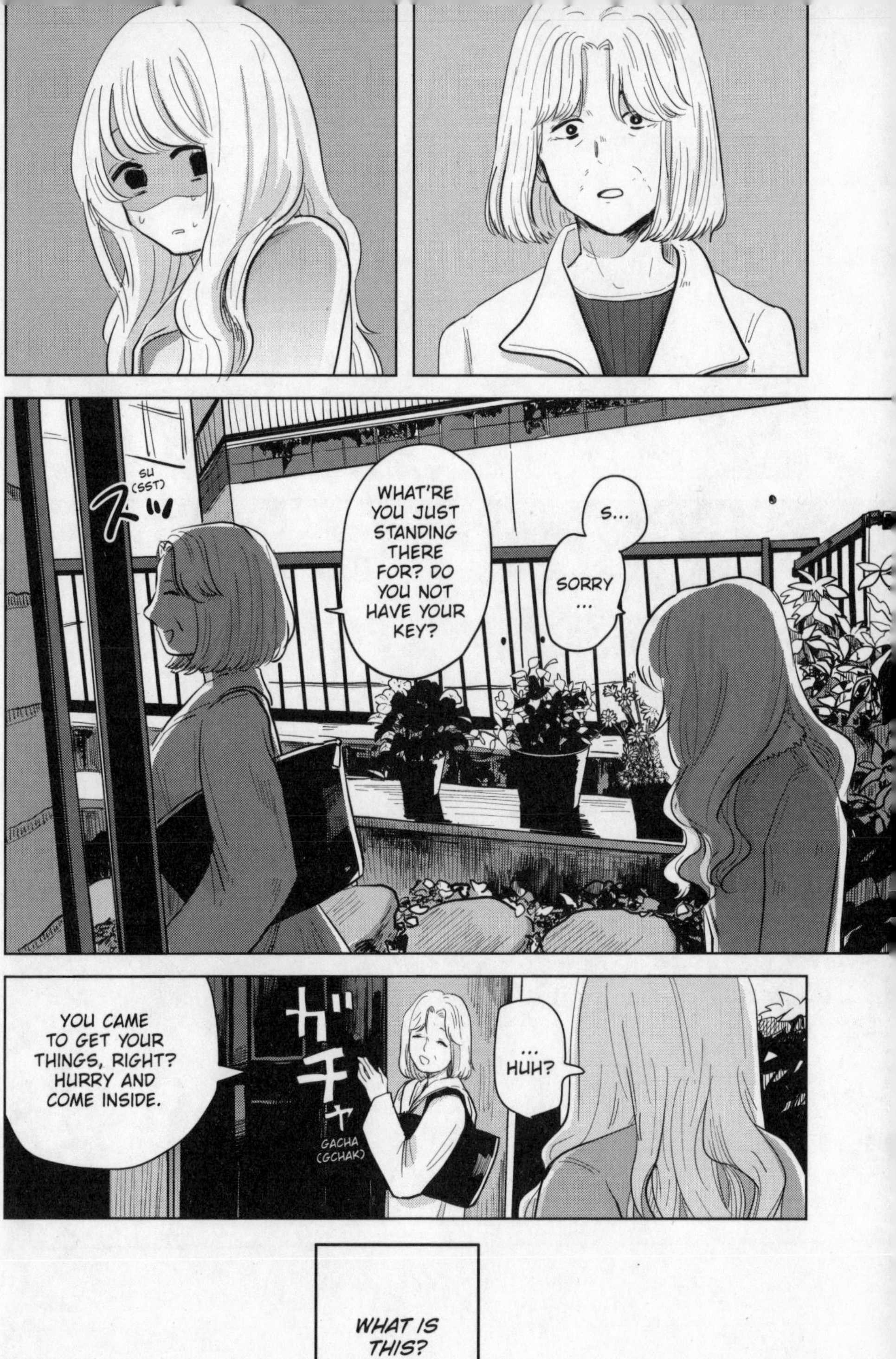
スッ
SU (SST)
WHAT'RE YOU JUST STANDING THERE FOR? DO YOU NOT HAVE YOUR KEY?
S... SORRY ...
ガチャ
GACHA (GCHAK)
YOU CAME TO GET YOUR THINGS, RIGHT? HURRY AND COME INSIDE.
... HUH?
WHAT IS THIS?

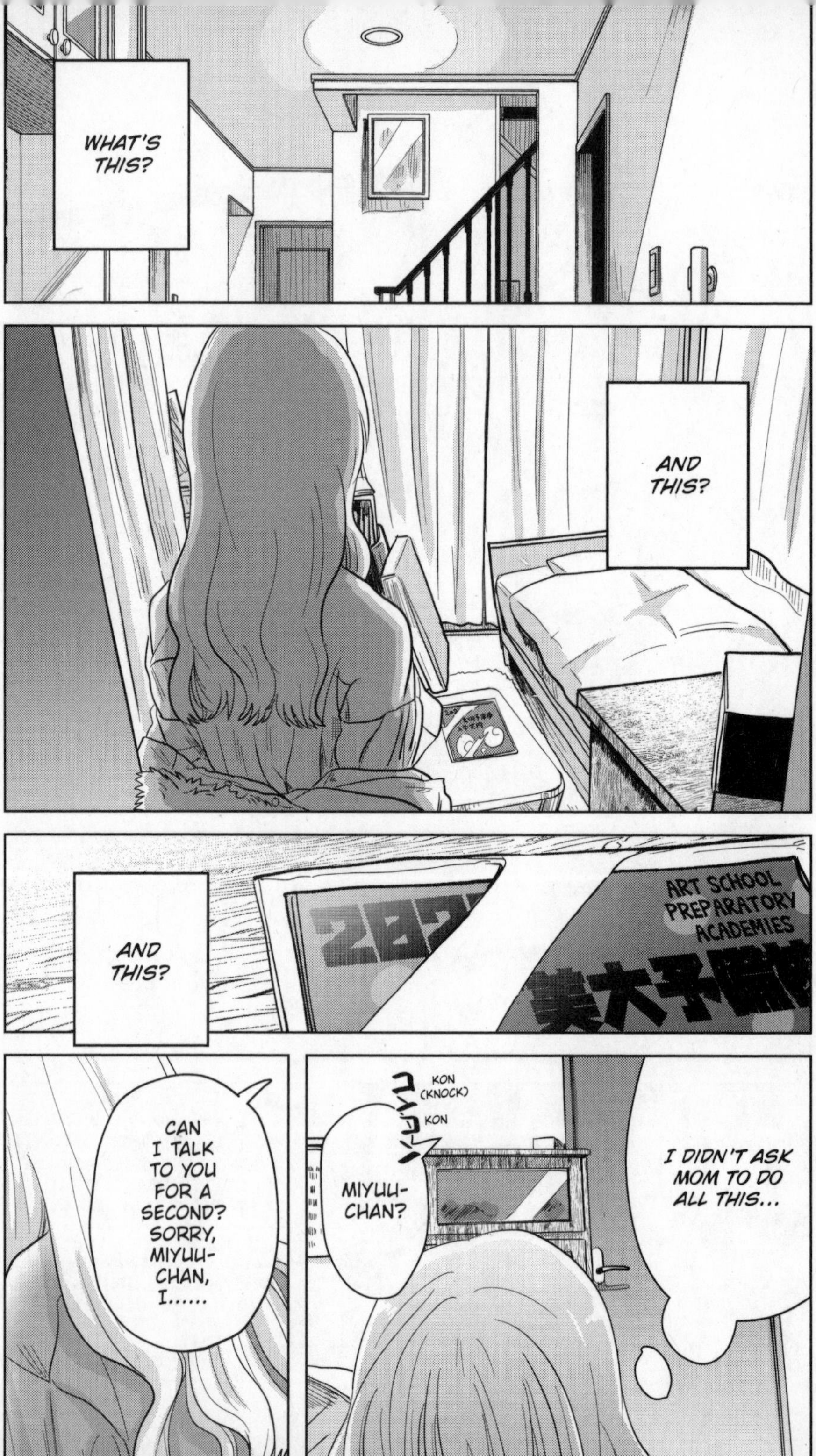
WHAT'S THIS?
AND THIS?
AND THIS?
ART SCHOOL PREPARATORY ACADEMIES
I DIDN'T ASK MOM TO DO ALL THIS...
KON (KNOCK) KON
MIYUU-CHAN?
CAN I TALK TO YOU FOR A SECOND? SORRY, MIYUU-CHAN, I......

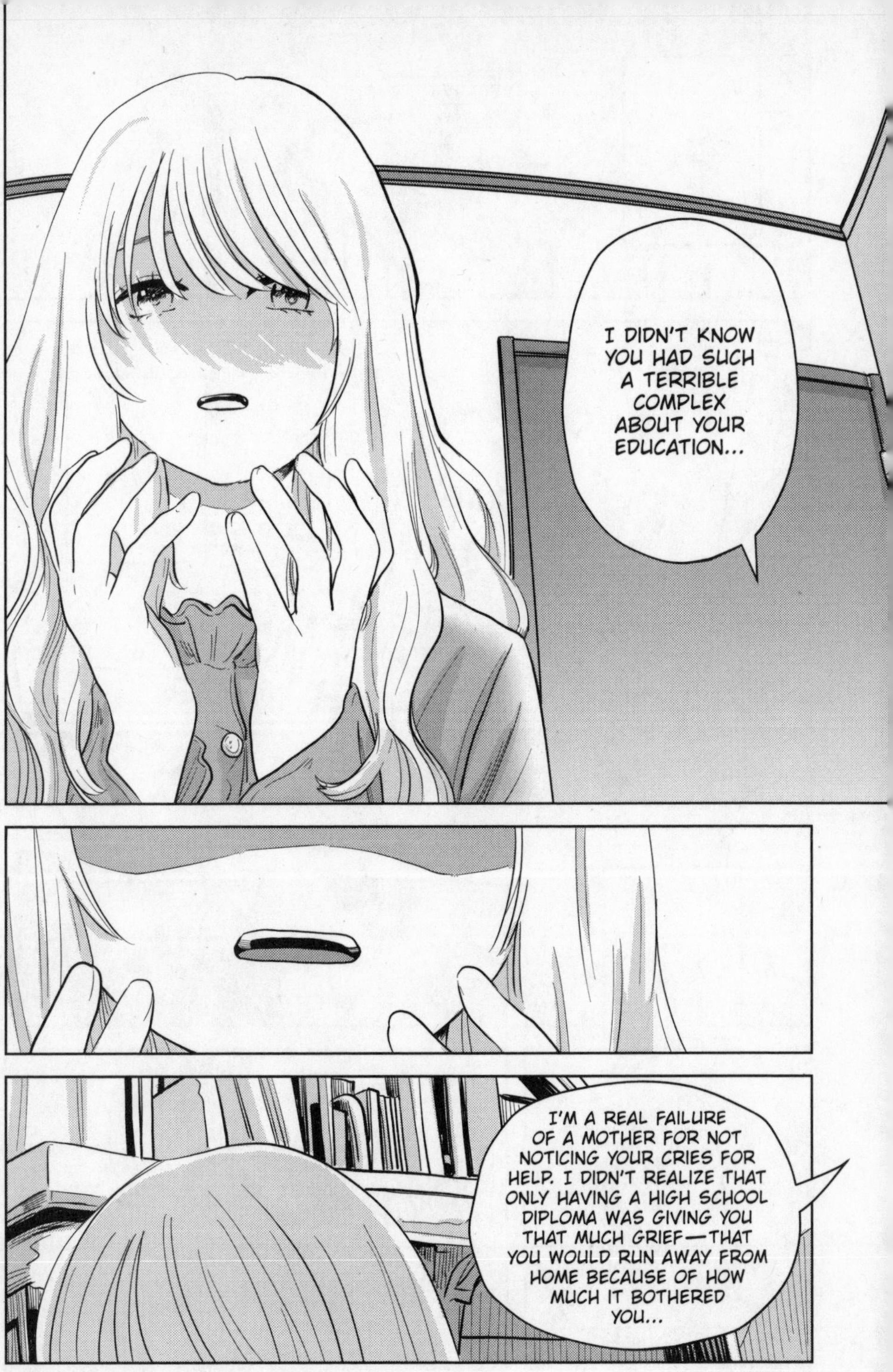
I DIDN'T KNOW YOU HAD SUCH A TERRIBLE COMPLEX ABOUT YOUR EDUCATION...
I'M A REAL FAILURE OF A MOTHER FOR NOT NOTICING YOUR CRIES FOR HELP. I DIDN'T REALIZE THAT ONLY HAVING A HIGH SCHOOL DIPLOMA WAS GIVING YOU THAT MUCH GRIEF—THAT YOU WOULD RUN AWAY FROM HOME BECAUSE OF HOW MUCH IT BOTHERED YOU...

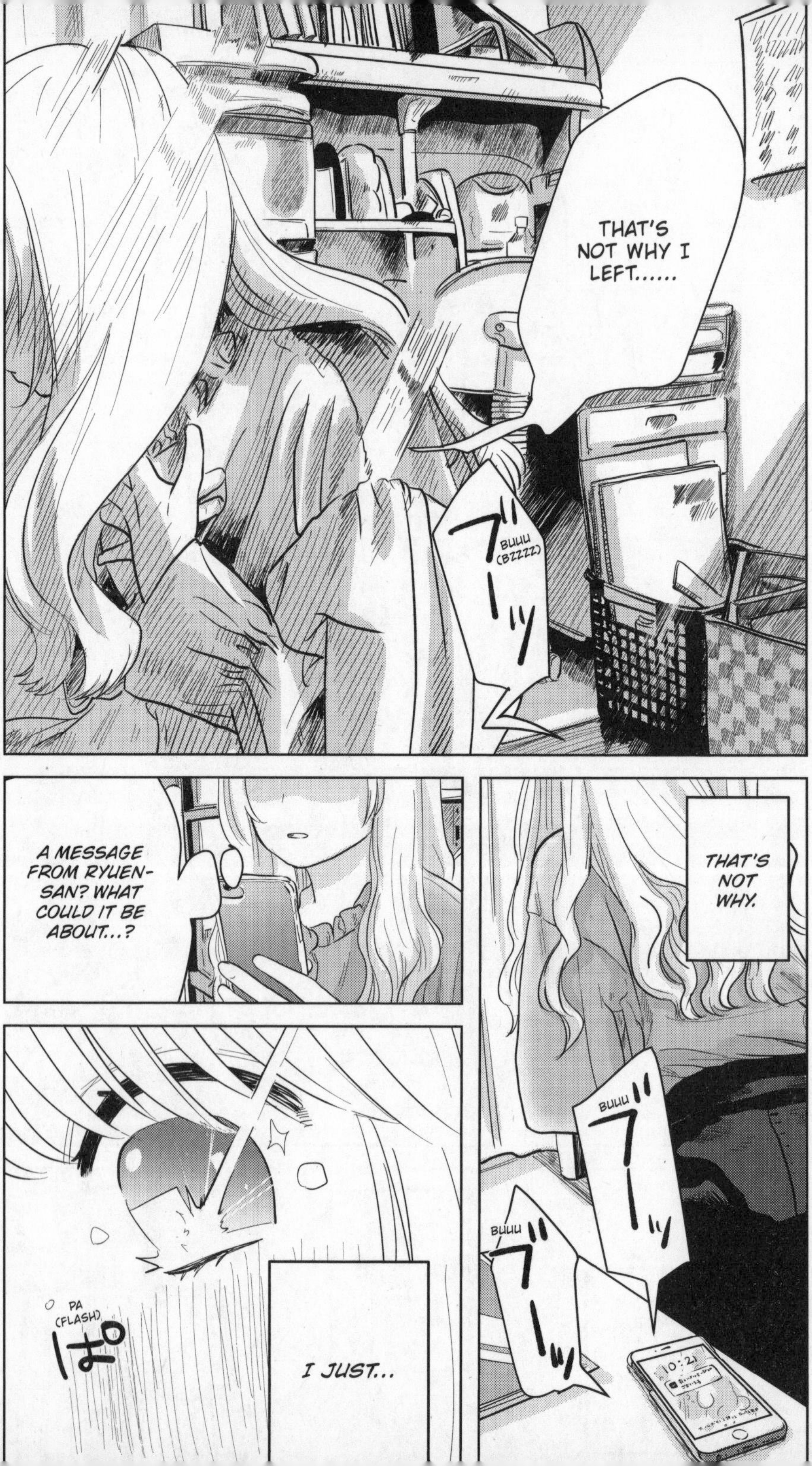
THAT'S NOT WHY I LEFT......
BUUU (BZZZZ)
ブーーッ
THAT'S NOT WHY.
BUUU
ブーッ
BUUU
ブーッ
A MESSAGE FROM RYUEN-SAN? WHAT COULD IT BE ABOUT...?
PA (FLASH)
ぱ
I JUST...

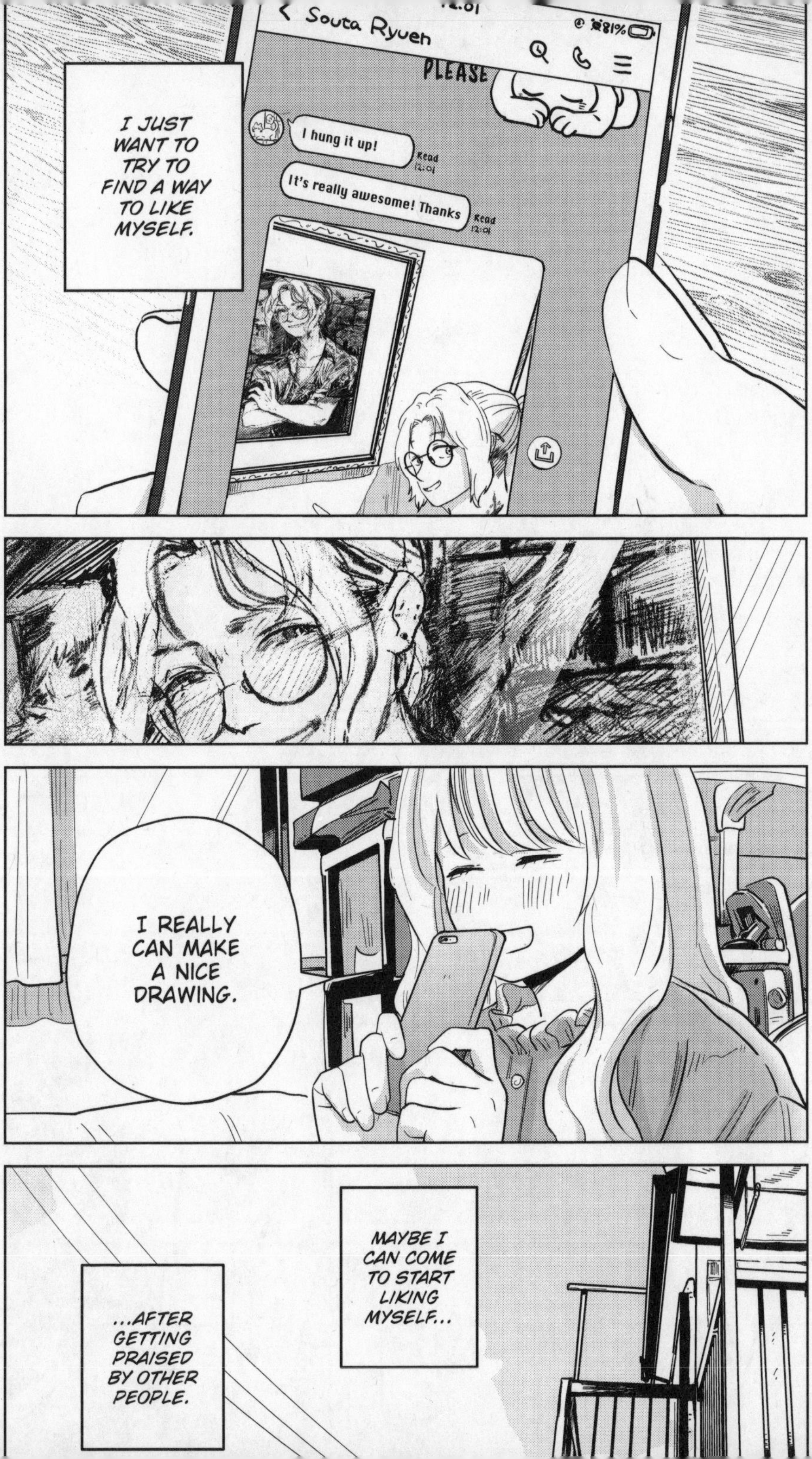
Souta Ryuen
PLEASE
I hung it up!
Read 12:01
It's really awesome! Thanks
Read 12:01
I JUST WANT TO TRY TO FIND A WAY TO LIKE MYSELF.
I REALLY CAN MAKE A NICE DRAWING.
MAYBE I CAN COME TO START LIKING MYSELF...
...AFTER GETTING PRAISED BY OTHER PEOPLE.

HOW WAS IT?

WERE YOU ABLE TO GET EVERYTHING YOU NEEDED?

OH, MIYUU-CHAN.

WELCOME BACK.

RYUEN-SAN.

I'M BACK.

?

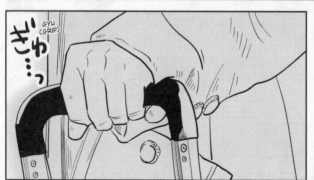

GYU (GRIP)

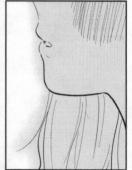

123

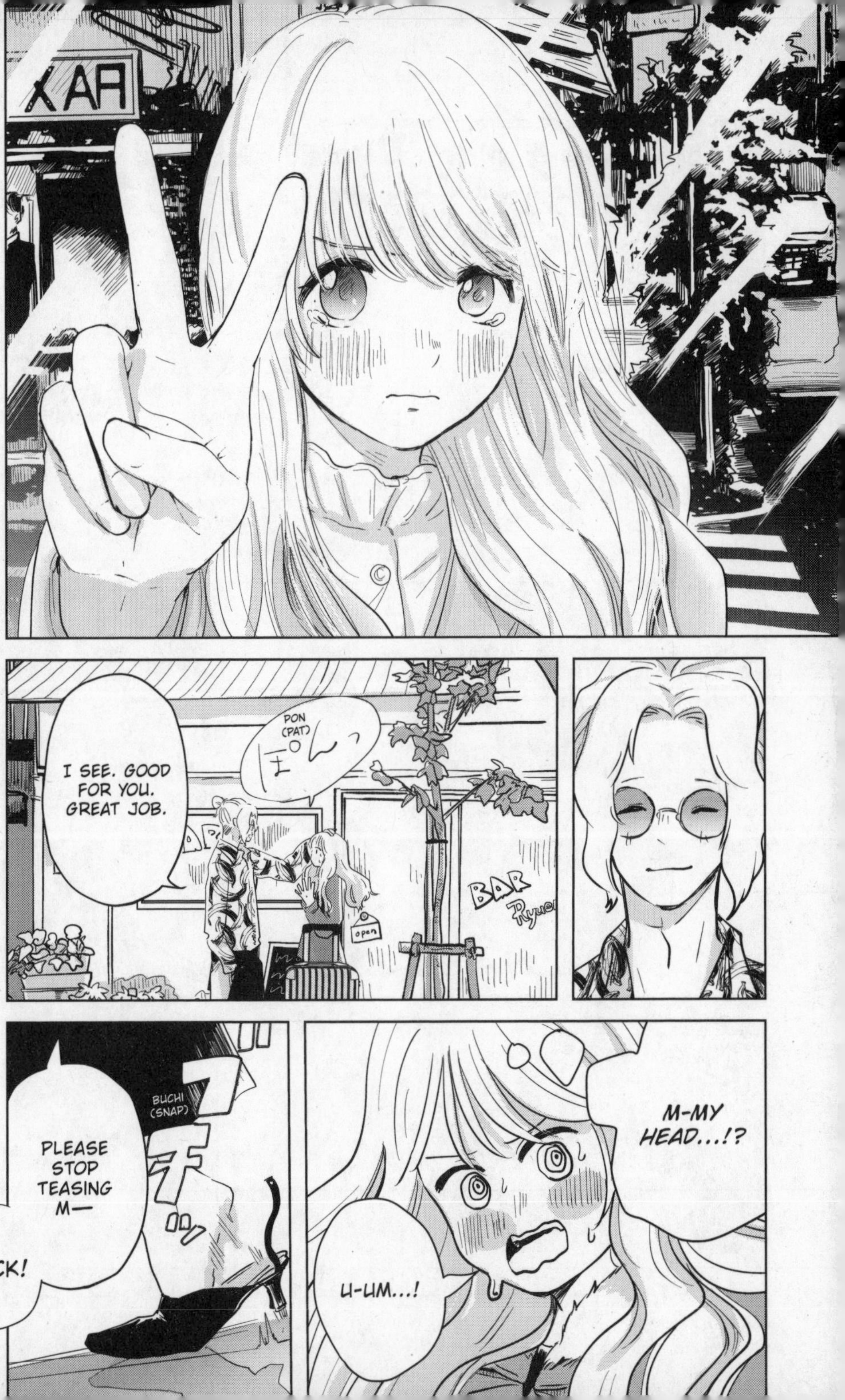

PON (PAT)
I SEE. GOOD FOR YOU. GREAT JOB.
BAR
open
M-MY HEAD...!?
U-UM...!
BUCHI (SNAP)
PLEASE STOP TEASING M—
ACK!

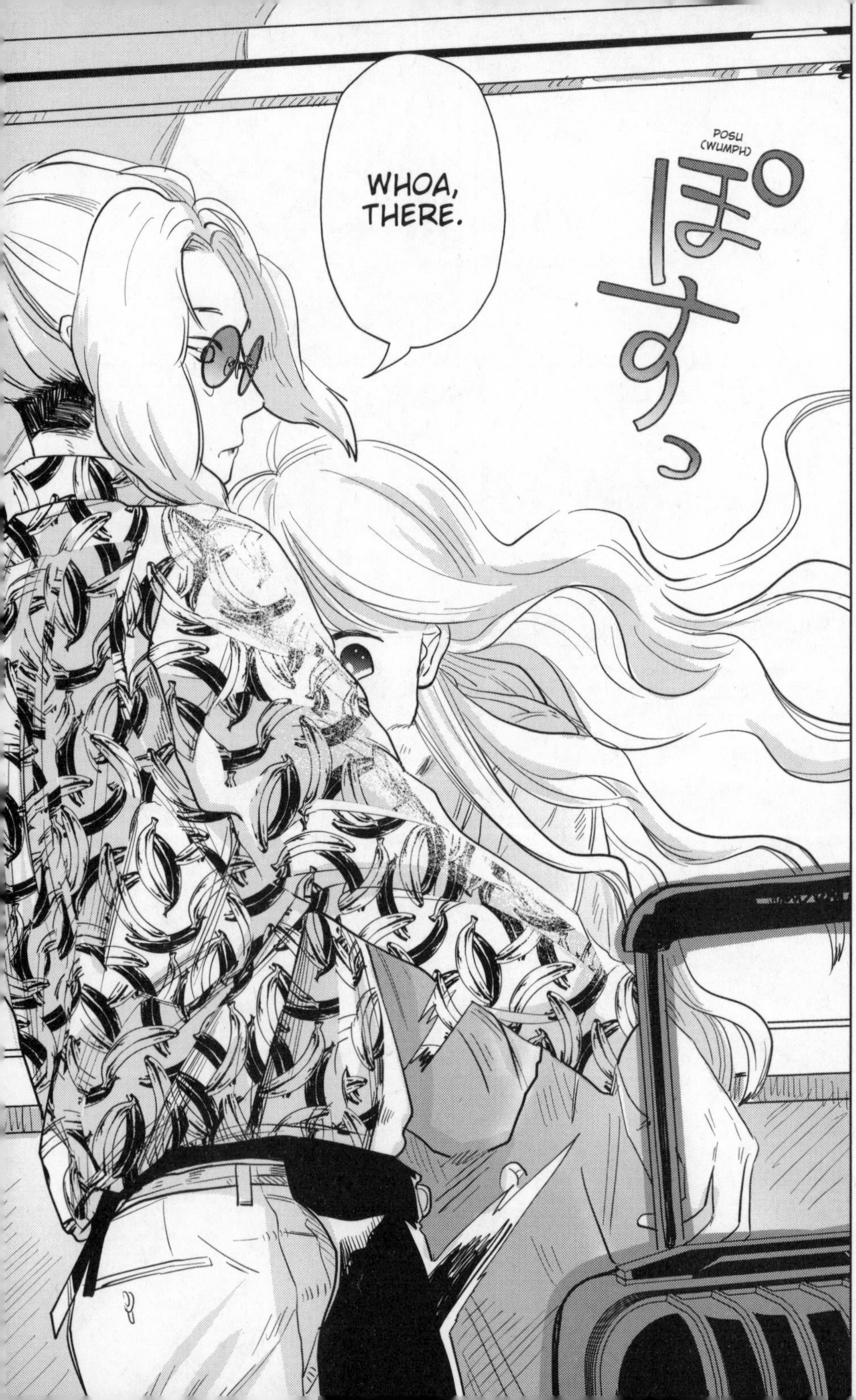
POSU
(WUMPH)
ぽすっ
WHOA, THERE.

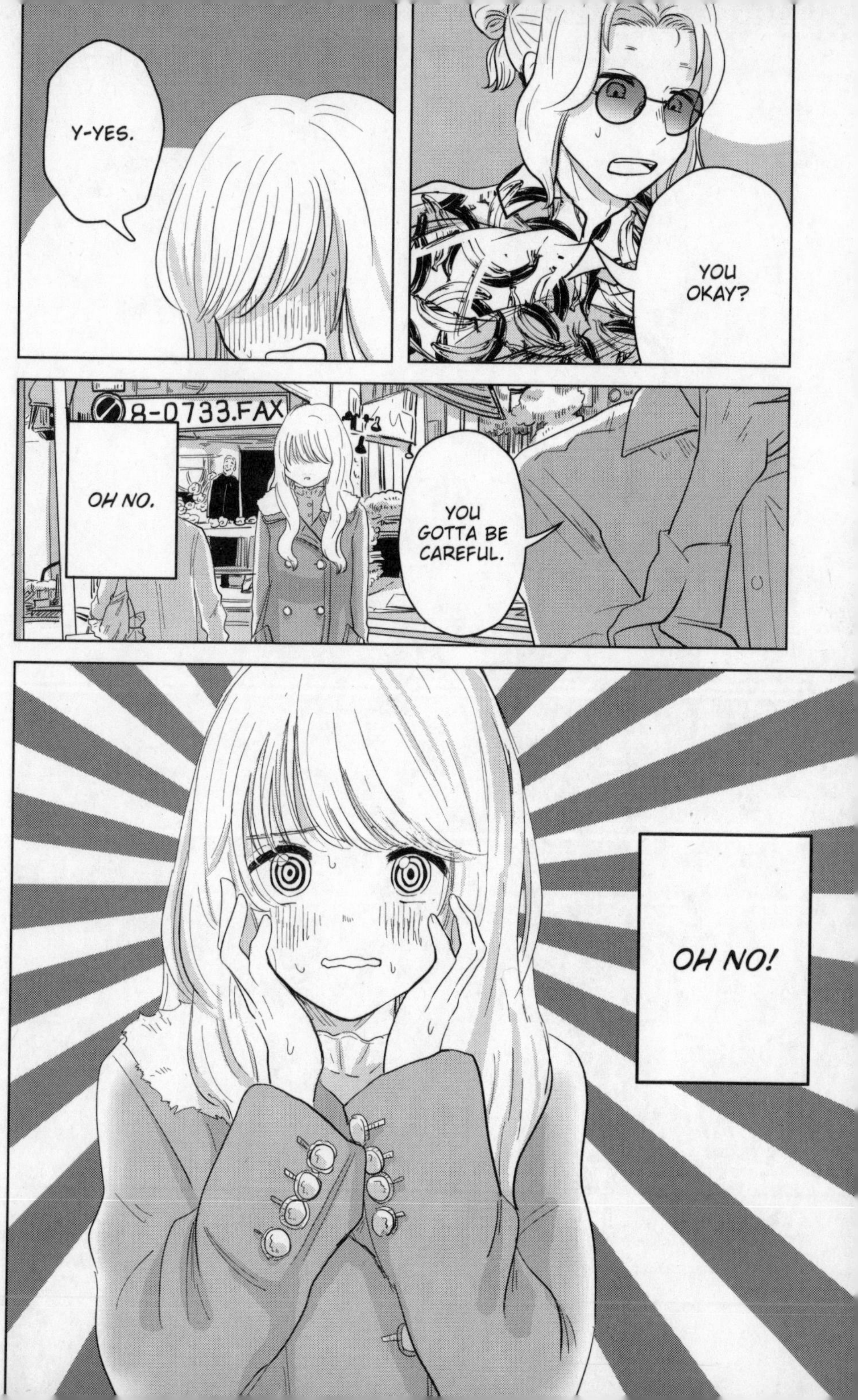
YOU OKAY?
Y-YES.
8-0733.FAX
YOU GOTTA BE CAREFUL.
OH NO.
OH NO!

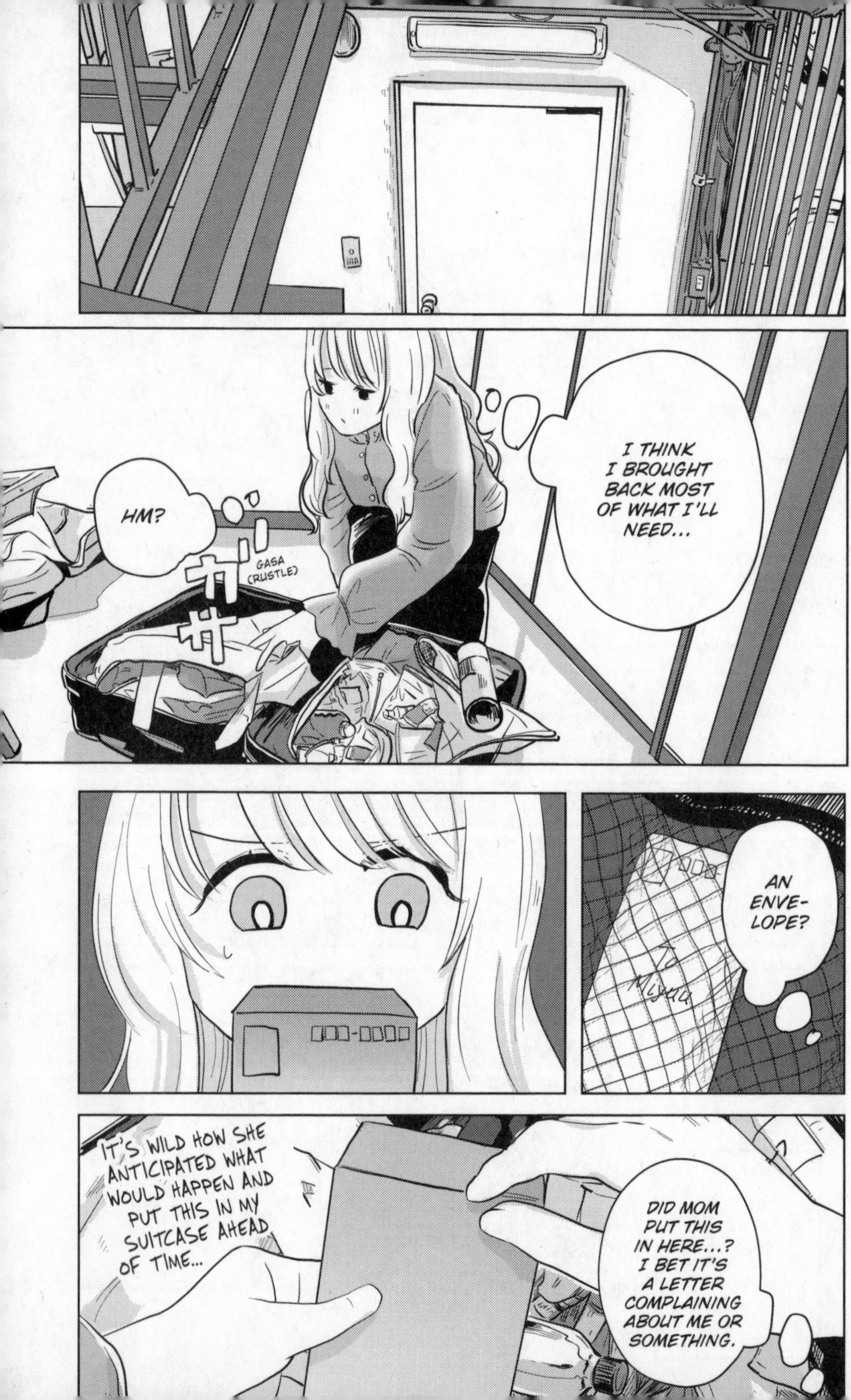
I THINK I BROUGHT BACK MOST OF WHAT I'LL NEED...
HM?
GASA (RUSTLE)
AN ENVE-LOPE?
DID MOM PUT THIS IN HERE...? I BET IT'S A LETTER COMPLAINING ABOUT ME OR SOMETHING.
IT'S WILD HOW SHE ANTICIPATED WHAT WOULD HAPPEN AND PUT THIS IN MY SUITCASE AHEAD OF TIME...

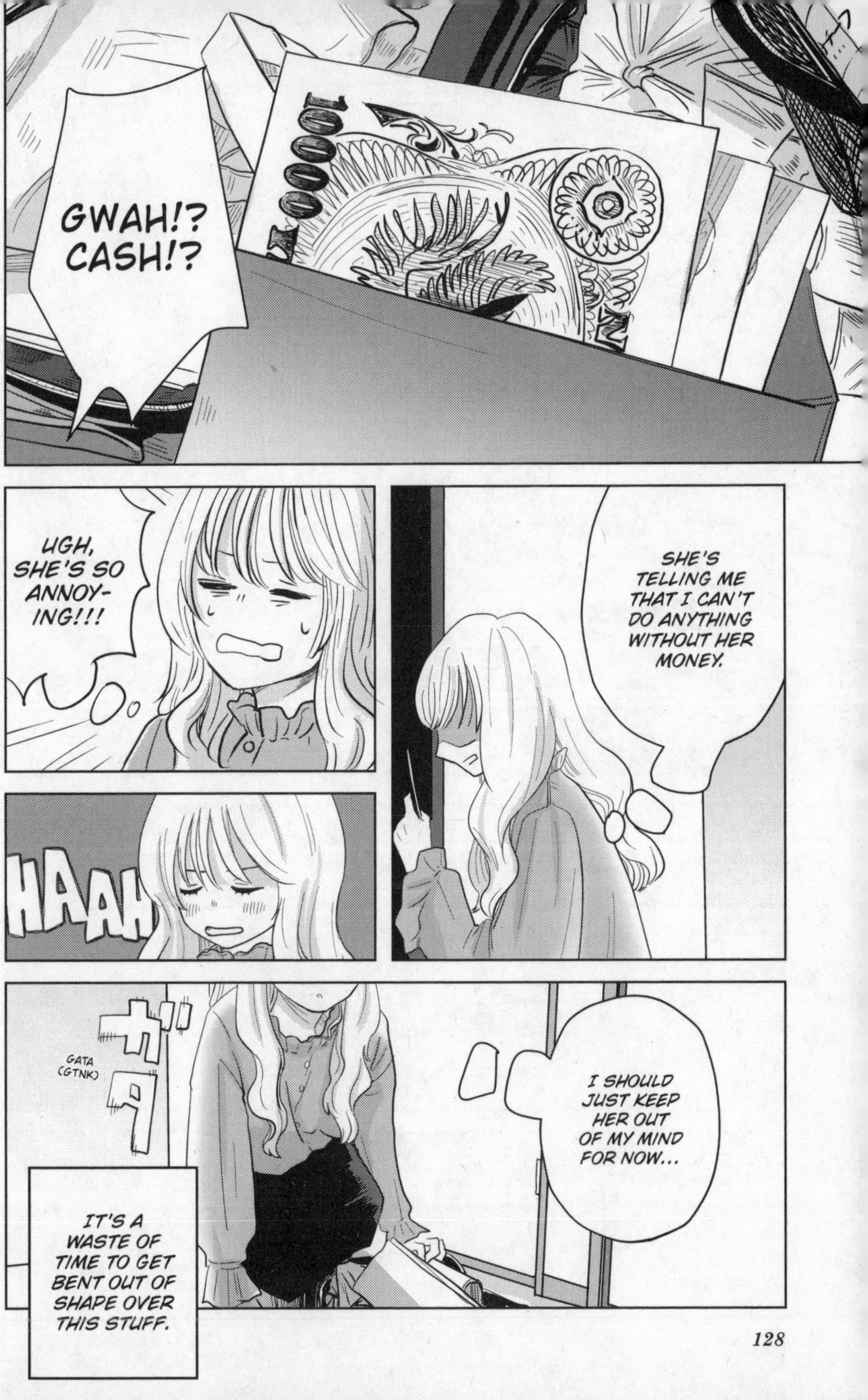
GWAH!? CASH!?
SHE'S TELLING ME THAT I CAN'T DO ANYTHING WITHOUT HER MONEY.
UGH, SHE'S SO ANNOY-ING!!!
HAAH
I SHOULD JUST KEEP HER OUT OF MY MIND FOR NOW...
GATA (GTNK)
IT'S A WASTE OF TIME TO GET BENT OUT OF SHAPE OVER THIS STUFF.

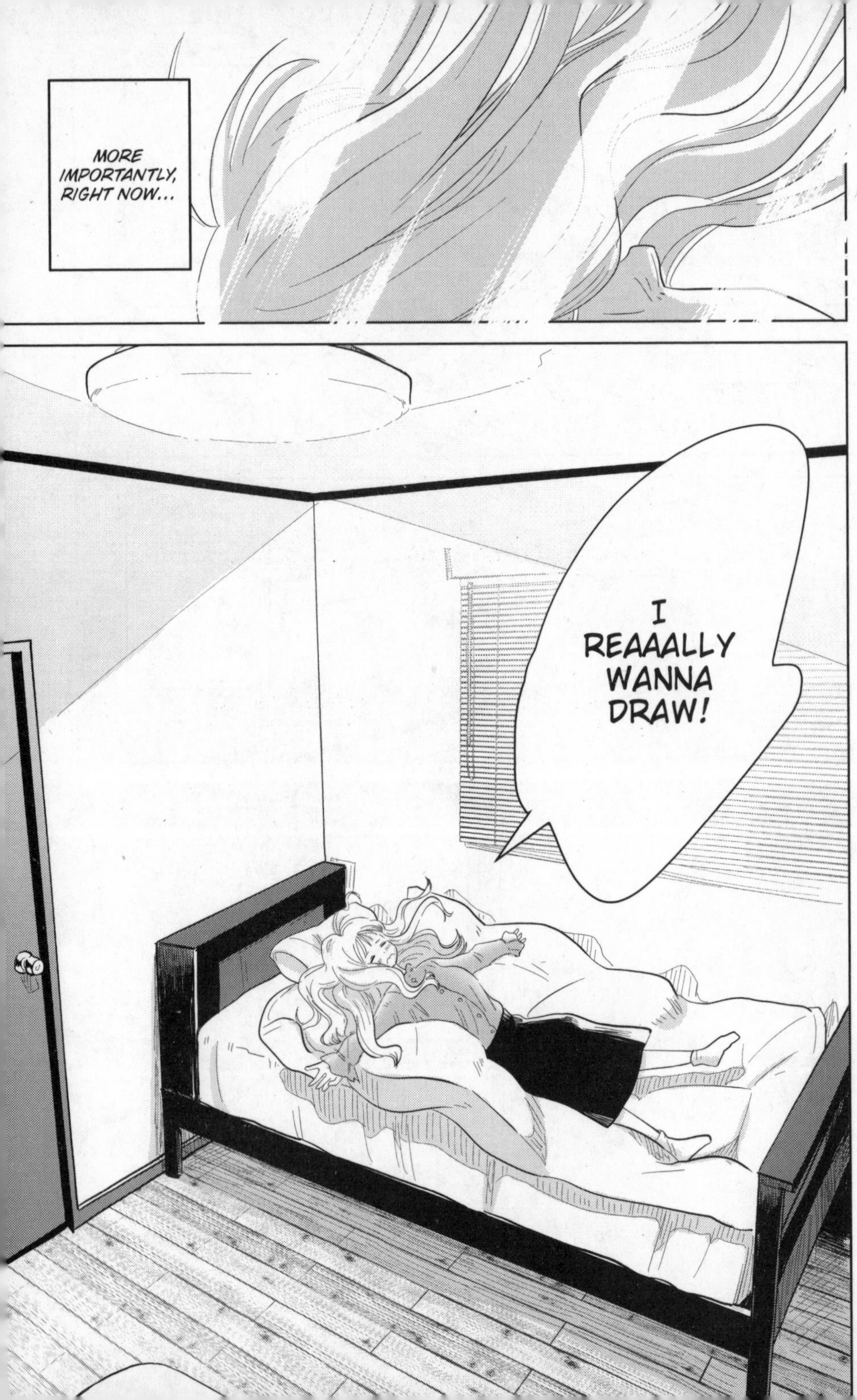
MORE IMPORTANTLY, RIGHT NOW...
I REAAALLY WANNA DRAW!

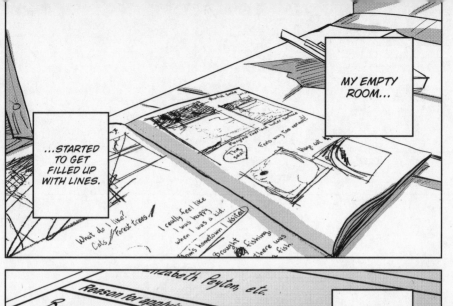

MY EMPTY ROOM...

...STARTED TO GET FILLED UP WITH LINES.

What do I like?
Cats /Forest trees./
I really feel like I was happy when I was a kid.
Mom's hometown I visited
Brought a fishing there was to fish.

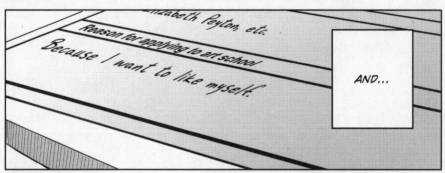

...Elizabeth Peyton, etc.

Reason for applying to art school

Because I want to like myself.

AND...

...SPRING WAS ALMOST HERE.

SIGN: JAPANESE PAINTING, OIL PAINTING, SCULPTURE / EAST NAKANO ART PREPARATORY ACADEMY, A.K.A. HIGABI

日本画
彫刻
油画
野美術予備校
HIG ABI
EXCUSE ME.
GOOD AFTERNOON. MAY I HELP YOU?
I'D LIKE TO APPLY FOR CLASSES...
FOR THE OIL PAINTING COURSE? ARE YOU LOOKING TO RETRY THE EXAMS?
I'M A WORKING ADULT.
TAKING THE ENTRANCE EXAM AS A WORKING ADULT, HUH. WILL YOU BE TAKING THE NIGHT COURSE? WHY DO YOU WANT TO DO THIS...?
ST NAKANO ART
PARATORY ACADEMY
OIL PAINTING
IGHT COURSE INSTRUCTOR
TOKEI UNIVERSITY OF THE ARTS
2ND YEAR
MIRAI TSUKIOKA

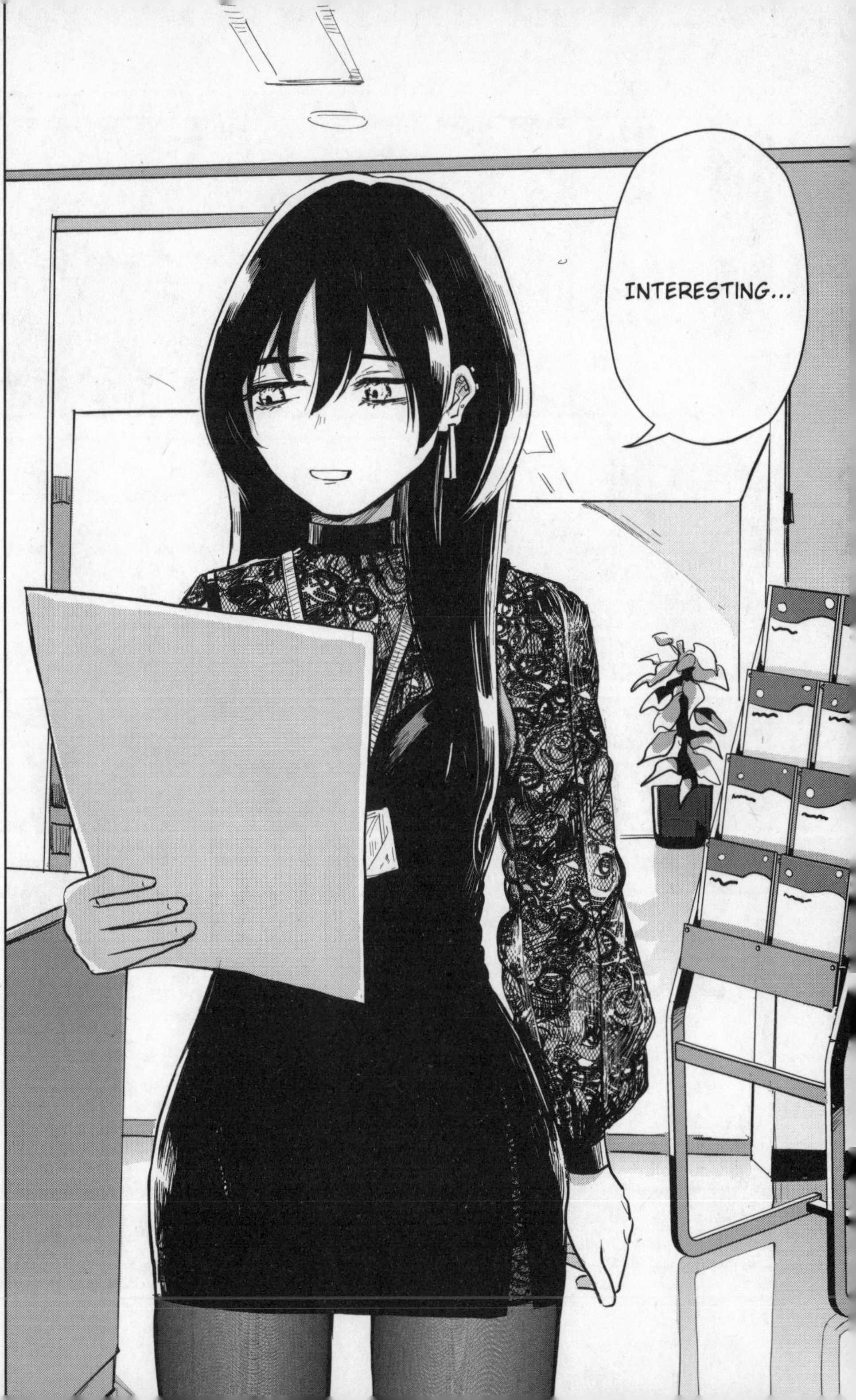
INTERESTING...

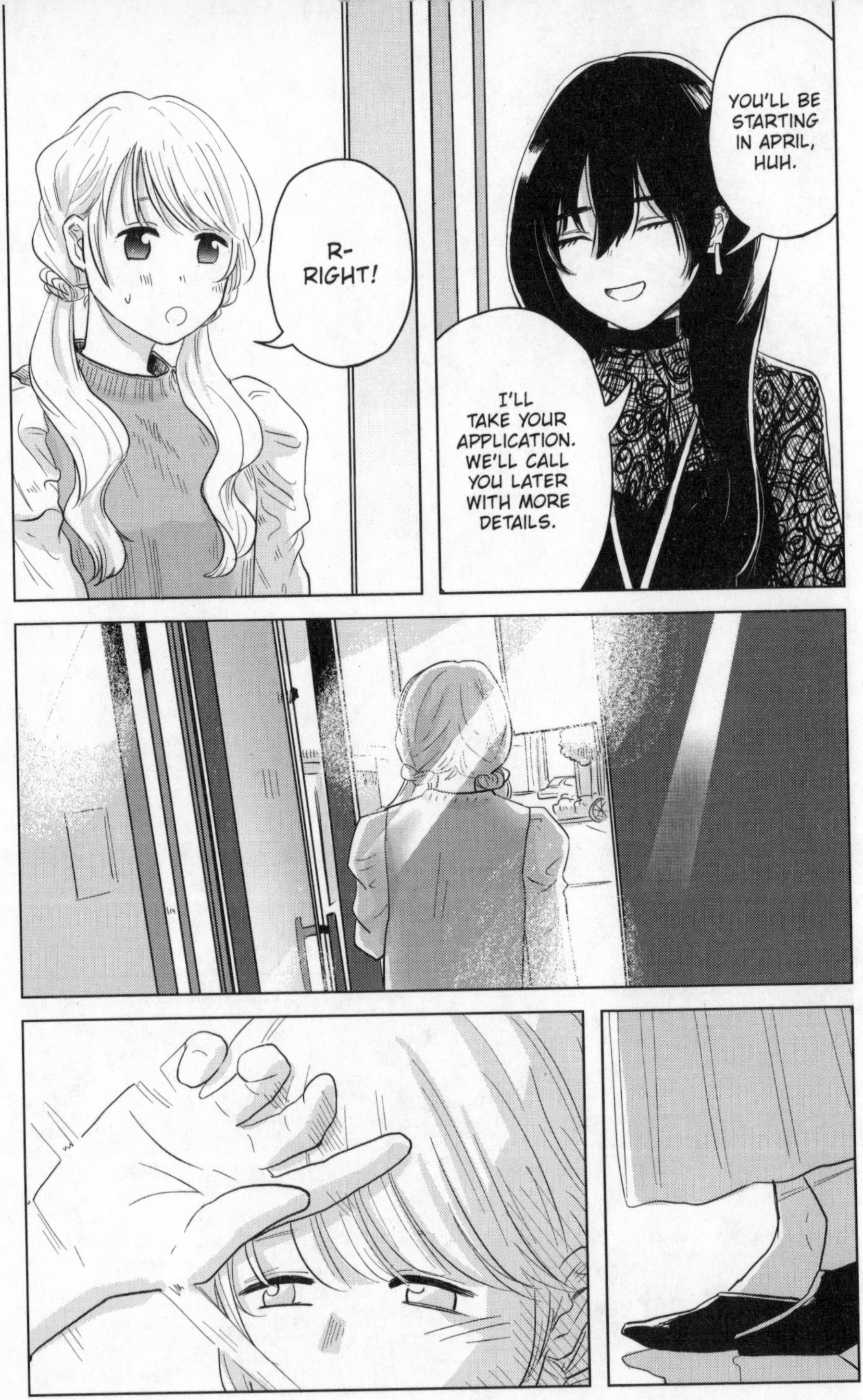
YOU'LL BE STARTING IN APRIL, HUH.
I'LL TAKE YOUR APPLICATION. WE'LL CALL YOU LATER WITH MORE DETAILS.
R-RIGHT!

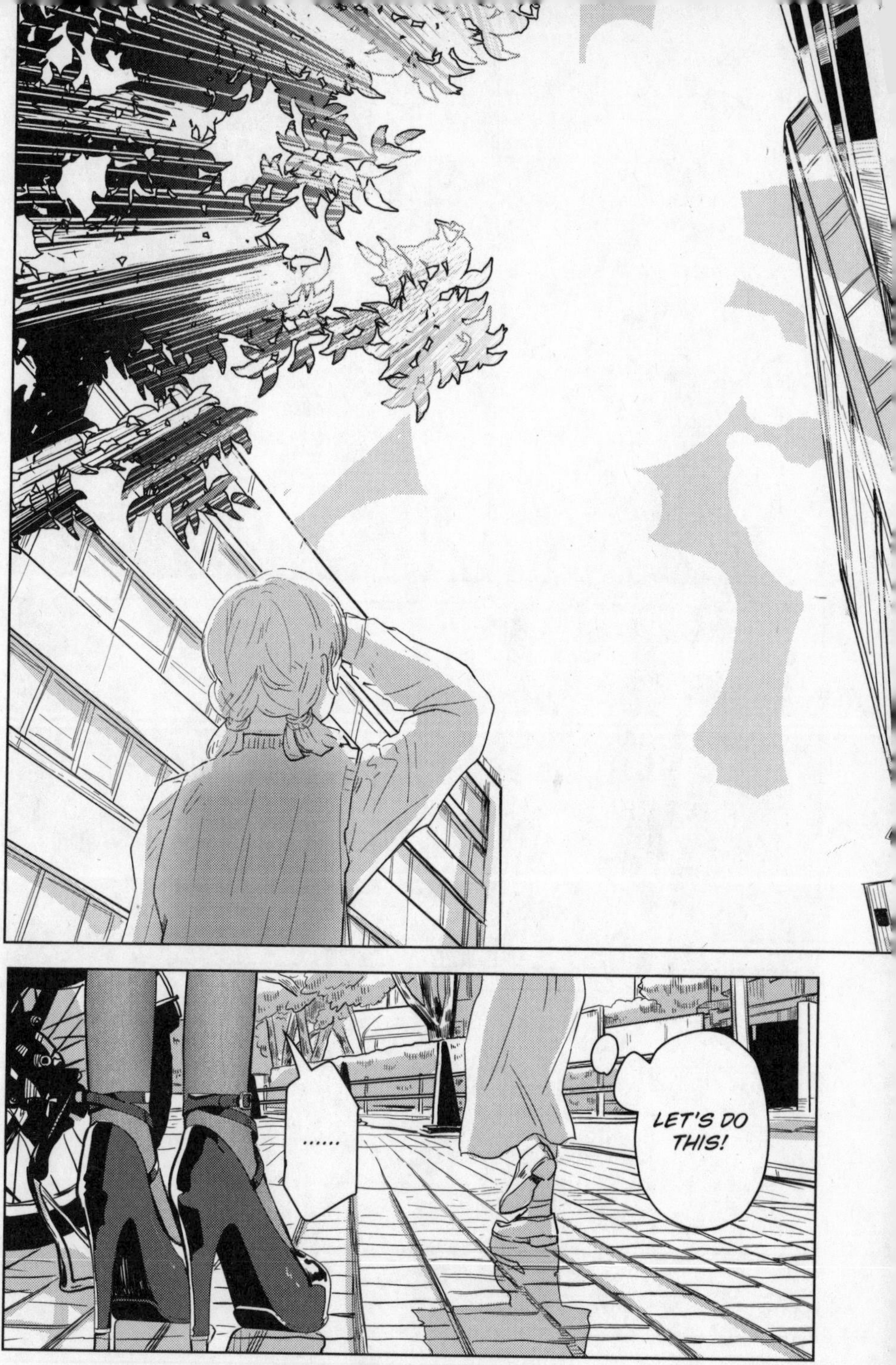
LET'S DO THIS!
......

Chapter 3 / END

Chapter 4

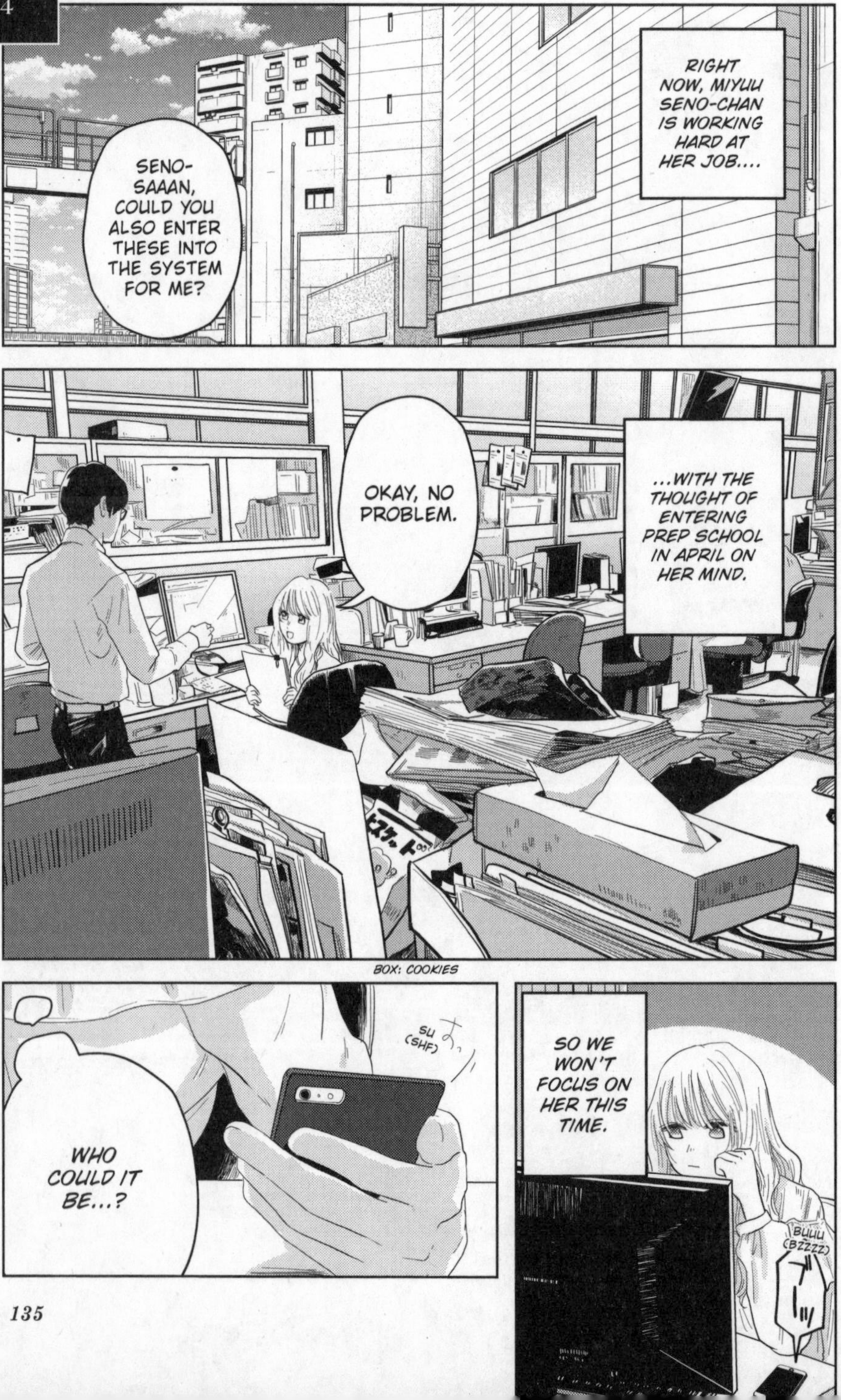
RIGHT NOW, MIYUU SENO-CHAN IS WORKING HARD AT HER JOB....
SENO-SAAAN, COULD YOU ALSO ENTER THESE INTO THE SYSTEM FOR ME?
...WITH THE THOUGHT OF ENTERING PREP SCHOOL IN APRIL ON HER MIND.
OKAY, NO PROBLEM.
BOX: COOKIES
SO WE WON'T FOCUS ON HER THIS TIME.
BUUU (BZZZZ)
SU (SHF)
WHO COULD IT BE...?

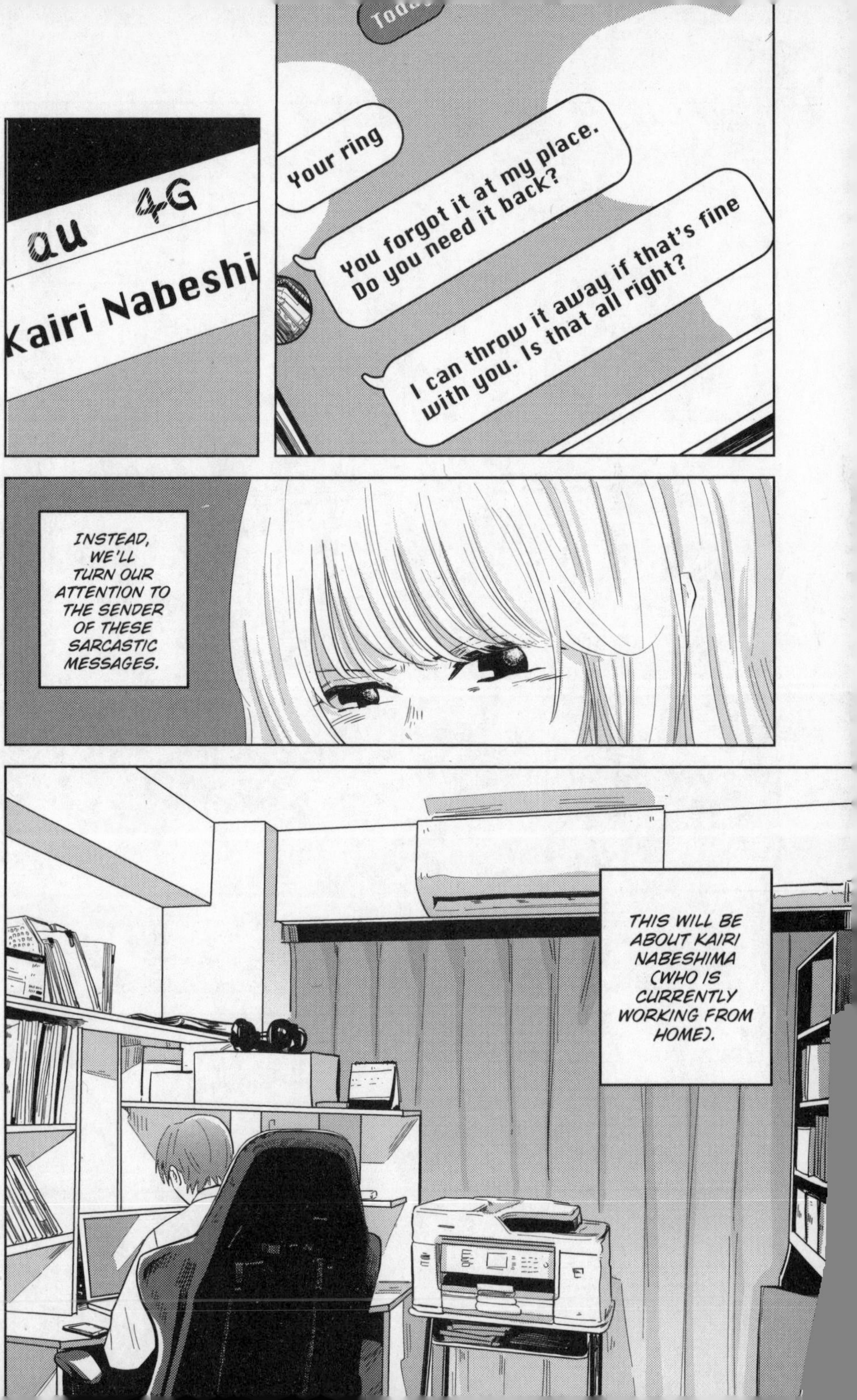
Your ring
You forgot it at my place. Do you need it back?
I can throw it away if that's fine with you. Is that all right?
au 4G
Kairi Nabeshi
INSTEAD, WE'LL TURN OUR ATTENTION TO THE SENDER OF THESE SARCASTIC MESSAGES.
THIS WILL BE ABOUT KAIRI NABESHIMA (WHO IS CURRENTLY WORKING FROM HOME).

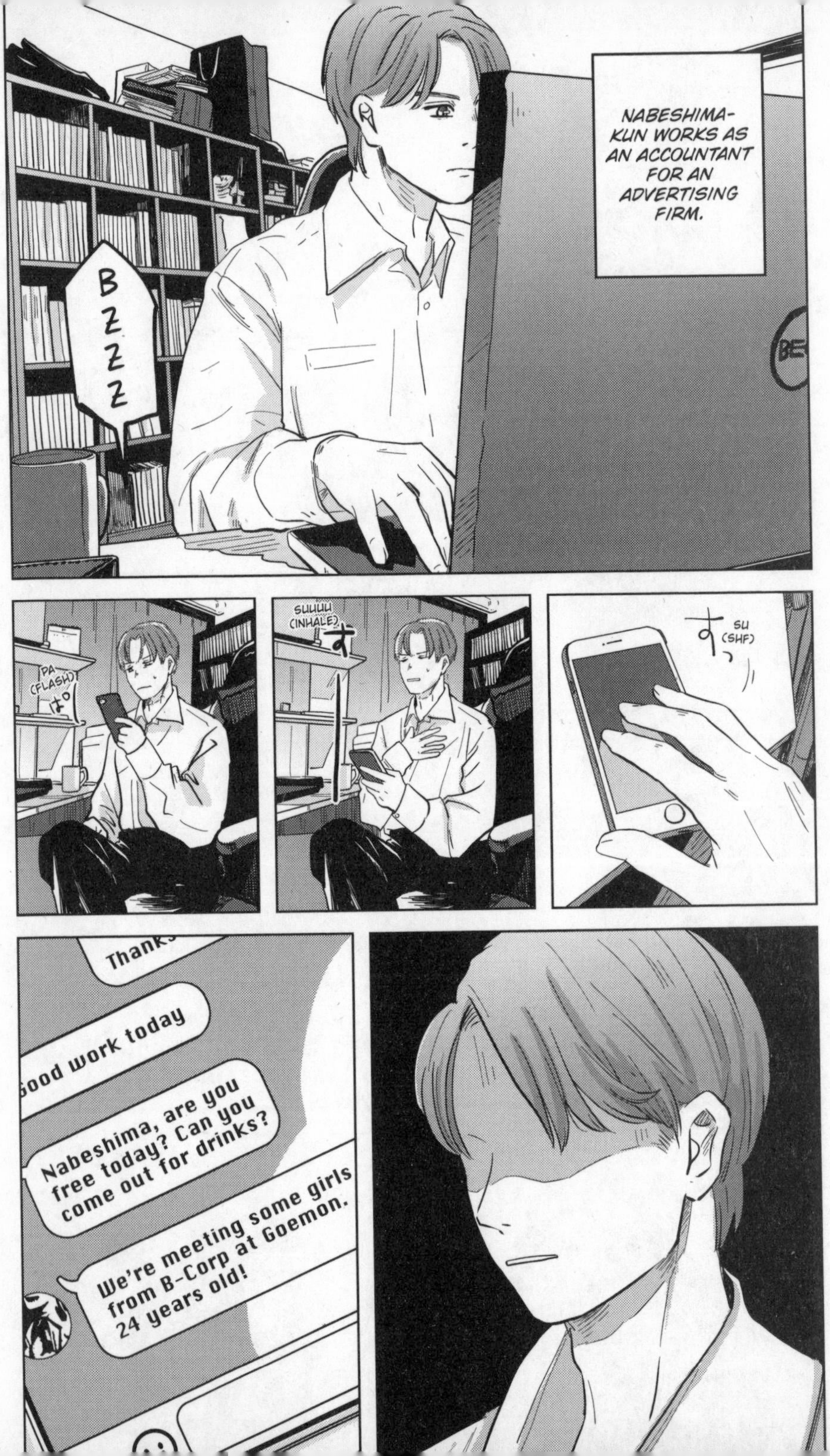
NABESHIMA-KUN WORKS AS AN ACCOUNTANT FOR AN ADVERTISING FIRM.
BZZZ
すっ
SU (SHF)
SUUUU (INHALE)
す
PA (FLASH)
ぱ
Thanks
Good work today
Nabeshima, are you free today? Can you come out for drinks?
We're meeting some girls from B-Corp at Goemon. 24 years old!

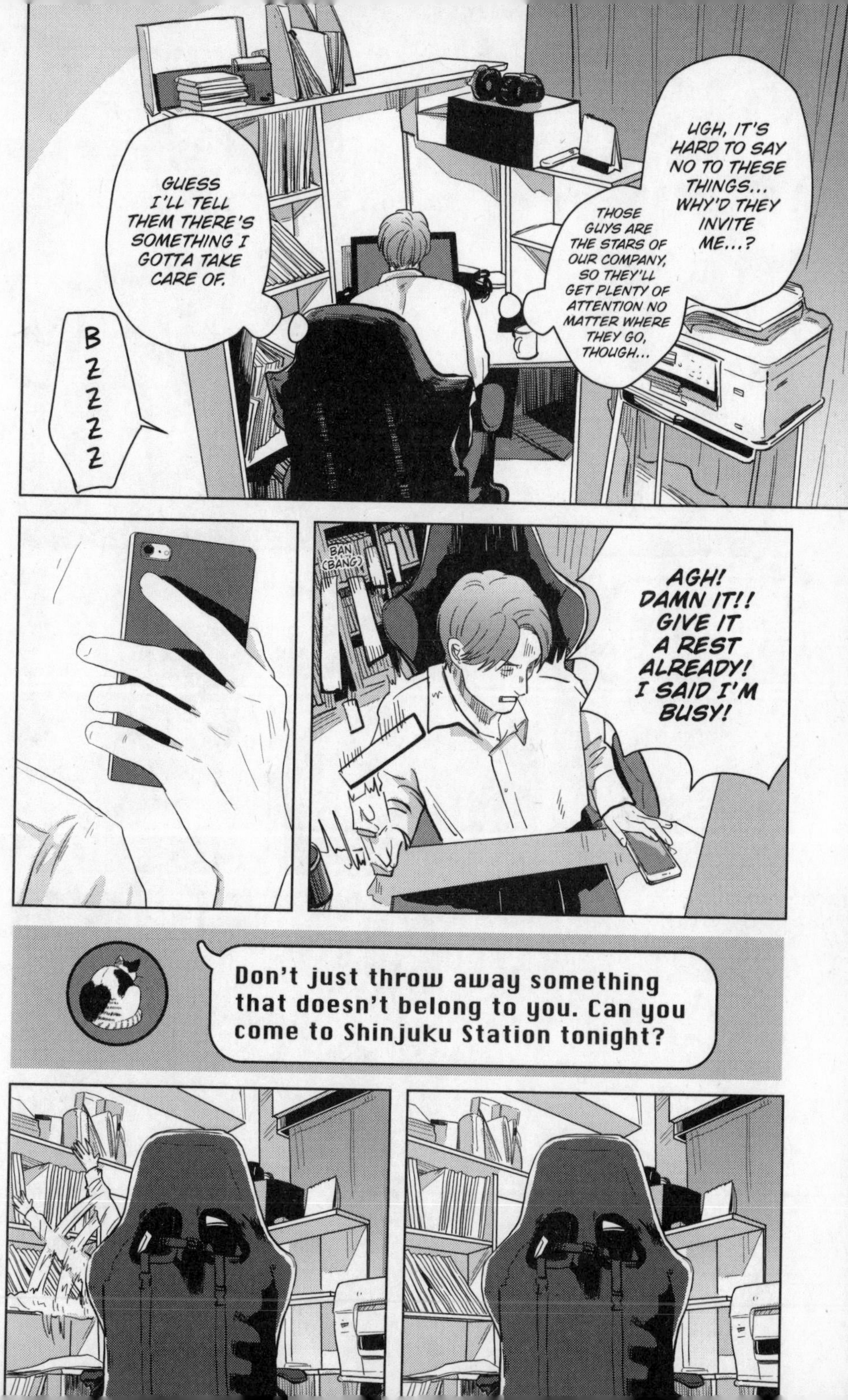
UGH, IT'S HARD TO SAY NO TO THESE THINGS... WHY'D THEY INVITE ME...?
THOSE GUYS ARE THE STARS OF OUR COMPANY, SO THEY'LL GET PLENTY OF ATTENTION NO MATTER WHERE THEY GO, THOUGH...
GUESS I'LL TELL THEM THERE'S SOMETHING I GOTTA TAKE CARE OF.
BZZZZ
BAN (BANG)
AGH! DAMN IT!! GIVE IT A REST ALREADY! I SAID I'M BUSY!
Don't just throw away something that doesn't belong to you. Can you come to Shinjuku Station tonight?

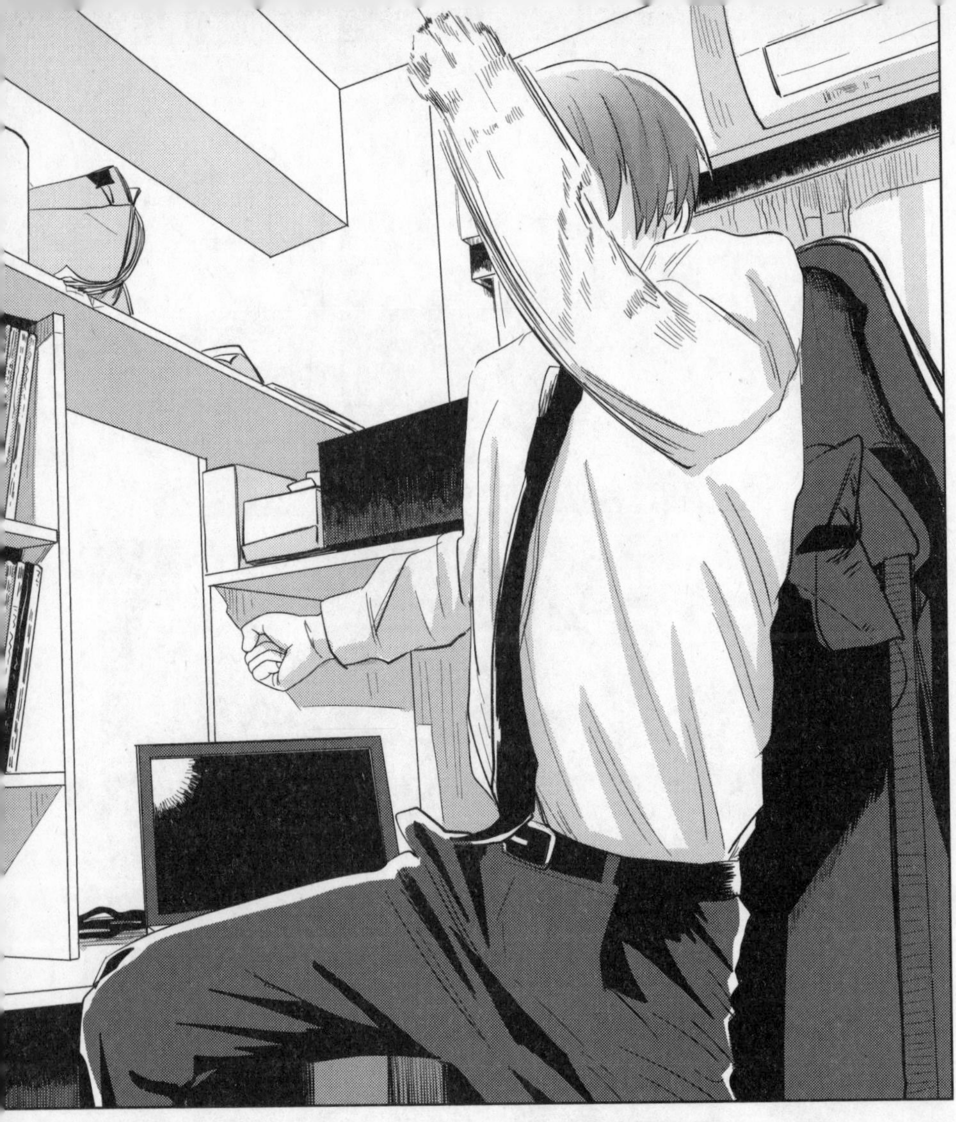

NABESHIMA-KUN...

...IS BAD AT SHOWING PEOPLE HIS TRUE FEELINGS.

GARA
(RTTL)

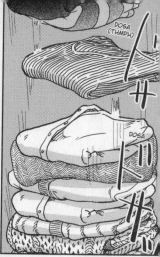

DOSA
(THMPH)

DOSA

THIS JACKET MIGHT BE A LITTLE TOO LOUD. PLUS, MIYUU-CHAN WILL BE ON HER WAY BACK FROM WORK......

HMMMM...

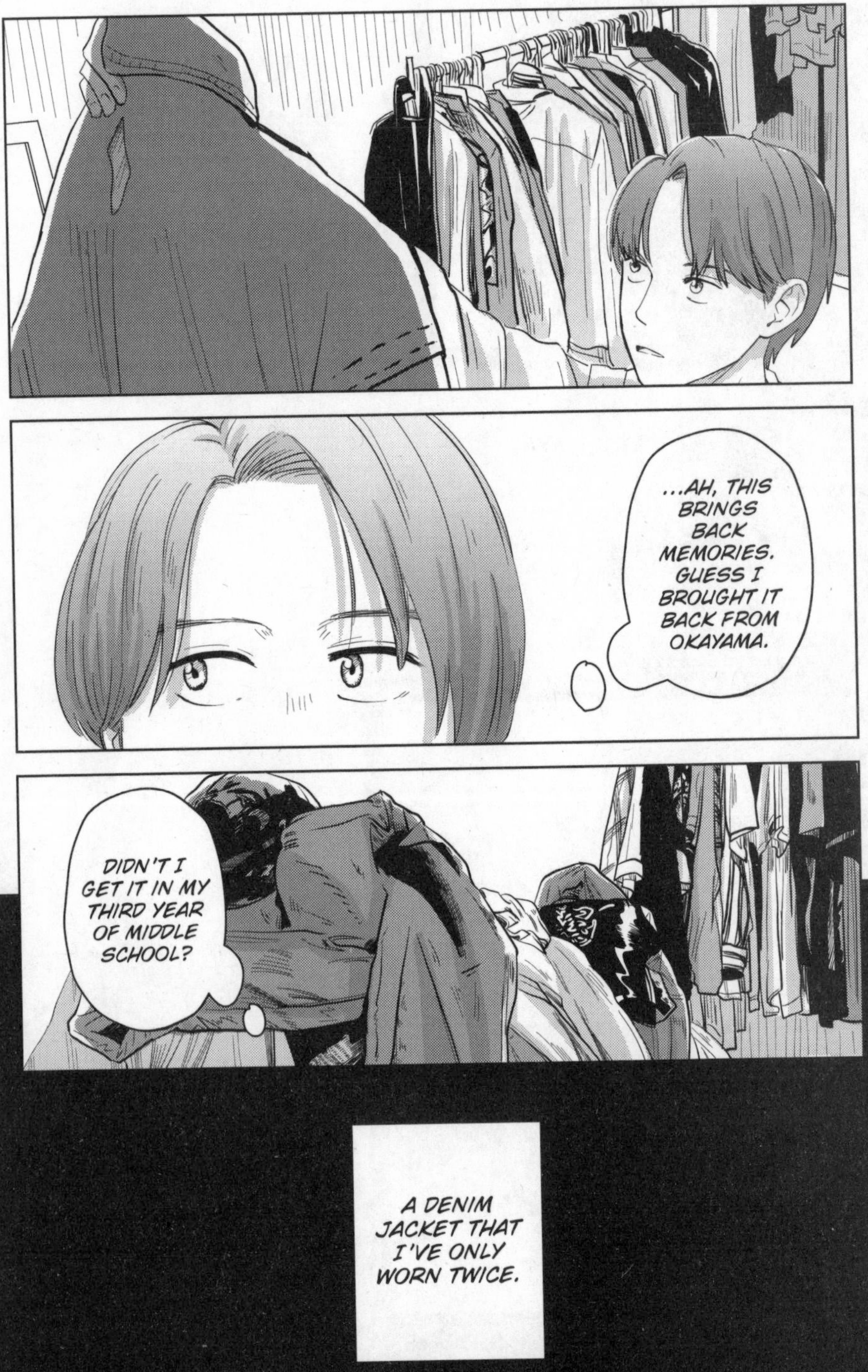
...AH, THIS BRINGS BACK MEMORIES. GUESS I BROUGHT IT BACK FROM OKAYAMA.
DIDN'T I GET IT IN MY THIRD YEAR OF MIDDLE SCHOOL?
A DENIM JACKET THAT I'VE ONLY WORN TWICE.

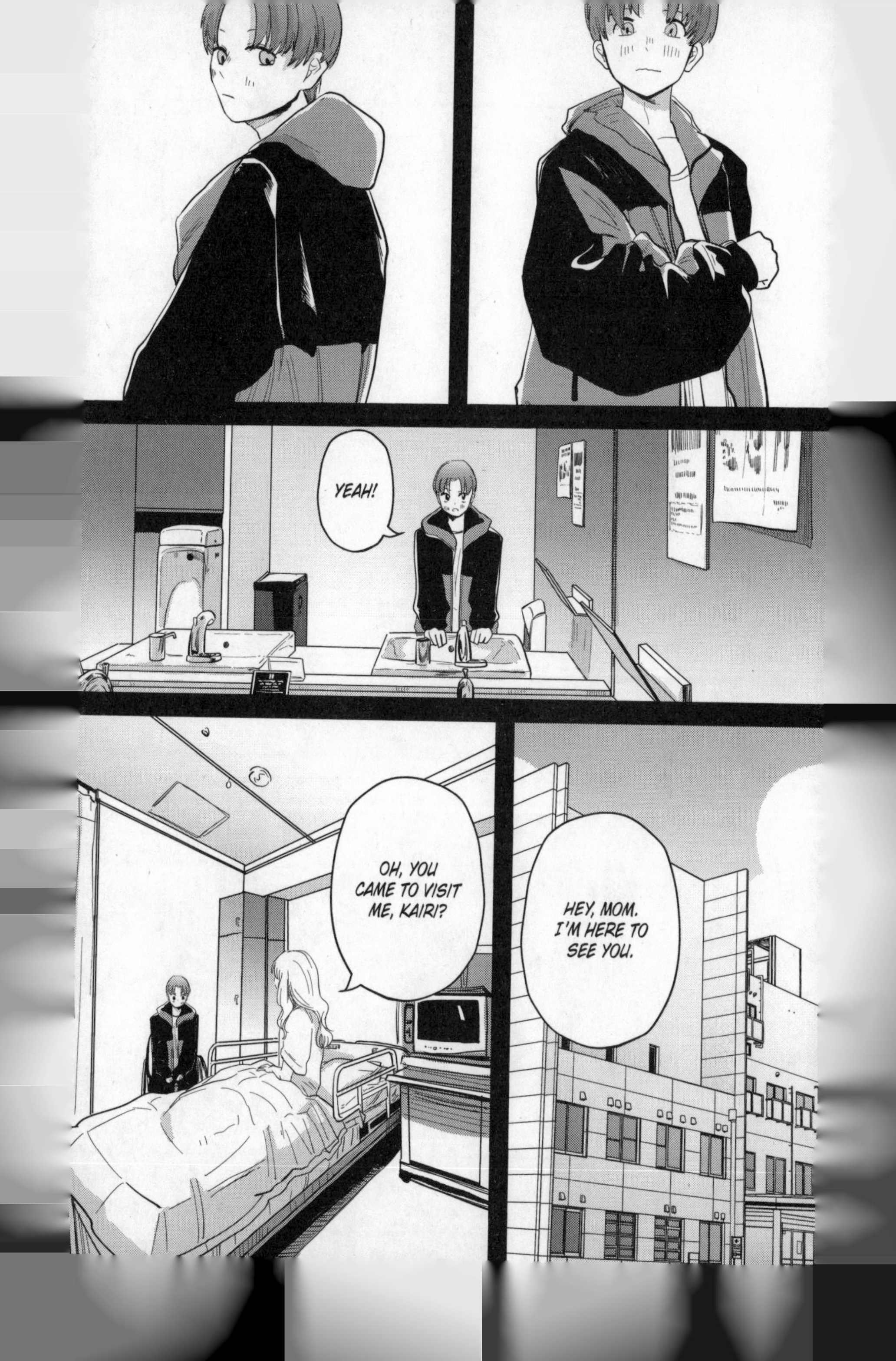
YEAH!
HEY, MOM. I'M HERE TO SEE YOU.
OH, YOU CAME TO VISIT ME, KAIRI?

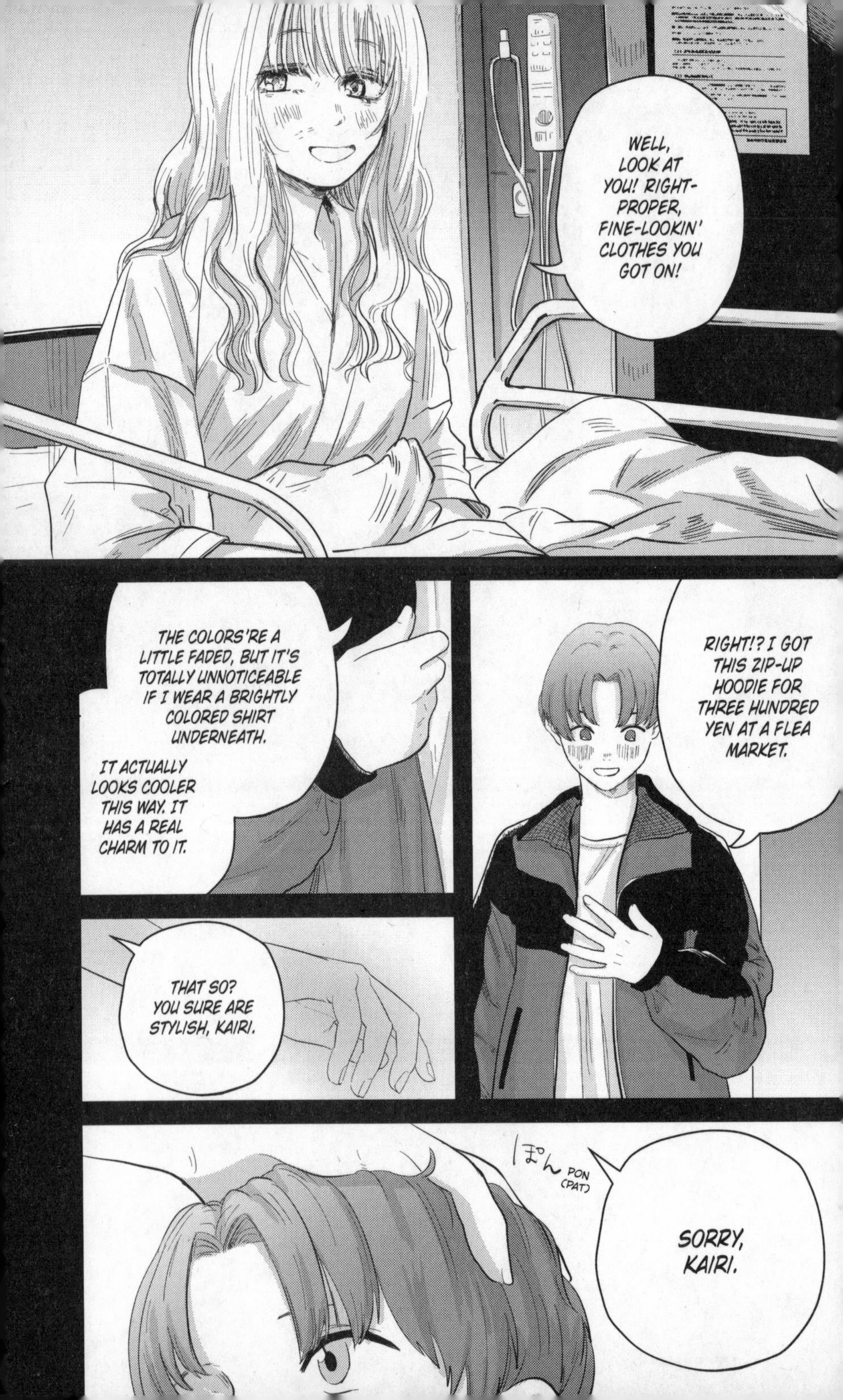
WELL, LOOK AT YOU! RIGHT-PROPER, FINE-LOOKIN' CLOTHES YOU GOT ON!
RIGHT!? I GOT THIS ZIP-UP HOODIE FOR THREE HUNDRED YEN AT A FLEA MARKET.
THE COLORS'RE A LITTLE FADED, BUT IT'S TOTALLY UNNOTICEABLE IF I WEAR A BRIGHTLY COLORED SHIRT UNDERNEATH.
IT ACTUALLY LOOKS COOLER THIS WAY. IT HAS A REAL CHARM TO IT.
THAT SO? YOU SURE ARE STYLISH, KAIRI.
ぽん PON (PAT)
SORRY, KAIRI.

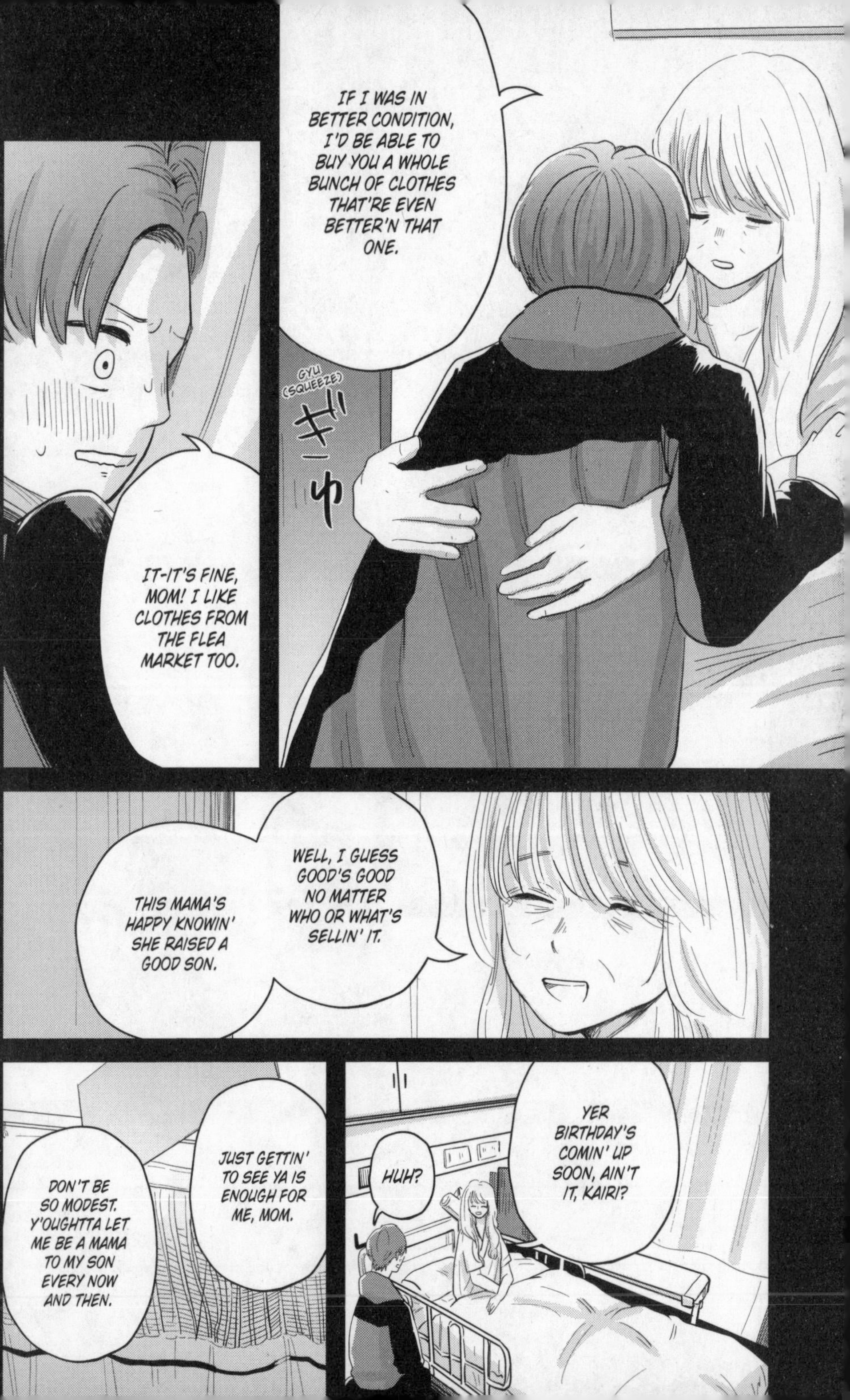
IF I WAS IN BETTER CONDITION, I'D BE ABLE TO BUY YOU A WHOLE BUNCH OF CLOTHES THAT'RE EVEN BETTER'N THAT ONE.
GYU (SQUEEZE)
IT-IT'S FINE, MOM! I LIKE CLOTHES FROM THE FLEA MARKET TOO.
WELL, I GUESS GOOD'S GOOD NO MATTER WHO OR WHAT'S SELLIN' IT.
THIS MAMA'S HAPPY KNOWIN' SHE RAISED A GOOD SON.
YER BIRTHDAY'S COMIN' UP SOON, AIN'T IT, KAIRI?
HUH?
JUST GETTIN' TO SEE YA IS ENOUGH FOR ME, MOM.
DON'T BE SO MODEST. Y'OUGHTTA LET ME BE A MAMA TO MY SON EVERY NOW AND THEN.

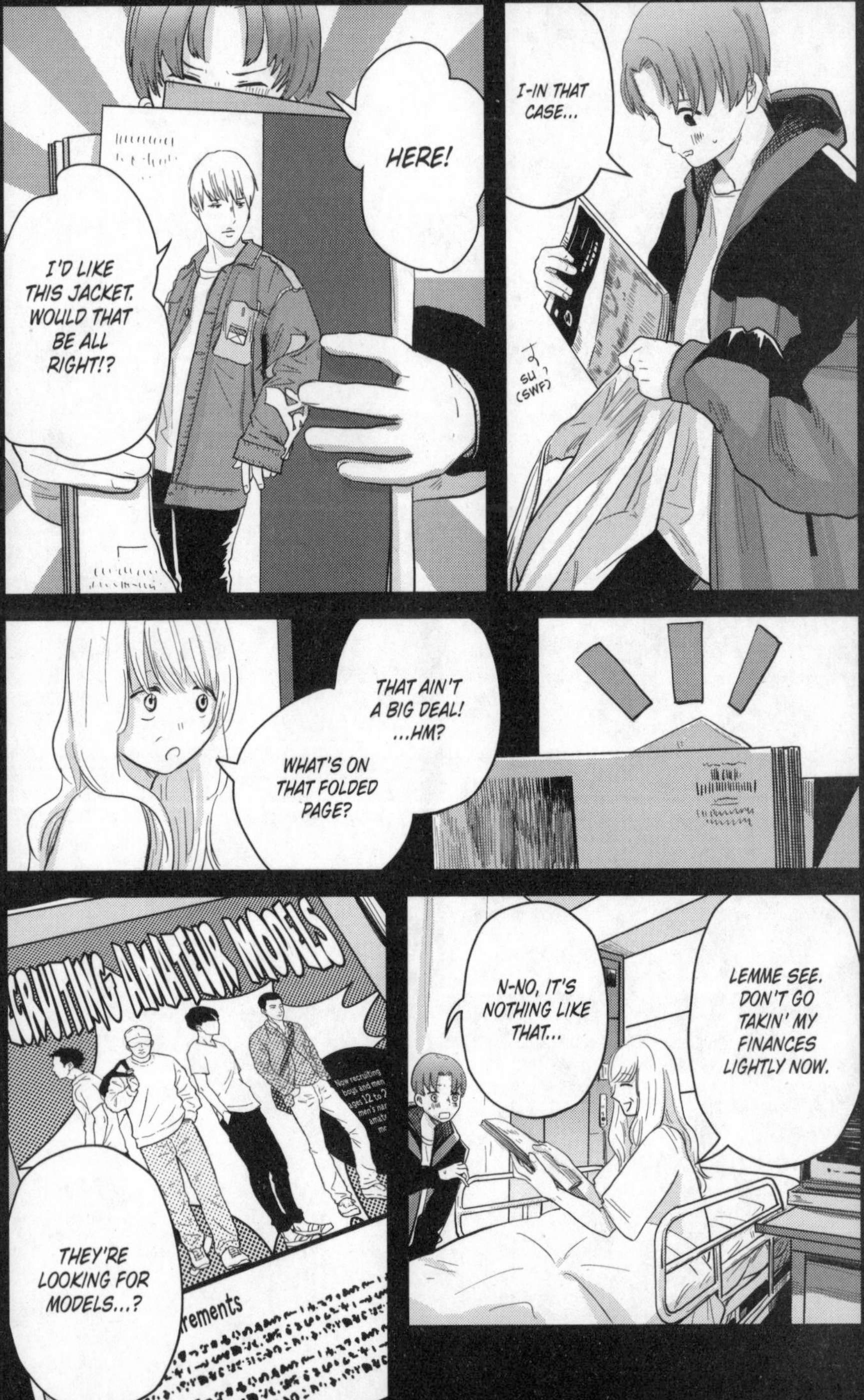
I-IN THAT CASE...
す
SU (SWF)
HERE!
I'D LIKE THIS JACKET. WOULD THAT BE ALL RIGHT!?
THAT AIN'T A BIG DEAL! ...HM?
WHAT'S ON THAT FOLDED PAGE?
LEMME SEE. DON'T GO TAKIN' MY FINANCES LIGHTLY NOW.
N-NO, IT'S NOTHING LIKE THAT...
THEY'RE LOOKING FOR MODELS...?

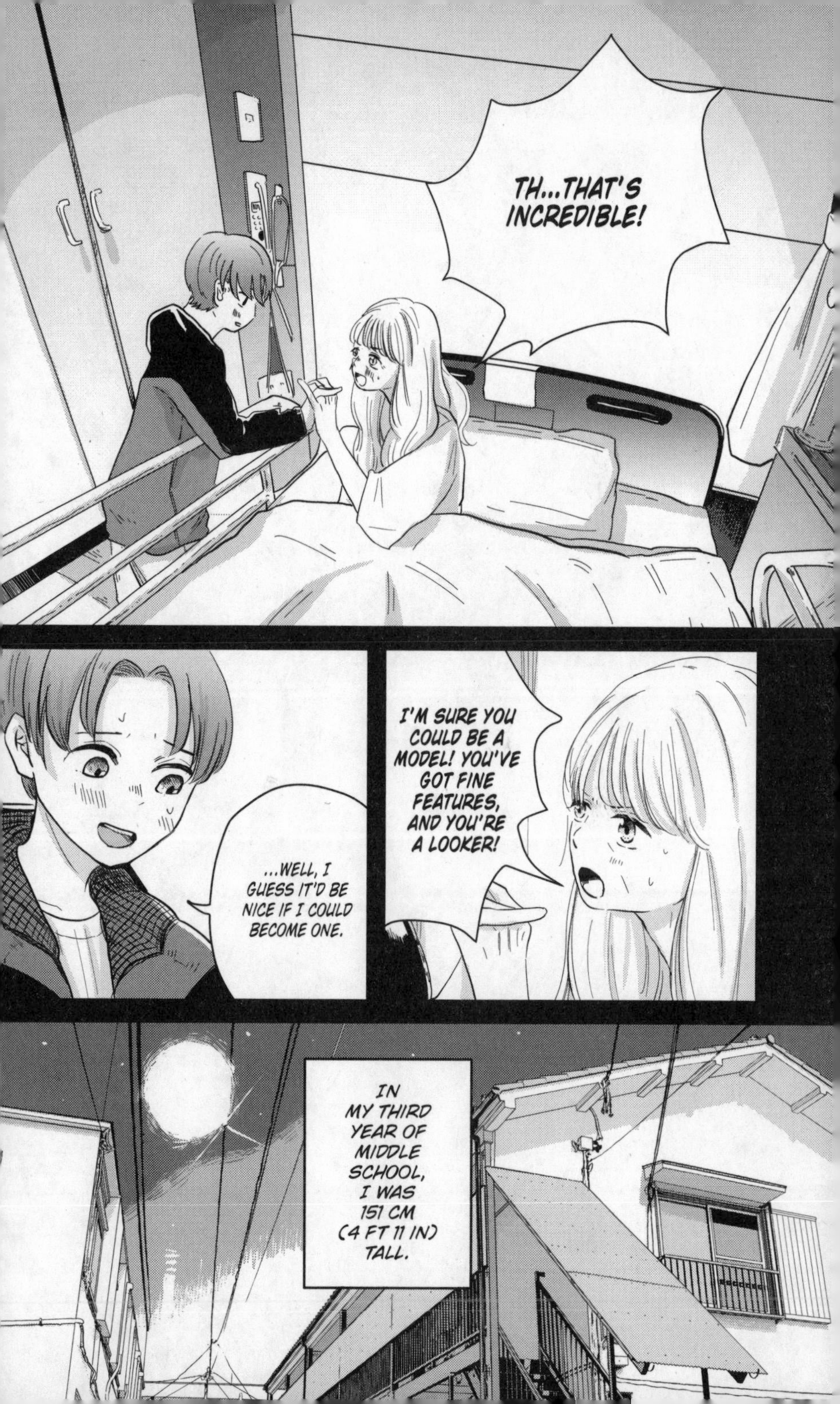
TH...THAT'S INCREDIBLE!
I'M SURE YOU COULD BE A MODEL! YOU'VE GOT FINE FEATURES, AND YOU'RE A LOOKER!
...WELL, I GUESS IT'D BE NICE IF I COULD BECOME ONE.
IN MY THIRD YEAR OF MIDDLE SCHOOL, I WAS 151 CM (4 FT 11 IN) TALL.

...OH, GUESS HE'S NOT BACK YET.

I'M HOME, DAD.

RIGHT-PROPER, FINE-LOOKIN' CLOTHES YOU GOT ON!

I LOVED MY MOM.

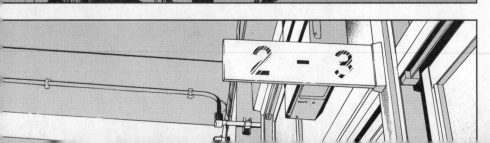

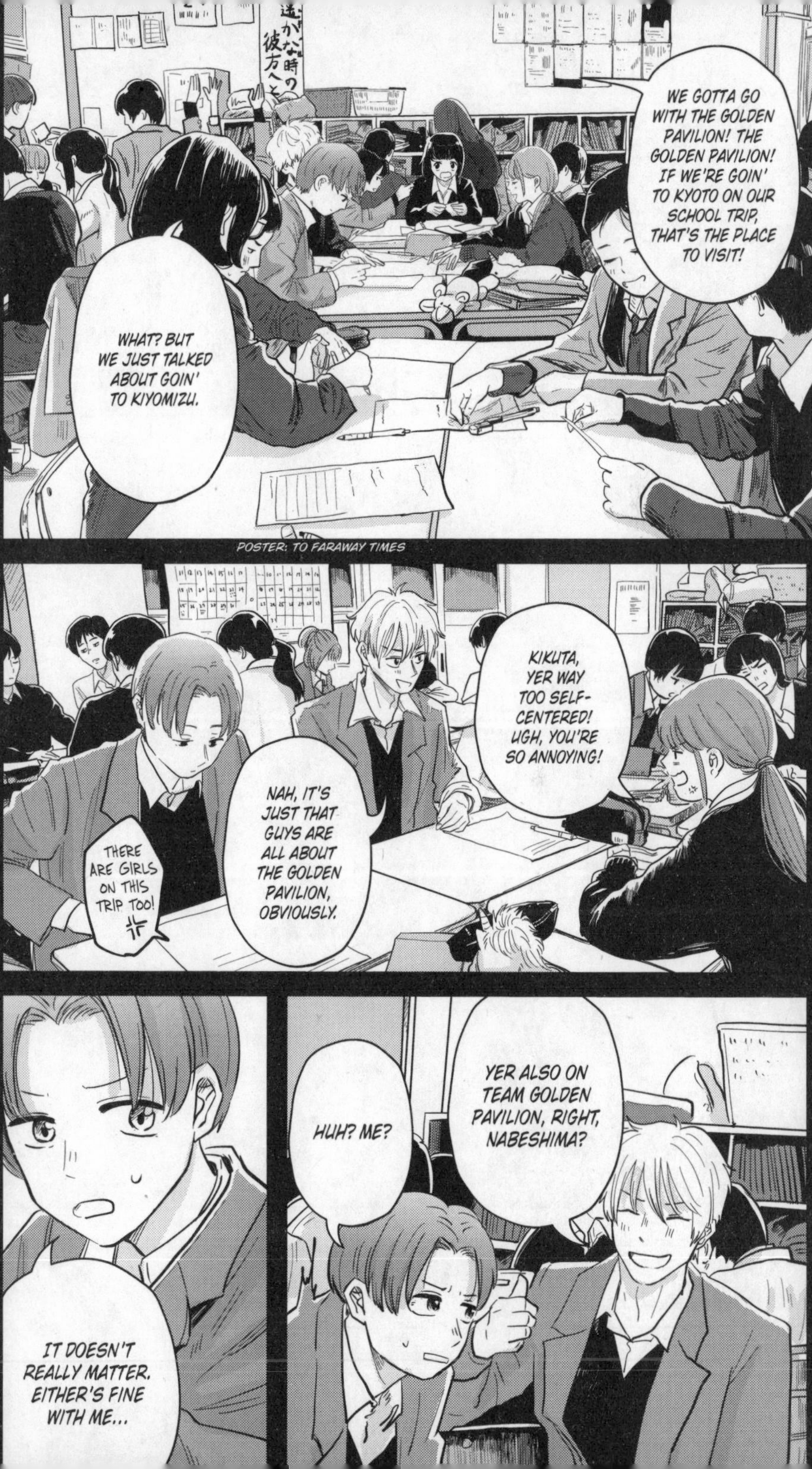
WE GOTTA GO WITH THE GOLDEN PAVILION! THE GOLDEN PAVILION! IF WE'RE GOIN' TO KYOTO ON OUR SCHOOL TRIP, THAT'S THE PLACE TO VISIT!
WHAT? BUT WE JUST TALKED ABOUT GOIN' TO KIYOMIZU.
POSTER: TO FARAWAY TIMES
KIKUTA, YER WAY TOO SELF-CENTERED! UGH, YOU'RE SO ANNOYING!
NAH, IT'S JUST THAT GUYS ARE ALL ABOUT THE GOLDEN PAVILION, OBVIOUSLY.
THERE ARE GIRLS ON THIS TRIP TOO!
YER ALSO ON TEAM GOLDEN PAVILION, RIGHT, NABESHIMA?
HUH? ME?
IT DOESN'T REALLY MATTER. EITHER'S FINE WITH ME...

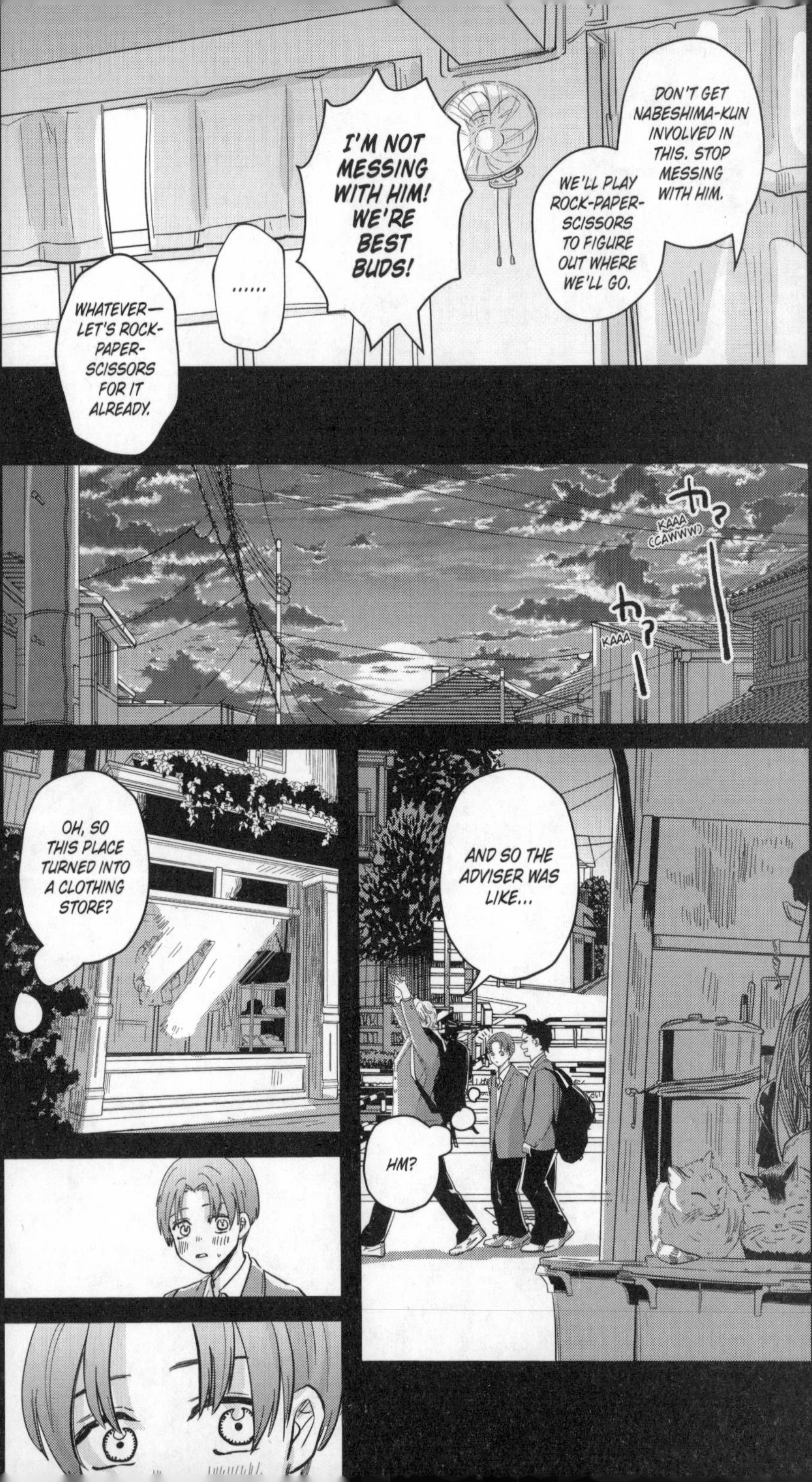
DON'T GET NABESHIMA-KUN INVOLVED IN THIS. STOP MESSING WITH HIM.
WE'LL PLAY ROCK-PAPER-SCISSORS TO FIGURE OUT WHERE WE'LL GO.
I'M NOT MESSING WITH HIM! WE'RE BEST BUDS!
......
WHATEVER—LET'S ROCK-PAPER-SCISSORS FOR IT ALREADY.
KAAA (CAWWW)
KAAA
AND SO THE ADVISER WAS LIKE...
HM?
OH, SO THIS PLACE TURNED INTO A CLOTHING STORE?

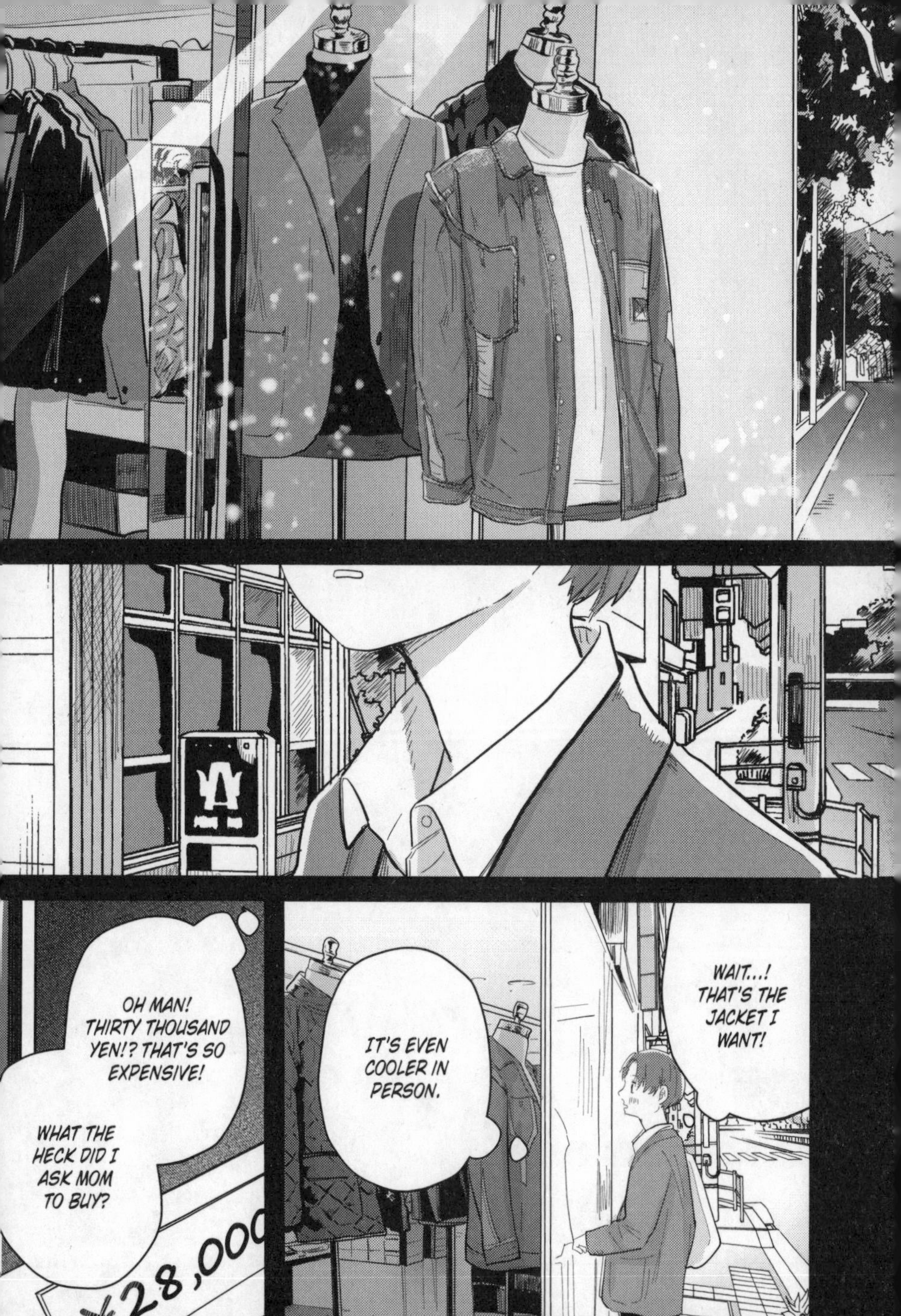
WAIT...! THAT'S THE JACKET I WANT!
IT'S EVEN COOLER IN PERSON.
OH MAN! THIRTY THOUSAND YEN!? THAT'S SO EXPENSIVE!
WHAT THE HECK DID I ASK MOM TO BUY?
¥28,000

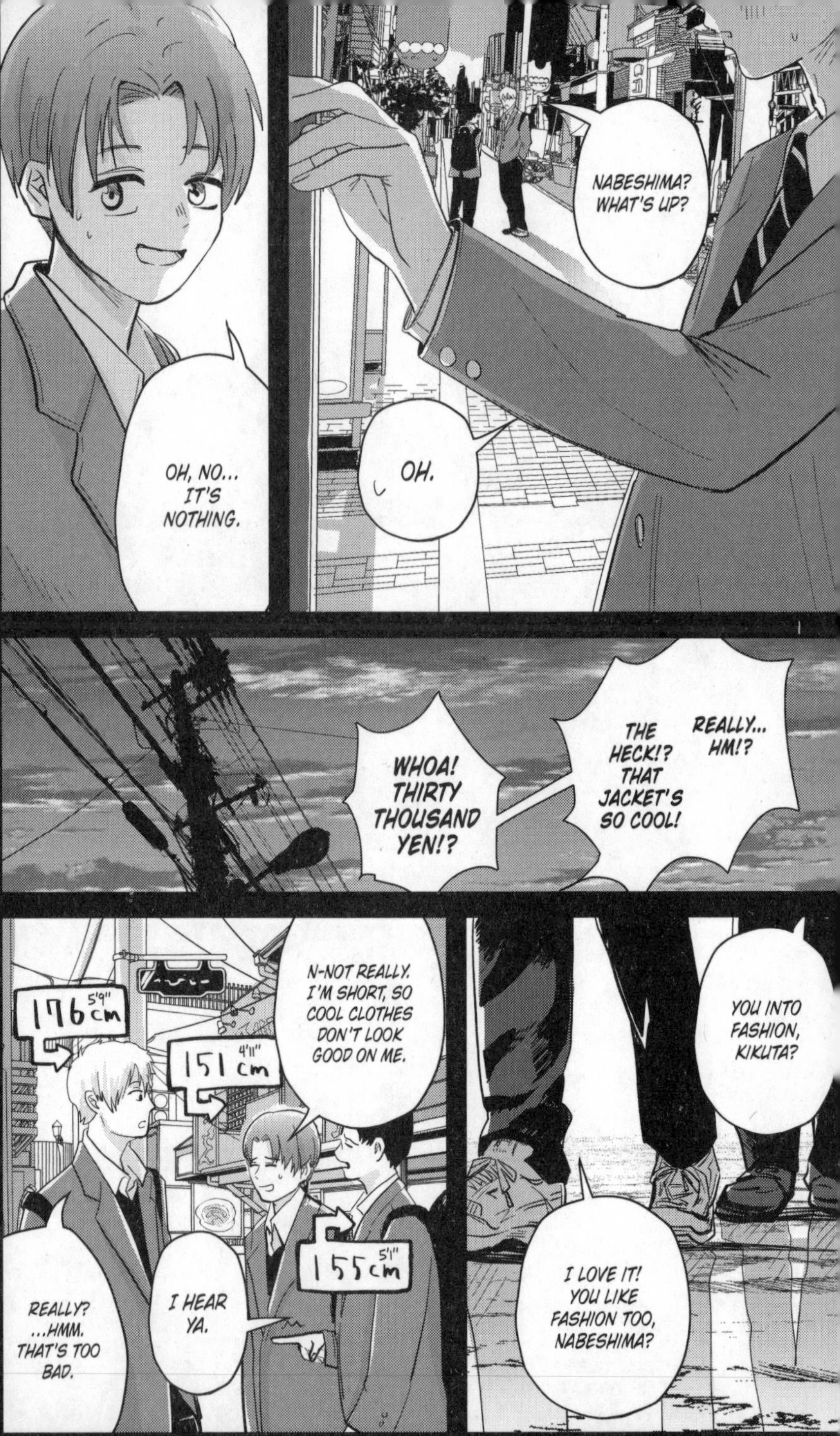
NABESHIMA? WHAT'S UP?
OH.
OH, NO... IT'S NOTHING.
REALLY... HM!?
THE HECK!? THAT JACKET'S SO COOL!
WHOA! THIRTY THOUSAND YEN!?
YOU INTO FASHION, KIKUTA?
I LOVE IT! YOU LIKE FASHION TOO, NABESHIMA?
N-NOT REALLY. I'M SHORT, SO COOL CLOTHES DON'T LOOK GOOD ON ME.
176cm 5'9"
151cm 4'11"
155cm 5'1"
I HEAR YA.
REALLY? ...HMM. THAT'S TOO BAD.

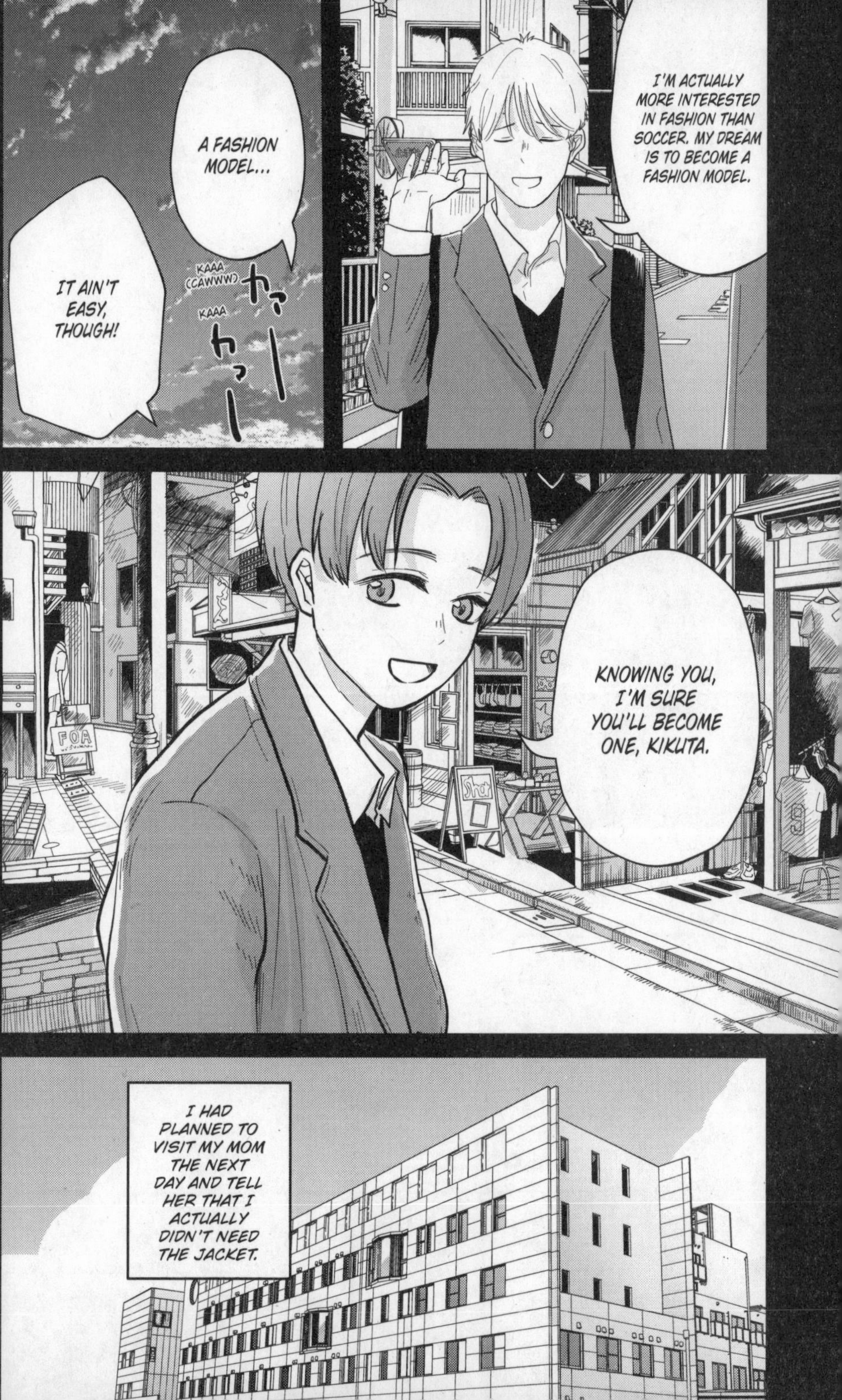
I'M ACTUALLY MORE INTERESTED IN FASHION THAN SOCCER. MY DREAM IS TO BECOME A FASHION MODEL.
A FASHION MODEL...
KAAA (CAWWW)
KAAA
IT AIN'T EASY, THOUGH!
KNOWING YOU, I'M SURE YOU'LL BECOME ONE, KIKUTA.
I HAD PLANNED TO VISIT MY MOM THE NEXT DAY AND TELL HER THAT I ACTUALLY DIDN'T NEED THE JACKET.

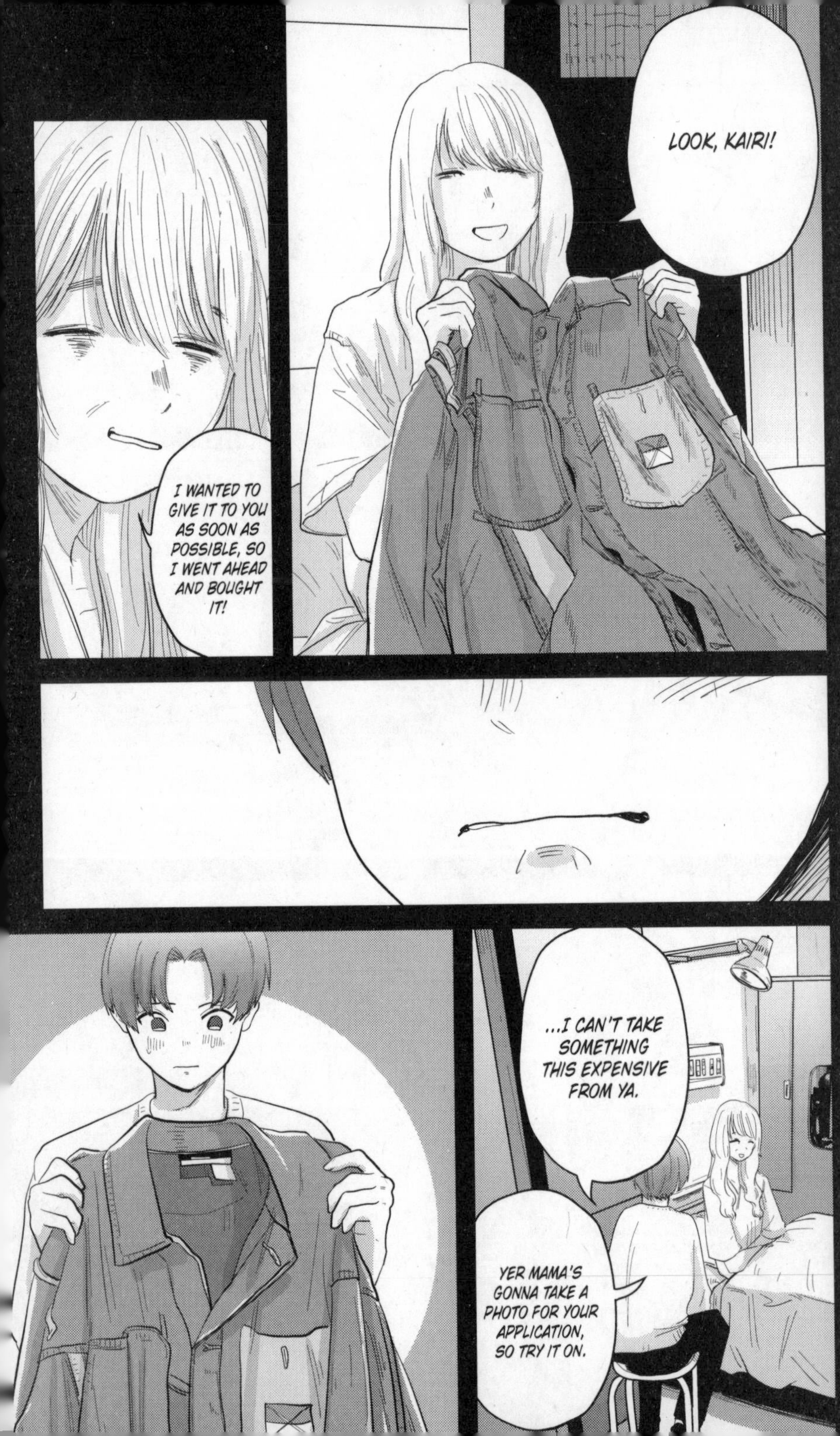
LOOK, KAIRI!
I WANTED TO GIVE IT TO YOU AS SOON AS POSSIBLE, SO I WENT AHEAD AND BOUGHT IT!
...I CAN'T TAKE SOMETHING THIS EXPENSIVE FROM YA.
YER MAMA'S GONNA TAKE A PHOTO FOR YOUR APPLICATION, SO TRY IT ON.

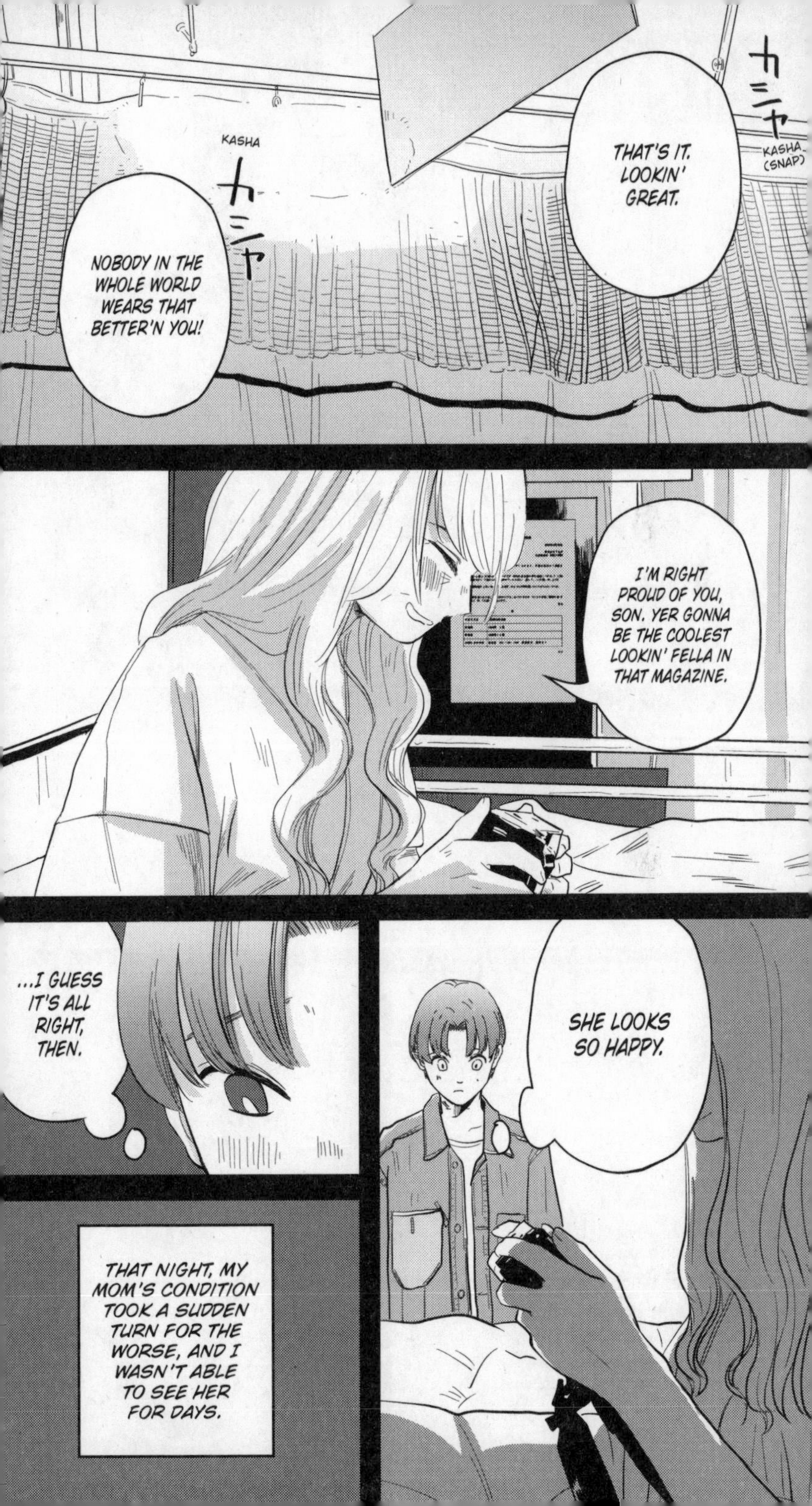
カシャ
KASHA (SNAP)
THAT'S IT. LOOKIN' GREAT.
KASHA
カシャ
NOBODY IN THE WHOLE WORLD WEARS THAT BETTER'N YOU!
I'M RIGHT PROUD OF YOU, SON. YER GONNA BE THE COOLEST LOOKIN' FELLA IN THAT MAGAZINE.
SHE LOOKS SO HAPPY.
...I GUESS IT'S ALL RIGHT, THEN.
THAT NIGHT, MY MOM'S CONDITION TOOK A SUDDEN TURN FOR THE WORSE, AND I WASN'T ABLE TO SEE HER FOR DAYS.

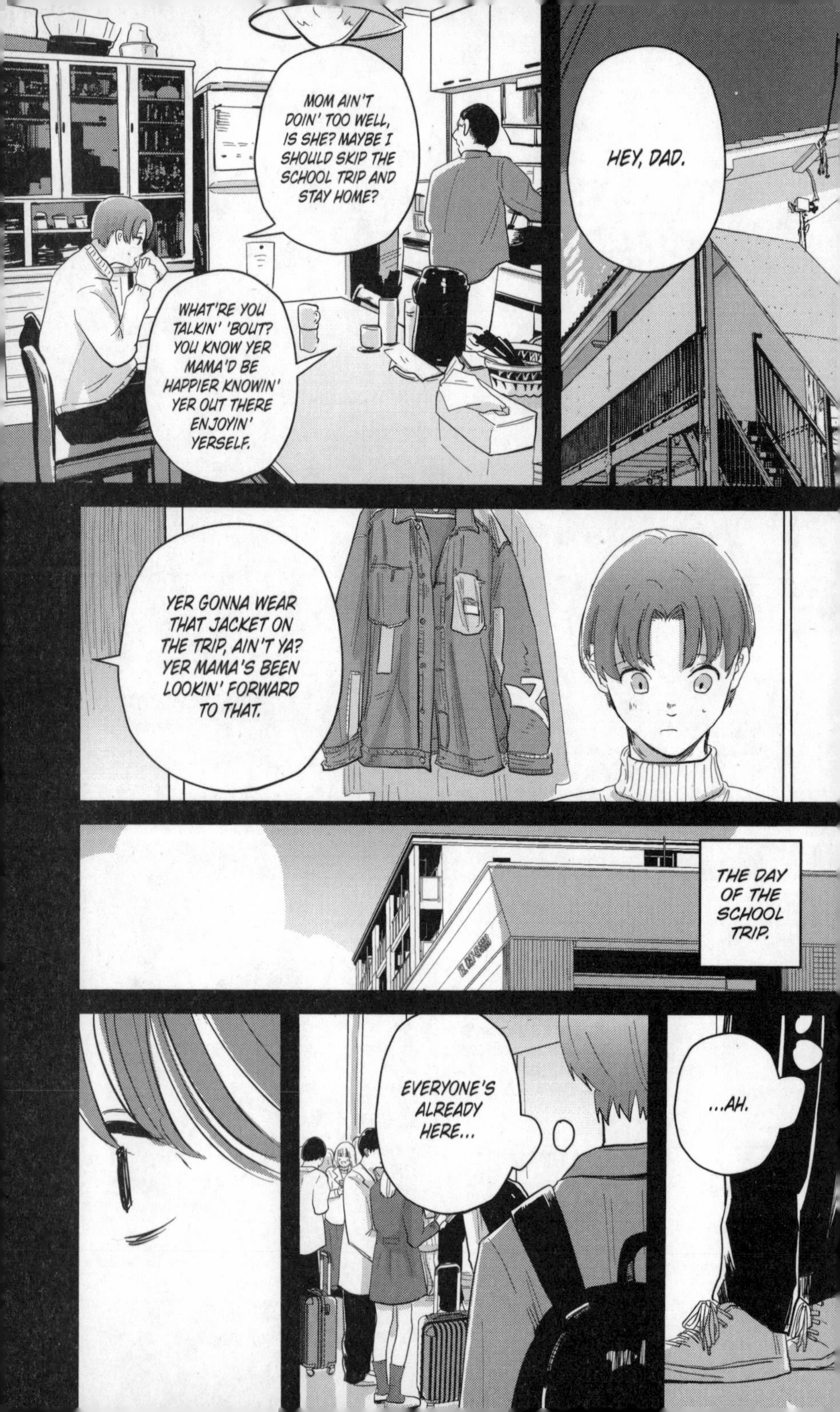
HEY, DAD.
MOM AIN'T DOIN' TOO WELL, IS SHE? MAYBE I SHOULD SKIP THE SCHOOL TRIP AND STAY HOME?
WHAT'RE YOU TALKIN' 'BOUT? YOU KNOW YER MAMA'D BE HAPPIER KNOWIN' YER OUT THERE ENJOYIN' YERSELF.
YER GONNA WEAR THAT JACKET ON THE TRIP, AIN'T YA? YER MAMA'S BEEN LOOKIN' FORWARD TO THAT.
THE DAY OF THE SCHOOL TRIP.
...AH.
EVERYONE'S ALREADY HERE...

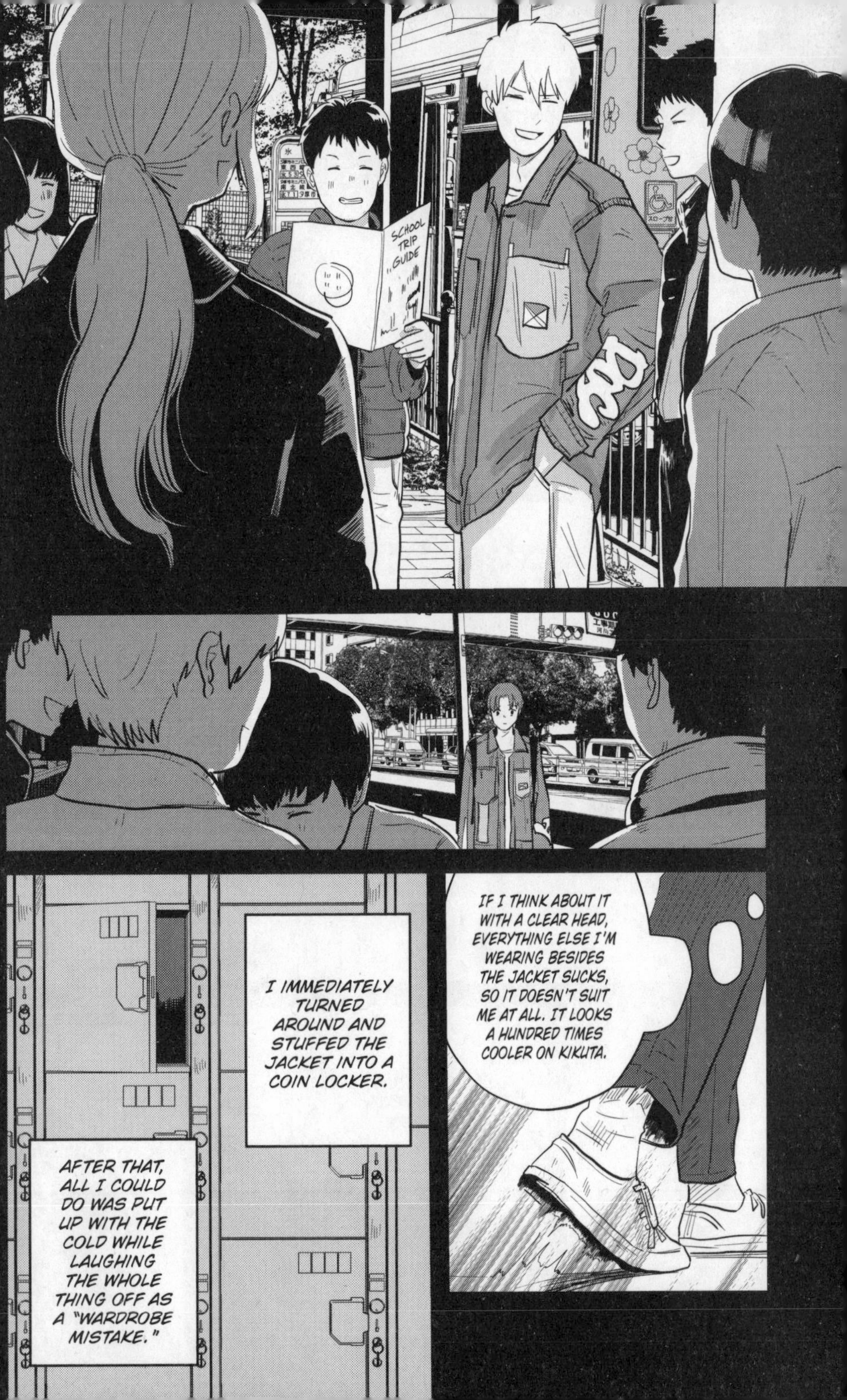
SCHOOL TRIP GUIDE
IF I THINK ABOUT IT WITH A CLEAR HEAD, EVERYTHING ELSE I'M WEARING BESIDES THE JACKET SUCKS, SO IT DOESN'T SUIT ME AT ALL. IT LOOKS A HUNDRED TIMES COOLER ON KIKUTA.
I IMMEDIATELY TURNED AROUND AND STUFFED THE JACKET INTO A COIN LOCKER.
AFTER THAT, ALL I COULD DO WAS PUT UP WITH THE COLD WHILE LAUGHING THE WHOLE THING OFF AS A "WARDROBE MISTAKE."

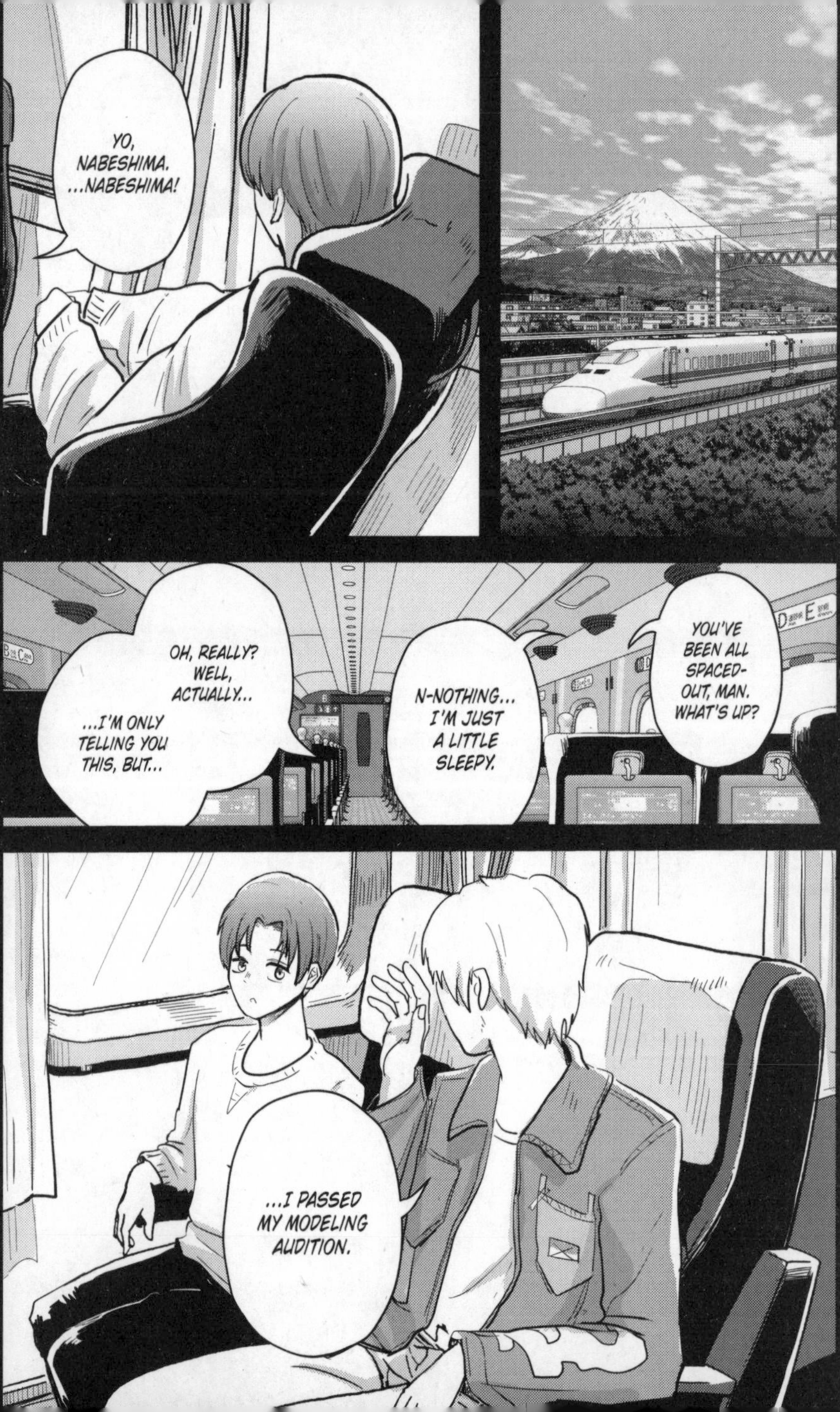
YO, NABESHIMA. ...NABESHIMA!
YOU'VE BEEN ALL SPACED-OUT, MAN. WHAT'S UP?
N-NOTHING... I'M JUST A LITTLE SLEEPY.
OH, REALLY? WELL, ACTUALLY...
...I'M ONLY TELLING YOU THIS, BUT...
...I PASSED MY MODELING AUDITION.

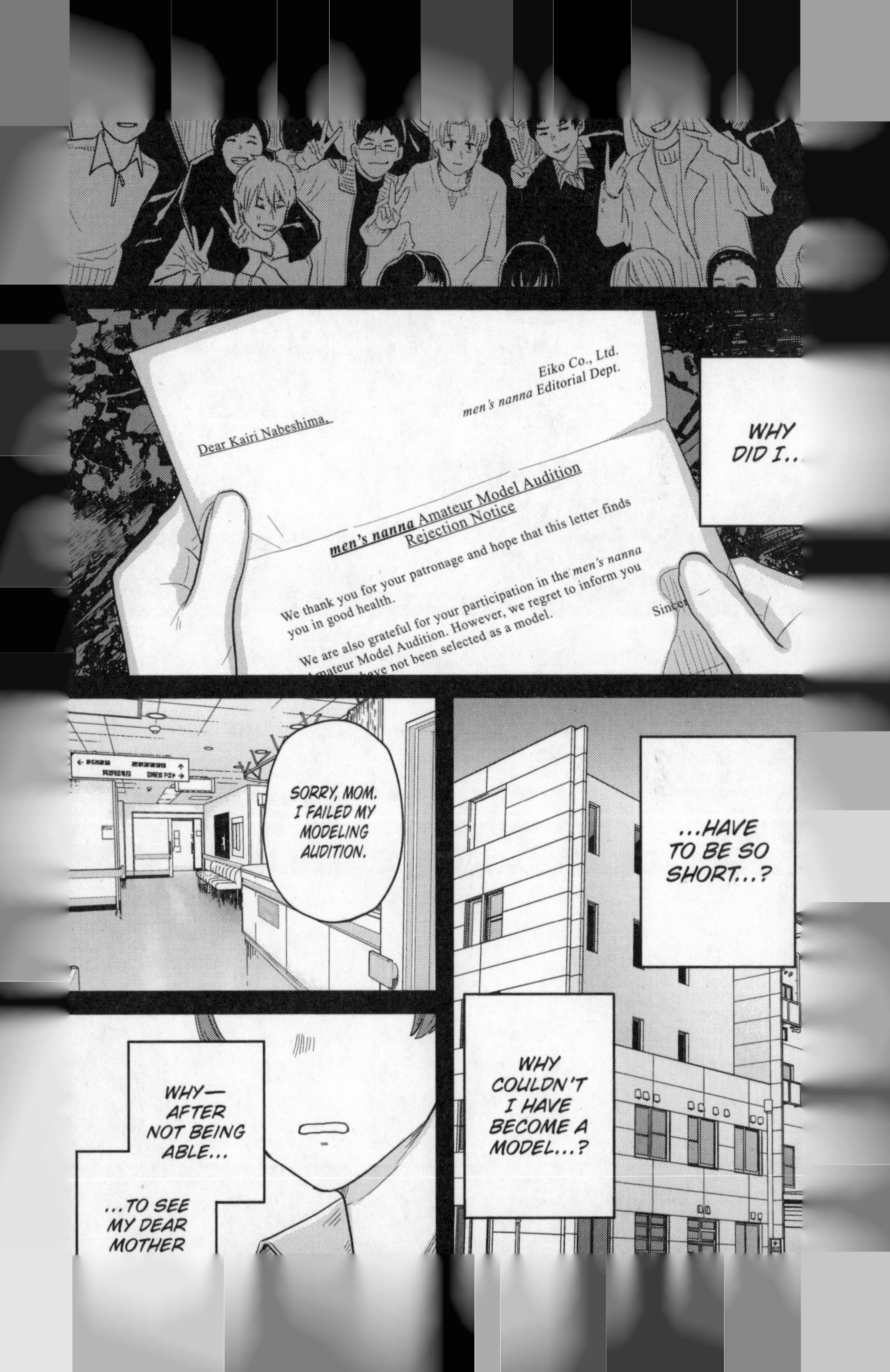
WHY DID I...
Eiko Co., Ltd.
men's nanna Editorial Dept.
Dear Kairi Nabeshima,
men's nanna Amateur Model Audition
Rejection Notice
We thank you for your patronage and hope that this letter finds
you in good health.
We are also grateful for your participation in the men's nanna
mateur Model Audition. However, we regret to inform you
have not been selected as a model.
...HAVE TO BE SO SHORT...?
WHY COULDN'T I HAVE BECOME A MODEL...?
SORRY, MOM. I FAILED MY MODELING AUDITION.
WHY— AFTER NOT BEING ABLE...
...TO SEE MY DEAR MOTHER

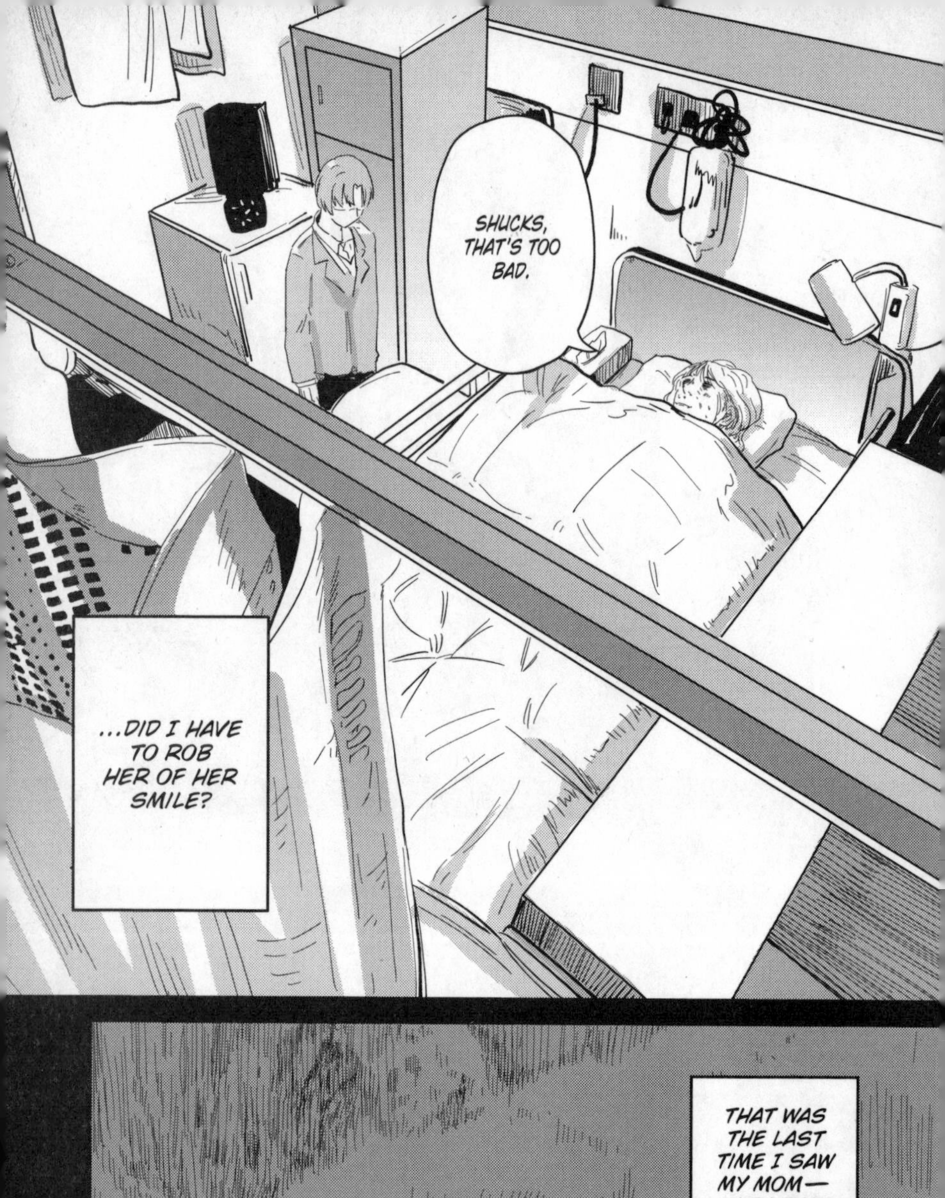
SHUCKS, THAT'S TOO BAD.
...DID I HAVE TO ROB HER OF HER SMILE?

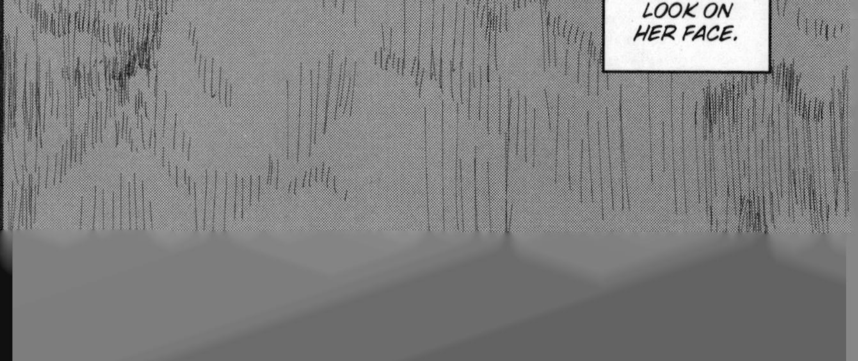
THAT WAS THE LAST TIME I SAW MY MOM— WITH THAT LOOK ON HER FACE.

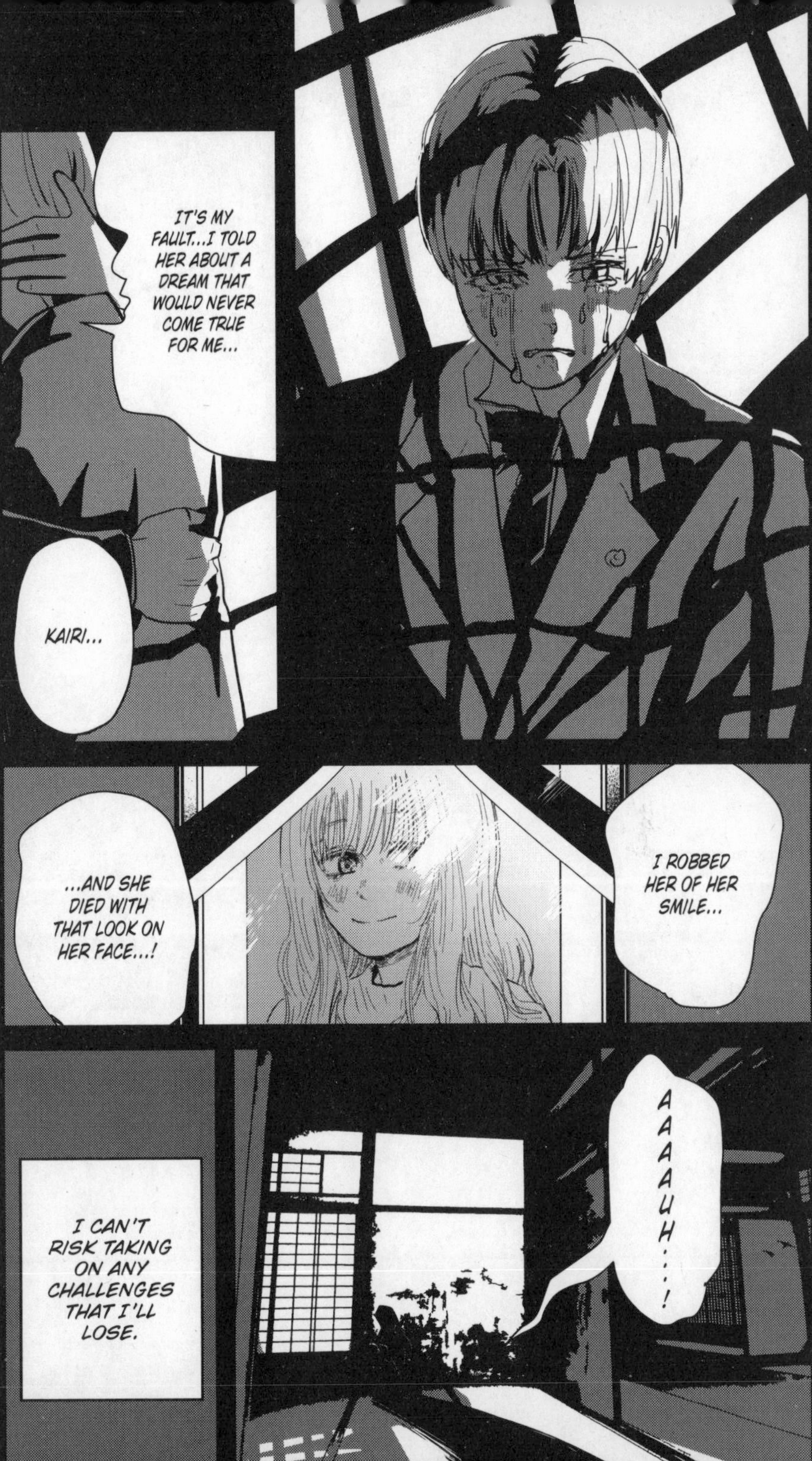
IT'S MY FAULT...I TOLD HER ABOUT A DREAM THAT WOULD NEVER COME TRUE FOR ME...
KAIRI...
I ROBBED HER OF HER SMILE...
...AND SHE DIED WITH THAT LOOK ON HER FACE...!
AAAAAUH...!
I CAN'T RISK TAKING ON ANY CHALLENGES THAT I'LL LOSE.

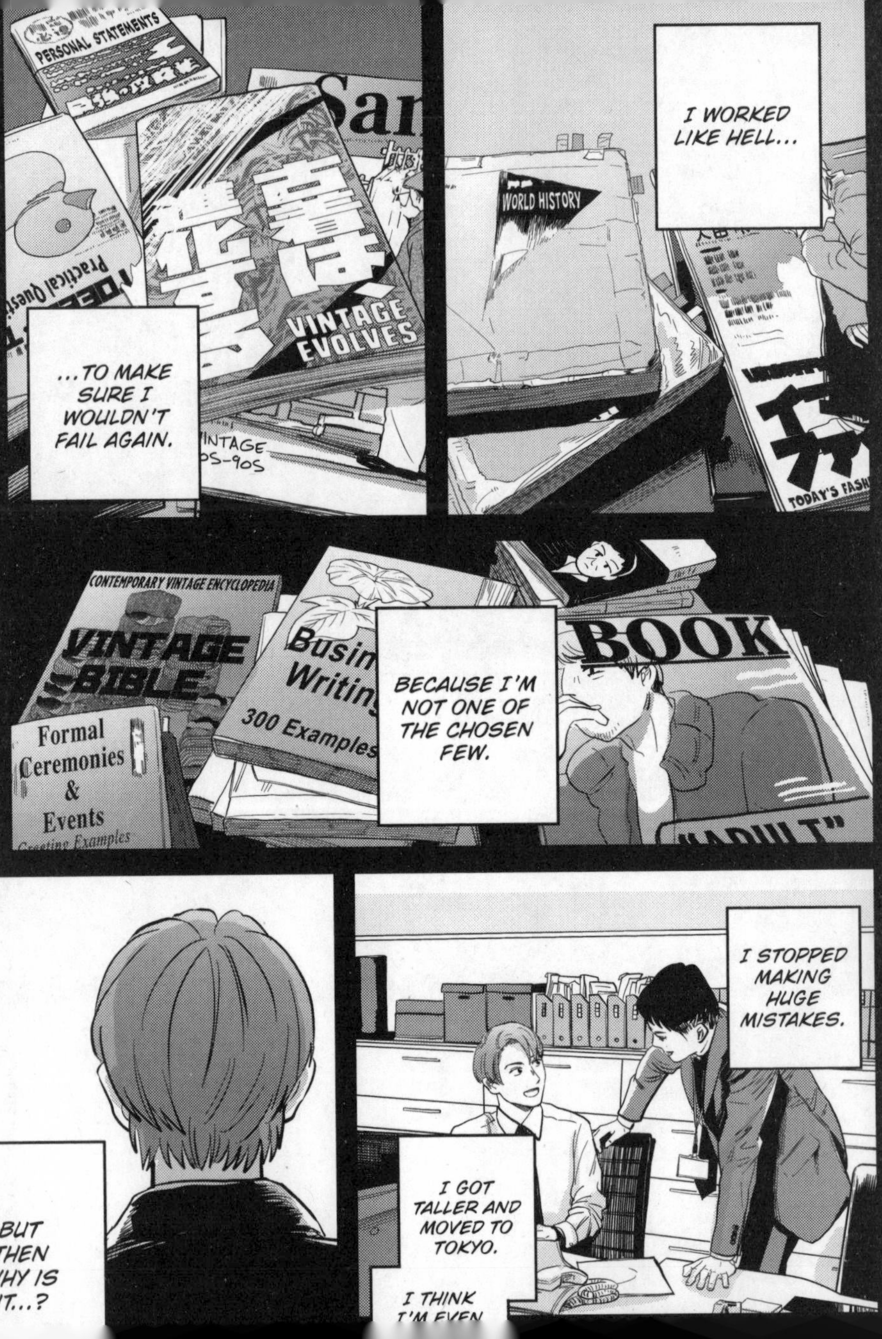
I WORKED LIKE HELL...
WORLD HISTORY
PERSONAL STATEMENTS
VINTAGE EVOLVES
...TO MAKE SURE I WOULDN'T FAIL AGAIN.
CONTEMPORARY VINTAGE ENCYCLOPEDIA
VINTAGE BIBLE
Formal Ceremonies & Events
300 Examples
BECAUSE I'M NOT ONE OF THE CHOSEN FEW.
BOOK
"ADULT"
I STOPPED MAKING HUGE MISTAKES.
I GOT TALLER AND MOVED TO TOKYO.
I THINK I'M EVEN
BUT THEN WHY IS IT...?

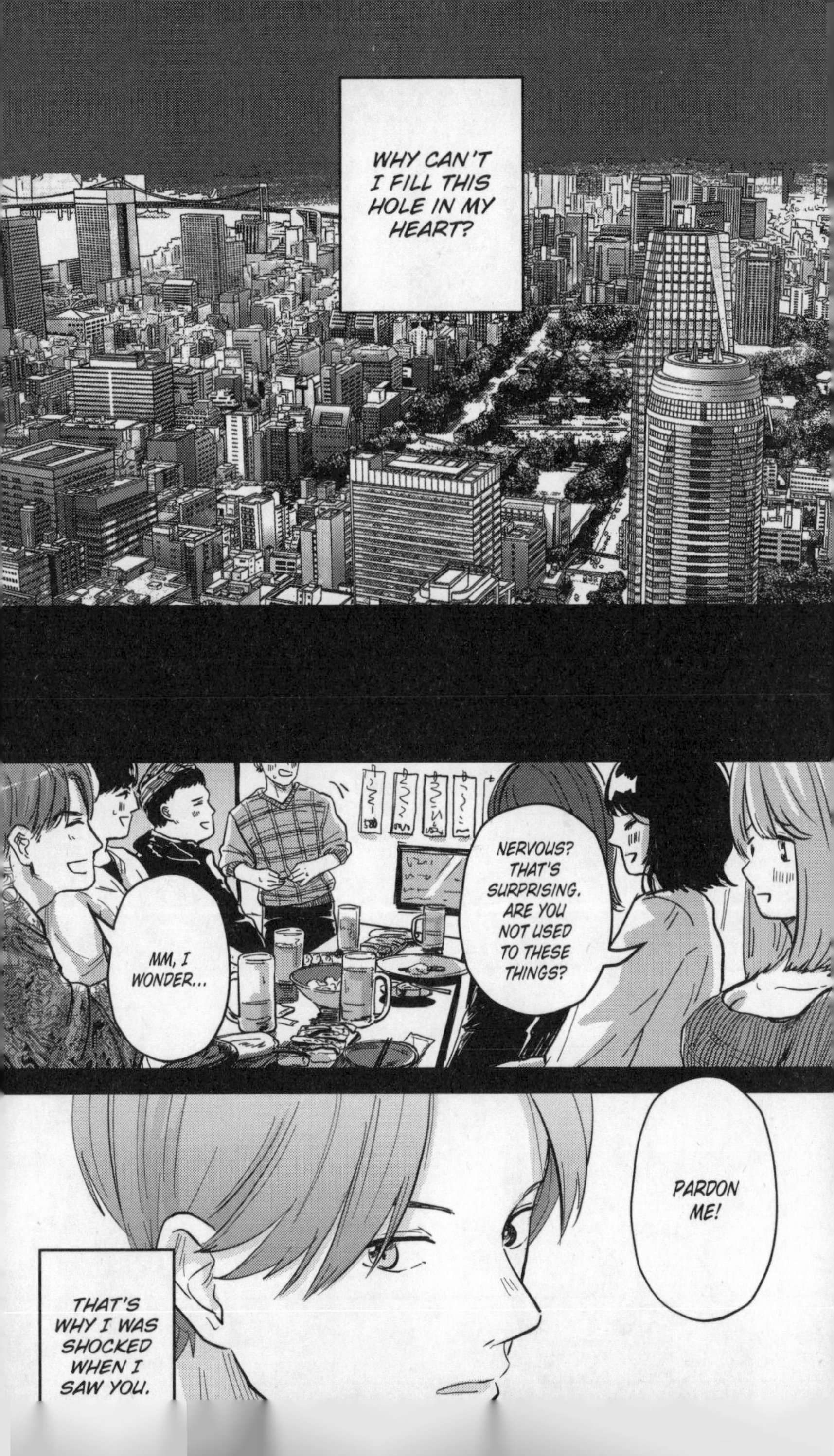
WHY CAN'T I FILL THIS HOLE IN MY HEART?
NERVOUS? THAT'S SURPRISING. ARE YOU NOT USED TO THESE THINGS?
MM, I WONDER...
PARDON ME!
THAT'S WHY I WAS SHOCKED WHEN I SAW YOU.

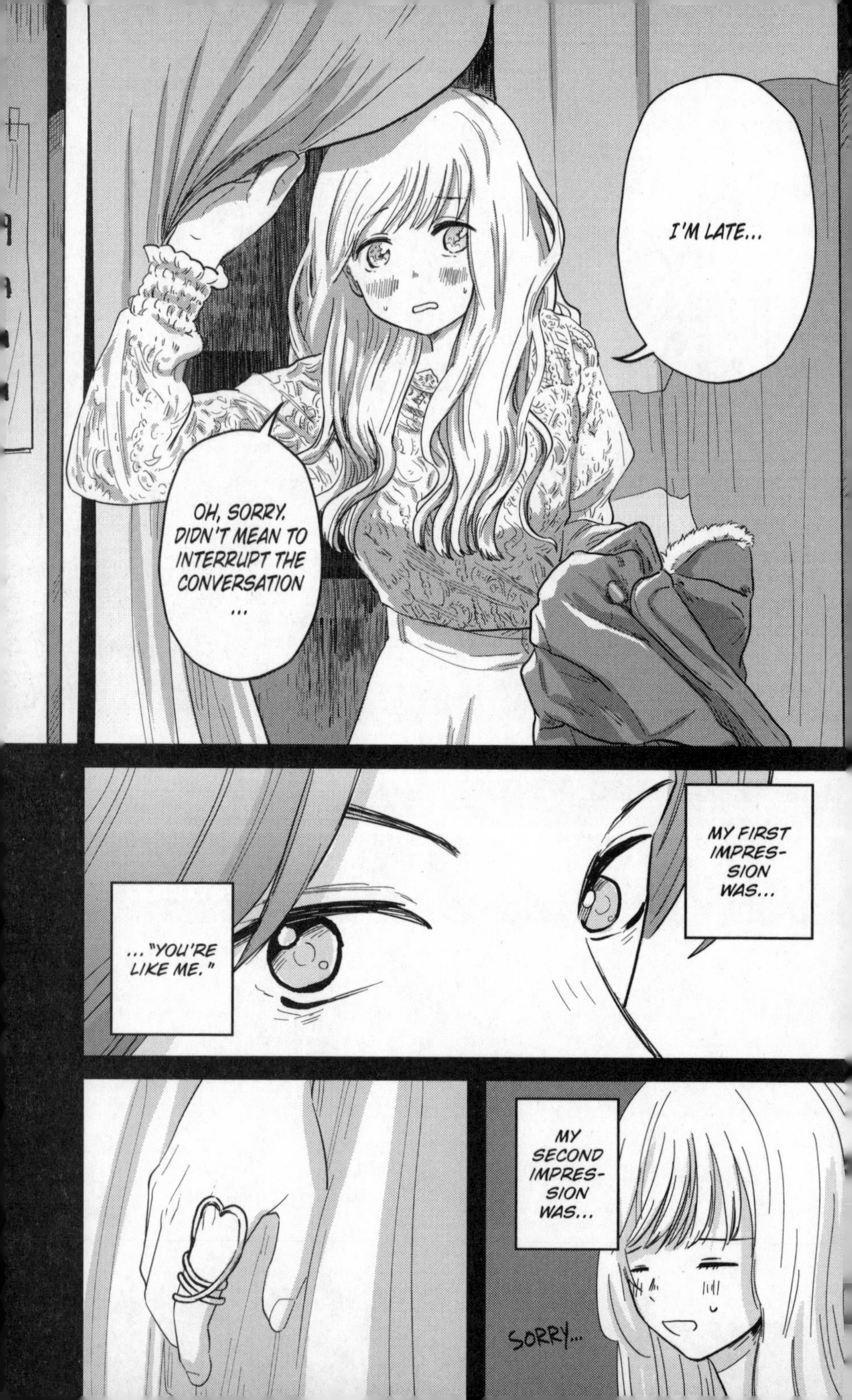
I'M LATE...
OH, SORRY. DIDN'T MEAN TO INTERRUPT THE CONVERSATION ...
MY FIRST IMPRES-SION WAS...
..."YOU'RE LIKE ME."
MY SECOND IMPRES-SION WAS...
SORRY...

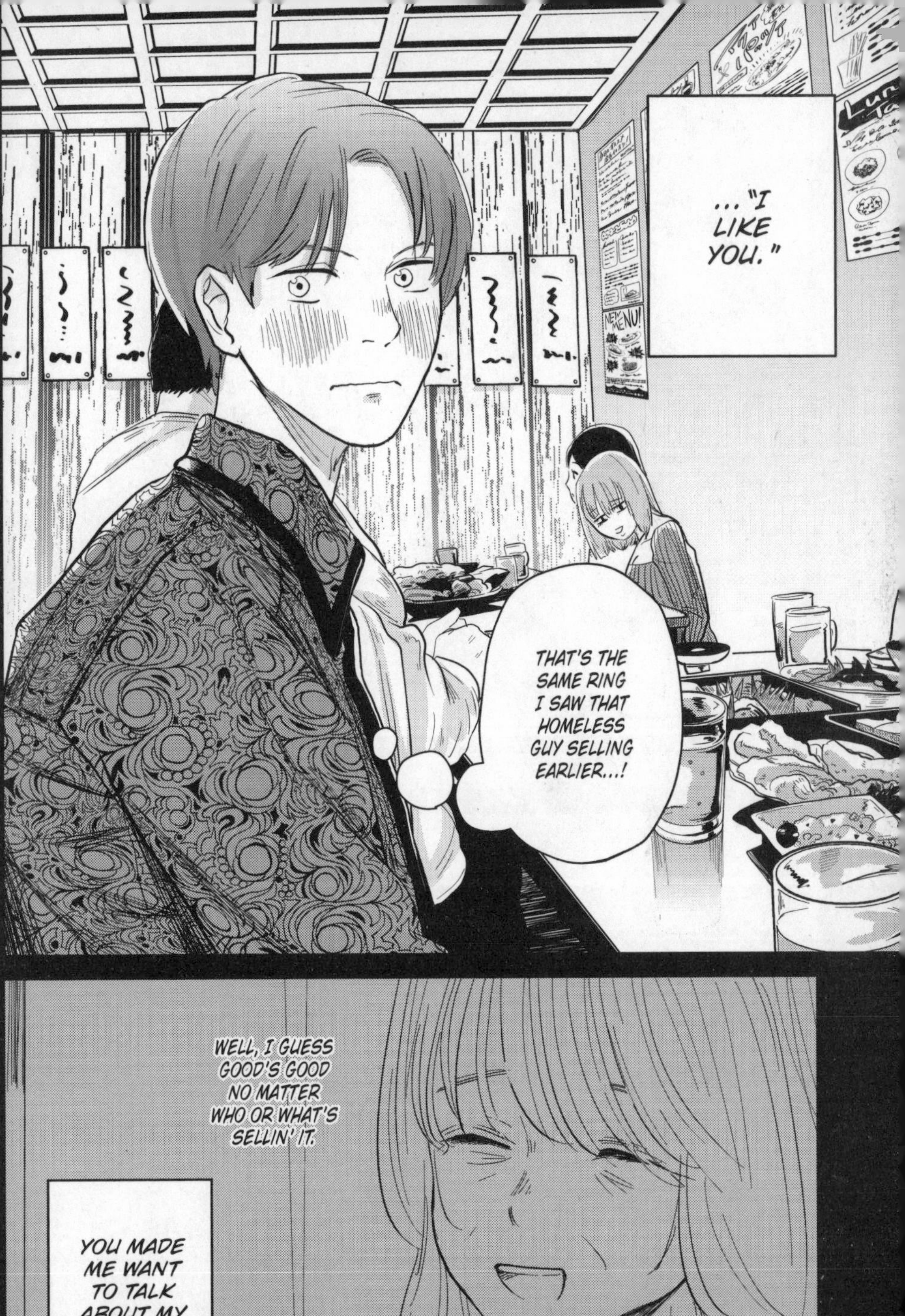
..."I LIKE YOU."
THAT'S THE SAME RING I SAW THAT HOMELESS GUY SELLING EARLIER...!
WELL, I GUESS GOOD'S GOOD NO MATTER WHO OR WHAT'S SELLIN' IT.
YOU MADE ME WANT TO TALK ABOUT MY PAST.

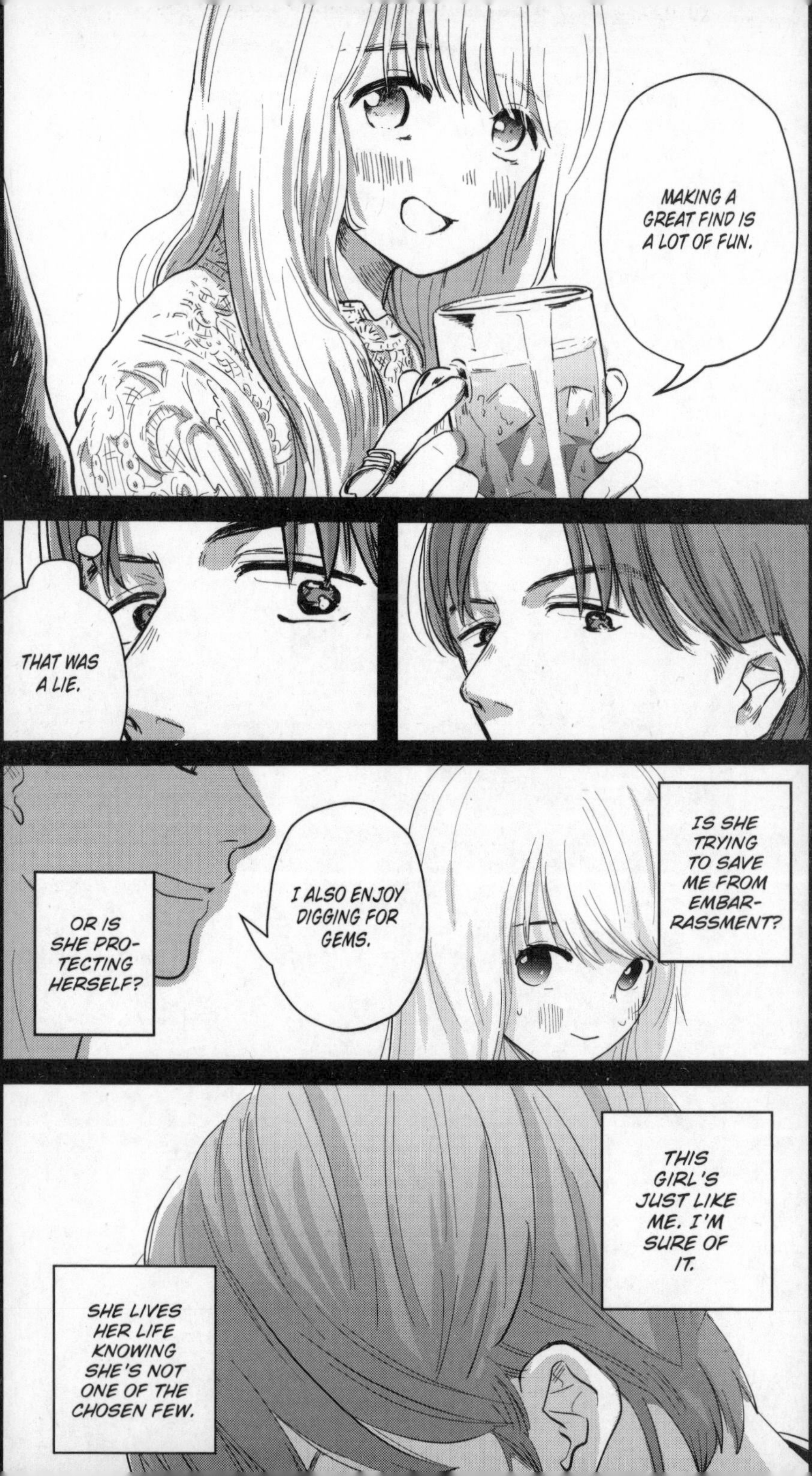
MAKING A GREAT FIND IS A LOT OF FUN.
THAT WAS A LIE.
IS SHE TRYING TO SAVE ME FROM EMBARRASSMENT?
I ALSO ENJOY DIGGING FOR GEMS.
OR IS SHE PROTECTING HERSELF?
THIS GIRL'S JUST LIKE ME. I'M SURE OF IT.
SHE LIVES HER LIFE KNOWING SHE'S NOT ONE OF THE CHOSEN FEW.

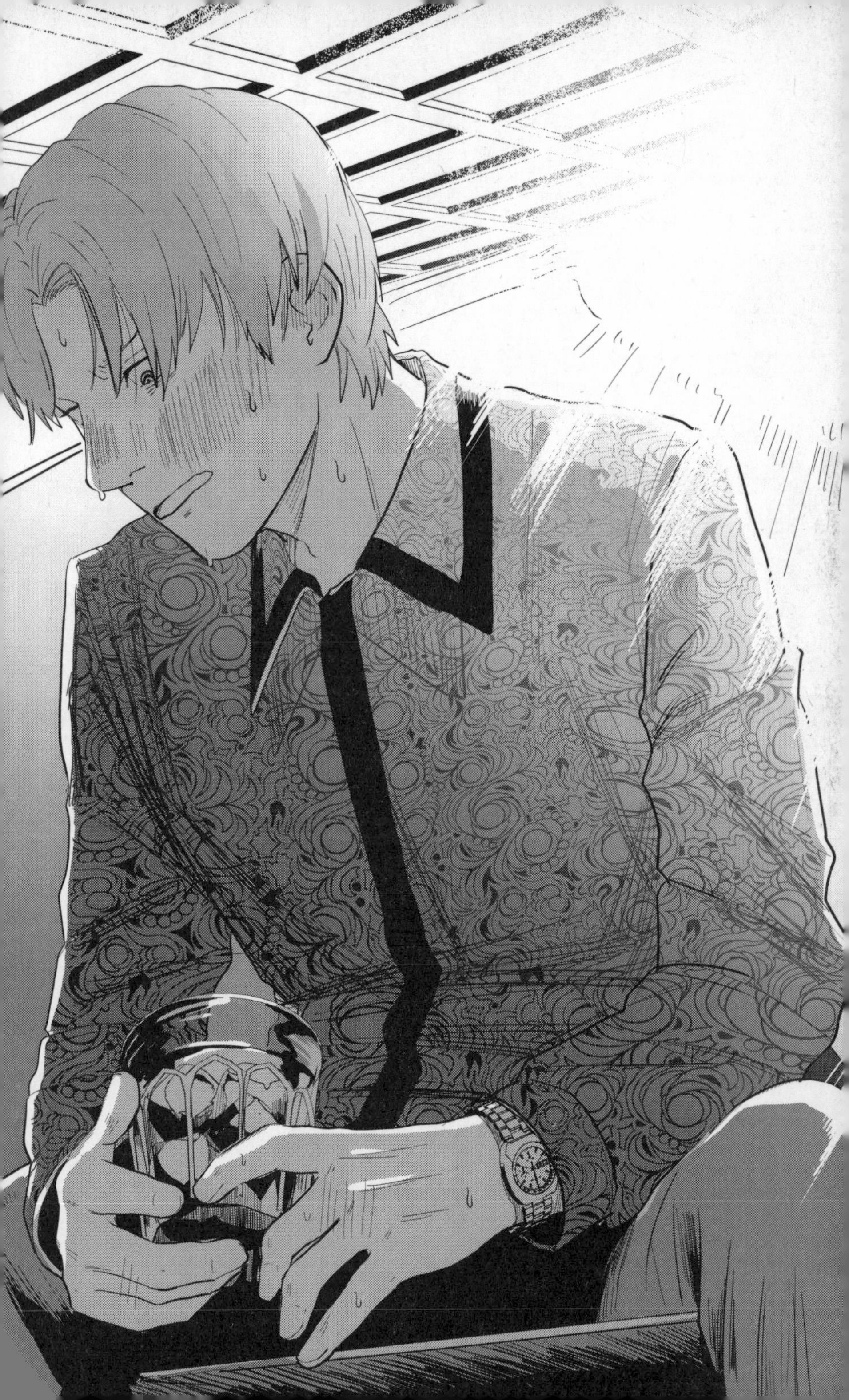

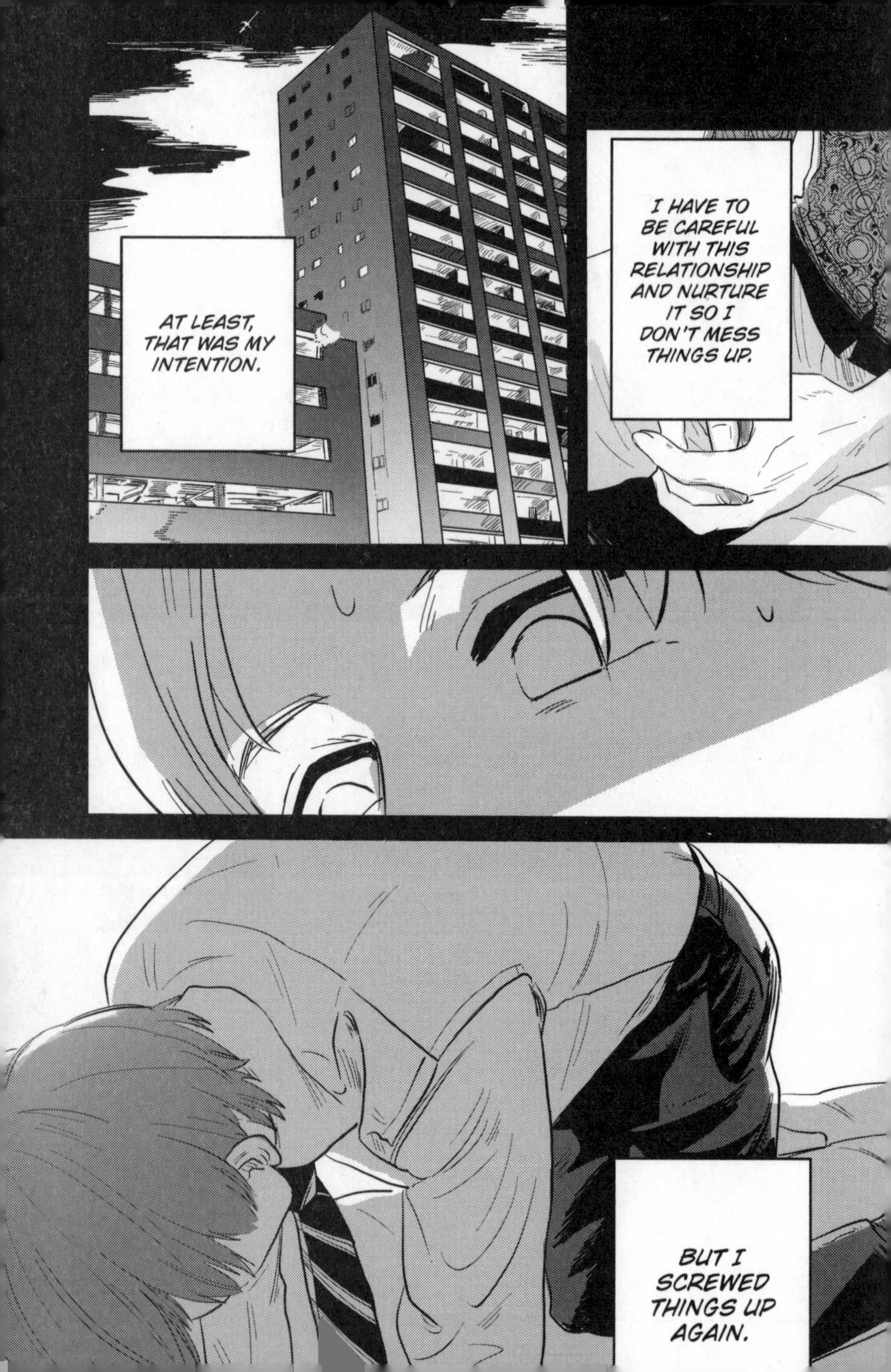
I HAVE TO BE CAREFUL WITH THIS RELATIONSHIP AND NURTURE IT SO I DON'T MESS THINGS UP.
AT LEAST, THAT WAS MY INTENTION.
BUT I SCREWED THINGS UP AGAIN.

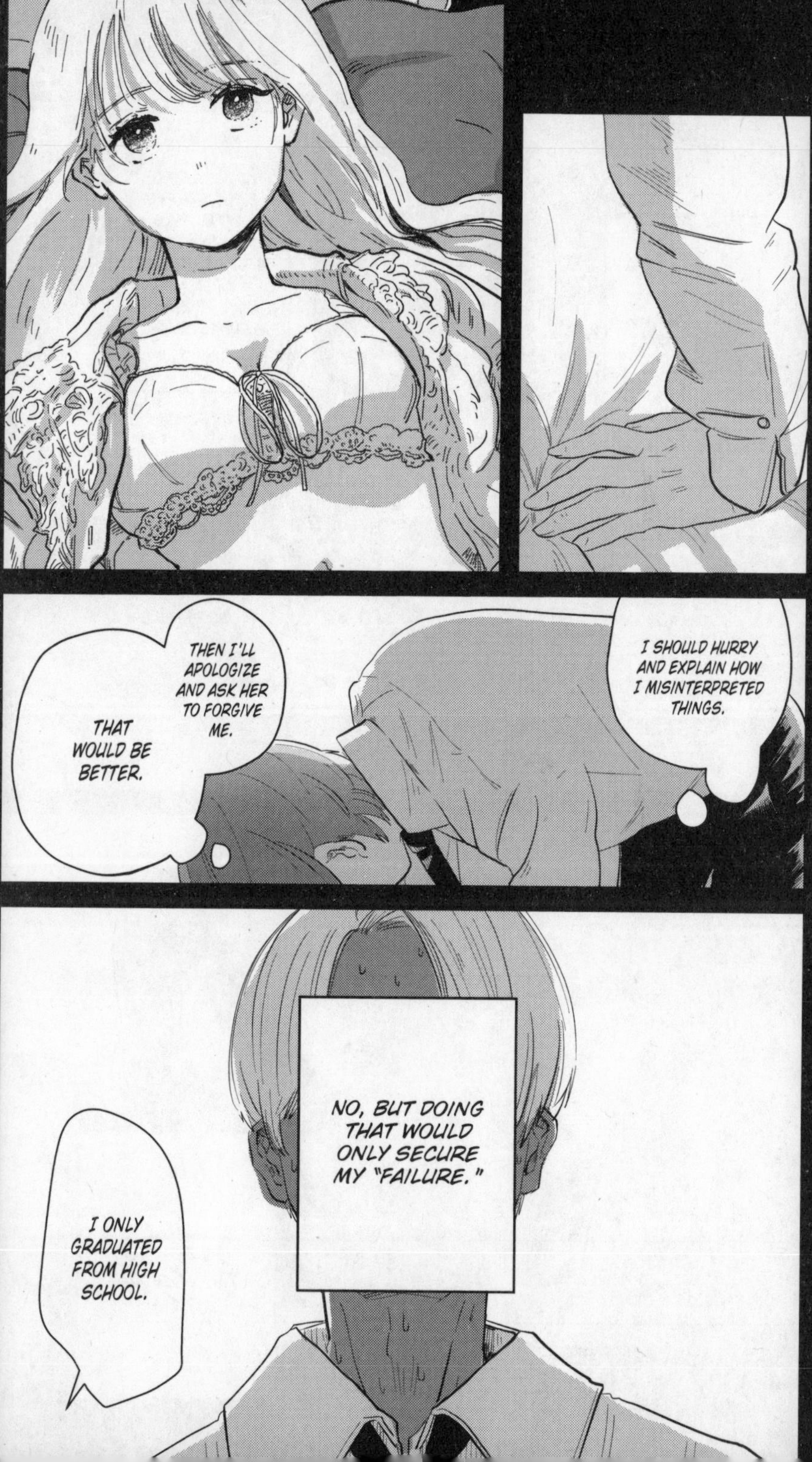
I SHOULD HURRY AND EXPLAIN HOW I MISINTERPRETED THINGS.
THEN I'LL APOLOGIZE AND ASK HER TO FORGIVE ME.
THAT WOULD BE BETTER.
NO, BUT DOING THAT WOULD ONLY SECURE MY "FAILURE."
I ONLY GRADUATED FROM HIGH SCHOOL.

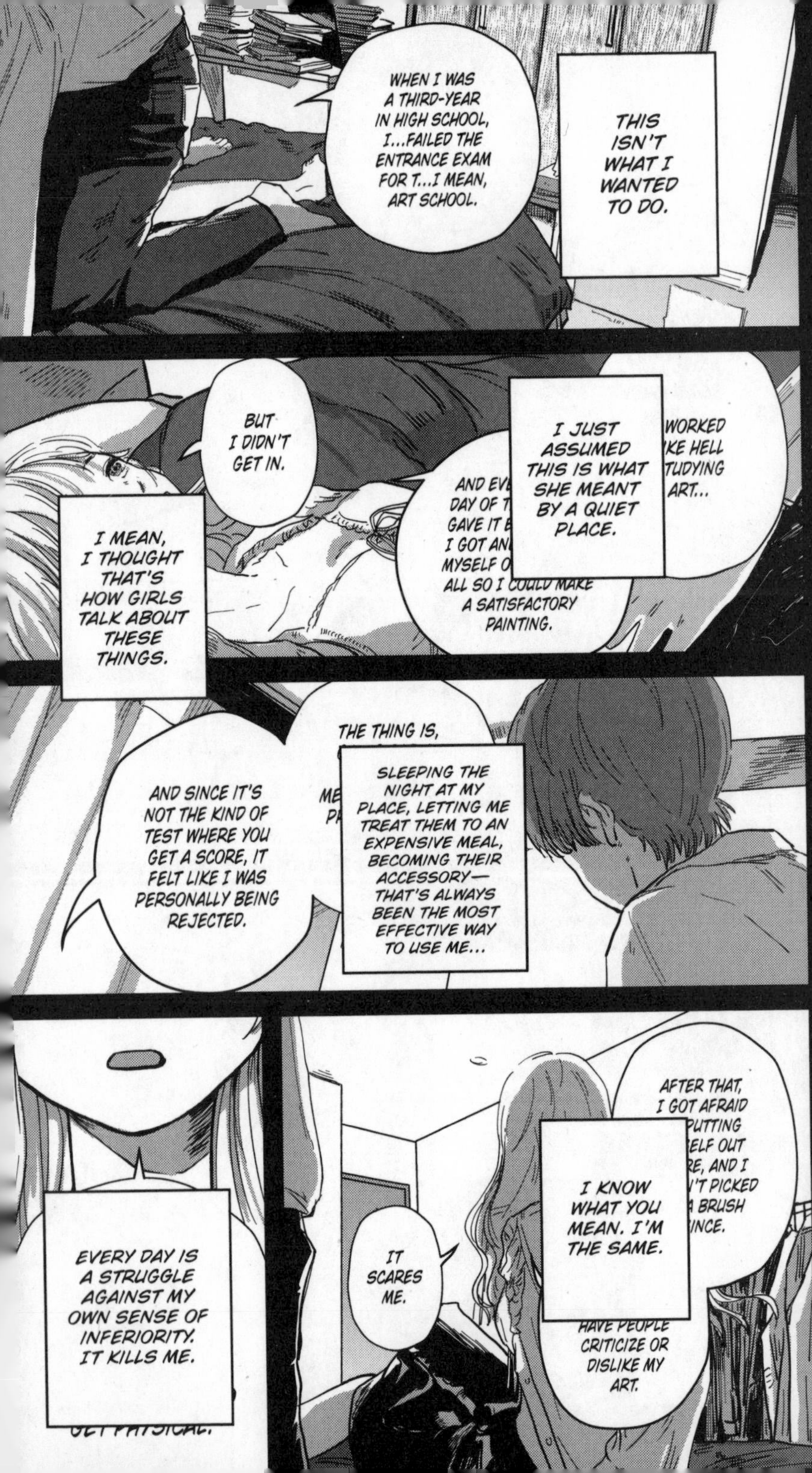

THIS ISN'T WHAT I WANTED TO DO.
WHEN I WAS A THIRD-YEAR IN HIGH SCHOOL, I...FAILED THE ENTRANCE EXAM FOR T...I MEAN, ART SCHOOL.
I JUST ASSUMED THIS IS WHAT SHE MEANT BY A QUIET PLACE.
BUT I DIDN'T GET IN.
I MEAN, I THOUGHT THAT'S HOW GIRLS TALK ABOUT THESE THINGS.
THE THING IS,
SLEEPING THE NIGHT AT MY PLACE, LETTING ME TREAT THEM TO AN EXPENSIVE MEAL, BECOMING THEIR ACCESSORY—THAT'S ALWAYS BEEN THE MOST EFFECTIVE WAY TO USE ME...
AND SINCE IT'S NOT THE KIND OF TEST WHERE YOU GET A SCORE, IT FELT LIKE I WAS PERSONALLY BEING REJECTED.
I KNOW WHAT YOU MEAN. I'M THE SAME.
CRITICIZE OR DISLIKE MY ART.
IT SCARES ME.
EVERY DAY IS A STRUGGLE AGAINST MY OWN SENSE OF INFERIORITY. IT KILLS ME.

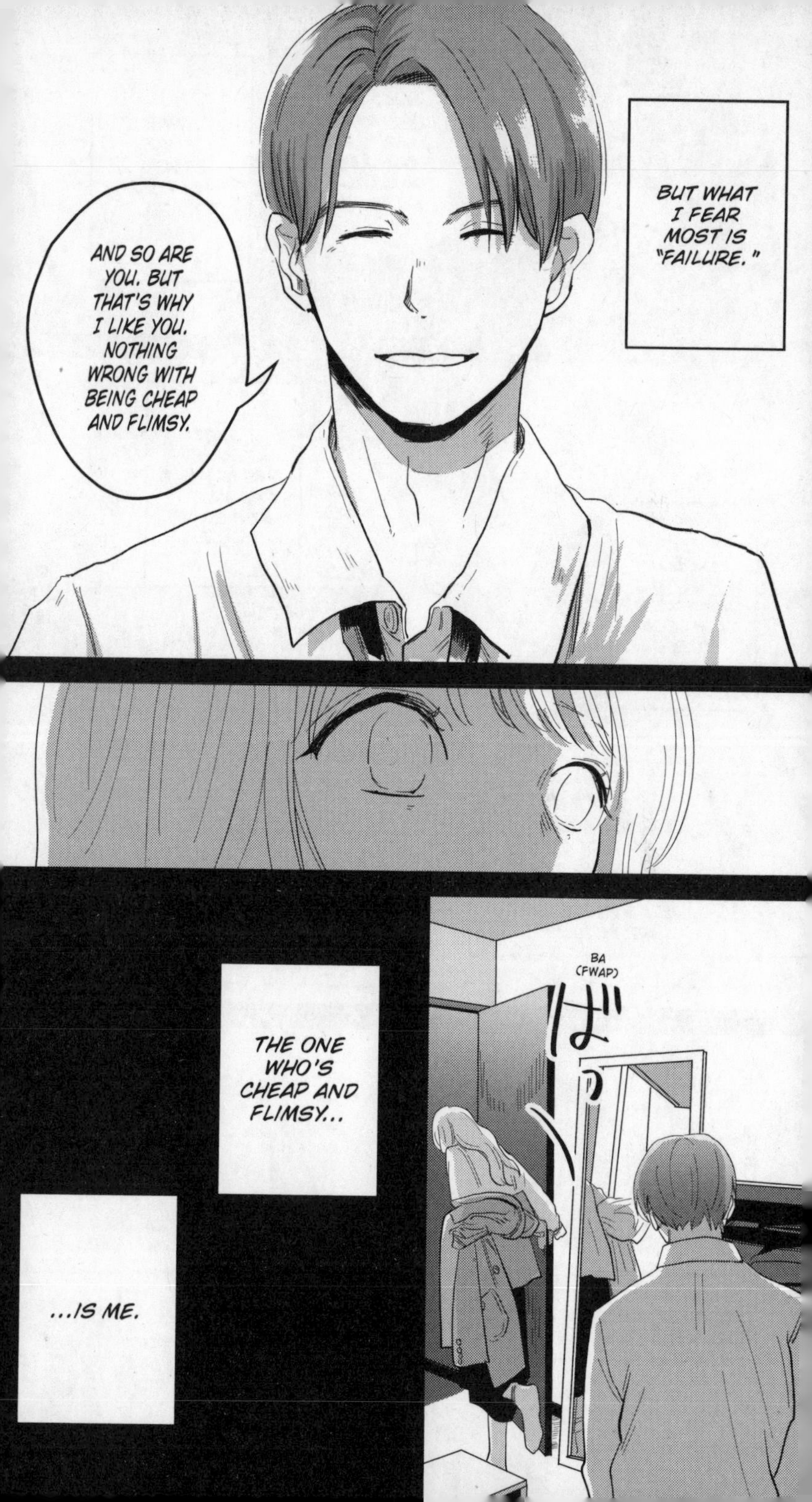
BUT WHAT I FEAR MOST IS "FAILURE."
AND SO ARE YOU. BUT THAT'S WHY I LIKE YOU. NOTHING WRONG WITH BEING CHEAP AND FLIMSY.
ばっ
BA (FWAP)
THE ONE WHO'S CHEAP AND FLIMSY...
...IS ME.

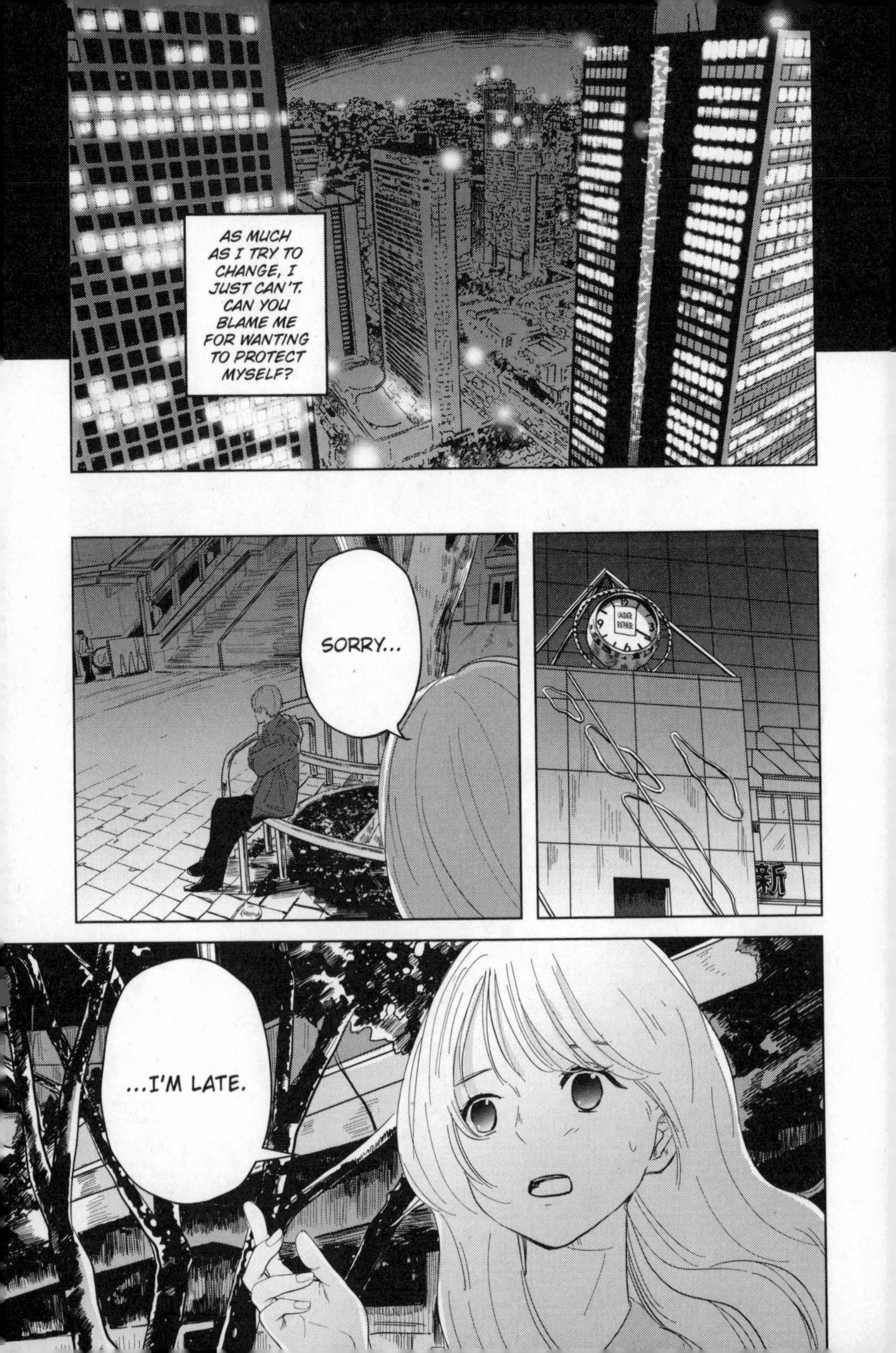
AS MUCH AS I TRY TO CHANGE, I JUST CAN'T. CAN YOU BLAME ME FOR WANTING TO PROTECT MYSELF?
UNDER REPAIR
新
SORRY...
...I'M LATE.

SORRY, I HAD TO DO SOME OVER-TIME...

NO, I JUST GOT HERE TOO.

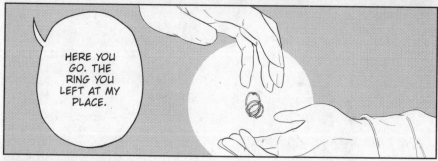

HERE YOU GO. THE RING YOU LEFT AT MY PLACE.

IF YOU DON'T MIND, HOW ABOUT GETTING SOMETHING TO EAT? MY TREAT.

HUH?

...THANK YOU.

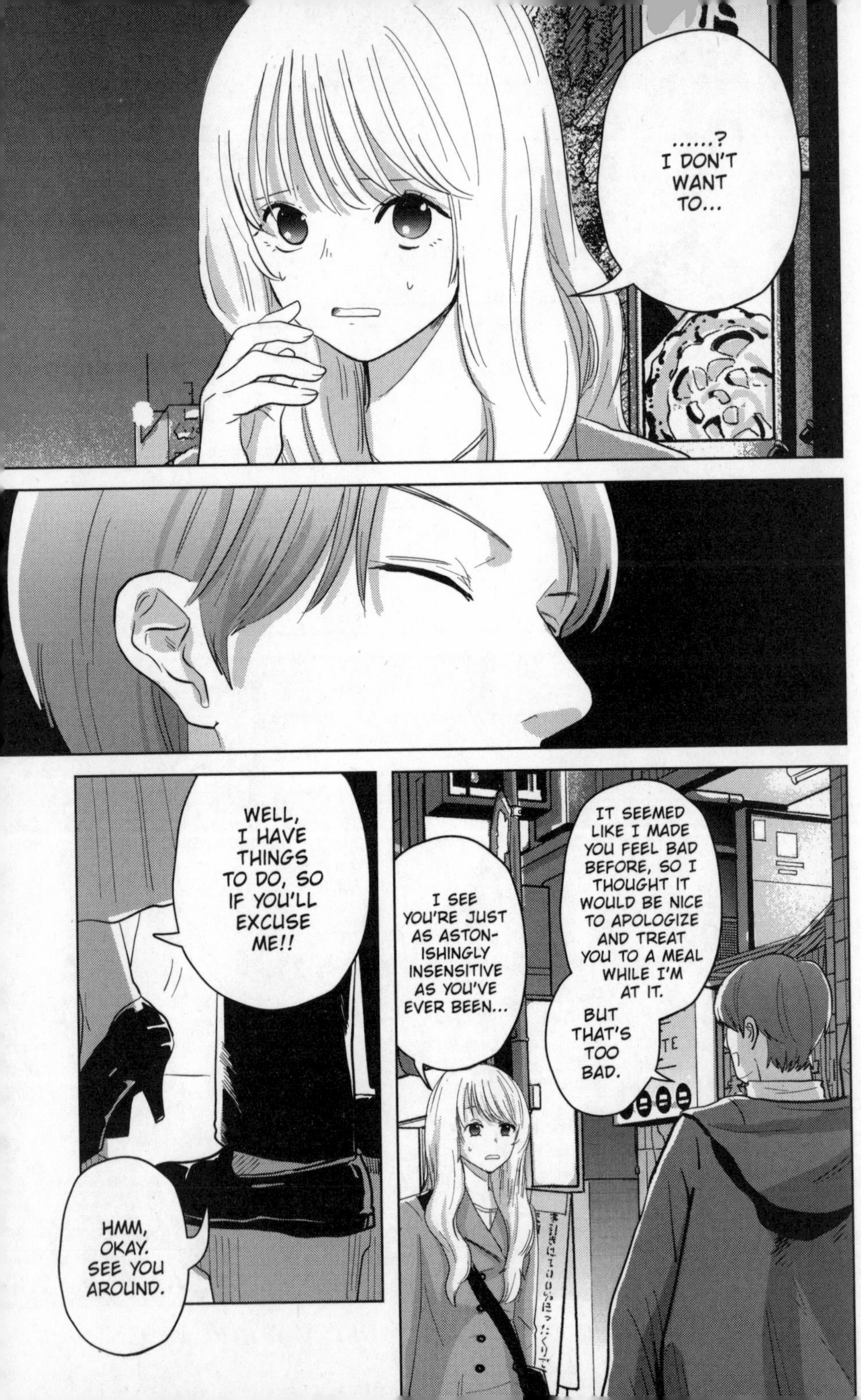
......? I DON'T WANT TO...
IT SEEMED LIKE I MADE YOU FEEL BAD BEFORE, SO I THOUGHT IT WOULD BE NICE TO APOLOGIZE AND TREAT YOU TO A MEAL WHILE I'M AT IT.
BUT THAT'S TOO BAD.
I SEE YOU'RE JUST AS ASTON-ISHINGLY INSENSITIVE AS YOU'VE EVER BEEN...
WELL, I HAVE THINGS TO DO, SO IF YOU'LL EXCUSE ME!!
HMM, OKAY. SEE YOU AROUND.

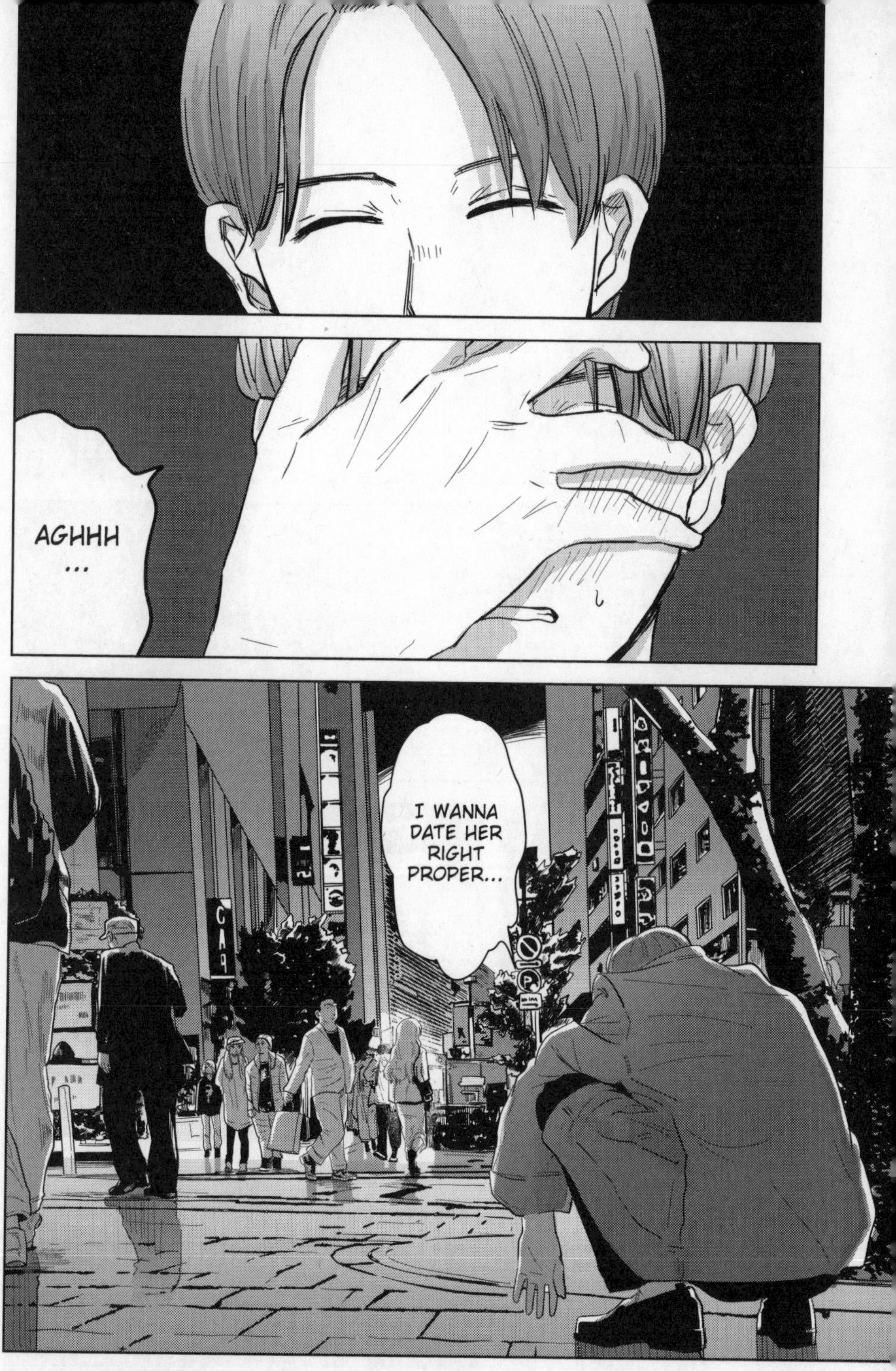
AGHHH ...
I WANNA DATE HER RIGHT PROPER...

The Essence of Being a Muse Volume 1 / END

The Essence of Being a Muse

The Essence of Being a Muse

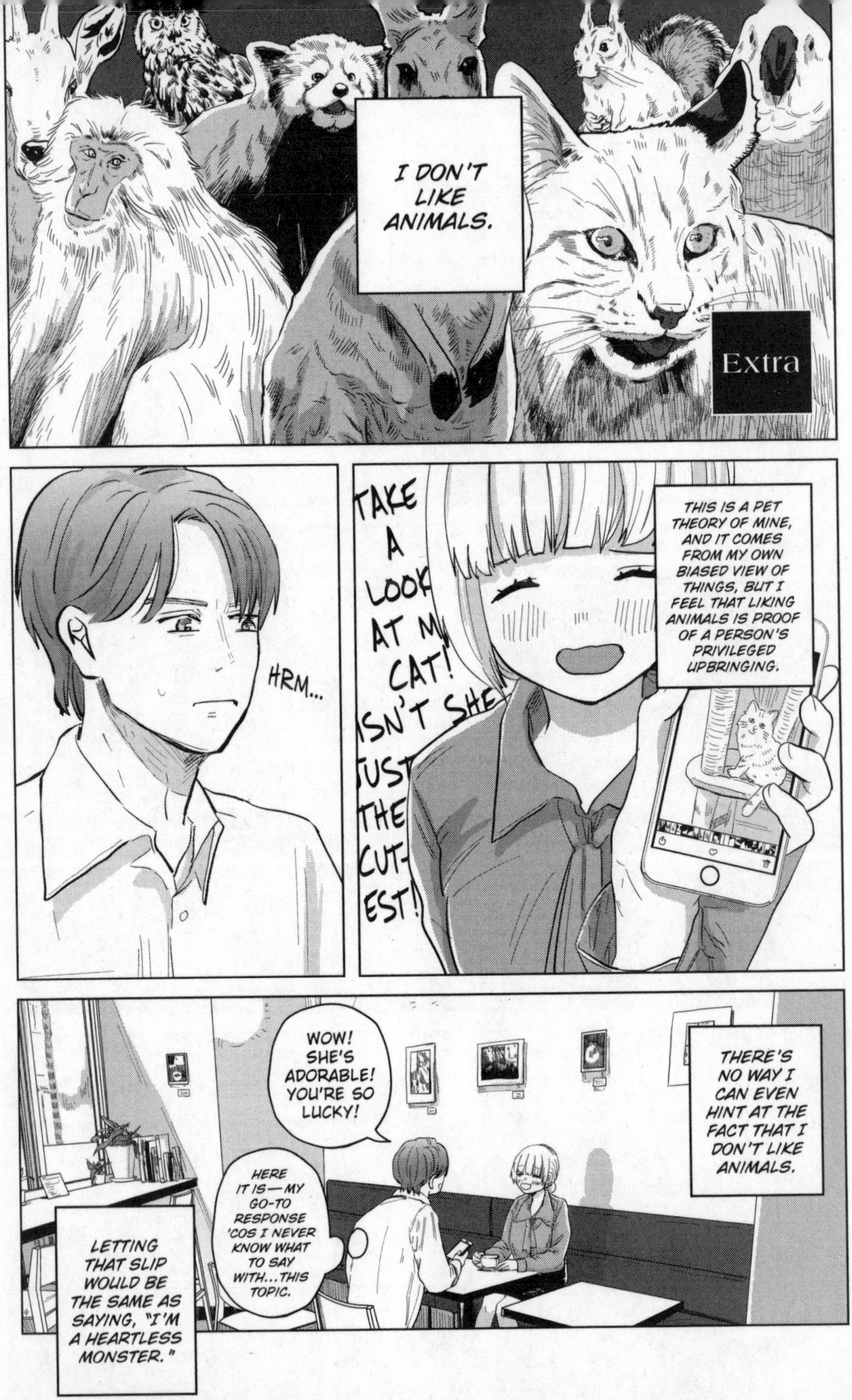
I DON'T LIKE ANIMALS.
Extra
THIS IS A PET THEORY OF MINE, AND IT COMES FROM MY OWN BIASED VIEW OF THINGS, BUT I FEEL THAT LIKING ANIMALS IS PROOF OF A PERSON'S PRIVILEGED UPBRINGING.
TAKE A LOOK AT MY CAT! ISN'T SHE JUST THE CUT-EST!
HRM...
THERE'S NO WAY I CAN EVEN HINT AT THE FACT THAT I DON'T LIKE ANIMALS.
WOW! SHE'S ADORABLE! YOU'RE SO LUCKY!
HERE IT IS—MY GO-TO RESPONSE 'COS I NEVER KNOW WHAT TO SAY WITH...THIS TOPIC.
LETTING THAT SLIP WOULD BE THE SAME AS SAYING, "I'M A HEARTLESS MONSTER."

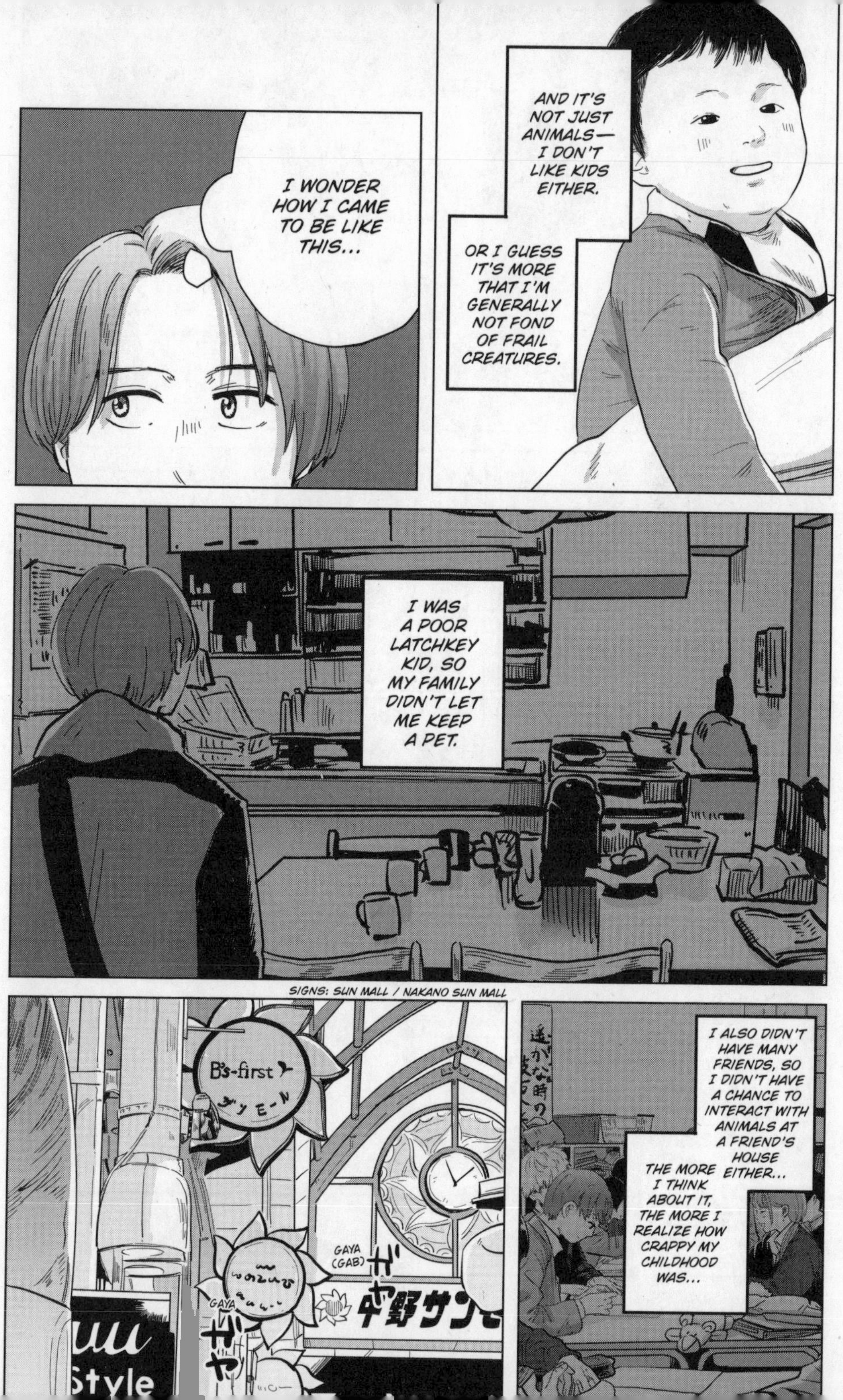
AND IT'S NOT JUST ANIMALS— I DON'T LIKE KIDS EITHER.
OR I GUESS IT'S MORE THAT I'M GENERALLY NOT FOND OF FRAIL CREATURES.
I WONDER HOW I CAME TO BE LIKE THIS...
I WAS A POOR LATCHKEY KID, SO MY FAMILY DIDN'T LET ME KEEP A PET.
I ALSO DIDN'T HAVE MANY FRIENDS, SO I DIDN'T HAVE A CHANCE TO INTERACT WITH ANIMALS AT A FRIEND'S HOUSE EITHER...
THE MORE I THINK ABOUT IT, THE MORE I REALIZE HOW CRAPPY MY CHILDHOOD WAS...
SIGNS: SUN MALL / NAKANO SUN MALL
B's-first
GAYA (GAB)
GAYA
中野サン
Style

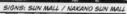

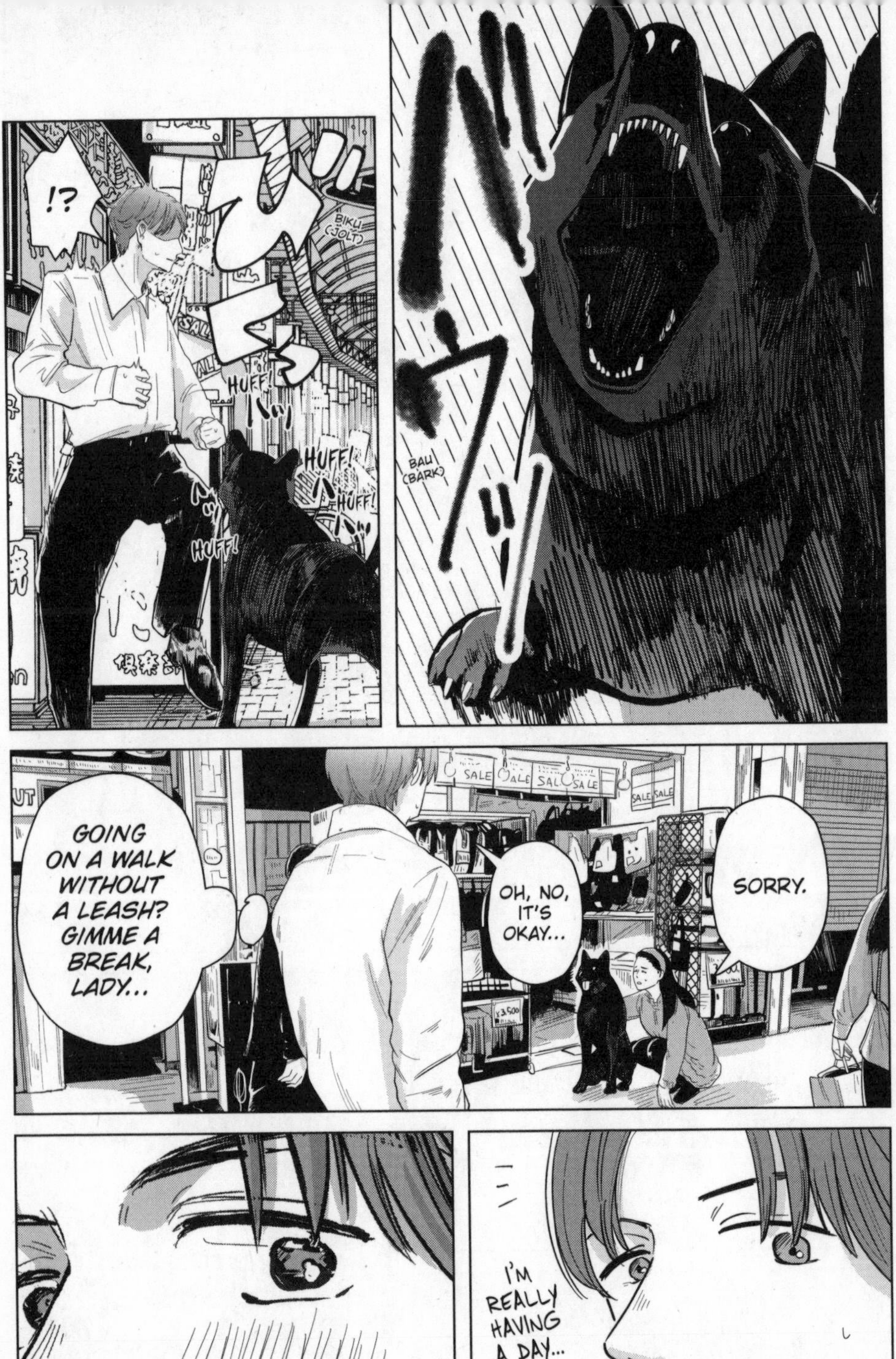
BAU (BARK)
!?
BIKU (JOLT)
HUFF!
HUFF!
HUFF!
HUFF!
SORRY.
OH, NO, IT'S OKAY...
GOING ON A WALK WITHOUT A LEASH? GIMME A BREAK, LADY...
I'M REALLY HAVING A DAY...

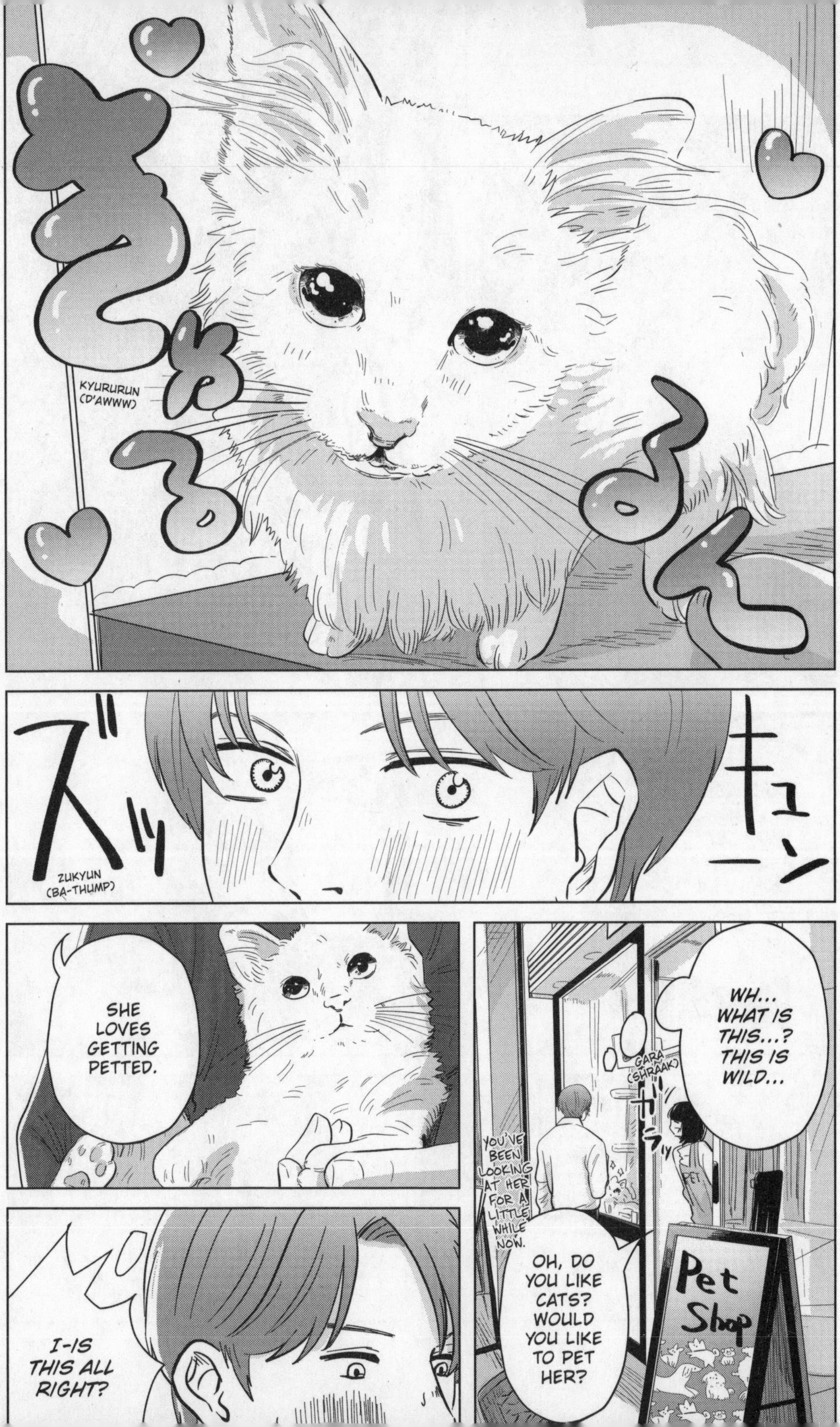
KYURURUN (D'AWWW)
ZUKYUN (BA-THUMP)
WH... WHAT IS THIS...? THIS IS WILD...
GARA (SHRAAK)
YOU'VE BEEN LOOKING AT HER FOR A LITTLE WHILE NOW.
OH, DO YOU LIKE CATS? WOULD YOU LIKE TO PET HER?
Pet Shop
SHE LOVES GETTING PETTED.
I-IS THIS ALL RIGHT?

WON'T I STRESS HER OUT OR BREAK HER OR SOMETHING IF I TOUCH HER!?

THIS SMALL, DELICATE LITTLE THING...

B-BUT...

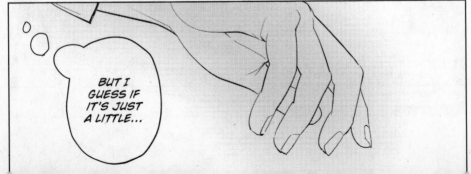

BUT I GUESS IF IT'S JUST A LITTLE...

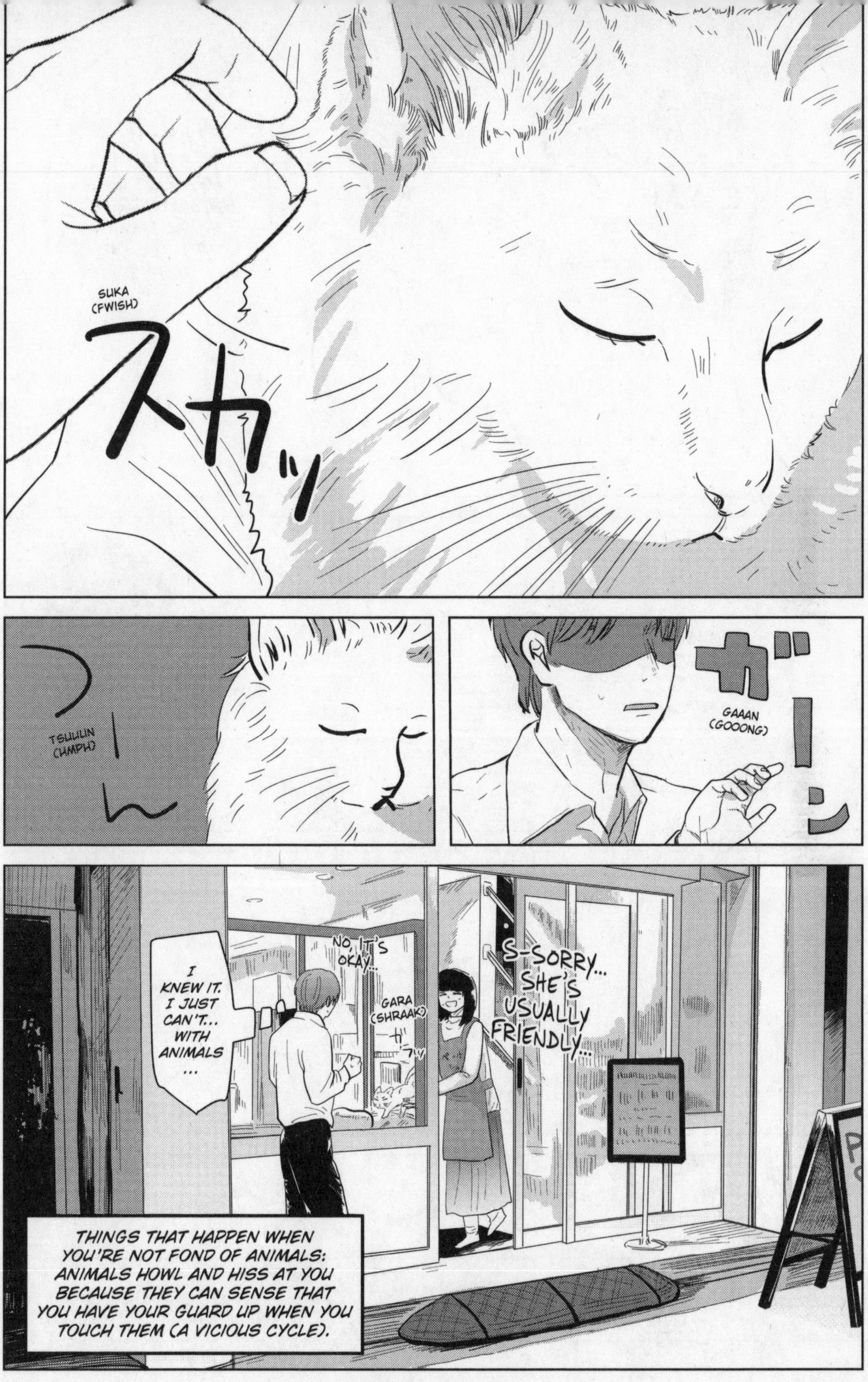

SUKA (FWISH)
スカッ
GAAAN (GOOONG)
ガーン
TSUUUN (HMPH)
つーん
S-SORRY... SHE'S USUALLY FRIENDLY...
NO, IT'S OKAY...
GARA (SHRAAK)
I KNEW IT. I JUST CAN'T... WITH ANIMALS...
THINGS THAT HAPPEN WHEN YOU'RE NOT FOND OF ANIMALS: ANIMALS HOWL AND HISS AT YOU BECAUSE THEY CAN SENSE THAT YOU HAVE YOUR GUARD UP WHEN YOU TOUCH THEM (A VICIOUS CYCLE).

Extra / END

Who is Miyuu's prince on a white horse...?

Miyuu takes another step forward after finishing her application for prep school.

Nabeshima is unable to be honest about his feelings despite his growing admiration for Miyuu.

Ryuen will always encourage Miyuu whenever she's about to lose heart.

Their individual feelings will entangle and converge into a single connecting thread...

To be continued in Volume 2

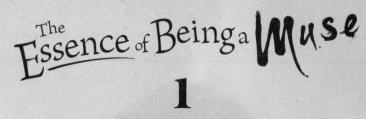

The Essence of Being a Muse

1

Aya Fumino

Translation by: Ajani Oloye   **Lettering by: Lys Blakeslee**

MUSE NO SHINZUI VOL.1
©Fumino Aya 2022
First published in Japan in 2022 by KADOKAWA CORPORATION, Tokyo.
English translation rights arranged with KADOKAWA CORPORATION, Tokyo
through TUTTLE-MORI AGENCY, INC., Tokyo.

Yen Press
150 West 30th Street, 19th Floor
New York, NY 10001

Visit us at:
yenpress.com • facebook.com/yenpress • twitter.com/yenpress
yenpress.tumblr.com • instagram.com/yenpress

First Yen Press Edition: June 2023
Edited by Yen Press Editorial: Carl Li, JuYoun Lee
Designed by Yen Press Design: Madelaine Norman

Library of Congress Control Number: 2023933179

ISBNs: 978-1-9753-6097-9 (paperback)
978-1-9753-6098-6 (ebook)

1 3 5 7 9 10 8 6 4 2

WOR

Printed in the United States of America